APPLIED MANAGEMENT ACCOUNTING

STUDY TEXT

Qualifications and Credit Framework

Q2022

The material in this book may support study for the following AAT qualifications:

AAT Level 4 Diploma in Professional Accounting

AAT Diploma in Professional Accounting at SCQF Level 8

KAPLAN PUBLISHING'S STATEMENT OF PRINCIPLES

LINGUISTIC DIVERSITY, EQUALITY AND INCLUSION

We are committed to diversity, equality and inclusion and strive to deliver content that all users can relate to.

We are here to make a difference to the success of every learner.

Clarity, accessibility and ease of use for our learners are key to our approach.

We will use contemporary examples that are rich, engaging and representative of a diverse workplace.

We will include a representative mix of race and gender at the various levels of seniority within the businesses in our examples to support all our learners in aspiring to achieve their potential within their chosen careers.

Roles played by characters in our examples will demonstrate richness and diversity by the use of different names, backgrounds, ethnicity and gender, with a mix of sexuality, relationships and beliefs where these are relevant to the syllabus.

It must always be obvious who is being referred to in each stage of any example so that we do not detract from clarity and ease of use for each of our learners.

We will actively seek feedback from our learners on our approach and keep our policy under continuous review. If you would like to provide any feedback on our linguistic approach, please use this form (you will need to enter the link below into your browser).

https://forms.gle/U8oR3abiPpGRDY158

We will seek to devise simple measures that can be used by independent assessors to randomly check our success in the implementation of our Linguistic Equality, Diversity and Inclusion Policy.

British Library Cataloguing-in-Publication Data

A catalogue record for this book is available from the British Library.

Published by
Kaplan Publishing UK
Unit 2, The Business Centre
Molly Millars Lane
Wokingham
Berkshire
RG41 2QZ

ISBN: 978-1-83996-046-8

Printed and bound in Great Britain.

CONTENTS

INTRODUCTION

HOW TO USE THESE MATERIALS

These Kaplan Publishing learning materials have been carefully designed to make your learning experience as easy as possible and to give you the best chance of success in your AAT assessments.

They contain a number of features to help you in the study process.

The sections on the Unit Guide, the Assessment and Study Skills should be read before you commence your studies.

They are designed to familiarise you with the nature and content of the assessment and to give you tips on how best to approach your studies.

STUDY TEXT

This study text has been specially prepared for the revised AAT qualification introduced in 2022.

It is written in a practical and interactive style:

- key terms and concepts are clearly defined
- all topics are illustrated with practical examples with clearly worked solutions based on sample tasks provided by the AAT in the new examining style
- frequent activities throughout the chapters ensure that what you have learnt is regularly reinforced
- 'pitfalls' and 'examination tips' help you avoid commonly made mistakes and help you focus on what is required to perform well in your examination
- 'Test your understanding' activities are included within each chapter to apply your learning and develop your understanding.

ICONS

The study chapters include the following icons throughout.

They are designed to assist you in your studies by identifying key definitions and the points at which you can test yourself on the knowledge gained.

Definition

These sections explain important areas of knowledge which must be understood and reproduced in an assessment.

Example

The illustrative examples can be used to help develop an understanding of topics before attempting the activity exercises.

Test your understanding

These are exercises which give the opportunity to assess your understanding of all the assessment areas.

Foundation activities

These are questions to help ground your knowledge and consolidate your understanding on areas you're finding tricky.

Extension activities

These questions are for if you're feeling confident or wish to develop your higher level skills.

Quality and accuracy are of the utmost importance to us so if you spot an error in any of our products, please send an email to mykaplanreporting@kaplan.com with full details.

Our Quality Co-ordinator will work with our technical team to verify the error and take action to ensure it is corrected in future editions.

Progression

There are two elements of progression that we can measure: first how quickly students move through individual topics within a subject; and second how quickly they move from one course to the next. We know that there is an optimum for both, but it can vary from subject to subject and from student to student. However, using data and our experience of student performance over many years, we can make some generalisations.

A fixed period of study set out at the start of a course with key milestones is important. This can be within a subject, for example 'I will finish this topic by 30 June', or for overall achievement, such as 'I want to be qualified by the end of next year'.

Your qualification is cumulative, as earlier papers provide a foundation for your subsequent studies, so do not allow there to be too big a gap between one subject and another.

We know that exams encourage techniques that lead to some degree of short term retention, the result being that you will simply forget much of what you have already learned unless it is refreshed (look up Ebbinghaus Forgetting Curve for more details on this). This makes it more difficult as you move from one subject to another: not only will you have to learn the new subject, you will also have to relearn all the underpinning knowledge as well. This is very inefficient and slows down your overall progression which makes it more likely you may not succeed at all.

In addition, delaying your studies slows your path to qualification which can have negative impacts on your career, postponing the opportunity to apply for higher level positions and therefore higher pay.

You can use the following diagram showing the whole structure of your qualification to help you keep track of your progress.

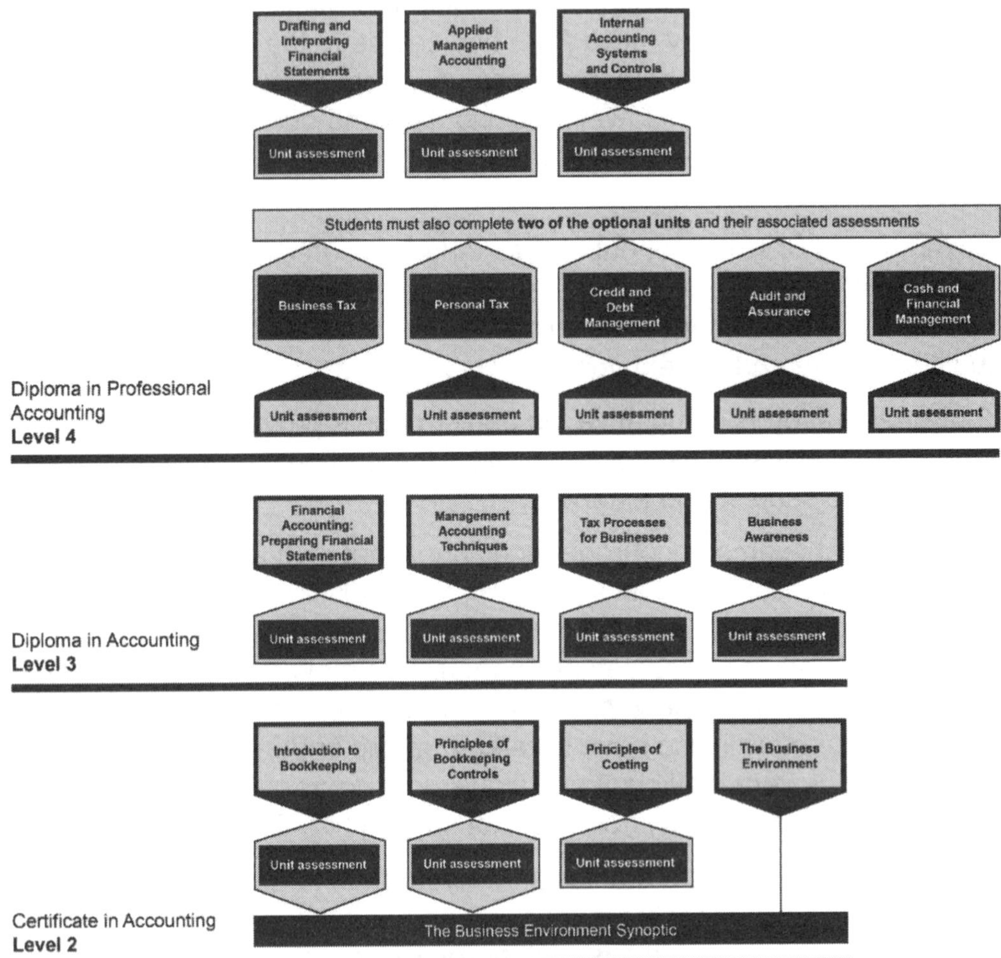

UNIT GUIDE

Introduction

In today's world, management accountants are not only required to interpret and analyse data to produce reports. They are also required to have the requisite skills to be able to relate their findings to the organisation and provide insightful feedback that will help the business to move forward and achieve its objectives. This unit focuses on the three fundamental areas of management accounting: planning, control and decision making. All organisations rely on the provision of accurate, business-focused information in order to make sound business judgements.

This unit will allow learners to understand how the budgetary process is undertaken. Learners will be able to construct budgets and then identify and report both on areas of success and on areas that should be of concern to key stakeholders. Learners will also gain the skills required to critically evaluate organisational performance.

Learners will be equipped with the knowledge and skills across a range of systems that will help to enhance the control environment of the organisation. Appreciating that there are many methods, and understanding how and when it is appropriate to use each of them, will allow learners to advise a business in a range of situations.

Learners will also gain an appreciation of the methods used to deal with the issues surrounding both short-term and long-term decision making. It is vitally important to understand the different challenges and uncertainties between the two types of decision making. Only by appreciating and incorporating those differences into the analysis produced can a management accountant consider themselves to be an integral part of the decision-making process.

This unit is mandatory in the Level 4 Diploma in Professional Accounting.

Learning outcomes

On completion of this unit the learner will be able to

- Understand and implement the organisational planning process
- Use internal processes to enhance operational control
- Use techniques to aid short-term and long-term decision making
- Analyse and report on business performance

Scope of content

To perform this unit effectively you will need to know and understand the following:

		Chapter
1	**Understand and implement the organisational planning process**	
1.1	**The budgetary process**	7
	Learners need to understand: • purposes of a budget • the budget cycle • types of budget: operating, capital, fixed and flexed • sources of data for budgeting • the principal budget factor.	
1.2	**Budgetary responsibilities and accountabilities**	7
	Learners need to understand: • the role of the budget committee • the duties and responsibilities of the budget accountant • the budgetary accountabilities of senior managers in organisations • the participatory alternatives: – top-down – bottom-up • the appropriate managers to provide information required to prepare budgets • how to identify appropriate responsibility centres and recovery methods for all types of indirect cost. Learners need to be able to: • classify and allocate direct costs to appropriate responsibility centres • apply the principle of responsibility accounting • apply responsibility accounting to controllable and uncontrollable costs.	

		Chapter
1.3	**Types of budgets and recommendations for their use**	7, 8

Learners need to understand:

- the features of the following budget types:
  - incremental
  - zero-based
  - priority-based
  - activity-based
  - rolling
  - contingency
- the comparative advantages of each method
- the circumstances in which each method should be recommended.

Learners need to be able to:

- prepare operating budgets incorporating the following types of cost:
  - direct
  - indirect
  - fixed
  - variable
  - semi-variable
  - stepped
  - capital
  - revenue
- prepare production budgets incorporating the following schedules:
  - production plan: inventory and sales
  - materials usage
  - materials purchases
  - labour costs
  - labour hours
  - plant utilisation

		Chapter
	• prepare cash flow forecasts/budgets allowing for: – time lags – changes in receivables – changes in payables – changes in inventory	
1.4	**Budgeting where resource constraints exist** Learners need to be able to: • identify budget limiting factors: – market share – access to finance – shortage of production resources – plant capacity – factory space • calculate the maximum level of production where a constraint exists.	9
1.5	**Impact of internal and external factors on forecasts** Learners need to understand:: • the stages and features of the product life cycle and their impact on income forecasts • market trends and competitive pressures • the expected impact of promotional activity • external events affecting the reliability of cost forecasts. Learners need to be able to: • advise on the reliability of forecasts	2, 7, 9

		Chapter
1.6	**Uncertainty in the budget setting process** Learners need to understand: • the methods of dealing with the uncertainty inherent in budgeting – planning models – regular re-forecasting – re-budgeting – rolling budgets.	7, 9
1.7	**Budget revision to reflect changing circumstances** Learners need to understand: • the key planning assumptions used in the budget • the potential threats to budget achievement • when a budget revision is appropriate. Learners need to be able to: • calculate the impact of changes to planning assumptions and forecasts • recalculate budgets accordingly.	9
2	**Use internal processes to enhance operational control**	
2.1	**Budgetary control** Learners need to understand: • the purpose of budget flexing as part of the control process • the limitations of budget flexing • the concept of feedback and feedforward control. Learners need to be able to: • flex budgets, adjusting each element of the budget correctly according to the original budget assumptions about revenue and cost behaviour. • provide potential reasons for variances (either calculated or given).	9, 10

		Chapter
2.2	**Standard costing**	10

Learners need to understand:

- different types of standards:
  - ideal
  - target
  - normal
  - basic
- the purpose of standard cost cards
- why variances occur
- courses of action to be taken to address divergences from standard
- the interaction of variances
- how different types of standards can have an impact on both behaviour and the level of the variance
- how the use of standard costing can complement budgetary control

Learners need to be able to:

- calculate the value of items to be included in standard cost cards
- calculate variances for revenue and costs:
  - total sales variance
  - sales price
  - sales volume
  - total material variance
  - material price
  - material usage
  - total labour variance
  - labour rate
  - labour efficiency
  - labour idle time
  - total variable overhead variance

		Chapter
	– variable overhead price – variable overhead efficiency – total fixed overhead variance – fixed overhead expenditure – fixed overhead efficiency • provide potential reasons for variances either calculated or given • incorporate standard costs into budgetary control calculations	
2.3	**Activity based costing** Learners need to understand: • the circumstances where activity based costing would be most appropriate • the benefits of activity based costing over traditional absorption costing • issues surrounding the introduction of activity based costing • the potential implications for unit selling prices and profitability where activity based costing leads to a different unit cost. Learners need to understand: • calculate product costs using activity based costing • compare product costs derived under activity based costing to those under traditional absorption costing.	1
2.4	**Target costing** Learners need to understand: • principles underpinning target costing • the concept of value analysis • the value engineering process • actions to take to reduce cost gaps.	2

		Chapter
	Learners need to be able to: • calculate: – target costs – any cost gap	
2.5	**Life cycle costing**	2, 13
	Learners need to understand: • principles underpinning life cycle costing • how life cycle costing contributes to operational control • the concepts of economies of scale, mechanisation and learning effect and how costs can switch between variable and fixed through the life cycle	
	Learners need to be able to: • identify the components of the life cycle cost of a product • calculate the discounted and non-discounted life cycle cost of a product • interpret the results of calculations of life cycle costs.	
2.6	**Technology and its impact on operational control**	14
	Learners need to understand: • technologies that are changing the way business collects and uses data: – cloud accounting – artificial intelligence – data analytics – visualisation • how these technologies can provide benefit to operational control processes • the challenges faced by business in adopting these technologies.	

		Chapter
3	**Use techniques to aid short-term and long-term decision making**	
3.1	**Comparison of short- and long-term decisions**	13

Learners need to understand:

- the fundamental differences between short-term and long-term decision making:
  - time frame
  - capital investment
  - risk

3.2	**Relevant costing**	5

Learners need to understand:

- how to identify relevant costs
- the concept of opportunity costs
- factors to be considered when a business decides to:
  - make or buy products
  - supply or buy-in services
  - continue or discontinue products
  - continue or discontinue services

Learners need to be able to:

- calculate relevant:
  - costs
  - revenues

3.3	**Key factor analysis**	3

Learners need to understand:

- the concept of scarce resources
- the concept of contribution
- when contribution should be used as part of the decision-making criteria.

		Chapter

Learners need to be able to:

- calculate the contribution per unit of scarce resources
- calculate the optimum production plan in situations where there is one scarce resource
- calculate total profit or total contribution based on the optimum production plan. .

3.4 Linear programming 4

Learners need to understand:

- the assumptions behind linear programming.

Learners need to be able to:

- calculate the optimum production plan in situations where there are multiple scarce resources
- calculate the optimum production plan using:
  - graphical approach
  - simultaneous equations.

3.5 Discount cash flows 13

Learners need to understand:

- the concept of the time value of money
- the benefits of discounted cash flows over non-discounted cash flows.

Learners need to be able to:

- calculate discounted cash flows.

3.6 Appraisal methods for long-term decisions 13

Learners need to understand:

- long-term investment appraisal techniques:
  - Net Present Value (NPV)
  - Internal Rate of Return (IRR)
  - Accounting Rate of Return (ARR)
  - payback period: non discounted and discounted
- strengths and weaknesses of each method.

		Chapter
	Learners need to be able to: • calculate net present values • use the IRR formula • calculate the ARR of projects • calculate the payback period of projects • compare NPV, IRR, ARR and payback period to support decision making.	
4	**Analyse and report on business performance**	
4.1	**Financial performance indicators** Learners need to understand: • what the performance indicator means • the impact on performance indicators due to: – learning effect – economies of scale • how some performance indicators interrelate with each other • how proposed actions may affect the indicator • actions that could be taken to improve the indicator Performance indicators: • Profitability: – gross profit margin – operating profit margin – return on capital employed (ROCE), calculated as operating profit / capital employed × 100 where capital employed = net assets. • Efficiency: – receivable period – payable period – inventory holding period – working capital cycle period	11

		Chapter
	– any cost as a percentage of revenue – asset turnover (AT), calculated as revenue / net assets. Learners need to be able to: • calculate key financial performance indicators • interpret financial performance ratios to evaluate organisational performance. .	
4.2	**Non-financial performance indicators**	11

Learners need to understand:

- costs of quality:
  - prevention
  - appraisal
  - internal failure
  - external failure
- how the behaviour of managers aiming to achieve a target can be affected by:
  - the ethical code of practice
  - commercial considerations
- non-financial performance indicators covering:
  - profitability
  - efficiency
  - productivity
  - quality
- measures that could be taken to improve performance
- balanced scorecards.

Learners need to be able to:

- calculate non-financial performance indicators
- interpret non-financial performance ratios to evaluate organisational performance
- evaluate results from a balanced scorecard.

		Chapter
4.3	**Divisional performance**	12

Learners need to understand:

- the differences between cost, profit and investment centres
- the issues of using return on investment and residual income as performance measures
- the options available to organisations when setting a transfer price and the potential issues that may arise.

Learners need to be able to:

- calculate:
  - return on investment
  - residual income

4.4	**Calculate forecasts**	6

Learners need to understand:

- elements of a time series
- the simple regression equation
- concept of expected values.

Learners need to be able to:

- calculate index numbers
- use moving averages to calculate the seasonal variations and trend from a time series
- use the simple regression equation to calculate total cost
- calculate forecasts of future performance based on historical data
- interpret statistical data calculated to evaluate organisational performance
- make recommendations based on results of sensitivity analysis.

Deliverying this unit

This unit has close links with:

Level 2 Principles of costing

Level 3 Management Accounting Techniques

Level 4 Internal Accounting Systems and Controls

Level 4 Cash and Financial Management

THE ASSESSMENT

Test specification for this unit assessment

Assessment type	Marking type	Duration of exam
Computer based unit assessment	Partially computer/ partially human marked	3 hours

	Learning outcomes	Weighting
1	Understand and implement the organisational planning process	25%
2	Use internal processes to enhance operational control	27%
3	Use techniques to aid short-term and long-term decision making	25%
4	Analyse and report on business performance	23%
Total		**100%**

UNIT LINK TO SYNOPTIC ASSESSMENT

To achieve the Professional Accounting Technician apprenticeship students must pass all of the assessments in the Diploma in Accounting, complete a portfolio and reflective discussion or written statement and complete a synoptic assessment.

The synoptic assessment is attempted following completion of the compulsory AAT units and it draws upon knowledge and understanding from those units. It will be appropriate for students to retain their study materials for individual units until they have successfully completed the synoptic assessment for that apprenticeship level.

With specific reference to this unit, the following learning objectives are also relevant to the synoptic assessment.

LO1 Understand and implement the organisational planning process

LO2 Use internal processes to enhance operation control

LO3 Use techniques to aid short-term and long-term decision making

LO4 Analyse and report on business performance

STUDY SKILLS

Preparing to study

Devise a study plan

Determine which times of the week you will study.

Split these times into sessions of at least one hour for study of new material. Any shorter periods could be used for revision or practice.

Put the times you plan to study onto a study plan for the weeks from now until the assessment and set yourself targets for each period of study – in your sessions make sure you cover the whole course, activities and the associated questions in the workbook at the back of the manual.

If you are studying more than one unit at a time, try to vary your subjects as this can help to keep you interested and to see the relationships between subjects.

When working through your course, compare your progress with your plan and, if necessary, re-plan your work (perhaps including extra sessions) or, if you are ahead, do some extra revision/practice questions.

Effective studying

Active reading

You are not expected to learn the text by rote, rather, you must understand what you are reading and be able to use it to pass the assessment and develop good practice.

A good technique is to use SQ3Rs – Survey, Question, Read, Recall, Review.

1 **Survey the chapter**

   Look at the headings and read the introduction, knowledge, skills and content, so as to get an overview of what the chapter deals with.

2 **Question**

   Whilst undertaking the survey ask yourself the questions you hope the chapter will answer for you.

3 **Read**

Read through the chapter thoroughly working through the activities and, at the end, making sure that you can meet the learning objectives highlighted on the first page.

4 **Recall**

At the end of each section and at the end of the chapter, try to recall the main ideas of the section/chapter without referring to the text. This is best done after short break of a couple of minutes after the reading stage.

5 **Review**

Check that your recall notes are correct.

You may also find it helpful to reread the chapter to try and see the topic(s) it deals with as a whole.

Note taking

Taking notes is a useful way of learning, but do not simply copy out the text. The notes must

- be in your own words
- be concise
- cover the key points
- well organised
- be modified as you study further chapters in this text or in related ones.

Trying to summarise a chapter without referring to the text can be a useful way of determining which areas you know and which you don't.

Three ways of taking notes

1 **Summarise the key points of a chapter**

2 **Make linear notes**

A list of headings, subdivided with sub-headings listing the key points.

If you use linear notes, you can use different colours to highlight key points and keep topic areas together.

Use plenty of space to make your notes easy to use.

3 Try a diagrammatic form

The most common of which is a mind map.

To make a mind map, put the main heading in the centre of the paper and put a circle around it.

Draw lines radiating from this to the main sub-headings which again have circles around them.

Continue the process from the sub-headings to sub-sub-headings.

Annotating the text

You may find it useful to underline or highlight key points in your study text – but do be selective.

You may also wish to make notes in the margins.

Revision phase

Kaplan has produced material specifically designed for your final examination preparation for this unit.

These include pocket revision notes and a bank of revision questions specifically in the style of the new syllabus.

Further guidance on how to approach the final stage of your studies is given in these materials.

Further reading

In addition to this text, you should also read the 'Student section' of the 'Accounting Technician' magazine every month to keep abreast of any guidance from the examiners.

TERMINOLOGY

There are different terms used to mean the same thing – you will need to be aware of both sets of terminology.

UK GAAP	IAS
Profit and loss	Income statement
Sales	Revenue
Balance sheet	Statement of financial position
Fixed assets	Non-current assets
Stock	Inventory
Trade debtors	Trade receivables
Trade creditors	Trade payables
Capital	Equity
Profit	Retained earnings

Activity based costing

1

Introduction

Overhead is the general term used to describe costs which are not direct costs of production. They are also known as indirect costs and they may be indirect production costs or indirect non-production costs. Traditionally when a management accountant has been trying to ascertain the cost of a product or service, there have been two approaches for dealing with overheads. The first is absorption costing, which involves apportionment and allocation of all production overheads to arrive at a 'full' cost per unit. The other approach is to use only direct costs to arrive at the cost per unit and leave indirect costs as a general overhead not related to units of output. This approach is known as marginal costing

In this chapter we look at a new technique. Changes in technology and processes mean that some organisations have a much higher proportion of overhead costs now and their management are not happy with the traditional approaches, so an approach called activity based costing has been developed. Read on to find out more.

ASSESSMENT CRITERIA

Activity based costing (LO 2.3)

CONTENTS

1 Modern production environments

1.1 Introduction

Modern manufacturing is different from traditional manufacturing techniques:

(a) much more machinery and computerised manufacturing systems are used

(b) smaller batch sizes are manufactured at the request of customers

(c) less use of 'direct' labour due to the higher use of computers and machinery.

This has had an impact on production costs:

- more indirect costs (overheads)
- less direct labour costs

This means that the traditional methods of costing using Absorption costing and Marginal costing are less useful.

- **Absorption costing** charges overheads to products in an arbitrary way – usually based on the volume of production in units or hours.
- **Marginal costing** values products based on the variable cost to produce them and fixed costs are treated as a period charge. In modern environments the variable costs might be small in comparison to the fixed costs and the fixed cost may not be truly fixed if considering all aspects of the production process.

1.2 Criticisms of absorption costs

Historically a direct labour rate for absorption of all fixed overheads was a very common method, as production tended to be highly labour-intensive. Items such as rent would be apportioned using the area involved, but the absorption rate would usually be labour hours. It was reasonable to assume that the more labour time spent on a product, the more production resources in general were being used. Thus a product with a higher labour content should be charged with a higher share of the overheads.

In this example, one solution would be to use machine hours as a basis. However, this still tries to relate all overhead costs, whatever their nature, to usage of one resource. This would not necessarily be appropriate for, say, costs of receiving and checking materials going into the production process. This will be more likely to depend upon the number of times an order of material is received into stores for a particular product.

2 Activity-based costing (ABC)

2.1 Activity-based costing (ABC) approach

Professors Robin Cooper and Robert Kaplan at the Harvard Business School developed a costing system called activity-based costing (ABC) which avoids the problems experienced by traditional costing methods. If management are keen to control costs, then it is vital that they should know the activities that cause costs to arise.

(a) **Cost drivers**

Those activities that are the significant determinants of cost are known as cost-drivers. For example, if production-scheduling cost is driven by the number of production set-ups, then that number is the cost-driver for the cost of production-scheduling. The cost-drivers represent the bases for charging costs in the ABC system, with a separate cost code established for each cost-driver.

(b) **Cost pools**

Where the costs with the same cost driver are accumulated (e.g. machine technician salary, machine programming costs and repairs) is known as a 'cost pools' and the total of the cost pool is absorbed by the volume of the cost driver say, machine set ups.

2.2 Mechanics of ABC

The mechanics of operating an ABC system are similar to a traditional costing system. The significant cost drivers need to be ascertained and a cost centre is established for each cost driver. Costs are allocated to products by dividing the cost centre costs by the number of cost driving activities undertaken.

For example, in Plant Y a production run set up would be a cost driver. The cost of the engineers who do the set ups would be a cost pool. If the cost of the engineers is say £280,000 and the number of sets ups is 500, then the charge out rate is $\frac{£280,000}{500} = £560$. A product which has a large number of small production runs will thus have a greater proportion of these costs relative to the quantity of the product produced, than a product with a small number of large production runs.

Other overheads will be allocated to products in a different way; which way depends upon the cost drivers which have been ascertained.

2.3 Calculating the full production cost per unit using ABC

There are five basic steps:

Step 1: Group production overheads into activities, according to how they are driven.

A cost pool is an activity which consumes resources and for which overhead costs are identified and allocated.

For each cost pool, there should be a cost driver. The terms 'activity' and 'cost pool' are often used interchangeably.

Step 2: Identify cost drivers for each activity, i.e. what causes these activity costs to be incurred.

A cost driver is a factor that influences (or drives) the level of cost.

Step 3: Calculate a cost driver rate for each activity.

The cost driver rate is calculated in the same way as the absorption costing OAR.

However, a separate cost driver rate will be calculated for each activity, by taking the activity cost and dividing by the total cost driver volume.

Step 4: Absorb the activity costs into the product.

The activity costs should be absorbed back into the individual products.

Step 5: Calculate the full production cost and/ or the profit or loss.

Some questions ask for the production cost per unit and/ or the profit or loss per unit.

Other questions ask for the total production cost and/ or the total profit or loss.

Example

Plant Y produces about one hundred products. Its largest selling product is Product A; its smallest is Product B. Relevant data is given below.

	Product A	**Product B**	**Total Plant Y**
Units produced pa	50,000	1,000	500,000
Material cost per unit	£1.00	£1.00	
Direct labour per unit	15 minutes	15 minutes	
Machine time per unit	1 hour	1 hour	
Number of set ups p.a.	24	2	500
Number of purchase orders for materials	36	6	2,800
Number of times material handled	200	15	12,000
Direct labour cost per hour			£5

Overhead costs

	£
Set up	280,000
Purchasing	145,000
Materials handling	130,000
Machines	660,000
	1,215,000

Total machine hours are 600,000 hours.

Traditional costing (absorbing overheads on machine hours):

Unit cost	*A*	*B*
	£	£
Material cost	1.00	1.00
Labour cost £5 × 15/60	1.25	1.25
Overhead per machine hour $\frac{1,215,000}{600,000} = 2.025$	2.025	2.025
	4.275	4.275

The above costings imply that we are indifferent between producing Product A and Product B.

Using an ABC approach would show:

Calculate the direct material and labour costs as for the traditional approach.

Unit cost	*A*	*B*
	£	£
Material cost	1.00	1.00
Labour cost	1.25	1.25
	2.25	2.25

Calculate the overheads that will be charged to each product by:

(a) Calculating the overhead cost per cost driver for each type of overhead (e.g. cost per set-up).

(b) Charge cost to each unit by calculating the unit cost accordingly.

	A	*B*
	£	£
Overheads:		
Set up		
£280,000/500 = £560 per set up		
(£560 × 24)/50,000 = £0.2688	0.27	
(£560 × 2)/1,000 = £1.12		1.12
Purchasing:		
£145,000/2,800 = £51.79 per purchase order		
(£51.79 × 36)/50,000 = £0.0372888	0.04	
(£51.79 × 6)/1,000 = £0.31074		0.31
Materials handling:		
£130,000/12,000 = £10.83 per time handled		
(£10.83 × 200)/50,000 = £0.04332	0.04	
(£10.83 × 15)/1,000 = £0.16245		0.16

Machines:		
£660,000/600,000 = £1.10 per machine hour	1.10	1.10
	1.45	2.69
Add: Direct material and labour costs	2.25	2.25
	£3.70	£4.94

Under ABC we can see that the company shouldn't be indifferent between which products to produce as they would've been when the costs were calculated using absorption costing based on machine hours.

This is an example of how using ABC can provide a better analysis of costs.

Common sense would lead us to conclude that ABC is a more accurate representation of the relative real costs of the two products.

2.4 ABC versus Absorption costing

Imagine the machining department of a business that makes clothing. In a traditional absorption costing system the overhead absorption rate would be based on machine hours because many of the overheads in the machining department would relate to the machines, for example power, maintenance, machine depreciation etc. Using only machine hours as the basis would seem fair, however not only does the machine department have machine related costs, but also in an absorption costing system it would have had a share of rent and rates, heating, lighting apportioned to it. These costs would also be absorbed based on machine hours and this is inappropriate as the machine hours are not directly responsible for the rent or rates.

ABC overcomes this problem by not using departments as gathering points for costs, but instead it uses activities to group the costs (cost pools) which are caused (driven) by an activity. There would be an activity that related to each of the following: power usage, machine depreciation and machine maintenance. Machining would not pick up a share of personnel costs or rent and rates as these would be charged to another activity. For example:

- the cost of setting up machinery for a production run might be driven by the number of set-ups (jobs or batches produced)

- the cost of running machines might be driven by the number of machine hours for which the machines are running
- the cost of order processing might be related to the number of orders dispatched or to the weight of items dispatched
- the cost of purchasing might be related to the number of purchase orders made.

ABCs flexibility reduces the need for arbitrary apportionments.

Using ABC should lead to more accurate product and/or service costs being calculated.

What must be considered, however, is whether the benefits of this approach outweigh the costs of implementing and applying the system. The following example again contrasts a traditional product costing system with an ABC system and shows that an ABC system produces much more accurate product costs.

Example

Mayes plc has a single production centre and has provided the following budgeted information for the next period.

	Product A	Product B	Product C	Total
Production and sales (units)	40,000	25,000	10,000	75,000
Direct material cost per unit	£25	£20	£18	£1,680,000
Direct labour hours per unit	3	4	2	240,000
Machine hours per unit	2	4	3	210,000
Number of production runs	5	10	25	40
Number of component receipts	15	25	120	160
Number of production orders	15	10	25	50

Direct labour is paid £8 per hour.
Overhead costs in the period are expected to be as follows:

	£	Cost driver
Set-up	140,000	Number of production runs
Machine	900,000	Number of machine hours
Goods inwards	280,000	Number of receipts
Packing	200,000	Number of production orders
Engineering	180,000	Number of production orders
	———	
	1,700,000	
	———	

What are the unit costs of each product using:

(a) the traditional approach absorbing overheads based on labour hours?

(b) the ABC method?

Solution

(a) A traditional costing approach would cost each product as follows:

	Product A	**Product B**	**Product C**
	£	£	£
Direct materials	25.00	20.00	18.00
Direct labour @£8 per hour	24.00	32.00	16.00
Overhead @£7.08 per hour(W1)	21.24	28.32	14.16
	–––––	–––––	–––––
Total cost	70.24	80.32	48.16
	–––––	–––––	–––––

(W1) Overhead recovery rate = $\frac{£1{,}700{,}000}{240{,}000}$

= £7.08 per direct labour hour

(b) **Step 1** – has been completed already.

Step 2 – an ABC system needs to identify the cost drivers for the indirect overheads not driven by production volume. Again, this has been completed already.

Step 3 – Calculate cost driver rates

Machine overhead = $\frac{£900{,}000}{210{,}000}$

= £4.29 per machine hour (after rounding).

The cost per activity for each of the other cost centres is as follows.

Set-up cost $\frac{£140{,}000}{40}$ = £3,500 per production run

Goods inwards $\frac{£280{,}000}{160}$ = £1,750 per component receipt

Packing $\frac{£200{,}000}{50}$ = £4,000 per production order

Engineering $\frac{£180{,}000}{50}$ = £3,600 per production order

Step 4 – Absorb the activity costs into the product:

	Product A	Product B	Product C
	£	£	£
Set-up costs			
5 × £3,500	17,500		
10 × £3,500		35,000	
25 × £3,500			87,500
Machine costs (rounded down)			
(2 × 40,000) × £4.29	343,200		
(4 × 25,000) × £4.29		429,000	
(3 × 10,000) × £4.29			128,700
Goods inwards costs			
15 × £1,750	26,250		
25 × £1,750		43,750	
120 × £1,750			210,000
Packing costs			
15 × £4,000	60,000		
10 × £4,000		40,000	
25 × £4,000			100,000
Engineering costs			
15 × £3,600	54,000		
10 × £3,600		36,000	
25 × £3,600			90,000
	———	———	———
Total overhead	500,950	583,750	616,200
	———	———	———
Average overhead per unit			
£500,950/40,000	£12.52		
£583,750/25,000		£23.35	
£616,200/10,000			£61.62
This compares to the traditional overhead absorption of:			
	£21.24	£28.32	£14.16

In this case, step 5 is not required.

It can be seen that product C is significantly under-costed under the traditional system, while products A and B are over-costed.

This situation arises because the large proportion of costs driven by product C is not picked up under the traditional costing system.

Since it is the cost-drivers identified in the ABC system which generate the costs in the first place, the ABC system will produce a more accurate final analysis.

Test your understanding 1

For an organisation with a high proportion of overheads to direct costs, which method of costing gives a more accurate product cost?

A Activity based costing

B Total absorption costing

C Marginal costing

D Standard costing

2.5 Advantages and disadvantages of activity based costing

ABC has a number of advantages:

- It provides a more accurate cost per unit. As a result, pricing, sales strategy, performance management and decision making should be improved.
- It provides much better insight into what causes (drives) overhead costs.
- ABC recognises that overhead costs are not all related to production and sales volume.
- In many businesses, overhead costs are a significant proportion of total costs, and management needs to understand the drivers of overhead costs in order to manage the business properly. Overhead costs can be controlled by managing cost drivers.
- It can be applied to calculate realistic costs in a complex business environment.
- ABC can be applied to all overhead costs, not just production overheads.
- ABC can be used just as easily in service costing as in product costing.

Disadvantages of ABC:

- ABC will be of limited benefit if the overhead costs are primarily volume related or if the overhead is a small proportion of the overall cost.
- It is impossible to allocate all overhead costs to specific activities.
- The choice of both activities and cost drivers might be inappropriate.
- ABC can be more complex to explain to the stakeholders of the costing exercise.
- The benefits obtained from ABC might not justify the costs.

2.6 The implications of switching to ABC

The use of ABC has potentially significant commercial implications:

- **Pricing can be based on more realistic cost data.**

  Pricing decisions will be improved because the price will be based on more accurate cost data.

- **Sales strategy can be more soundly based.**

  More realistic product costs as a result of the use of ABC may enable sales staff to:

  – target customers that appeared unprofitable using absorption costing but may be profitable under ABC

  – stop targeting customers or market segments that are now shown to offer low or negative sales margins.

- **Decision making can be improved.**

  Research, production and sales effort can be directed towards those products and services which ABC has identified as offering the highest sales margins.

- **Performance management can be improved.**

  Performance management should be enhanced due to the focus on selling the most profitable products and through the control of cost drivers.

  ABC can be used as the basis of budgeting and longer term forward planning of overhead costs. The more realistic budgeted overhead cost should improve the system of performance management.

Test your understanding 2

Which of the following statements are correct?

Tick all that apply

	Correct?
(i) A cost driver is any factor that causes a change in the cost of an activity.	☐
(ii) For long-term variable overhead costs, the cost driver will be the volume of activity.	☐
(iii) Traditional absorption costing tends to under-allocate overhead costs to low-volume products.	☐

 Test your understanding 3

The accounting technician and the planning engineer have recently analysed the value adding processes at their organisation. They have identified various activities, cost drivers within those activities and current volumes of production and decided to apply the ABC methodology.

Budget 20X3

	Activity	Cost pool	Cost driver volume
		£	
(1)	Process set up	260,000	200 set ups
(2)	Material procurement	74,000	50 purchase orders
(3)	Maintenance	64,000	12 maintenance plans
(4)	Material handling	120,000	2,500 material movements
(5)	Quality costs	80,000	200 inspections
(6)	Order processing	30,000	1,000 customers
		628,000	

The company plans to produce 1,000 tonnes per month of a product which will require the following:

17 set ups

4 purchase orders

1 maintenance plan

210 material movements

16 inspections

80 customers

Task

(a) Calculate the cost driver rates.

(b) Determine the amount of overhead to be recovered per tonne of product.

Solution

(a) Cost driver rates:

Activity	**Cost pool**	**Cost driver volume**	**Cost driver rate**
	£		
Process set up			
Material procurement			
Maintenance			
Material handling			
Quality costs			
Order processing			

(b) Using the ABC method, the following overhead would be recovered for each 1,000 tonnes of output:

				£
	set ups	×		
	purchase orders	×		
	maintenance plan	×		
	material movements	×		
	inspections	×		
	customers	×		
				———
				———

Thus the overhead cost per tonne of product would be:

£ ____________ per tonne.

3 Implications for pricing

3.1 Pricing considerations

The use of marginal cost is simpler as there is no need for the absorption of fixed overheads and could be argued to be more consistent with the use of contribution in decision making. The main difficulty lies in setting an appropriate margin or mark-up as this will need to ensure that fixed costs are covered. In practice the danger is often that prices are set too low. Marginal costing is particularly useful in short-term decisions concerning the use of excess capacity or one off contracts.

The use of full absorption cost ensures that all costs are incorporated into the pricing decision, so should ensure a profit is made, provided the target volume is achieved. However, to calculate the fixed cost per unit an assumption must be made concerning sales volumes, which in turn depend on the price, which depends on the cost per unit. A further criticism is that the method of absorbing overheads is somewhat arbitrary, so the prices obtained may not be very realistic when compared with what customers are willing to pay.

The use of ABC cost has the similar benefit to absorption costing in that all costs are incorporated into the pricing decision, so should ensure a profit is made. It is probably the most accurate cost and so therefore pricing, sales strategy, performance management and decision making should be improved. The issues are the same as listed earlier around complexity and ability to accurately allocate all overheads to specific activities.

Test your understanding 4

Cabal makes and sells two products, Plus and Doubleplus. The direct costs of production are £12 for one unit of Plus and £24 per unit of Doubleplus.

Information relating to annual production and sales is as follows:

	Plus	**Doubleplus**
Annual production and sales	24,000 units	24,000 units
Direct labour hours per unit	1.0	1.5
Number of orders	10	140
Number of batches	12	240
Number of setups per batch	1	3
Special parts per unit	1	4

Information relating to annual production and sales is as follows:

	Cost driver	Annual cost
		£
Setup costs	Number of setups	73,200
Special parts handling	Number of special parts	60,000
Other materials handling	Number of batches	63,000
Order handling	Number of orders	19,800
Other overheads	–	216,000
		432,000

Other overhead costs do not have an identifiable cost driver and, in an ABC system, these overheads would be recovered on a direct labour hours basis.

Task

(a) Calculate the production cost per unit of Plus and of Doubleplus if the company uses traditional absorption costing and the overheads are recovered on a direct labour hours basis.

(b) Calculate the production cost per unit of Plus and of Doubleplus if the company uses ABC.

(c) Comment on the reasons for the differences in the production cost per unit between the two methods.

(d) What are the implications for management of using an ABC system instead of an absorption costing system?

Solution

(a) Traditional absorption costing:

Budgeted direct labour hours

Budgeted overhead costs

Recovery rate per direct labour hour

	Plus	Doubleplus
	£	£
Direct costs		
Production overhead		
Full production cost		

(b) ABC:

Workings

	Plus	Doubleplus	Total
Batches			
Setups			
Special parts			
Orders			
Direct labour hours			

Cost driver rates	Working	Rate per driver
Set ups		
Special parts handling		
Order handling		
Materials handling		
Other overheads		

	Plus	Doubleplus	Total
Setup costs			73,200
Special parts handling costs			60,000
Order handling costs			19,800
Materials handling costs			63,000
Other overheads			216,000
			432,000

	Plus	Doubleplus
Number of units	24,000	24,000
	£	£
Direct cost per unit		
Overhead cost per unit		
Full cost		

(c) **The reasons for the difference in the production cost per unit between the two methods**

(d) **What are the implications for management of using an ABC system instead of an absorption costing system?**

Test your understanding 5

P Ltd operates an activity based costing (ABC) system to attribute its overhead costs to cost objects.

In its budget for the year ending 31 August 20X6, the company expected to place a total of 2,895 purchase orders at a total cost of £110,010. This activity and its related costs were budgeted to occur at a constant rate throughout the budget year, which is divided into 13 four-week periods.

During the four-week period ended 30 June 20X6, a total of 210 purchase orders were placed at a cost of £7,650.

The over-recovery of these costs for the four-week period was:

A £330

B £350

C £370

D £390

4 Summary

This chapter has covered the cost accounting topic of activity based costing, in particular we considered:

- circumstances it would be appropriate
- benefits and issues with ABC
- issues surrounding introducing it
- implications for selling prices
- the calculations
- comparing costs under ABC principles to traditional methods.

Test your understanding answers

Test your understanding 1

A For an organisation with a high proportion of overheads to direct costs ABC gives the most accurate product cost.

Test your understanding 2

Which of the following statements are correct (tick all that apply)?

		Correct?
(i)	A cost driver is any factor that causes a change in the cost of an activity.	☑
(ii)	For long-term variable overhead costs, the cost driver will be the volume of activity.	☑
(iii)	Traditional absorption costing tends to under-allocate overhead costs to low-volume products.	☑

Statement (i) provides a definition of a cost driver. Cost drivers for long-term variable overhead costs will be the volume of a particular activity to which the cost driver relates, so statement (ii) is correct. statement (iii) is also correct. In traditional absorption costing, standard high-volume products receive a higher amount of overhead costs than with ABC. ABC allows for the unusually high costs of support activities for low volume products (such as relatively higher set-up costs, order processing costs and so on).

Test your understanding 3

(a) Cost driver rates:

Activity	Cost pool	Cost driver volume	Cost driver rate
	£		
Process set up	260,000	200 set ups	£1,300/set up
Material procurement	74,000	50 purchase orders	£1,480 per purchase order
Maintenance	64,000	12 maintenance plans	£5,333 per plan
Material handling	120,000	2,500 material movements	£48 per movement
Quality costs	80,000	200 inspections	£400 per inspection
Order processing	30,000	1,000 customers	£30 per customer

(b) Using the ABC method, the following overhead would be recovered for each 1,000 tonnes of output:

			£
17 set ups	×	£1,300	22,100
4 purchase orders	×	£1,480	5,920
1 maintenance plan	×	£5,333	5,333
210 material movements	×	£48	10,080
16 inspections	×	£400	6,400
80 customers	×	£30	2,400
			£52,233

Thus the overhead cost per tonne of product would be:

£52,233/1,000 = £52.23 per tonne.

Test your understanding 4

Solution

(a) Traditional absorption costing:

Budgeted direct labour hours	60,000
(24,000 × 1.0) + (24,000 × 1.5)	
Budgeted overhead costs	£432,000
Recovery rate per direct labour hour	£7.20

	Plus	**Doubleplus**
	£	£
Direct costs	12.00	24.00
Production overhead	7.20	10.80
	19.20	34.80
Full production cost		

(b) ABC:

Workings

	Plus	**Doubleplus**	**Total**
Batches	12	240	252
Setups			
Plus: 1 set up per batch	12		732
Doubleplus: 3 setups per batch		720	
Special parts	24,000	96,000	120,000
Orders	10	140	150
Direct labour hours	24,000	36,000	60,000

Cost driver rates

Setups	£73,200/732	£100 per setup
Special parts handling	£60,000/120,000	£0.50 per part
Materials handling	£63,000/252	£250 per batch
Order handling	£19,800/150	£132 per order
Other overheads	£216,000/60,000	£3.60 per labour hour

	Plus	Doubleplus	Total
Setup costs	1,200	72,000	73,200
Special parts handling costs	12,000	48,000	60,000
Materials handling costs	3,000	60,000	63,000
Order handling costs	1,320	18,480	19,800
Other overheads	86,400	129,600	216,000
	103,920	328,080	432,000

Number of units	24,000	24,000
	£	£
Direct cost	12.00	24.00
Overhead cost per unit	4.33	13.67
Full cost	16.33	37.67

Note: In the example above the full production costs were:

	Plus	Doubleplus
Using traditional absorption costing	£19.20	£34.80
Using ABC	£16.33	£37.67
Assume the selling prices are	£25.00	£40.00
Using absorption costing sales margins are	23.2%	13.0%
ABC sales margins are	34.7%	5.8%

(c) **The reasons for the difference in the production cost per unit between the two methods**

- The allocation of overheads under absorption costing was unfair. This method assumed that all of the overheads were driven by labour hours and, as a result, the Doubleplus received 1.5 times the production overhead of the Plus.
- However, this method of absorption is not appropriate. The overheads are in fact driven by a number of different factors. There are five activity costs, each one has its own cost driver. By taking this into account we end up with a much more accurate production overhead cost per unit.

- Using ABC, the cost per unit of a Doubleplus is significantly higher. This is because the Doubleplus is a much more complex product than the Plus. For example, there are 140 orders for the Doubleplus but only 10 for the Plus and there are 4 special parts for the Doubleplus compared to only one for the Plus. As a result of this complexity, the Doubleplus has received more than three times the overhead of the Plus.
- This accurate allocation is important because the production overhead is a large proportion of the overall cost.

(d) **What are the implications for management of using an ABC system instead of an absorption costing system?**

Pricing – pricing decisions will be improved because the price will be based on more accurate cost data.

- Decision making – this should also be improved. For example, research, production and sales effort can be directed towards the most profitable products.
- Performance management – should be improved. ABC can be used as the basis of budgeting and forward planning. The more realistic overhead should result in more accurate budgets and should improve the process of performance management. In addition, an improved understanding of what drives the overhead costs should result in steps being taken to reduce the overhead costs and hence an improvement in performance.
- Sales strategy – this should be more soundly based. For example, target customers with products that appeared unprofitable under absorption costing but are actually profitable, and vice versa.

Test your understanding 5

A

Cost driver rate = £110,010 ÷ 2,895 = £38 for each order

	£
Cost recovered: 210 orders × £38	7,980
Actual costs incurred	7,650
Over-recovery of costs for four-week period	330

Target costing and life cycle costing

2

Introduction

Target costing involves setting a target cost by subtracting a desired profit from a competitive market price. It has been described as a cost management tool for reducing the overall cost of a product over its entire life-cycle with the help of production, engineering, research and design. Real world users include Sony, Toyota and the Swiss watchmakers, Swatch. In effect it is the opposite of conventional 'cost plus pricing'.

Some costs change when activity levels change, whilst others do not. The ability to isolate cost elements by behaviour is essential to management who are concerned with predicting future costs as part of the planning and decision making processes.

Life cycle considers the big picture in terms of all the costs incurred by an organisation relating to a product or opportunity from inception through to abandonment. This increased awareness helps improve decision making.

ASSESSMENT CRITERIA

Impact of internal and external factors on forecasts (LO 1.5)

Target costing (LO 2.4)

Life cycle costing (LO 2.5)

CONTENTS

1 Cost reduction

1.1 Introduction

There are few organisations which would not benefit from real efforts to keep costs to a minimum. Businesses will make more money that way, assuming quality is not compromised.

Not-for-profit organisations will make their funds go further in providing necessary services, and will be better able to meet the requirements for 'good stewardship' normally imposed on them.

Definitions

Cost reduction is a process which leads to the achievement of real and permanent reductions in the unit costs of goods manufactured or services rendered without impairing their suitability for the use intended.

Cost control, on the other hand, aims simply to achieve the target costs originally accepted.

Note that cost reduction is aiming to reduce unit costs, i.e. the cost per item of output. (It would be possible for a cost reduction programme to increase the total costs incurred if the output volume rose even higher, so that the unit cost was reduced.)

1.2 Implementing a cost reduction programme

Once an organisation has adopted an objective of reducing costs, the following conditions need to apply if it is to be successful.

- A clear purpose – say, to reduce labour costs by 20%, or materials costs by 15%.
- A good reason – economic survival, say, or the ability in the future to compete with competitors with a lower cost base.
- Commitment and involvement by senior managers.
- Excellent and positive communication with workforce and, if possible, consultation.
- Gradual introduction.

2 Target costing

2.1 Introduction

Target costing involves setting a target cost by subtracting a desired profit from a competitive market price. Real world users include Sony, Toyota and the Swiss watchmakers, Swatch.

In effect it is the opposite of conventional 'cost plus pricing'.

Target costing starts by subtracting a desired profit margin from the market price at which an item can be sold; this gives the target cost. It is then up to the designers to plan how the product can be manufactured for that cost. If the product is currently planned to cost more than the target cost, then the plan must be modified (which may mean that it is abandoned).

For example, if customers have indicated that they would pay £100 for a new product, and the company that developed it aims to make a 20% profit margin on each product they sell, then the product would have to be manufactured for £80. If this was impossible, then the product would not make it as far as the production stage.

Example – traditional pricing

Music Matters manufactures and sells vinyl records for a number of popular artists. At present, it uses a traditional cost-plus pricing system

Cost-plus pricing system

(1) The cost of the vinyl record is established first. This is £14 per unit.

(2) A profit of £5 per unit is added to each vinyl record.

(3) This results in the current selling price of £19 per unit.

However, cost-plus pricing ignores:

- The price that customers are willing to pay – pricing the vinyl records too high could result in low sales volumes and profits.
- The price charged by competitors for similar products – if competitors are charging less than £19 per vinyl records for similar vinyl records then customers may decide to make their purchases from the competitor companies.
- Cost control – the cost of the vinyl record is established at £14 but there is little incentive to control this cost.

2.2 Steps used in deriving a target cost

Step 1: A market based target price is set, based on the customers' perceived value of the product.

Step 2: The required target operating profit per unit is then calculated. This could be based on the return on sales, or return on investment.

Step 3: The target cost per unit is calculated by subtracting the target profit per unit from the target price.

Step 4: Any **cost gap** is then calculated.

Target cost gap = Estimated product cost per unit – Target cost

Step 5: If there is a cost gap, attempts will be made to close it using some of the techniques which will be outlined later. These techniques include value engineering and value analysis. The ultimate aim is to reduce cost while still satisfying customer needs.

In certain very rare situations negotiation with the customer may take place before deciding whether to go ahead with the project. This would be if it was a one of contract, and could be around the features required on the product. It is unlikely that a multinational organisation selling multiple product ranges would negotiate with their customer base.

Example – target costing

Target costing

Music Matters could address the problems discussed above through the implementation of target costing:

(1) The first step is to establish a competitive market price. The company would consider how much customers are willing to pay and how much competitors are charging for similar products. Let's assume this is £15 per vinyl record.

(2) Music Matters would then deduct their required profit from the selling price. The required profit may be kept at £5 per vinyl record.

(3) A target cost is arrived at by deducting the required profit from the selling price, i.e. £15 – £5 = £10 per vinyl record.

(4) The cost gap can then be identified. In this case the current cost per vinyl record of £14 must be reduced to the target cost of £10. A gap of £4 per vinyl record must be closed.

(5) Steps must then be taken to close the target cost gap (see below for further details).

2.3 Closing the target cost gap

The target cost gap is established in step 4 of the target costing process.

Target cost gap = Estimated product cost per unit – Target cost

It is the difference between what an organisation thinks it can currently make a product for, and what it needs to make it for, in order to make a required profit.

Alternative product designs should be examined for potential areas of cost reduction that will not compromise the quality of the products.

Questions that a manufacturer may ask in order to close the gap include:

- Can any materials be eliminated, e.g. cut down on packing materials?
- Can a cheaper material be substituted without affecting quality?
- Can labour savings be made without compromising quality, for example, by using lower skilled workers?
- Can productivity be improved, for example, by improving motivation?
- Can production volume be increased to achieve economies of scale?
- Could cost savings be made by reviewing the supply chain?
- Can part-assembled components be bought in to save on assembly time?
- Can the incidence of the cost drivers be reduced?
- Is there some degree of overlap between the product-related fixed costs that could be eliminated by combining service departments or resources?

A key aspect of this is to understand which features of the product are essential to customer perceived quality and which are not. This process is known as '**value analysis**'. Attention should be focused more on reducing the costs of features perceived by the customer not to add value.

Note: Closing the cost gap by increasing the selling price is not a viable option as the price is determined by market forces rather than the company.

2.4 Value engineering

Value engineering is a philosophy of designing products which meet customer needs at the lowest cost while assuring the required standard of quality and reliability. The idea is to understand what it is that customers want from your products, and save costs by eliminating items that add no value in customers' eyes. For example, a manufacturer of computer components may decide that its customers place no value on a paper instruction manual or on elaborate packaging, and will decide to sell its products with no manual and in a plain cardboard box.

2.5 Value analysis

Value analysis is similar to value engineering, but relates to existing products, while value engineering relates to products that have not yet been produced. A company may sell a product with a feature that they discover adds no value to the customer, but incurs cost to include in the product. Using value analysis they would remove this feature, thus saving money, without harming the value of the product to the customer.

A cost advantage may be obtained in many ways, for example:

- economies of scale
- the experience (or learning curve) of workers
- product design innovations
- the use of 'no frills' product offering

Each provides a different way of competing on the basis of cost advantage.

2.6 Value enhancement

The 'flip side' of cost reduction is value enhancement namely, getting the best value from the resources that are used in the organisation. Value added can be defined as revenue less the cost of bought in materials. Use of performance indicators that we will see later on (for example productivity and efficiency) provides useful comparative measures to assess value enhancement before and after an active 'value-for-money' programme. It should be emphasised that cost reduction and value enhancement are not just the responsibility of the accounts department of a business. All of the functional specialists (designers, marketing, engineering, quality control, etc) must pool their knowledge and work side-by-side to achieve the required objectives.

2.7 Benchmarking

One way of closely monitoring one's own business is to compare the results in your business by department or division (internal benchmarking) or against a competitor (competitive benchmarking).

Benchmarking is the establishment of targets and comparators, through whose use relative levels of performance (particularly areas of under-performance) can be identified. By the adoption of identified best practices it is hoped that performance can be improved.

One common example is internal benchmarking, where a company is split up into business divisions, all operating in more or less the same industry, and performance indicators are calculated and compared for each division. Perhaps it is then found that one division has receivables of four months revenue, while all the other divisions have receivables of less than two months revenue. The division with abnormally high receivables should be able to improve its liquidity by tightening up its credit control procedures.

Test your understanding 1

Revenue less the cost of bought-in materials and services is called:

- Value added ☐
- Cost reduction ☐
- Value enhancement ☐

Test your understanding 2

A cost reduction method whereby the starting point is the selling price followed by the deduction of a margin is called?

- Target costing ☐
- Loss leading ☐
- Competitor pricing ☐

Test your understanding 3

A new product has been developed. After extensive research it has been estimated that the future selling price will be £200 with a demand of 1,000 units. Other useful information is below:

Material	4 litres at £10 per litre
Labour	5 hours
Fixed costs	£10 per unit
Profit margin required	25%

Calculate the target labour cost per hour.

	£
Selling price	
Profit margin at 25%	
Total costs	
Material cost	
Fixed costs	
Maximum labour cost	
Target labour cost per hour	

Test your understanding 4

Company Cee is currently considering expansion into manufacturing two new products, a printer and a digital camera.

Company Cee normally uses a pricing policy of a 10% mark-up on standard prime cost on its products. However, as both the printing and camera markets are highly competitive, the finance director is considering using a target costing approach but wants to retain the same mark-up.

Printers

The maximum price the market will support is £200 per unit of the new printer. 60% of the direct cost of each printer is expected to be a specific material called polymer.

(a) **What is the target cost of the polymer used in the manufacture of printers?**

	£
Target selling price	
Profit	
Direct cost	
Target cost of polymer	

Digital cameras

40% of the direct cost of each digital camera is expected to be software. The minimum price Company Cee can source the software necessary to make one digital camera is currently £76, which has been built into the budget. On this basis, Company Cee has determined that the cost gap between the budgeted cost per digital camera and the target cost per digital camera is £23.70.

(b) **Assuming that target costing principles are adopted, what is the maximum selling price that Company Cee can charge per digital camera?**

	£
Software cost	
Direct cost	
Cost gap	
Target cost	
Mark up	
Selling price	

3 Life cycle costing

3.1 Life cycle costing

Traditional costing techniques based around annual periods may give a misleading impression of the costs and profitability of a product. This is because systems are based on the financial accounting year, and dissect the product's lifecycle into a series of annual sections. Usually, therefore, the management accounting systems would assess a product's profitability on a periodic basis, rather than over its entire life.

Lifecycle costing, however, tracks and accumulates costs and revenues attributable to each product over its entire product lifecycle.

$$\text{Lifecycle cost of Product A} = \frac{\text{Total costs of Product A over its entire lifecycle}}{\text{Total number of units of A}}$$

Then, the **total** profitability of any given product can be determined.

A product's costs are not evenly spread through its life.

According to Berliner and Brimson (1988), companies operating in an advanced manufacturing environment are finding that about **90% of a product's lifecycle costs are determined by decisions made early in the cycle**. In many industries, a large fraction of the life-cycle costs consists of costs incurred on product design, prototyping, programming, process design and equipment acquisition.

This had created a need to ensure that the tightest controls are at the design stage, i.e. before a launch, because most costs are committed, or 'locked in', at this point in time.

Management accounting systems should therefore be developed that aid the planning and control of product lifecycle costs and monitor spending and commitments **at the early stages of a product's life cycle**.

Please note that the approach to life cycle costing involving discounting will be covered in a later chapter.

Example

The following details relate to a new product that has finished development and is about to be launched

	Costs to date	Year 1	Year 2	Year 3	Year 4
R&D costs (£ million)	20				
Marketing costs (£ million)		5	4	3	0.9
Production cost per unit (£)		1.00	0.90	0.80	0.90
Production volume (millions)		1	5	10	4
Clean up costs (£ million)					1

The launch price in the first year is proving a contentious issue between managers.

The marketing manager is keen to start with a low price of around £8 to gain new buyers and achieve target market share.

The accountant is concerned that this does not cover costs during the launch phase and has produced the following schedule to support this:

Year 1		£ million
Amortised R&D costs	(£20,000,000/4 years)	5.0
Marketing costs		5.0
Production costs	1,000,000 × £1.00 per unit	1.0
Total		11.0
Total production units	1 million	
Cost per unit =	11,000,000/1,000,000 = **£11.00**	

Prepare a revised cost per unit schedule looking at the whole lifecycle and comment on the implications of this cost with regards to the pricing of the product during the launch phase.

Solution

Lifecycle costs		£ million
Total R&D costs		20.0
Total marketing costs	5 + 4 + 3 + 0.9	12.9
Total production costs	(1 × 1) + (5 × 0.9) + (10 × 0.8) + (4 × 0.9)	17.1
Clean up costs		1.0
Total life cycle costs		51.0
Total production units =	1 + 5 +10 + 4 = 20 million	
Cost per unit =	51,000,000/20,000,000 = **£2.55**	

Comment

The cost was calculated at £11 per unit during the launch phase. Based on this cost, the accountant was right to be concerned about the launch price being set at £8 per unit.

However, looking at the whole lifecycle the marketing manager's proposal seems more reasonable.

The average cost per unit over the entire life of the product is only £2.55 per unit. Therefore, a starting price of £8 per unit would seem reasonable and would result in a profit of £5.45 per unit.

3.2 The advantages of life cycle costing

Life cycle costing has the following advantages:

- the forecast profitability of a given product over its entire life is determined before production begins
- accumulated costs at any stage can be compared with life cycle budgeted costs, product by product, for the purposes of planning and control

We can compare this approach with more traditional management accounting practices.

- Most traditional accounting reporting systems are based upon periodic accounts, reporting product profitability in isolated calendar-based amounts, rather than focusing on the revenues and costs accumulated over the life cycle to date.
- Recognition of the commitment needed over the entire life cycle of a product will generally lead to more effective resource allocation than the traditional annual budgeting system.
- Research and development, design, production set-up, marketing and customer service costs are traditionally reported on an aggregated basis for all products and recorded as a period expense. Life cycle costing traces these costs to individual products over their entire life cycles, to aid comparison with product revenues generated in later periods.
- Relationships between early decisions on product design and production methods and ultimate costs can therefore be identified and used for subsequent planning.

With decreasing product lives, it is important to recognise and monitor the relatively high pre-production and early stage costs product by product.

3.3 Implications of life cycle costing

There are a number of factors that need to be managed in order to maximise a product's return over its lifecycle, these include:

Design costs out of the product

Around 90% of a product's costs are often incurred at the design and development stages of its life. Decisions made then commit the organisation to incurring the costs at a later date, because the design of the product determines the number of components, the production method, etc. It is absolutely vital therefore that design teams do not work in isolation but as part of a cross functional team in order to minimise costs over the whole life cycle.

Minimise the time to market

In a world where competitors watch each other keenly to see what new products will be launched, it is vital to get any new product into the marketplace as quickly as possible. The competitors will monitor each other closely so that they can launch rival products as soon as possible in order to maintain profitability. It is vital, therefore, for the first organisation to launch its product as quickly as possible after the concept has been developed, so that it has as long as possible to establish the product in the market and to make a profit before competition increases. Often it is not so much costs that reduce profits as time wasted.

Maximise the length of the life cycle itself

Generally, the longer the life cycle, the greater the profit that will be generated. This assumes that production ceases once the product goes into decline and becomes unprofitable. One way to maximise the life cycle is to get the product to market as quickly as possible because this should maximise the time in which the product generates a profit.

Another way of extending a product's life is to find other uses, or markets, for the product. Other product uses may not be obvious when the product is still in its planning stage and need to be planned and managed later on. On the other hand, it may be possible to plan for a staggered entry into different markets at the planning stage.

Many organisations stagger the launch of their products in different world markets in order to reduce costs, increase revenue and prolong the overall life of the product. A current example is the way in which new films are released in the USA months before the UK launch. This is done to build up the enthusiasm for the film and to increase revenues overall. Other companies may not have the funds to launch worldwide at the same moment and may be forced to stagger it. Skimming the market is another way to prolong life and to maximise the revenue over the product's life.

Pricing

Pricing decisions can be based on total life-cycle costs rather than simply the costs for the current period.

Decision making

In deciding to produce a product, a timetable of life-cycle costs helps to show what costs need to be allocated to a product so that an organisation can recover its costs. If all costs cannot be recovered, it would not be wise to produce the product or service.

Life-cycle costing allows an analysis of links between business functions, e.g. a decision taken now to reduce research and development costs may lead to a fall in sales in the future.

Performance management

Improved control – as many companies have found that 90% of the product's life-cycle costs are determined by decisions made in the development and launch stages. Focusing on costs after the product has entered production results in only a small proportion of life-cycle costs being manageable. Life-cycle costing thus reinforces the importance of tight control over locked-in costs, such as research and development in the development stage.

Improved reporting – costs such as research and development and marketing are traditionally reported on an aggregated basis for all products and recorded as a period expense. Life-cycle costing traces these costs to individual products over their entire life cycles, to aid comparison with product revenues generated in later periods.

4 Product lifecycle

4.1 Revenue forecasts

When forecasting revenue figures, consideration should be given to the position of the product within its lifecycle. Some products have a limited life and there are generally thought to be five stages of the product lifecycle – development, launch (or introduction), growth, maturity and decline, each of which will have different characteristics.

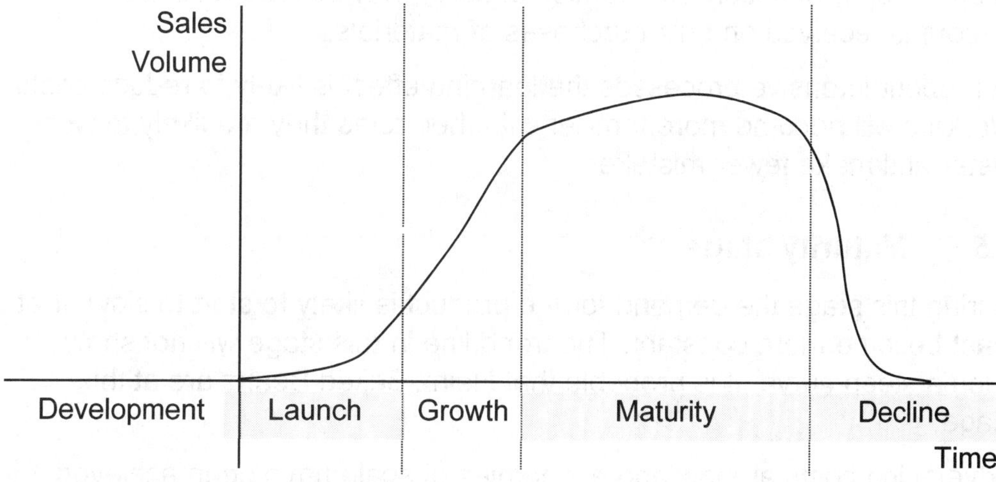

4.2 Development stage

During this time of the product's life there is likely to be a large amount of cost incurred on research and development but no revenue will be generated yet.

4.3 Launch stage

In the early stages of the product's life, immediately after its launch, sales volume is likely to be at a low level whilst the product establishes itself in the market place. In addition, potential customers may not be fully aware of the existence of the product or may be reluctant to try a new product, preferring to remain loyal to the products already established in the market place. However, some eagerly awaited products, for example the PlayStation 3 games console, have had incredibly high sales levels in the launch stage.

Advertising costs will be very high, as will production costs building up inventory ready for the launch.

4.4 Growth stage

If the product is successfully launched then the product is likely to show fairly large increases in revenue indicated by a steep upward trend. However, such large revenue increases are unlikely to continue indefinitely.

As revenues increase, production will increase in order to match demand. Mechanisation may be preferred over labour intensive processes in order to speed up production. Economies of scale may be achieved through discounts received on bulk purchases of materials.

For labour intensive processes the learning effect is likely to reduce costs. Workers will become more familiar with their roles they are likely to work faster and make fewer mistakes.

4.5 Maturity stage

During this stage the demand for the product is likely to start to slow or at least become more constant. The trend line in this stage will not show such a steep curve. It is probable that Heinz Baked Beanz are at this stage.

Advertising costs are low and economies of scale have been achieved, any further cost reduction from the learning effect will likely cease at this stage. There will probably be a switch from traditionally variable costs to fixed costs, for materials and labour, as production levels are now stable. Profits are probably maximised in this stage.

At this stage some form of modification may be required to prevent the product from going into the final stage. Considering the example of Heinz Baked Beanz, they have modified the product to include different flavours like Spanish Beanz, Five Beanz, Fiery Chilli Beanz and different sizes like 200g Snap Pots and a 1kg Fridge Pack.

4.6 Decline stage

Most products will eventually reach the end of their life and revenues will begin to decline, with the trend line now also declining. The product may have become outdated or unfashionable, or new products may have entered the market and attracted customers away.

Costs will also fall as production stops and the remaining inventory is sold off. Profits will reduce considerably possibly to a loss.

4.7 Time series analysis and product lifecycle

Due to the changes in sales demand throughout the lifecycle of a product, care should be taken when using time series analysis to estimate the trend of future revenues. If the time series figures are based upon the growth stage then the trend line in this stage is unlikely to continue but will be likely to become less steep.

Test your understanding 5

Enrono is an accounting software package which has a six year product lifecycle. The following are the yearly costs, estimated for the entire length of the packages life:

Costs in £000	*Year 1*	*Year 2*	*Year 3*	*Year 4*	*Year 5*	*Year 6*
R&D costs	275					
Design costs		120				
Production cost			120	200	200	
Marketing cost			125	170	130	60
Distribution cost			20	20	15	10
Customer service cost			5	15	30	45

The company that make Enrono expect to sell 150,000 units across its entire life.

(a) Calculate the life cycle cost per unit.

Life cycle costs	£000
R&D costs	
Design costs	
Production cost	
Marketing cost	
Distribution cost	
Customer service cost	
Total life cycle cost	

(b) Comment on the uses of this information for the company.

(c) Comment on the implications for planning at the different stages of the products life.

Introduction	**Growth**	**Maturity**	**Decline**

Test your understanding 6

The stage in the product lifecycle with the highest unit sales is:

Introduction ☐

Growth ☐

Maturity ☐

Decline ☐

5 Summary

Target costing reverses the traditional approach to setting a selling price, by identifying a competitive selling price and the desired profit first then working backwards to get the target cost.

One of the key components is the process involved in making sure the company achieve that target cost, by using cost reduction, value engineering and value analysis.

Lifecycle costing and how it can be used to aid cost management has been considered.

This chapter has also considered the product lifecycle and how costs will change throughout the life of a product.

Answers to chapter test your understandings

Test your understanding 1

Value added equals revenue less the cost of bought-in materials and services.

Test your understanding 2

Target costing is the idea of identifying the cost at which a product must be made, and then choosing a design and production method that will meet that cost. This differs from the traditional idea of producing an item, seeing how much it has cost, and then adding a profit margin to set the selling price.

Test your understanding 3

	£
Selling price	200
Profit margin at 25%	(50)
Total costs	150
Material cost	(40)
Fixed costs	(10)
Maximum labour cost	100
Target labour cost per hour	20

Test your understanding 4

(a)

	%	£
Target selling price	110	200.00
Profit	10	18.18
Direct cost	100	181.82
Target cost of polymer	60	109.09

Polymer costs represent 60% of direct cost, so 60% × £181.82 = £109.09 per printer.

(b)

	%	£
Software cost	40	76.00
Direct cost	100	190.00
Cost gap		23.70
Target cost	100	166.30
Mark up	10	16.63
Selling price	110	182.93

Software represents 40% of direct cost, so total direct cost £76/0.40 = £190. Cost gap at present is £23.70;

Therefore target cost = £190 – £23.70 = £166.30.

£166.30 × (1 + 10% mark-up) = £182.93

Test your understanding 5

(a)

Life cycle costs	£000
R&D costs	275
Design costs	120
Production cost	520
Marketing cost	485
Distribution cost	65
Customer service cost	95
Total life cycle cost	1,560

Lifecycle cost per unit = 1,560,000/150,000 = £10.40

(b) Lifecycle costing clearly takes into consideration the costs of the package incurred during the entire lifecycle – over £1.5 m. accordingly, from lifecycle costing, the management can know whether the revenue earned by the product is sufficient to cover the whole costs incurred during its life cycle.

When viewed as a whole, there are opportunities for cost reduction and minimisation (and thereby scope for profit maximisation) in several categories of cost:

For example, initiatives could be taken to reduce testing costs and therefore the 'Research and Development' category.

Likewise, proper planning and a tight control on transportation and handling costs could minimise distribution costs.

(c) These opportunities for cost reduction are unlikely to be found when management focuses on maximising profit in a period by period basis. Only on knowing the lifecycle costs of a product can a business decide appropriately on its price. This, coupled with planning of the different phases of the product's life, could give rise to the following tactics:

Introduction	**Growth**	**Maturity**	**Decline**
High prices to recoup high development costs; high returns before competitors enter the market.	Competition increases; reduce price to remain competitive.	Sales slow down and level off; the market price is maintained. Upgrades and/or new markets should be considered.	Superior products appear – our prices must be cut to maintain sales.

Test your understanding 6

The maturity stage has the highest unit sales.

Limiting factor analysis

3

Introduction

We all face limits on our lives, from not having the money to buy all the food or possessions we want, to not having the time to do all the things we'd like to do. Organisations are the same too, they face many constraints on their activity and in the same way that we prioritise activities or purchases so to do organisations.

For an organisation the constraints could be anything from access to finance, plant capacity and factory space, to shortage of production resources like labour or materials.

Assessment questions will focus on the problem of scarce resources that prevent the normal plan from being achieved. As an example, it may be that a firm is facing a labour shortage this month due to sickness and, as a result, cannot produce the number of units that it would like to. The challenge for accounting technicians is how the production plan for the organisation should be revised.

ASSESSMENT CRITERIA

Key factor analysis (LO 3.3)

CONTENTS

1 Contribution

1.1 Introduction

Contribution is defined as the difference between the selling price and the variable cost of producing and selling the item. This is in contrast to profit per unit, which is the difference between the selling price and the total absorption cost of producing and selling that item, which includes an element of fixed cost.

It is called contribution since it tells us how much each product contributes towards paying for the fixed costs of the business.

Fixed costs, by definition, are unavoidable and do not change with the level of production. Therefore, in any decision which is connected with varying the levels of production, fixed costs are not a relevant cost as they do not change regardless of which course of action is taken.

Test your understanding 1

R Ltd makes a single product, the Morton. During 20X9 R Ltd plans to make and sell 10,000 Mortons and accordingly has estimated the cost of each to be £50 (see below). Each Morton sells for £75.

	£
Materials	12
Labour	24
Variable overheads	10
Fixed overheads	4
Total absorption cost	50

Required:

(a) Calculate the contribution earned by each Morton.

(b) Calculate the total profit if R Ltd sells 2,000 Mortons.

Solution

(a) **Contribution per unit**

Selling price per unit – Variable cost per unit

= £__________

(b) **Profit**

Total contribution – Fixed costs

= £__________

Test your understanding 2

Blidworth Loam Ltd manufacture a single product, the 'Cricketloam', and supply this product to cricket clubs.

Its cost specification includes the following budgeted details for the current year:

Direct labour hours	4.5
Labour rate per hour	£8.50
Direct material	1.1 tonnes per tonne of saleable output
Material cost	£25 per tonne
Variable production overheads (total)	£378,000
Fixed production overheads (total)	£250,000
Selling price per tonne	£132
Production volume	12,000 tonnes
Sales volume	11,500 tonnes

Task

Considering the above information, what is the budgeted marginal cost per tonne of product?

A £65.75

B £59.00

C £97.25

D £118.08

	£
Direct labour	
Direct material	
Variable overhead	
Marginal cost = Total variable costs per tonne	

Test your understanding 3

Task

Using the information in test your understanding 2, what is the contribution per tonne of product?

A £66.25

B £73.00

C £13.92

D £34.75

2 The concept of a scarce resource

2.1 Scarce resources

As we discussed in the introduction to this chapter we, as individuals, have to make decisions on a daily basis about how we will use our money or our time, what television show we will stream. We generally make a choice based around Maslow's hierarchy of needs, satisfying our basic needs first of all with food, water, warmth and safety, then onto psychological needs relating to friendship and feelings of accomplishment, through to self-fulfilment and carrying out creative activities linked to our interests.

For an organisation, it is more likely to be related to the level of activity they would be able to achieve. Limitations may be imposed, for example, by:

- market demand for its products or services
- the number of skilled employees available
- the availability of material supplies
- the space available either as a working area or for the storage of goods
- the amount of cash or credit facilities available to finance the business.

Questions will focus on the problem of scarce resources that prevent the normal plan from being achieved. For example, an organisation is facing a labour shortage this month due to sickness and, as a result, cannot produce the number of units that it would like to. You may be asked to consider how that organisation's production plan should be revised.

3 Limiting factor analysis

3.1 Single limiting factor

Limiting factor analysis can also be referred to as key factor analysis or principal budget factor analysis.

Since most overheads are fixed the decision to make one extra unit of production will not affect that cost, so it should be ignored. Only the marginal cost of making one extra unit should be considered in decision making and therefore should be added to the cost unit.

This approach to costing enables us to make decisions when there is a scarcity of resources, which is when the shortage of one resource means that that resource limits the entire capacity of the operation: this is the limiting factor.

A company may produce two products, each requiring materials and labour. There may be a limit as to the amount of labour or materials that is available for the coming month. How can the company make the most profit when subject to such a constraint?

Since fixed costs are independent of production they are irrelevant (they will have to be paid however many units of each product are manufactured). The above problem therefore requires us to maximise contribution taking into account the limiting factor.

3.2 Identifying the single limiting factor

For limiting factor analysis, one of the skills that may be tested is identifying which resource is the limiting factor. To do this, we must consider what the organisation would do if the resources were unlimited. This is generally to produce to demand levels or desired production levels.

As in life, in assessment questions we'll know what limits we have, we'll either be told in the question or given enough information to work out what the limitations are. The key, for this area of the syllabus, is that there will only be one resource that actually stops the organisation from achieving the demand levels, budget or plan.

Example

Two products, Chaffinch and Greenfinch, are made of Material X and require skilled labour in the production process.

The product details are as follows:

	Chaffinch	**Greenfinch**
	£	£
Selling price	10.00	15.00
Variable cost	6.00	7.50
Contribution	4.00	7.50
Material X required per unit	2 kg	4 kg
Skilled labour time required per unit	1 hour	3 hours

The maximum demand per week is 30 units of Chaffinch and 10 units of Greenfinch.

There is a restriction on the availability of both Material X and skilled labour.

There are 150 kg of material available per week and 45 hours of skilled labour available per week.

Identify the limiting factor.

	Chaffinch	**Greenfinch**	**Total**
Maximum demand (units)	30	10	
Material X required per unit (kg)	2	4	
Material X required for maximum demand (kg)	60	40	100
Total available kg			150
Labour time per unit (hours)	1	3	
Skilled labour time required for maximum demand (hours)	30	30	60
Total available hours			45

Material X requirement (100 kg) is less than the amount of Material X available in a week (150 kg).

Material X does not, therefore, limit the activities of the organisation.

60 hours of skilled labour are required in order to produce the maximum number of units of each product demanded each week.

However, only 45 hours of skilled labour are available and so skilled labour is the limiting factor in this situation because it limits the organisation's activities.

Example

The following data relates to Products H and B.

	H	B
Direct materials cost per unit	£10	£30
Direct labour:		
Sawing department £5 per hour	7 hours per unit	5 hours per unit
Smoothing department £7.50 per hour	15 hours per unit	9 hours per unit
Selling price per unit	£206.50	£168.00
Budgeted production	1,200 units	600 units
External demand for the period	1,500 units	800 units

Notes

(1) No opening or closing inventory is anticipated.

(2) The skilled labour used for the sawing processes is highly specialised and in short supply, although there is just sufficient to meet the budgeted production. However, it will not be possible to increase the supply for the budget period.

Determine the amount of the scarce resource that is available.

The limiting factor is time in the sawing department.

There is 'just sufficient to meet the budgeted production'.

Using this as our guide:

	H	B	Total
Budgeted production units	1,200	600	
Sawing hours per unit	7	5	
Hours required for budgeted production	8,400	3,000	11,400

That means there are 11,400 hours available in the sawing department.

Test your understanding 4

An organisation intends to sell 500 units in the month and has identified the availability of the resources required to make the product as follows.

Resource	Usage		Maximum availability
Materials	2	litres per unit	890 litres
Labour	1	hour per unit	600 hours
Machine time	0.1	hours per unit	50 hours

No more resources are available.

Which resource is the limiting factor for production in the month, and how many units can be produced and sold?

Solution

The resource that limits production in the month is ___________ .

The maximum number of units that can be made in the month is ______ units.

3.3 Step by step approach

If there is one limiting factor, then the problem is best solved using key factor analysis:

Step 1 Identify the scarce resource.

Step 2 Calculate the contribution per unit for each product.

Step 3 Calculate the contribution per unit of the scarce resource for each product.

Step 4 Rank the products in order of the contribution per unit of the scarce resource.

Step 5 Allocate resources using this ranking and answer the question.

Example

Barbecue Limited manufactures two products for which the following details are available.

	Product X		Product Y
Selling price	£38		£38
Direct materials 8 kgs @ £1	£8	4 kgs @ £1	£4
Labour 4 hours @ £2	£8	6 hours @ £2	£12
Variable overhead 4 machine hours @ £3	£12	3 machine hours @ £3	£9
Fixed overheads	£5		£7

Maximum demand for X is 2,500 units.

Maximum demand for Y is 2,000 units.

Required

Calculate the optimum production plan for Barbecue in each of the following two situations:

(a) Labour in the next period is limited to 16,000 hours, with no limit on machine hours.

(b) Machine hours in the next period are limited to 12,000 hours, with no limit on labour hours.

Solution

We would like to produce Xs and Ys up to the point where maximum demand is reached. (There is no point producing beyond this, because customers do not want any more.) So ideally we would like to produce 2,500 X and 2,000 Y.

To do this we would require the following resources.

	Labour hours	Machine hours
2,500 X	10,000	10,000
2,000 Y	12,000	6,000
	22,000	16,000

If labour is limited to 16,000 hours we will not have enough labour hours to achieve this. Similarly, if machine hours are limited to 12,000 our production will be restricted.

To tackle this problem we begin by calculating the contribution earned per unit of each product.

Contribution for each unit of X = £ (38 – 8 – 8 – 12) = £10 per unit

Contribution for each unit of Y = £ (38 – 4 – 12 – 9) = £13 per unit

(a) Labour is limited so we calculate the contribution earned per labour hour for each product.

X = £10/4 hours = £2.50 per labour hour

Y = £13/6 hours = £2.17 per labour hour

You get more contribution per labour hour for each unit of X produced than for Y so make as many Xs as possible.

Available hours = 16,000

2,500 Xs require 10,000 hrs

The remaining hours are all used to make as many Ys as possible.

Remaining Ys will take six hours each to make so produce 6,000/6 = 1,000 Ys.

Contribution = (2,500 × £10) + (1,000 × £13) = £38,000

(b) In this case, machine hours are the scarce resource so we calculate contribution per machine hour.

X = £10/4 hours = £2.50 per machine hour

Y = £13/3 hours = £4.33 per machine hour

Now it is better to make Ys. Making 2,000 Ys requires 2,000 × 3 = 6,000 machine hours. That leaves us a further 6,000 machine hours for making Xs.

6,000 remaining hours for X means making 6,000/4 = 1,500 Xs

Contribution = (1,500 × £10) + (2,000 × £13) = £41,000

Note that, in the assessment, if you are told the maximum demand for a product it is a big hint that this method should be used.

One final point, if no demand levels are given in the scenario, then the assumption is that an unlimited amount of units can be sold of every product. In this situation, an organisation wishing to maximise profits would make as many units as it possibly could of the product ranked 1st in step 4.

Test your understanding 5

Q Ltd makes three products – X Y and Z. In the next year Q Ltd would like to make 500 of each product.

	X	Y	Z
	£	£	£
Selling price	90	80	75
Materials (£3 per kg)	15	18	12
Labour	15	12	24
Variable overheads	8	6	10
Fixed overheads	4	4	4

Required

(a) Calculate the contribution earned by each product.

(b) If material supplies are limited to 7,000 kg calculate the production plan which will optimise Q Ltd's profit for the year.

Solution

(a) Contribution per unit = Selling price per unit – Variable cost per unit

	X	Y	Z
	£	£	£
Selling price			
Materials			
Labour			
Variable overhead			
Contribution			

(b)

Contribution			
Limiting factor			
Contribution per kg			
Rank			

Make	______	first using		kg
Make	______	next using		kg
			______	
				kg left
			______	
Available			7,000 kg	
			______	

The optimal production plan is ________________

Test your understanding 6

Revisiting the example from earlier where an organisation produces products H and B.

	H	**B**
Direct materials cost per unit	£10	£30
Direct labour:		
Sawing department £5 per hour	7 hours per unit	5 hours per unit
Smoothing department £7.50 per hour	15 hours per unit	9 hours per unit
Selling price per unit	£206.50	£168.00
Budgeted production	1,200 units	600 units
External demand for the period	1,500 units	800 units

Notes

(1) No opening or closing inventory is anticipated.

(2) The skilled labour used for the sawing processes is highly specialised and in short supply, although there is just sufficient to meet the budgeted production. However, it will not be possible to increase the supply for the budget period.

Earlier we calculated that there are 11,400 hours available in the sawing department.

An accounting technician has suggested that the current budgeted production plan is not the best use of the resources available. Calculate the optimum production plan to check if they are correct.

Complete the following table:

	H	B
Contribution per unit (£)		
Sawing hours per unit (hours)	7	5
Contribution per sawing hour (£)		

Calculate the current optimum production plan:

	H	B
Ranking		
Optimum production plan (units)		

3.4 Opportunity costs of limited resources

It may be possible to buy extra materials or get extra time. An organisation would need to consider what was stopping them from producing more, for example if a company had more materials than they needed, there would be no value in buying anymore.

If materials was the limiting factor and there was the opportunity to buy more, perhaps from a different supplier, the key consideration would be how much the company would be willing to pay for it.

The calculation to work it out would be: (the contribution generated per kg plus the variable cost per kg) multiplied by the number of kg they were buying.

For labour, the calculation would be: (the contribution generated per hour plus the variable cost per hour) multiplied by the number of hours they required.

Example

Revisiting the earlier example with two products, Chaffinch and Greenfinch, where skilled labour was the limiting factor.

The product details are as follows:

	Chaffinch	**Greenfinch**
	£	£
Selling price	10.00	15.00
Material @ £1 per kg	2.00	4.00
Labour @ £1 per hour	1.00	3.00
Other variable expenses	0.00	0.50
Contribution	4.00	7.50
Material X required per unit	2 kg	4 kg
Skilled labour time required per unit	1 hour	3 hours

The maximum demand per week is 30 units of Chaffinch and 10 units of Greenfinch.

The limiting restriction is 45 hours of skilled labour available per week.

What would be the value of 15 additional hours of labour?

Solution.

	Chaffinch	**Greenfinch**	**Total**
Contribution per unit (£)	4.00	7.50	
Contribution per labour hour (£)	4.00	2.50	
Ranking	1	2	

This means that the Chaffinch would be made to demand levels (30 units @ 1 hour = 30 hours) and the additional time would be spent making Greenfinches (the remaining 15 hours).15 hours would make 5 Greenfinches (15 hours/ 3 hours per unit). There will still be unsatisfied demand for 5 units of the Greenfinch.

We therefore need to determine the opportunity cost of having more labour hours available in which the remaining 5 units could be produced. Effectively we are calculating how much the company would be willing to pay in order to obtain additional labour hours.

At present, the direct labour costs £1 per hour. However, we know that we are able to generate additional contribution of £7.50 for each unit of the Greenfinch that we make and sell. As each unit requires 3 labour hours, then this means we earn £7.50/ 3 hours = £2.50 additional contribution for each labour hour that is available.

The company would therefore be willing to pay up to £2.50 MORE per labour hour that is available. This gives an opportunity cost of £1 + £2.50 = £3.50 per direct labour hour. If the cost was above £3.50 per hour, then a loss would be made and so this wouldn't be worthwhile.

As unsatisfied demand is for 5 units, and each unit requires 3 labour hours, then this is a total opportunity cost of 5 × 3 × £3.50 = £52.50.

The opportunity cost = (the contribution generated per hour plus the variable cost per hour) multiplied by the number of hours they required.

The labour cost per hour is £1 and the contribution per hour of time spent on Greenfinch is £2.50.

The opportunity cost = (£2.50 + £1) × 15 = £52.50

Test your understanding 7

A manufacturing business has correctly scheduled production of its two products, so as to maximise profits, using the 7,500 labour hours currently available.

The standard information per unit is as follows:

	A	B
	£	£
Selling price	82	75
Direct material	25	25
Labour (@ £10 per hour)	15	20
Variable overhead	12	16
Fixed overhead	8	10
Profit per unit	22	4
Maximum demand (units)	5,200	3,800

Complete the following table:

	A	**B**
Contribution per unit (£)		
Labour hours per unit (hours)		
Contribution per labour hour (£)		

Calculate the current optimum production plan:

	A	B
Ranking		
Optimum production plan (units)		

What would be the opportunity cost if 500 additional labour hours became available?

4 Summary

In this chapter we have looked at a fundamental problem that we all face, how to deal with limitations. We've looked at it from a financial viewpoint, revising the key concept of **contribution**.

We have also looked at how we identify what limits us, and also how much that limitation is.

Finally we have reviewed the approach that most organisations would use to resolve this issue and maximise their profitability. The process of limiting factor analysis.

Test your understanding answers

Test your understanding 1

(a) **Contribution per unit**

Selling price per unit – Variable cost per unit

£75 – £12 – £24 – £10 = £29

(b) **Profit**

Total contribution – Fixed costs

(£29 × 2,000 units) – £40,000 = £18,000

Test your understanding 2

Answer is C.

		£
Direct labour	4.5 hours × £8.50 per hour	38.25
Direct material	1.1 tonnes × £25 per tonne	27.50
Variable overhead	£378,000/12,000 tonnes	31.50
Marginal cost = Total variable costs per tonne		£97.25

Test your understanding 3

Answer is D.

Contribution per tonne	=	Selling price – Variable cost
	=	£132 – £97.25
	=	£34.75

Test your understanding 4

500 units would require 2 litres per unit, being a total of 1,000 litres. As there are only 890 available then materials are limited

The resource that limits production in the month is **materials**.

The maximum number of units that can be made in the month is **445** units.

890 litres of material will produce 890/2 = 445 units, so production is limited to this quantity.

Materials is the limiting factor, and only 445 units can be made and sold.

The maximum labour will produce 600 units, and so does not limit production. The maximum machine time will be enough to produce 500 units if and when more material becomes available

Test your understanding 5

(a) **Contribution per unit**

Selling price per unit – Variable cost per unit

	X	Y	Z
	£	£	£
Selling price	90	80	75
Materials	(15)	(18)	(12)
Labour	(15)	(12)	(24)
Variable overhead	(8)	(6)	(10)
Contribution	52	44	29

(b)

Contribution	£52	£44	£29
Limiting factor	£15/£3 = 5 kg	£18/£3 = 6 kg	£12/£3 = 4 kg
Contribution per kg	£10.40	£7.33	£7.25
Rank	1	2	3

Make 500 X first using 500 × 5 kg =	2,500 kg
Make 500 Y next using 500 × 6 kg =	3,000 kg
	5,500 kg
1,500 kg left	1,500 kg
Available	7,000 kg

Each Z requires 4 kg; therefore (1,500 kg/4 kg) = 375 Z can be produced.

Optimal production plan is 500 X, 500 Y and 375 Z.

Test your understanding 6

Workings:

	H	B
	£	£
Selling price per unit	206.50	168.00
Direct materials cost per unit	10.00	30.00
Direct labour:		
Sawing department £5 per hour	35.00	25.00
Smoothing department £7.50 per hour	112.50	67.50
	49.00	45.50

Completed table:

	H	B
Contribution per unit (£) 2DP	**49.00**	**45.50**
Sawing hours per unit (hours)	7	5
Contribution per sawing hour (£) 2DP	**7.00**	**9.10**

Calculate the current optimum production plan (in round units):

	H	B
Ranking	**2**	**1**
Optimum production plan (units)	**1,057**	**800**

Workings

B = 800 units × 5 hours per unit = 4,000 hours

11,400 – 4,000 = 7,400 hours remaining

H = 7,400 hours / 7 hours per unit = 1,057.142857 units.

Test your understanding 7

	A	**B**
Contribution per unit (£)	30	14
Labour hours per unit (hours)	1.5	2
Contribution per labour hour (£)	20	7

Calculate the current optimum production plan:

	A	B
Ranking	1	2
Optimum production plan	5,000	0

What would be the opportunity cost if 500 additional labour hours became available?

If 500 extra labour hours were available then the manufacturing business would make the remaining 200 units of A, using 1.5 hours per unit, so 300 hours. Leaving 200 hours to make B. Each unit of B takes 2 hours, meaning 100 units could be made of B.

The opportunity cost = (the contribution generated per hour plus the variable cost per hour) multiplied by the number of hours they required

Opportunity cost of A = (£20 + £10) × 300 hours = £9,000

Opportunity cost of B = (£7 + £10) × 200 hours = £3,400

Therefore the opportunity cost of 500 hours would be £12,400.

Linear programming

4

Introduction

In the previous chapter we looked at how an organisation solves the problem of a single scarce resource. In reality, there is often more than one thing that limits an organisation's ability to meet demand.

In this chapter we look at a technique which can help an organisation prioritise their operations if they had more than one resource constraint. The technique used is linear programming.

ASSESSMENT CRITERIA

Linear programing (LO 3.4)

CONTENTS

1 Linear programming

1.1 Introduction

When there is only one scarce resource, we have seen that limiting factor analysis (key factor analysis) can be used to solve the problem.

Linear programming is a technique for decision making in the context of two or more scarce resources. If only one resource is in short supply then key factor analysis is the preferred method.

In assessment questions linear programming is used for an organisation that makes two products with multiple limiting factors to identify the optimum solution:

- maximise contribution and/or
- minimise costs

1.2 Limitations of linear programming

While linear programming is a very useful tool, it does have its limitations. It is based on a number of assumptions that in reality are not always the case.

Assumptions:

- There is a single quantifiable objective, e.g. maximise contribution. In reality there may be multiple objectives such as maximising return while simultaneously minimising risk.
- Each product always uses the same quantity of the scarce resource per unit. In reality this may not be the case. For example, learning effects may be enjoyed.
- The contribution per unit is constant in linear programming. In reality this may not be the case, for example the selling price may have to be lowered to sell more or there may be economies of scale, for example a discount for buying in bulk.
- Products are independent – in reality customers may expect to buy both products together or the products may be manufactured jointly together. For example, razors and razor blades, no-one would buy the blades if the razor had not been made first.
- The scenario is short term. This allows us to ignore fixed costs.

These assumptions apply to the analysis used when there is one limiting factor or if there are multiple limiting factors.

In the AMAC assessment there will only be two products or variables.

2 Graphical approach

2.1 Introduction

The graphical approach involves drawing a graph with one product represented on the x axis and one product represented by the y axis. Then straight lines are drawn onto the graph using linear equations that represent the limitations that the organisation faces with regards to resources and also demand.

2.2 Step by step approach

In this chapter we'll work through this step by step guide to solving linear programming problems.

Step 1: define the variables.

Step 2: define and formulate the objective.

Step 3: formulate the constraints.

Step 4: draw a graph identify the feasible region.

Step 5: solve for the optimal production plan.

Step 6: answer the question set.

2.3 Step 1: define the variables

This first step is like a key for a diagram. In the formulation of the problem we're be using a letter to represent one unit of one of the products.

For example, if our organisation makes cups and saucers then we won't refer to cups and saucers while we're working through the problem, we will refer to letters to represent them. We can choose any letter that we want, so we could say c = one cup, and s = one saucer. Given that they will be represented on a graph, people often use x and y, as one product will be represent on the x axis and one on the y axis, so in this case we could say:

Let x = one cup and let y = one saucer

2.4 Step 2: define and formulate the objective

The objective will be financial and the organisation will be trying to either minimise cost, or more likely trying to maximise the profit they make in the coming period. As in the last chapter, fixed costs are unlikely to change depending on the output, so they are not relevant to our problem, so the objective therefore becomes to maximise contribution.

Each unit of product will make a standard amount of contribution, or have a standard cost to produce.

The aim will be to make the contribution as big a number as is feasibly possible given the limitations. Alternatively, the aim will be to make the variable cost as small as is possible given the commitments that the organisation must honour.

The cost or the contribution can be denoted as c in the objective function.

2.5 Step 3: formulate the constraints

The constraints will represent the limitations that the organisation faces. These are likely to be the same as we saw when looking at limiting factor analysis, except that with linear programming there will be more than one:

- labour time
- material requirements
- machine time
- financial resources
- plant capacity
- factory space.

For each limitation a linear equation is written to express the limitation.

These first three steps are the formulation of the linear programming problem.

There is always one constraint that exists in manufacturing, and that is that the lowest amount that can be made of something is zero. This constraint is called non-negativity and is written as $x, y \geq 0$.

 **Example**

Linear programming

A company produces two musical instruments in three departments. Details are shown below regarding the time per unit required in each department, the available hours in each department and the contribution per unit of each product:

	xylophone	yueqin	Available hours
Department A	8	10	11,000
Department B	4	10	9,000
Department C	12	6	12,000
Contribution per unit	£4	£8	

There is also a limit on the number of yueqins that will be demanded in any period, that maximum demand is 600.

Formulate the problem to be solved by linear programming.

Solution

Step 1: define the variables

In this case what varies is how many units of the two different musical instruments the company will make.

The variables will be how many of units of each of the two musical instruments the company will make. From now on:

The xylophone will be referred to as x

The yueqin will be referred to as y.

Step 2: define and formulate the objective

As we are given no cost data and only the contribution per unit, the aim for this company must be to maximise contribution.

Contribution = C

As each unit of x makes £4 of contribution and each unit of y makes £8 of contribution our objective function is:

Maximise C = 4x + 8y

Step 3: formulate the constraints.

There are three things limiting us in this question, the amount of labour time in each of the three departments, therefore our constraints are:

Dept A: $8x + 10y \leq 11{,}000$

Dept B: $4x + 10y \leq 9{,}000$

Dept C: $12x + 6y \leq 12{,}000$

Demand: $y \leq 600$

Non-negativity: $x, y \geq 0$

Test your understanding 1

A smoothie manufacturer makes two types of smoothie, the 'Orange one' and the 'Green one'. For a single batch of the 'Orange one' they require 3kg of mango, 7kg of oranges, 2kg of bananas and 3kg of apples, while for a single batch of the 'Green one' they require 1kg of oranges, 11kg of apples, 4kg of bananas and 2kg of kiwis. The manufacturer makes £100 contribution on a batch of the 'Orange one' and £120 contribution on a batch of the 'Green one'. This week, the smoothie manufacturer has access to 500kg of apples, 1,000kg of bananas, 200kg of oranges, 100kg of mangoes and 50kg of kiwis.

Let x = number of batches of the 'Orange one'

Let y = number of batches of the 'Green one'

Requirements

(i) State the objective function

(ii) State the constraints

2.6 Step 4: draw a graph identify the feasible region

In the assessment you won't be required to draw a graph, but you may need to interpret one, and so having an understanding of how it is constructed is beneficial to your understanding of the topic as a whole. Each of the constraints represents a straight line that will form the highest (≤) amount that can be produced on a constraint or the lowest amount (≥) that can be produced while satisfying that constraint.

Example

To draw the line $8x + 10y \leq 11{,}000$ we turn it into an equation:

$$8x + 10y = 11{,}000$$

We then need two points on that straight line. Usually the easiest thing to do is identify the ends of the line, or where it crosses the x and y axis.

We do this as follows:

If x = 0, substituting into the equation gives 10y = 11,000, so y = 1,100.

Likewise, if y = 0, then 8x = 11,000, so x = 1,375.

This means that two possible production plans that are possible in department A would be to make zero xylophones and 1,100 yueqins; or alternatively we could make 1,375 xylophones and zero yueqins.

The following graph shows the constraint for department A, the line of the constraint 8x + 10y = 11,000

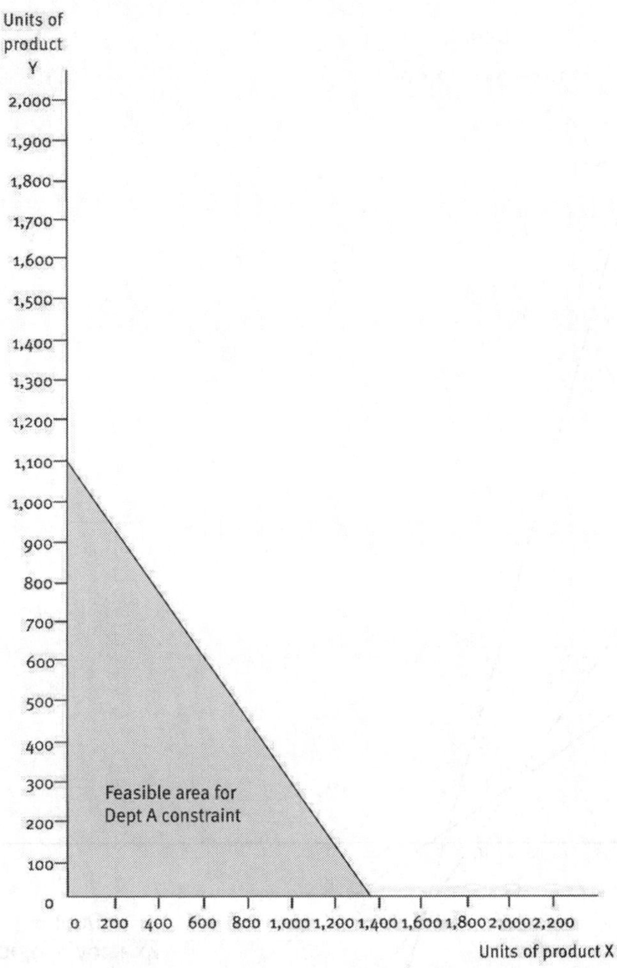

All combinations of x and y 'above' or 'to the right of' the line would **not** be feasible, as they would require more than the available 11,000 hours in department A.

Example

We do this for each individual constraint:

Dept B: 4x + 10y ≤ 9,000

4x + 10y = 9,000

When x = 0, y = 900 and when y = 0 x = 2,250

Dept C: 12x + 6y ≤ 12,000

12x + 6y = 12,000

When x = 0, y = 2,000 and when y = 0, x = 1,000

y = 600 is a straight line, perpendicular to the y access when y = 600.

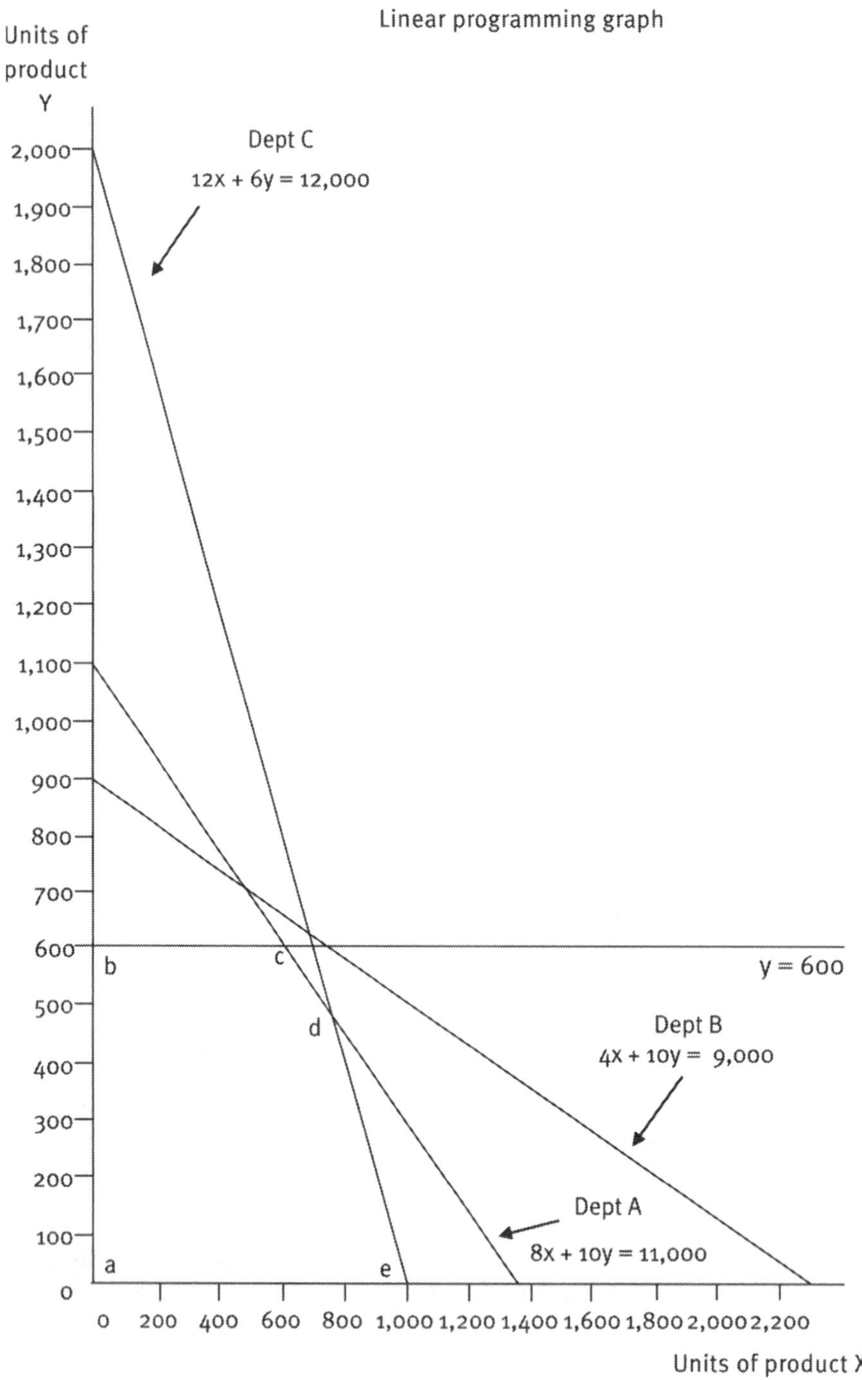

In the AMAC assessment it would not be possible to draw the graph, but the process has been included here to try to help understanding.

It could however be a requirement to identify the feasible region. The feasible region is the area on the graph that satisfies all the constraints that have been drawn.

Where there is a '≥' constraint, this means that all the equation is satisfied by all points either on the line, or in the area above the line.

Make sure that you pay attention to the direction of the inequality, as this will determine on which side of the line your feasible region will fall.

In the example for xylophones and yueqins, the original constraints were all '≤' types, so the feasible region is shown by the shaded area formed by the points a, b, c, d and e. All of the possible solutions (production plans) within this area are possible given the time limitations in each of the three production departments.

2.7 Step 5: solve for the optimal production plan

Knowing what is possible is useful for the organisation, but knowing what is the best plan of all the possible ones is even better. There are two approaches to this final stage.

(1) Using an iso-contribution line

We do not know the maximum value of the objective function. However, we can draw an **iso-contribution line** that shows all the combinations of x and y that provide the same total value for the objective function.

(2) Using simultaneous equations

The maximum contribution will lie on one of the corners of the feasible region. In this method we calculate the coordinates of each vertex (furthest points) on the feasible region. Then calculate the contribution (using the objective function) at each vertex. We will look at this method further in the next section.

2.8 Using an iso-contribution line

To use the iso contribution line, we need to put the objective equal to a contribution figure. Once we have this we will be able to draw the line onto the graph and use it to help us identify the optimum point.

Example

We know that our objective function is to maximise contribution £4x + £8y. To help us identify how many units of x and y that we should produce in order to do this, we can draw a line on the graph that shows combinations of values for x and y that give the same total contribution, when x has a contribution of £4 and y has a contribution of £8. Any total contribution figure can be picked to help us to draw this line, but a multiple of £4 and £8 is easiest.

- For example, assume 4x + 8y = £4,000. This iso-contribution line could be found by joining the points on the graph x = 0, y = 500 and x = 1,000 and y = 0.

- Instead, we might select a total contribution value of 4x + 8y = £8,000. This iso-contribution line could be found by joining the points on the graph x = 0, y = 1,000 and x = 2,000 and y = 0.
- When drawing both of these iso-contribution lines on a graph, we find that the two lines are parallel and the line with the higher total contribution value for values x and y (£8,000) is further away from the origin of the graph (point 0,0).

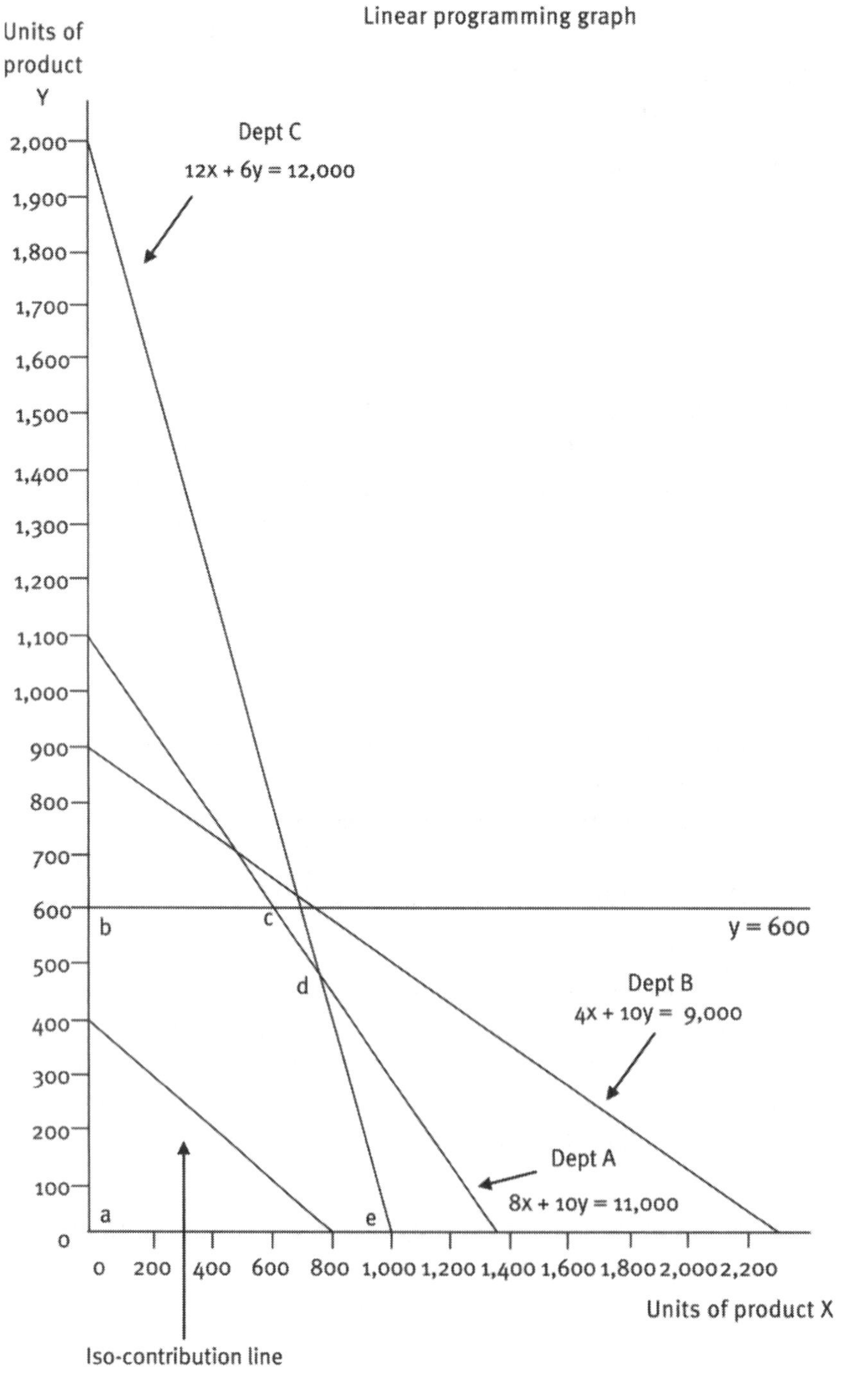

- This iso-contribution line can then be used to identify the solution to a linear programming problem.
- The process is to look at the slope of the iso-contribution line and visualise the line 'moving' across the page, towards the top right of the page and away from the origin, maintaining the same gradient at all times. As it moves, the line will pass over the corners of the feasible region. The optimal point will be at the final vertex which the iso-contribution line passes before it leaves the feasible region completely. The coordinates of x and y at this vertex provide the solution to the linear programming problem. Some students find it helps to hold a ruler along the iso-contribution line, and then to 'slide' this across the page.

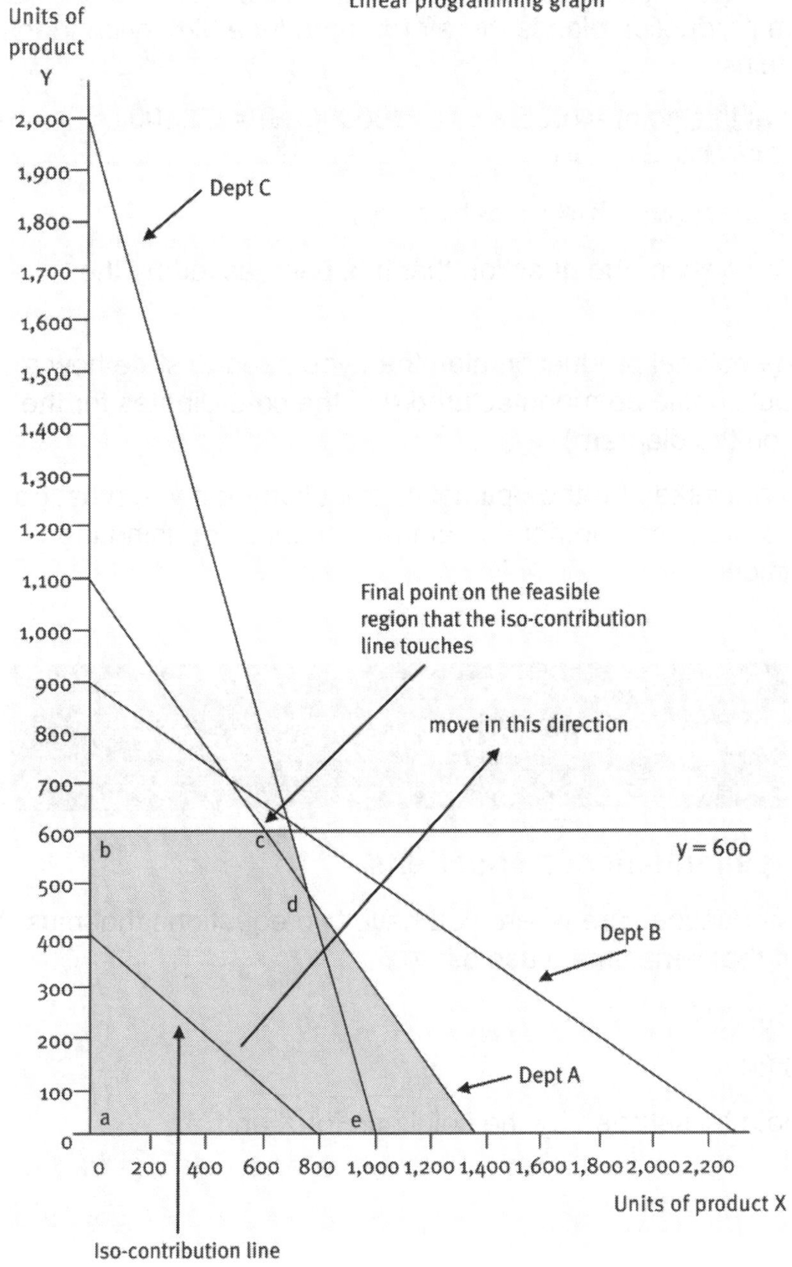

Example

The line plotted from point 400 on the y axis to point 800 on the x axis is the iso-contribution line. If you were to put a ruler along this line and move it outwards in parallel to that line, the last point that you would meet on the feasible region would be point c. This tells us that the optimal point in the feasible region in our illustration is at point c.

The solution could be read directly from the graph at the point of intersection to find that x = 625 and y = 600.

Alternatively, we could then use simultaneous equations (see the next section) to determine the co-ordinates for this point.

The optimum production plan is therefore to produce 625 xylophones and 600 yueqins.

Contribution at this point = (625 × £4) + (600 × £8) = £7,300.

2.9 Step 6: answer the question set

Ensure that you answer the question that has been asked by the examiner.

If asked for the optimal production plan then you need to state how much of each product should be manufactured (i.e. the co-ordinates for the optimal point on the diagram)

If instead you are asked for the optimal contribution then you must go further and calculate the contribution at the optimal point using the objective function.

3 Simultaneous equations

3.1 Using simultaneous equations

Simultaneous equations are where you have two equations that must both be satisfied at the same time, such as:

$3X + 4Y = 18$ (i)

$5X + 2Y = 16$ (ii)

which must both be satisfied by the solutions for X and Y.

Provided you multiply both sides of an equation by the same amount, it continues to be true. In the solution of these equations, one or both of the equations are multiplied by numbers chosen so that either the X or the Y terms in the two equations become numerically identical.

We have labelled the equations (i) and (ii) for clarity. Suppose we were to multiply (i) by 5 and (ii) by 3. Both equations would contain a 15X term that we could eliminate by subtraction, it being the case that you can add or subtract two equations and the result remains true.

In this case, however, the simplest method is to multiply equation (ii) by 2, so that both equations will contain 4Y and we can subtract to eliminate Y. The full solution is shown below.

$3X + 4Y = 18$ (i)

$5X + 2Y = 16$ (ii)

Multiply (ii) by 2 to give:

$10X + 4Y = 32$ (iii)

Subtract (i) from (iii):

$(10X - 3X) + (4Y - 4Y) = (32 - 18)$

$7X + 0 = 14$

$X = 14 \div 7 = 2$

Substitute X = 2 into (i) to find Y

$(3 \times 2) + 4Y = 18$

$6 + 4Y = 18$

$4Y = 18 - 6 = 12$

$Y = 12 \div 4 = 3$

You can check the results by substituting the values for X and Y into either of the initial equations, (i) or (ii). Using (ii) gives:

$5X + 2Y = 16$

$(5 \times 2) + (2 \times 3) = 16$

The equation does indeed equal 16 when X=2 and Y=3 are substituted in.

The solution is therefore X = 2, Y = 3. These are the values of X and Y where both equations are satisfied.

Had we chosen to substitute X = 2 into equation (ii) it would not have affected the result but we would then have checked in the other equation (i).

Example

Using the example from earlier.

Point d occurs where the constraints for Dept A and Dept C intersect. Because the point is at the furthest point of each of the lines we know that all of the constraint is being used and the less than or equal to sign in the equations can be converted to an equal sign:

Dept A: $8x + 10y = 11{,}000$

Dept C: $12x + 6y = 12{,}000$

We need to use simultaneous equations to solve this problem and find the coordinates of x and y where they intersect:

$8x + 10y = 11{,}000$ (call this equation 1)

$12x + 6y = 12{,}000$ (call this equation 2)

If we multiply equation 1 by 6, and equation 2 by 10 we would have 60y in both equations.

Multiply equation 1 by 6 gives:

$48x + 60y = 66{,}000$ (call this equation 3)

Multiply equation 2 by 10 gives:

$120x + 60y = 120{,}000$ (call this equation 4)

If we now subtract equation 3 from equation 4 we get:

$(120x – 48x) + (60y – 60y) = (120{,}000 – 66{,}000)$

$72x = 54{,}000$

$x = 54{,}000/72 = 750$

We can now substitute this value of x back into either of the two equations (let's use equation 1), to find the value for y:

$8x + 10y = 11{,}000$

$(8 \times 750) + 10y = 11{,}000$

$6{,}000 + 10y = 11{,}000$

$10y = 11{,}000 – 6{,}000 = 5{,}000$

$y = 5{,}000/10 = 500$

The intersection of the constraint lines for Dept A and Dept C is therefore at the point x=750, y=500. If we substitute these values into the objective function the total contribution is $(4 \times 750) + (8 \times 500) =$ £7,000.

Test your understanding 2

The constraints for Dept A and Dept B intersect:

Dept A: 8x + 10y = 11,000

Dept B: 4x + 10y = 9,000

Using simultaneous equations, identify the production plan at this point and the amount of contribution that would be made using this production plan.

Test your understanding 3

Given the following equations:

25x + 50y = 350

15x + 20y = 180

Solve the equations simultaneously.

4 Minimisation problems

4.1 Minimisation problems

Linear programming enables organisations to find optimal solutions to economic decisions. Generally, this means maximising profits but it could aim to minimise costs instead. In such situations, rather than finding a contribution line touching the feasible region at a tangent as far away from the origin as possible, the aim is to find a total cost line touching the feasible polygon at a tangent as close to the origin as possible.

Suppose we had a minimisation problem and had identified the feasible region as being the shaded area in the diagram below. As we are looking to minimise costs, we would identify the optimal solution by moving the iso-contribution line towards the origin. The optimal point would be the final vertex on the feasible region that the line crosses as it moves towards the origin:

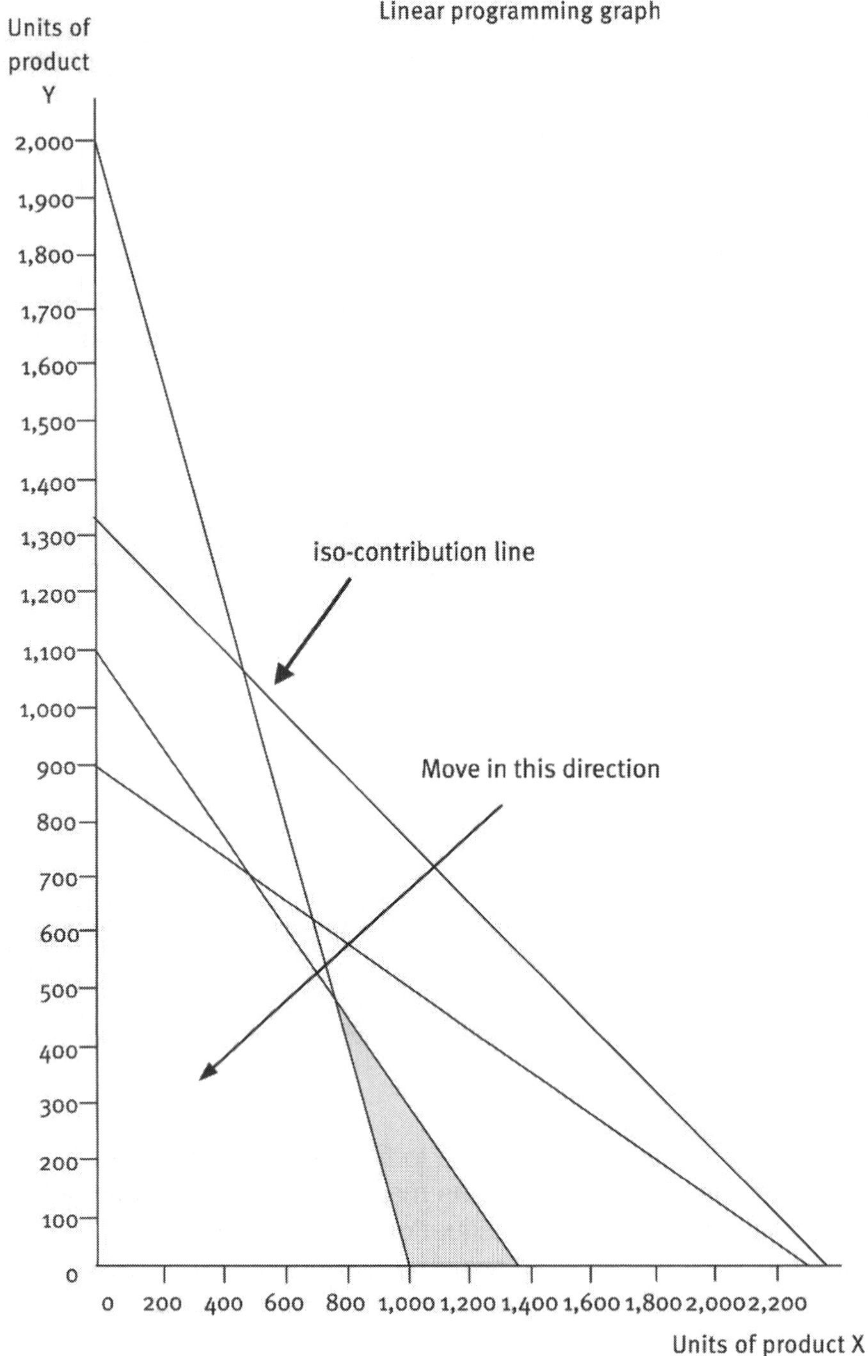
Linear programming graph
Units of product Y
2,000
1,900
1,800
1,700
1,600
1,500
1,400
1,300
1,200
1,100
1,000
900
800
700
600
500
400
300
200
100
0
iso-contribution line
Move in this direction
0 200 400 600 800 1,000 1,200 1,400 1,600 1,800 2,000 2,200
Units of product X

Test your understanding 4

A coffee shop makes two types of cheesecake, the Regular and the Premium. For a single batch of Regular cheesecakes they require 3kg of butter and 7kg of cream cheese, while for a single batch of the Premium cheesecakes they require 11kg of butter and 13kg of cream cheese. The coffee shop makes £65 contribution on a batch of Regular cheesecakes and £90 contribution on a batch of Premium cheesecakes. This week, the coffee shop has access to 700kg of butter and 1,150kg of cream cheese.

Let x = number of batches of Regular cheesecake produced

Let y = number of batches of Premium cheesecake produced

Requirements

(i) State the objective function

(ii) State the constraints

(iii) Determine how many batches of the Regular and Premium cheesecakes that the coffee shop should make this week in order to maximise profits.

5 Summary

This chapter has covered linear programming from the principles of how it works and the limitations of it to the overall process.

That process goes from formulation of the problem, to displaying the problem graphically and solving it, either using the graph, simultaneous equations or a combination of the two.

Test your understanding answers

Test your understanding 1

(i) State the objective function

The objective is to maximise contribution. Each batch of the 'Orange one' (x) generates contribution of £100 and each batch of the 'Green one' (y) generates contribution of £120. The objective function is therefore:

$C = 100x + 120y$

(ii) State the constraints

Production is limited by the availability of the fruits used to make the smoothies.

Each batch of the 'Orange one' requires 7kg of oranges and each batch of the 'Green one' requires 1kg of oranges. Oranges are limited to 200kg. This constraint is therefore:

$7x + 1y \leq 200$

Note, when there is just 1, then we don't need to put 1y and can just put y

So the constraint would be:

$7x + y \leq 200$

Each batch of the 'Orange one' requires 2kg of bananas and each batch of the 'Green one' requires 4kg of bananas. Bananas are limited to 1,000kg. This constraint is therefore:

$2x + 4y \leq 1,000$

Each batch of the 'Orange one' requires 3kg of apples and each batch of the 'Green one' requires 11kg of apples. Apples are limited to 500kg. This constraint is therefore:

$3x + 11y \leq 500$

Each batch of the 'Orange one' requires 3kg of mangoes and each batch of the 'Green one' requires no mangoes. Mangoes are limited to 100kg. This constraint is therefore:

$3x \leq 100$

Each batch of the 'Orange one' requires no kiwis and each batch of the 'Green one' requires 2kg of kiwis. Kiwis are limited to 50kg. This constraint is therefore:

$2y \leq 50$

Non-negativity constraint: $x, y \geq 0$

Test your understanding 2

$8x + 10y = 11,000$ (call this equation 1)

$4x + 10y = 9,000$ (call this equation 2)

As we have matching values of y in each equation, we can now subtract equation 2 from equation 1, to get:

$(8x - 4x) + (10y - 10y) = (11,000 - 9,000)$

$4x = 2,000$

$x = 2,000/4 = 500$

Substituting x = 500 back into equation 1 gives us:

$8x + 10y = 11,000$

$(8 \times 500) + 10y = 11,000$

$4,000 + 10y = 11,000$

$10y = 11,000 - 4,000 = 7,000$

$y = 7,000/10 = 700$

The intersection of the constraint lines for Dept A and Dept B is therefore at the point **x = 500, y = 700**.

If we substitute these values into the objective function the total contribution is (4 × 500) + (8 × 700) = **£7,600**.

This is greater than the contribution from the optimum plan, but the intersection lies outside of the feasible region.

Test your understanding 3

We need to use simultaneous equations to solve the equations:

25x + 50y = 350 (call this equation 1)

15x + 20y = 180 (call this equation 2)

As we need to have 'matching' values for either x or y in both equations, we can multiply equation 1 by 2 to and equation 2 by 5 as this will give 100y in each equation, as follows:

(25x × 2) + (50y × 2) = (350 × 2)

(15x × 5) + (20y × 5) = (180 × 5)

50x + 100y = 700 (call this equation 3)

75x + 100y = 900 (call this equation 4)

Now we can subtract equation 3 from equation 4, to get:

(75x – 50x) + (100y – 100y) = (900 – 700)

25x = 200

x = 200/25 = 8

We now just substitute the x value into either of the original equations to find y. Let's substitute into equation 1:

25x + 50y = 350

(25 × 8) + 50y =350

200 + 50y = 350

50y = 350 – 200

50y = 150

y = 150/50 = 3

We can check whether these values of x and y are correct by substituting back into either of the original equations to see if the equation is satisfied:

15x + 20y = 180

(15 × 8) + (20 × 3) = 180

Test your understanding 4

(i) State the objective function

The objective is to maximise profits. Each batch of Regular cheesecake (x) generates contribution of £65 and each batch of Premium cheesecake (y) generates contribution of £90. The objective function is therefore:

C = 65x + 90y

(ii) State the constraints

Production is limited by the availability of butter and cream cheese.

Each batch of Regular cheesecakes requires 3kg of butter and each Premium requires 11kg of butter. Butter is limited to 700kg. This constraint is therefore:

$3x + 11y \leq 700$

Each batch of Regular cheesecakes requires 7kg of cream cheese and each Premium requires 13kg. Cream cheese is limited to 1,150kg. This constraint is therefore:

$7x + 13y \leq 1,150$

Non-negativity constraint: $x, y \geq 0$

(iii) Production plan to maximise profits

If you sketch the graph of the feasible region you can see that it is the area between the origin and points a, b and c on the graph below.

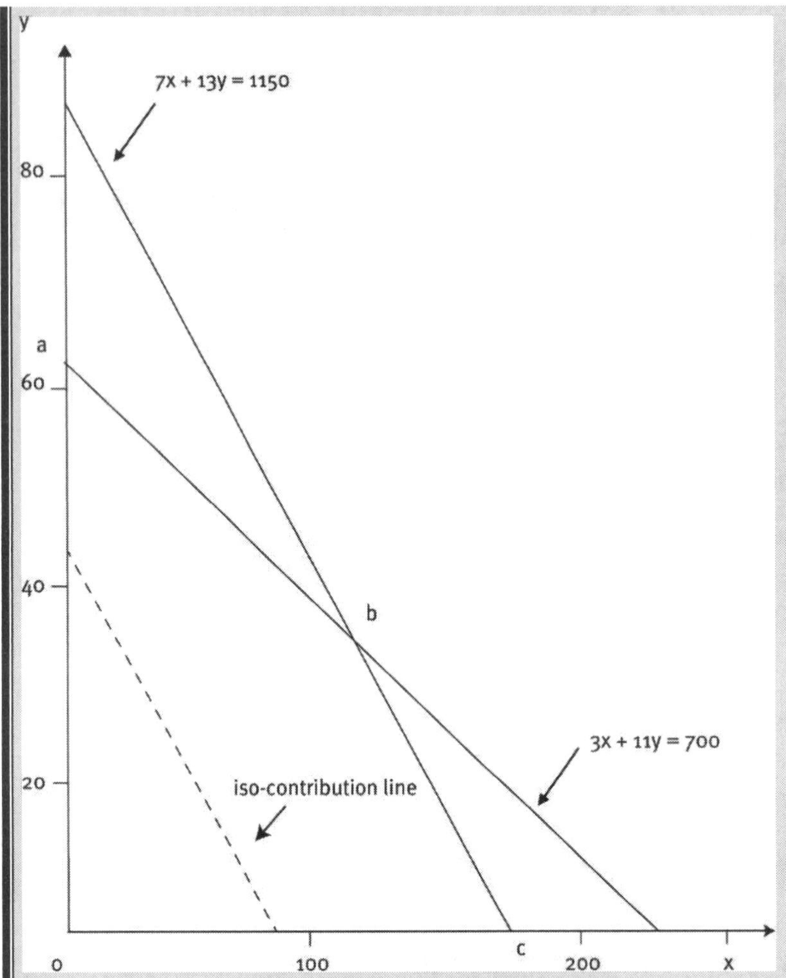

The optimal solution lies at one of the vertices. We can solve this by using the iso-contribution line.

C = 65x + 90y, if we put it equal to 5,850

When x = 0, 90y = 5,850 so y = 65, so one point is 0, 65

When y = 0, 65x = 5,850 so x = 90, so the other point is 90, 0

If this is moved away from the origin, the final point on the feasible region that the line will touch will be point c. This is where the line 7x + 13y = 1,150 crosses the x axis. On the x axis, the value for y is zero. We therefore substitute y=0 into the constraint to find the corresponding value for x:

7x + 13y = 1,150

7x = 1,150

x = 1,150/7 = 164.3

We need to round this down to 164, as we cannot make part-batches.

The optimal solution is therefore to make zero batches of the Premium cheesecake and 164 batches of the Regular cheesecake.

Short term decision making 5

Introduction

In the section on limiting factor analysis and linear programming we used the key concept of contribution to assist in decision making. If a decision has to be made it is sensible only to take into account those costs which will actually be affected by the decision.

Within this chapter we will consider a number of different techniques that can help a company make a decision.

ASSESSMENT CRITERIA

Relevant costs (LO 3.2)

CONTENTS

1 Relevant costing

1.1 Introduction

When assisting management in making **short term** decisions only costs or revenues that are **relevant** to the decision should be considered. Any form of decision-making involves making a choice between two or more alternatives.

For decision making, it is necessary to identify the costs and revenues that will be affected as a result of taking one course of action rather than another. The costs that would be affected by a decision are known as relevant costs.

Since relevant costs and revenues are those which are affected by the decision, the term effectively means costs and revenues which change as a result of a decision.

Even though the costs and revenues are only being estimated it is important to ensure that the calculations are made with as much detail as possible or that any assumptions are stated. This will maintain the integrity of the information and should demonstrate professional competence.

1.2 Relevant costs and revenues

Definition

Relevant costs and revenues are those costs and revenues that **change as a direct result of a decision that is taken**.

A relevant cost is a **future, incremental, cash flow** arising as a direct result of a decision being taken:

- **Future costs and revenues** – costs and revenues that are going to be incurred sometime in the future due to the decision being taken.
- **Incremental costs and revenues** – any extra cost or revenue generated by the decision that would not arise otherwise e.g. an extra amount of fixed costs due to making the decision.
- **Cash flows rather than profits** – actual cash being spent or received should be used when making the decision. Profits can be manipulated by accounting concepts like depreciation. Cash flows are more reliable.

A relevant cost or revenue could also be referred to as an avoidable cost.

Definition

An **avoidable cost** is any cost that would only occur as a result of taking the decision. If the decision did not go ahead then the cost would not be incurred so it is avoidable.

1.3 Non-relevant costs and revenues

Costs or revenues that can be ruled out when making a decision come under the following categories:

- **Sunk costs** – past or historic costs that cannot be changed e.g. any cost incurred due to research and development that has already been carried out will not apply after the decision has been made.
- **Committed costs** – costs that, while they occur in the future, are **unavoidable** not incremental and will be incurred whether or not the project is done. This means they do not have all three characteristics of a relevant cost. An example would be a fixed cost of a building that a firm already rented, but was just being used for a different purpose.
- **Non-cash flow costs** – depreciation and carrying amounts are accounting concepts, not actual cash flows and are not relevant costs. An example would be the net book value (NBV) of a piece of machinery that was being considered for sale.

1.4 Variable costs

It is usually assumed that a **variable cost** will be **relevant** to a decision as when activity increases the total variable cost incurred also increases. There is a direct relationship between production activity and variable costs. However there are some situations where this may not be true.

To consider this in more detail we'll look at materials and labour cost separately.

Firstly, we'll look at **materials**, the diagram that follows summarises most of the key considerations.

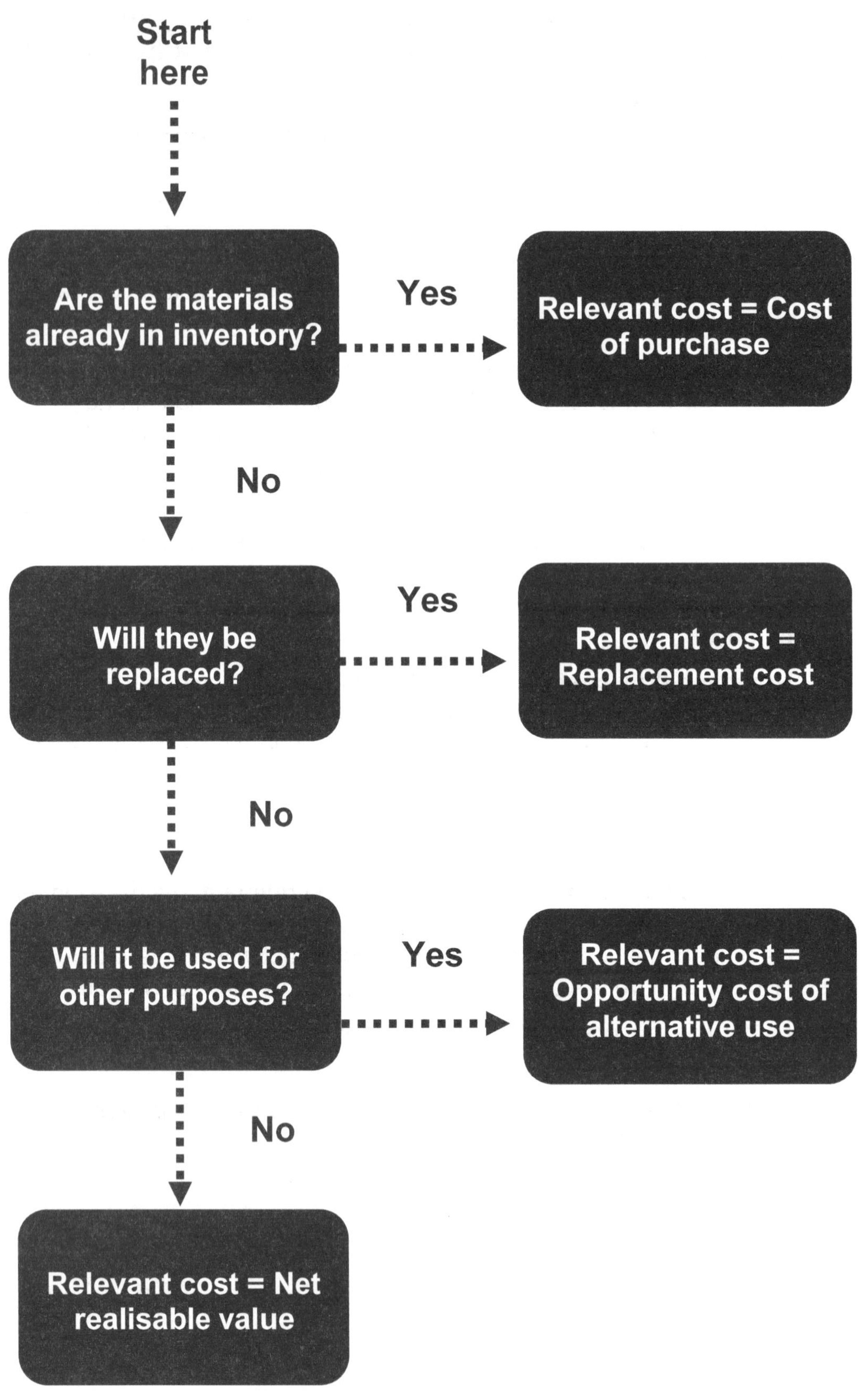
Start here
Are the materials already in inventory?
Yes
Relevant cost = Cost of purchase
No
Will they be replaced?
Yes
Relevant cost = Replacement cost
No
Will it be used for other purposes?
Yes
Relevant cost = Opportunity cost of alternative use
No
Relevant cost = Net realisable value

Example

A company is considering a short-term pricing decision for a contract that would use 1,000 kg of material A. There are 800 kg of material A in inventory, which was bought some time ago for £3 per kg. The material in inventory could be sold for £3.50 per kg. The current purchase price of material A is £4.50.

What is the relevant cost of material A for this contract?

Solution

The cost per kg of material is considered to be a variable cost but you also need to consider whether the cost is a future cost for it to be relevant.

The company has already got 800 kg in inventory so this does not need to be purchased. The £3 per kg is an old purchase price i.e. a sunk cost so it is not relevant. The material would therefore be valued at the current re-sale value of £3.50 per kg.

The company will need to buy a further 200 kg to complete the contract. This would be valued at the current purchase price of £4.50.

The total relevant cost of material A is:

800 kg × £3.50 = £2,800

200 kg × £4.50 = £900

Total = £3,700

For **labour**, we can use a similar diagram to summarise the common considerations

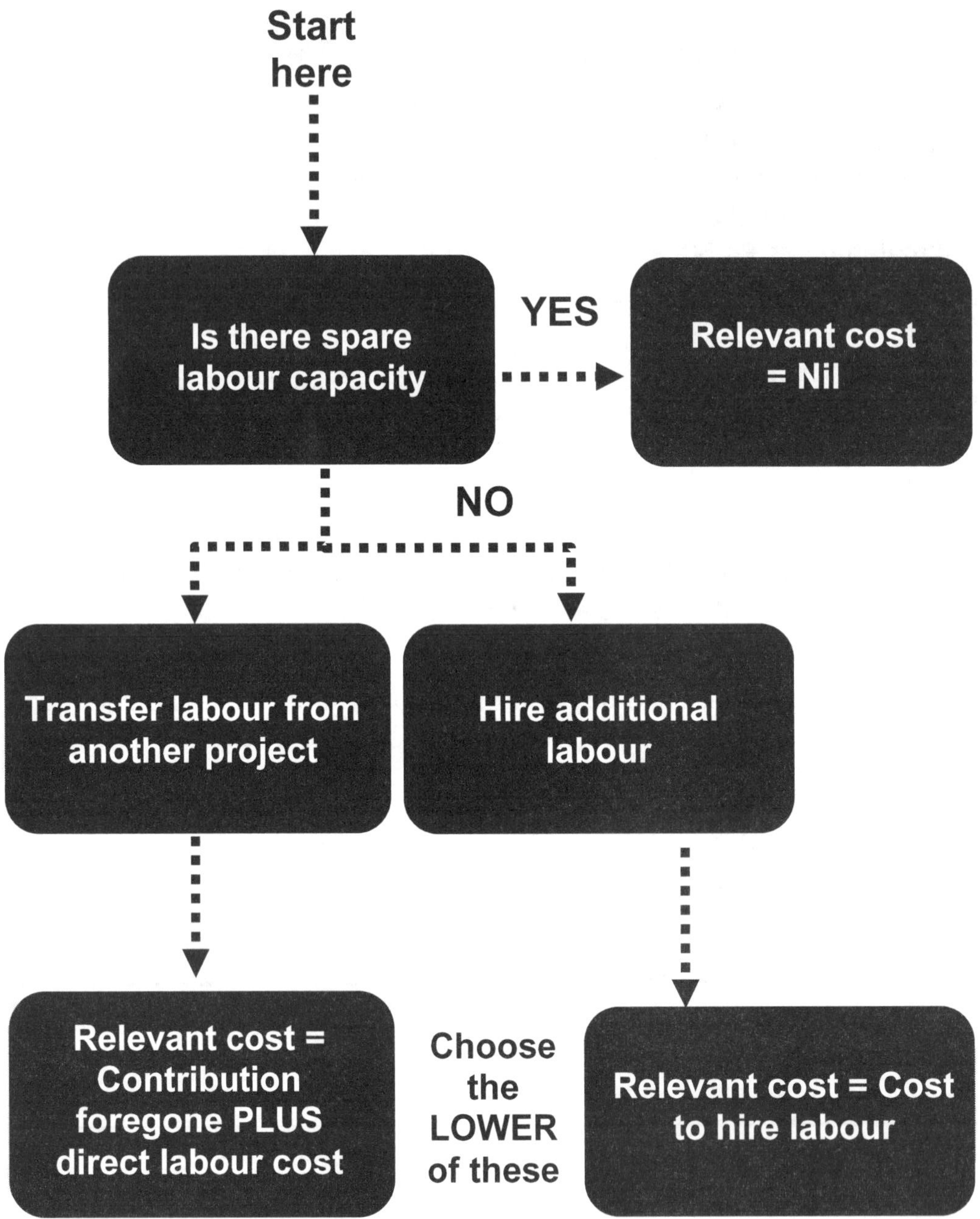

Not all scenarios will include all these options, but applying these thought processes to the given situation should lead to the correct answer in most situations.

Example

100 hours of skilled labour are needed for a special contract. The staff are working at full capacity at the moment and the workers would have to be taken off production of a different product in order to work on the special contract. The details of the other product are shown below:

	£/unit
Selling price	60
Direct material	10
Direct labour 1 hour @ £10 per hour	10
Variable overheads	15
Fixed overheads	15

The skilled workers' pay rate would not change, regardless of which product they worked on.

What would be the relevant cost?

Solution

Using our diagram, there is no spare capacity, no alternative source of labour is mentioned, and so we would need to take workers off the alternative product.

Relevant cost = Contribution foregone PLUS direct labour cost

Existing product earns a contribution per hour of £60 – £10 – £10 – £15 = £25

Relevant cost	= Contribution forgone PLUS direct labour cost	
	= £25 + £10	
	= £35 per hour	
Total cost	= £35 × 100 hours	= £3,500

Unless told otherwise variable costs and the variable element of the semi-variable costs are relevant to a decision.

1.5 Fixed costs

Fixed costs tend to come under the umbrella of committed costs so are not relevant. Be careful though because if the fixed cost were to step up as a direct result of a decision taken then the extra cost would be relevant as it is an incremental cost.

Example

MDCL Plc absorbs overheads on a machine hour rate, currently £20 per hour, of which £7 is for variable overheads and £13 is for fixed overheads. The company is deciding whether to undertake a contract in the coming year. If the contract is accepted it is estimated that the fixed costs will increase by £3,200 for the duration.

What are the relevant overhead costs for this decision?

Solution

The variable cost per hour is relevant as this cost would be avoided if the contract were not undertaken. The relevant cost is therefore £7 per machine hour.

The fixed cost per hour is an absorption rate. This is not an indication of how much actual overheads would increase by. The £3,200 extra fixed cost is relevant as it is an incremental or extra cost.

With regards to short-term decision making we assume that on the whole **fixed costs** are **non-relevant** costs so we can approach decisions using the **marginal costing technique**.

Test your understanding 1

As part of a new product development a company has employed a building consultant to perform an initial survey. This initial survey has cost £40,000. But there will be an ongoing need for her services if the company decides to proceed with the project. This work will be charged at a fixed rate of £20,000 per annum.

What relevant cost should be included for the building consultant's services in the first year when considering whether the project should proceed?

A £0

B £20,000

C £40,000

D £60,000

Test your understanding 2

A company which manufactures and sells one single product is currently producing 102,000 units per month and has capacity to produce up to 18,000 more. The current total monthly costs of production amount to £330,000, of which £75,000 are fixed and are expected to remain unchanged for all levels of activity up to full capacity.

A new potential customer has expressed interest in taking a regular monthly delivery of 12,000 units at a price of £2.80 per unit.

All existing production is sold each month at a price of £3.25 per unit, the variable cost of production is £2.50 per unit. If the new business is accepted, existing sales are expected to fall by 2 units for every 15 units sold to the new customer.

What is the overall increase in monthly profit which would result from accepting the new business?

Test your understanding 3

A company is considering a short-term pricing decision to utilise some spare capacity. The item to be manufactured and sold would use 1,500 kgs of raw material Q.

Material Q is in regular use by the company. It currently has 1,000 kgs in inventory, which was purchased last month at a cost of £4 per kg. The current replacement cost of material Q is £4.80 per kg and the current inventory could be sold for £4.30 per kg.

Calculate what the relevant cost of material Q is for the purposes of this decision.

Test your understanding 4

JB absorbs overheads on a machine hour rate, currently £50/hour, of which £17.50 is for variable overheads and £32.50 for fixed overheads.

The company is deciding whether to undertake a contract in the coming year. If the contract is undertaken, it is estimated that fixed costs will increase for the duration of the contract by £8,000. The contract would require 2,000 hours of machine time

What is the relevant cost of overheads for the contract?

Test your understanding 5

Equipment owned by a company has a net book value of £1,800 and has been idle for some months. It could now be used on a six months contract that is being considered. If not used on this contract, the equipment would be sold now for a net amount of £2,000. After use on the contract, the equipment would have no resale value and would be dismantled.

What is the total relevant cost of the equipment to the contract?

2 Make or buy decisions

2.1 Make or buy?

Sometimes a business will have to decide whether to make a product themselves or whether to buy it in from another company. This may be, for example, because they are already busy or because another company could produce it more cheaply or because the other company is a specialist.

Relevant costing should be used to resolve this decision. Make or buy decisions can include differences in variable costs and differences in directly attributable fixed costs.

2.2 Other considerations and risks associated with the decision

In addition to the relative cost of buying externally compared to making in-house, management must consider a number of other issues before a final decision is made.

- Reliability of external supplier: can the outside company be relied upon to meet the requirements in terms of:
  - quantity required
  - quality required
  - delivering on time
  - price stability.
- Specialist skills: the external supplier may possess some specialist skills that are not available in-house.
- Alternative use of resource: outsourcing will free up resources which may be used in another part of the business.
- Social: will outsourcing result in a reduction of the workforce? Redundancy costs should be considered.
- Legal: will outsourcing affect contractual obligations with suppliers or employees?
- Confidentiality: is there a risk of loss of confidentiality, especially if the external supplier performs similar work for rival companies?
- Customer reaction: do customers attach importance to the products being made in-house?

Example

Make or buy?

Dogbone makes two products X and Y. Next year the costs are expected to be:

	X	Y
Production (units)	1,000	2,000
	£	£
Direct materials	14	15
Direct labour	8	9
Variable production overhead	2	3
Directly attributable fixed costs	1,000	3,000

A subcontractor has offered to supply Dogbone with units of X and/or Y for £20 and £30 respectively. Should Dogbone make or buy the units?

	X	Y
	£	£
Variable cost of making	24	27
Variable cost of buying	20	30
Differential variable cost	4	(3)
Production (units)	1,000	2,000
Saving in variable cost by buying	4,000	(6,000)
Fixed cost saved by buying	1,000	3,000
Saving in total costs by buying	5,000	(3,000)

Dogbone should buy in units of X but should make units of Y.

Other considerations

- Is the supplier reliable with regards to delivery times and quality?
- Dogbone may have spare capacity now, which may lead to future job losses if other profitable activities cannot be found.
- Are the attributable fixed cost estimates reliable?

Test your understanding 6

P Limited is considering whether to continue making a component or buy it from an outside supplier. It uses 12,000 of the components each year.

The internal manufacturing cost comprises:

	£/unit
Direct materials	3.00
Direct labour	4.00
Variable overhead	1.00
Specific fixed cost	2.50
Other fixed costs	2.00
	12.50

If the direct labour were not used to manufacture the component, it would be used to increase the production of another item for which there is unlimited demand. This other item has a contribution of £10.00 per unit but requires £8.00 of labour per unit.

What is the maximum price per component at which buying is preferable to internal manufacture?

3 Discontinue a section of the business

3.1 Decisions about closure

The following difficult decisions might need to be made by a management accountant:

(a) Whether to close down a product line, service or department, perhaps because it appears to be making losses

(b) If the decision is to discontinue or shut down, is it temporary or permanent?

A closure might result in

- savings in annual operating costs for a number of years
- unwanted non-current assets becoming available for sale
- employees being made redundant, relocated, re-trained or offered early retirement. There will be lump-sum cash outflows involved.

Example

Shut down?

Dogbone makes two products X and Y. This year's annual profits are:

	X	**Y**	**Total**
	£	£	£
Sales	50,000	60,000	110,000
Variable costs	(30,000)	(40,000)	(70,000)
Contribution	20,000	20,000	40,000
Fixed costs	(15,000)	(25,000)	(40,000)
Profit / (loss)	5,000	(5,000)	Nil

Dogbone is concerned about Y's poor performance and is considering ceasing production of Y.

£15,000 of Y's fixed costs could be saved if production ceased i.e. there are some directly attributable fixed costs.

By stopping production of Y there would be a loss in profit of £5,000:

	£
Loss of contribution	(20,000)
Savings in fixed costs	15,000
Incremental loss	(5,000)

Another way of looking at this is that product X would now have to absorb some of Y's non-attributable fixed costs.

	£
Profit made by X	5,000
Companywide fixed costs previously charged to Y (£25,000 – £15,000 attributable fixed costs)	(10,000)
Incremental loss (as above)	(5,000)

Based on financial grounds, Y should not be discontinued as the profit that is made by Dogbone would be reduced by £5,000.

3.2 Other considerations and risks associated with the decision

Qualitative factors should be taken in to account alongside any numeric calculations, such as:

- Impact on employee morale
- Competitor reaction
- Customer reaction.

Non quantifiable costs and benefits of a discontinuation:

- Some of the costs and benefits discussed above may be non-quantifiable at the point of making the discontinuation decision:
  - penalties and other costs resulting from the closure (e.g. redundancy, compensation to customers) may not be known with certainty
  - reorganisation costs may not be known with certainty
  - additional contribution from the alternative use for resources released may not be known with certainty.
- Knock-on impact of the shut-down decision. For example, supermarkets often stock some goods which they sell at a loss. This is to get customers through the door, who they then hope will purchase other products which have higher profit margins for them. If the decision is taken to stop selling these products, then the customers may no longer come to the store.

3.3 Automation

Similar to closure of a business segment and with links to make or buy is automation.

Automation of a production process could involve closing down a production department to be replaced by a piece of machinery. The decision here could be whether to continue as we are now and incur the associated costs; or whether to automate the process and incur the associated costs.

As with earlier decisions in this chapter the business would need to consider other factors such as employee morale and customer reaction.

Test your understanding 7

The management of MD Ltd is considering the closure of one of its operations, department 3, based on the information included within the following report:

	1	2	3	Total
Sales units	5,000	6,000	2,000	13,000
Sales (£)	150,000	240,000	24,000	414,000
Cost of sales (£)				
Direct material	75,000	150,000	8,000	233,000
Direct labour	25,000	30,000	8,000	63,000
Production overhead	5,769	6,923	2,308	15,000
	–––––	–––––	–––––	–––––
Gross profit (£)	44,231	53,077	5,692	103,000
Expenses (£)	15,384	18,461	6,155	40,000
	–––––	–––––	–––––	–––––
Net profit (£)	28,847	34,616	(463)	63,000

Additional information:

- Total production overheads have been apportioned to the three departments on the basis of sales volume. However, upon further investigation it has been determined that only 50% of the production overheads can be directly traced to the departments in the proportion 2:2:1.
- Total expenses are head office overheads, again apportioned to the departments on the basis of sales volume. It has since been determined that only 60% of these can be directly traced to the departments, in the ratio 3:3:2.

Complete the following to restate the financial position in terms of the controllable profit made by each department and advise whether department 3 should be closed?

	1	2	3	Total
Sales units	5,000	6,000	2,000	13,000
Sales (£)	150,000	240,000	24,000	414,000
Cost of sales (£)				
Direct material	75,000	150,000	8,000	233,000
Direct labour	25,000	30,000	8,000	63,000
Production overhead				
Expenses				
	–––––	–––––	–––––	–––––
Controllable profit (£)				
Other costs (£)				
Overhead (50%)				
Expenses (40%)				
				–––––
Net profit (£)				63,000

Complete the following sentence:

Looking at the restated figures, department 3 should be ___________ (closed/kept open). The department is making a _________ **(positive/negative)** contribution towards the overall profit of the business.

4 Further processing

4.1 Decisions about further processing

Another type of decision to consider is whether a semi-finished product should be sold part way through production or whether it could be processed further and then sold at a higher price.

When deciding whether to process a particular product further or to sell at the end of the original processing **only future incremental cash flows** should be considered:

- Any difference in revenue and any extra costs associated with further processing.

- Any costs of making the original product are sunk at this stage and thus not relevant to the decision. (Note: if we are considering the viability of the whole process, then the costs to make the basic product would be relevant).

For example a piece of cheese can be sold as a block, or it could be cut into slices or grated for the customer.

Slicing or grating the cheese is processing the basic product further and will incur additional costs (potentially labour time or use of machinery), but the sliced or grated cheese will command a higher price for the convenience it provides to the customer.

 **Example**

Further processing?

A firm makes three basic products, X, Y and Z, at a joint cost of £400,000. Joint costs are apportioned on the basis of weight. Products X and Z are currently processed further.

Product	Weight of basic product	Further processing costs (variable)	Sales revenue
	tonnes	£000	£000
X	600	800	980
Y	200	–	120
Z	200	400	600

An opportunity has arisen to sell all three products as the basic product for the following prices.

	£000
X	200
Y	120
Z	160

Which of the products, if any, should the firm process further?

Solution

The joint costs are not incremental and so can be ignored. The only incremental cash flows are as follows:

Product	X	Y	Z
	£000	£000	£000
Additional revenue from further processing	780	n/a	440
Less: additional cost from further processing	(800)	n/a	(400)
Benefit/(cost) of further processing	(20)		40

On financial grounds, only Z should be processed further.

Other considerations

- Are the products linked in anyway? By not processing X further the demand for Z could be reduced.
- Customer reaction, customers may be upset that the further processed version of X is no longer available.
- Use of spare capacity, the company could put the resources that previously processed X further to another use.

Test your understanding 8

Z is one of a number of companies that produce three products for an external market. The three products, R, S and T may be bought or sold in this market. Details of the inputs and outputs for March 20X7 is shown below:

Input	Kg	£
Material A	1,000	3,500
Material B	2,000	2,000
Material C	1,500	3,000
Direct labour		6,000
Variable overhead		2,000
Fixed cost		1,000
		17,500

Output	**Units**	**£**
Product R	800	3,500
Product S	2,000	8,750
Product T	1,200	5,250
		17,500

Z can sell products R, S or T after this common process or they can be individually further processed and sold as RZ, SZ and TZ respectively. The market prices for the products at the intermediate stage and after further processing are (market prices per unit):

Product	**£**
R	3.00
S	5.00
T	3.50
RZ	6.00
SZ	5.75
TZ	6.75

The specific costs of the three individual further processes are:

Process R to RZ – variable cost of £1.40 per unit, no fixed costs

Process S to SZ – variable cost of £0.90 per unit, no fixed costs

Process T to TZ – variable cost of £1.00 per unit, fixed cost of £600 per month

Complete the following table to determine whether any of the intermediate products should be further processed before being sold.

Product	**Incremental revenue (£)**	**Incremental cost (£)**	**Impact on profit (£)**
RZ			
SZ			
TZ			

Complete the following sentences:

On financial grounds R _________ (**should/should not**) be processed further to RZ.

On financial grounds S _________ (**should/should not**) be processed further to SZ.

On financial grounds T _________ (**should/should not**) be processed further to TZ.

Test your understanding 9

The CS group is planning its annual marketing conference for its sales executives and has approached the VBJ Holiday Company (VBJ) to obtain a quotation. VBJ has been trying to win the business of the CS group for some time and is keen to provide a quotation which the CS group will find acceptable in the hope that this will lead to future contracts.

The manager of VBJ has produced the following cost estimate for the conference:

	£
Coach running costs	2,000
Driver costs	3,000
Hotel costs	5,000
General overheads	2,000
Subtotal	12,000
Profit (30%)	3,600
Total	15,600

You have considered this cost estimate but you believe that it would be more appropriate to base the quotation on relevant costs. You have therefore obtained the following further information:

Coach running costs represent the fuel costs of £1,500 plus an apportionment of the annual fixed costs of operating the coach. No specific fixed costs would be incurred if the coach is used on this contract. If the contract did not go ahead, the coach would not be in use for eight out of the ten days of the conference. For the other two days a contract has already been accepted which contains a significant financial penalty clause. A replacement coach could be hired for £180 per day.

Driver costs represent the salary and related employment costs of one driver for 10 days. If the driver is used on this contract the company will need to replace the driver so that VBJ can complete its existing work on the contract mentioned above. The replacement driver would be hired from a recruitment agency that charges £400 per day for a suitably qualified driver.

Hotel costs are the expected costs of hiring the hotel for the conference.

General overheads are based upon the overhead absorption rate of VBJ and are set annually when the company prepares its budgets.

The only general overhead cost that can be specifically identified with the conference is the time that has been spent in considering the costs of the conference and preparing the quotation. This amounted to £250.

Complete the statement showing the total relevant cost of the contract.

	£
Coach running costs	
Driver costs	
Hotel costs	
General overheads	
	______
Subtotal	
Profit	
	______
Total	
	______

Explain clearly the reasons for each of the values in your quotation and for excluding any of the costs (if appropriate).

5 Summary

This chapter has reviewed the key topic of relevant costing and several different types of short term decisions that an organisation might have to make:

- make or buy decisions
- discontinuation of a business segment
- further processing

Answers to chapter test your understandings

Test your understanding 1

The correct answer is B.

The initial £40,000 fee will be deemed to be a sunk cost – it has already been committed and won't be affected by any decision to proceed from this point.

The £20,000 is a future cost. Despite the fact that it is called a fixed cost it will only be incurred if the project proceeds. It is therefore an extra, or incremental, cost of the project and should be included in any future decision making.

Test your understanding 2

As the spare capacity is 18,000 units, there is sufficient slack to meet the new order.

Variable cost per unit = £2.50

Contribution per unit from existing product = £3.25 – £2.50 = £0.75

Contribution per unit from new product = £2.80 – £2.50 = £0.30

	£
Increase in contribution from new product:	
£0.30 × 12,000 units	3,600
Fall in contribution from existing product:	
£0.75 × (12,000 × 2/15)	(1,200)
Net gain in contribution	2,400

Test your understanding 3

Material Q is in regular use, so relevant cost = replacement cost

Replacement cost for Q = 1,500 kgs × £4.80 = £7,200

Test your understanding 4

The variable cost per hour of overhead is relevant since this cost would be avoidable if the contract were not undertaken. The relevant cost of variable overheads is therefore £17.50 per machine hour.

The fixed cost per hour is an absorption rate. Actual fixed costs would not increase by £32.50 per hour, but by £8,000 in total. The incremental relevant cost of fixed overheads is therefore £8,000.

This would make the total cost = (2,000 hours of machine time for variable overheads @ £17.50 per hour) + £8,000 or fixed overheads = £43,000.

Test your understanding 5

Net book values are not a relevant cost, therefore the relevant cost is the opportunity cost of £2,000 of not selling the equipment.

Test your understanding 6

The relevant cost of making the product is the variable cost of £3, £4 and £1 AND the specific fixed cost of £2.50.

In addition there is another cost – an opportunity cost – every unit of the component that we make uses £4 of labour. If £8 of labour were used on the other product contribution would increase by £10.

So therefore there is an extra opportunity cost of £5 per £4 of labour

Test your understanding 7

	1	2	3	Total
Sales units	5,000	6,000	2,000	13,000
Sales (£)	150,000	240,000	24,000	414,000
Cost of sales (£)				
Direct material	75,000	150,000	8,000	233,000
Direct labour	25,000	30,000	8,000	63,000
Production overhead (Note 1)	3,000	3,000	1,500	7,500
Expenses (Note 2)	9,000	9,000	6,000	24,000
Controllable profit (£)	38,000	48,000	500	86,500
Other costs (£)				
Overhead (50%)				7,500
Expenses (40%)				16,000
Net profit (£)				63,000

Completed sentence:

Looking at the restated figures, department 3 should be **kept open**. The department is making a **positive** contribution towards the overall profit of the business.

The apparent loss arises purely due to inappropriate apportionment of overheads and head office expenses.

(Note 1)

Only 50% of the existing production overhead charge should be included as only 50% is controllable.

50% of production overhead = £15,000 × 0.5 = £7,500.

Proportion 2:2:1 = £3,000:£3,000:£1,500

(Note 2)

60% of expenses = £40,000 × 0.6 = £24,000.

Proportion 3:3:2 = £9,000:£9,000:£6,000

Test your understanding 8

Product	Incremental revenue (£)	Incremental cost (£)	Impact on profit (£)
RZ	800 × (£6.00 – £3.00) = **2,400**	800 × £1.40 = **1,120**	1,280
SZ	2,000 × (£5.75 – £5.00) = **1,500**	2,000 × £0.90 = **1,800**	(300)
TZ	1,200 × (£6.75 – £3.50) = **3,900**	(1,200 × £1.00) + £600 = **1,800**	2,100

On financial grounds R **should** be processed further to RZ.

On financial grounds S **should not** be processed further to SZ.

On financial grounds T **should** be processed further to TZ.

Test your understanding 9

	£
Coach running costs: 1,500 + 360	1,860
Driver costs	800
Hotel costs	5,000
General overheads	–
	–––––
Subtotal	7,660
Profit	–
	–––––
Total	7,660
	–––––

Coach running costs

The £1,500 fuel cost is directly traceable to the contract and is therefore relevant. The apportionment of annual fixed costs for operating the coach are not relevant. The total fixed cost would remain the same whether they accept the contract or not.

The company should hire a replacement coach for two days @ £180 per day. This will ensure that any benefit on the other contract continues to be received. 2 × £180 = £360

Driver costs

The company's employed driver will be paid whether VBJ wins the contract or not. As a consequence of winning the contract, it would become necessary to hire a replacement driver for two days @ £400 per day to cover the existing work.

This incremental cost is relevant. 2 × £400 = £800

Hotel costs

The hotel cost is directly attributable to the contract and is therefore relevant.

General overheads

The general overhead that has been traced to the contract (£250) should be ignored as this cost is sunk.

Profit

The profit is not a relevant cost.

Calculating forecasts

Introduction

From your PCTN studies a forecast is the prediction of future events over which little or no control is exercised. Parts of budgets are also based on forecasts. This means it is useful for organisations to be able to predict these events and we use a variety of tools to help calculate forecasts of what will happen in the future, from time series techniques, expected values, indices to linear regression.

In your assessment you may be asked to use the results of the linear regression technique to produce a trend for a series of data.

You should be able to not only use the time series techniques to forecast future trends and seasonal variations but also understand the weaknesses of time series analysis and the problems of using historical data to predict the future.

Regression analysis is a technique for estimating the line of best fit, given a series of data. It is essentially a statistical technique and the description that follows in this chapter is sufficient in depth for applying the technique in the assessment.

There are other methods of indicating the trend of figures for income or costs and we will also look at the use of index numbers.

ASSESSMENT CRITERIA

Calculate forecasts (LO 4.4)

Uncertainty in the budget setting process (LO 1.6)

CONTENTS

1 Time series analysis

1.1 Introduction

The process of forecasting will inevitably involve some analysis of historic data (revenues, costs, share prices, etc) in order that future values may be predicted.

The data may concern the economy as a whole, the particular industry with which the organisation is involved (or wants to be) or the organisation itself.

Definitions

A **time series** is a set of values for some variable (e.g. monthly production) which varies with time. The set of observations will be taken at specific times, usually at regular intervals. Examples of figures which can be plotted as a time series are:

- monthly rainfall in London
- daily closing price of a share on the Stock Exchange
- monthly revenues of an online retailer.

Time series analysis takes historic data and breaks it down into component parts that are easier to extrapolate (predict future values of). In particular, it will isolate the underlying trend.

1.2 Plotting the graph of a time series

The pattern of a time series can be identified by plotting points of the values on a graph, such as below.

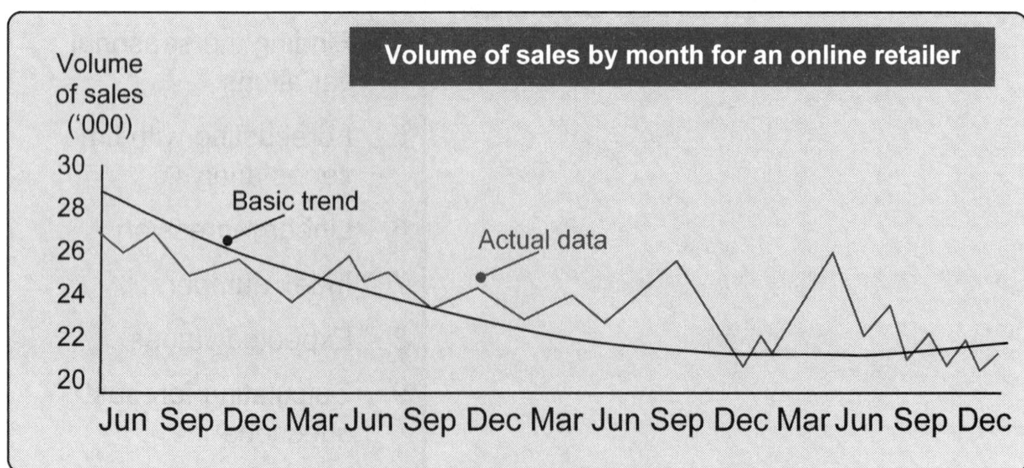

In such a graph time is always plotted on the horizontal x axis. Each point is joined by a straight line hence the typically 'jagged' appearance. Don't try to draw a smooth curve which will pass through all the points on a time series graph. You will find it practically impossible and, in any case, it is incorrect to do so. The only reason for joining the points at all is to give a clearer picture of the pattern, which would be more difficult to interpret from a series of dots.

On the graph above you will see that, having completed the time series graph, we have sketched in a 'basic trend' line. But what does it tell us? We need to look in more detail at what factors are at play in a time series.

1.3 Characteristic time series components

Analysis of time series has revealed certain characteristic movements or variations, the components of the time series. Analysis of these components is essential for forecasting purposes.

The four main types of component are as follows:

- basic trend (long-term)
- cyclical variations (medium-term)
- seasonal variations (short-term)
- random variations (short-term).

1.4 Basic trend

The basic trend refers to the general direction in which the graph of a time series goes over a long interval of time once the short-term variations have been smoothed out. This movement can be represented on the graph by a basic trend curve or line.

1.5 Cyclical variations

Cyclical variations refer to long term swings around the basic trend. These cycles may or may not be periodic; they do not necessarily follow exactly similar patterns after equal intervals of time. In business and economic situations movements are said to be cyclical if they recur at time intervals of more than one year. A good example is the trade cycle, representing intervals of boom, decline, recession, and recovery which has, historically, followed an approximate seven year cycle.

1.6 Seasonal variations

Seasonal variations are the identical, or almost identical, patterns which a time series follows during corresponding intervals of successive periods. Such movements are due to recurring events such as the sudden increase in department store sales before Christmas. Although, in general, seasonal movements refer to a period of three months, this is not always the case and periods of hours, days, weeks and months, may also be considered depending on the type of data available.

Having isolated the trend we need to consider how to deal with the seasonal variations. We will look at two models – the additive model and the multiplicative model.

The additive model is the simplest model and is satisfactory when the variations around the trend are within a constant range. If, as is more usual, the variations around the trend increase as the trend itself rises, it is better to use the multiplicative model.

1.7 Random variations

Random variations are the sporadic motions of time series due to chance events such as floods, strikes or elections.

By their very nature they are unpredictable and therefore cannot play a large part in any forecasting, but it is possible to isolate the random variations by calculating all other types of variation and removing them from the time series data. It is important to extract any significant random variations from the data before using them for forecasting.

Random and cyclical variations will not feature in your assessment.

2 Isolating the trend

2.1 Introduction

There are three main ways of isolating the trend:

- using a line of best fit
- using moving averages
- using linear regression.

2.2 Line of best fit – sketching a basic trend line

A basic trend line was drawn in on the time series graph shown earlier in this chapter. Indeed one way of isolating the trend is simply to draw it in freehand on the graph. This is called a 'line of best fit'.

This is actually a very helpful method. Once a time series has been prepared as a graph, it is usually a fairly simple matter to sketch in a basic trend line which manages to echo the overall long-term trend of the time series. There are some advantages to doing it this way:

- It is quick and easy.
- It allows one to interpolate a value easily. If you have monthly data for, say, Months 1, 3, 5, 7, 9 and 11 only, plotting those values and sketching a trend line will allow you to see what the likely value for months 2, 4, 6, 8 and 10 might have been. On the graph below you will see that we have interpolated the values of £125,000 for Month 6 of 20X4, and £175,000 for Month 12 of 20X4.
- It is possible to extrapolate a figure past the end of the data available (see the dotted line on the graph below). It is always worth bearing in mind, however, that data cannot be extrapolated very far ahead. Common sense suggests, for instance, that the trend line in the graph below is unlikely to continue in a horizontal line for very long – it is bound either to rise or fall. So the extrapolation of £175,000 for Month 7 in 20X5 is not unreasonable, but it would not be helpful to extrapolate the line and make the same prediction for, say, Month 1 of 20X6.

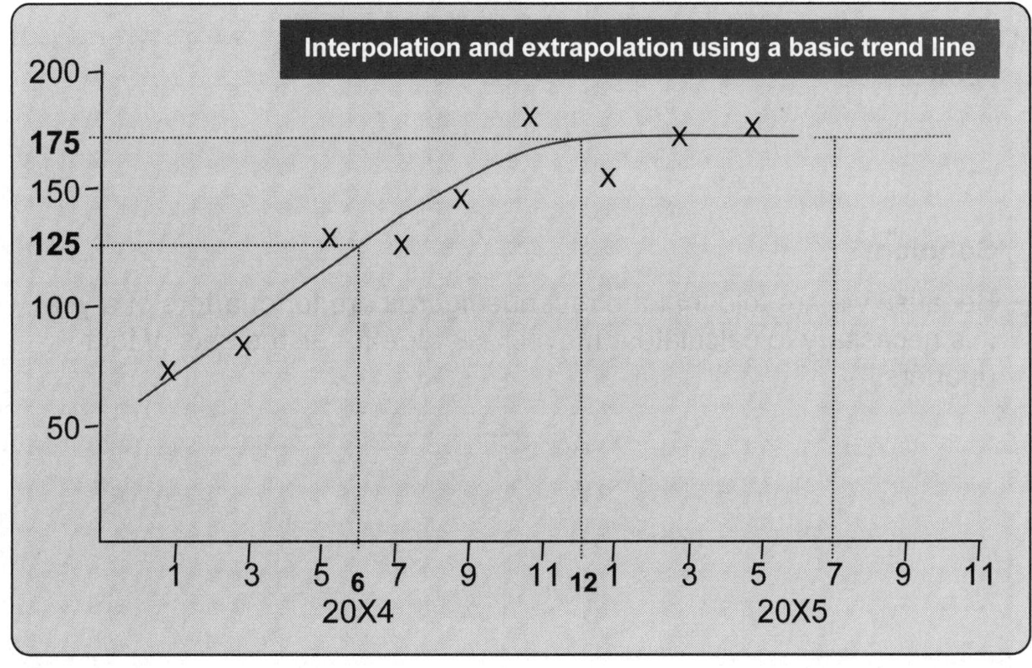

3 Moving averages

3.1 Introduction

By using moving averages, the effect of any seasonal variation in a time series can be eliminated to show the basic trend. This elimination process will only work if the moving average is calculated over the correct number of values (being the number of values in one complete cycle). For instance, if a seasonal variation present in a time series is repeated every fourth period, then moving averages with a cycle of four should be used.

This will become clearer as you follow through this simple example.

Example

The following time series shows a set of revenue figures for eight quarters which are clearly increasing. At first sight, however, this increase appears to be quite erratic. We can however produce the trend by the use of moving averages.

Year	Quarter	Revenues £000
20X4	1	3
	2	5
	3	5
	4	5
20X5	1	7
	2	9
	3	9
	4	9

Solution

Because we are told that the revenue figures are for quarters of a year, it is necessary to calculate a moving average for all the sets of four quarters.

Year	Quarter	Revenues	4-quarter moving average
		£000	£000
20X4	1	3	
	2	5	
			4.5 (W1)
	3	5	
			5.5
	4	5	
			6.5
20X5	1	7	
			7.5
	2	9	
			8.5
	3	9	
	4	9	

Workings:

The moving average for the first four quarters is calculated as

$$\frac{3+5+5+5}{4} = 4.5$$

Each moving average value is calculated and then placed in the centre of the numbers that were used in the calculation. For example, the first 4-value moving average is calculated as the average of the first four numbers, and then placed mid-way between the 2nd and 3rd quarter values of 20X4.

The moving average of four values captures the steadily increasing basic trend.

It will usually be fairly obvious which is the appropriate order in an examination question due to the way in which the data are presented, e.g. in 'quarters' (order 4) or days of the working week (order 5).

Be sure that you have understood the positioning of the moving averages in the above table. Each average has been written exactly opposite the middle of the figures from which it has been calculated. This results in the moving averages for even numbers of values (four in this case) being suspended halfway between two of the original figures.

Where you have a moving average for an even number of values, it is necessary to realign the moving averages so that they fall opposite the original values by calculating a centred moving average for every two moving average values.

Year	Quarter	Original time series	Moving average (4 values)	Centred moving average order 4
20X4	1	3		
	2	5		
			4.5	
	3	5		5 (W)
			5.5	
	4	5		6
			6.5	
20X5	1	7		7
			7.5	
	2	9		8
			8.5	
	3	9		
	4	9		

As you can see by the centring process, the centred moving average is the basic trend.

(W) (4.5 + 5.5) ÷ 2 = 5

Once we have the trend we can then use it to forecast/predict what will happen in future periods. In this case we can see that the trend is increasing by 1 each quarter. Going back to the start of this example that is revenue is increasing by £1,000 each quarter.

We can see that the underlying trend for Qtr 2 20X5 is 8, so the revenue trend for the next four quarters would be expected to continue as follows:

Qtr 3 20X5 = 8 +1 = 9, i.e. £9,000

Qtr 4 20X5 = 9 + 1 = 10, i.e. £10,000

Qtr 1 20X6 = 10 + 1 = 11, i.e. £11,000

Qtr 2 20X6 = 11 + 1 = 12, i.e. £12,000

We can then identify the seasonal variation (see later), allowing us to make a reasonable forecast.

3.2 Disadvantages of moving averages

- Values at the beginning and end of the series are lost – therefore the moving averages do not cover the complete period.
- The moving averages may generate cycles or other variations that were not present in the original data.
- The averages are strongly affected by extreme values. To overcome this a 'weighted' moving average is sometimes used giving the largest weights to central items and small weights to extreme values.

Test your understanding 1

Using the table below, calculate the moving average of the following sales figures to:

(a) order 3

(b) order 4.

Month	Value
	£
1	10
2	12
3	14
4	17
5	21
6	19
7	17
8	17

Solution

Month	Value £000	Moving average order 3	Moving average order 4
1	10		
2	12		
3	14		
4	17		
5	21		
6	19		
7	17		
8	17		

Test your understanding 2

Ski Fun Ltd owns a number of chalets in Switzerland that it lets out for holidays. Given below is data showing the number of people who stayed in the chalets each quarter.

	Quarter 1	Quarter 2	Quarter 3	Quarter 4
20X1			92	195
20X2	433	324	95	202
20X3	486	347	98	218
20X4	499	360	104	236

Calculate the trend of the number of visitors. Use a four-period moving average and round to the nearest whole number where necessary.

Ski Fun Ltd

Quarter		Numbers	Four-period moving total Step 1	Four-period moving average Step 2	Trend Step 3
20X1 –	3	92			
	4	195			
20X2 –	1	433			
	2	324			
	3	95			
	4	202			
20X3 –	1	486			
	2	347			
	3	98			
	4	218			
20X4 –	1	499			
	2	360			
	3	104			
	4	236			

4 Finding the seasonal variations

4.1 Introduction

Having isolated the trend we need to consider how to deal with the seasonal variations. We will look at two models – the additive model and the multiplicative model.

The additive model is the simplest model and is satisfactory when the variations around the trend are within a constant range.

4.2 The additive model – finding the seasonal variations

The additive model we will use expresses variations in absolute terms, with above and below average figures being shown as positives or negatives.

The four components of a time series (T = trend; S = seasonal variation; C = cyclical variation; R = random variation) are expressed as absolute values which are simply added together to produce the actual figures:

Actual data (time series) = T + S + C + R

For unsophisticated analyses over a relatively short period of time cyclical variations (C) and random variations (R) are ignored. Random variations are ignored because they are unpredictable and would not normally exhibit any repetitive pattern, whereas cyclical variations (long-term oscillations) are ignored because their effect is negligible over short periods of time. The model therefore simplifies to:

Actual data = T + S

The seasonal variation is therefore the difference between the computed trend figure and the original time series figure. Thus:

S = Actual – T

Example

The seasonal variations can be extracted by subtracting each trend value from its corresponding time series value.

Solution

Quarter	Original time series	Underlying trend	Seasonal variation (S)
	(a)	(b)	(a) – (b)
3	94	100	(6)
4	134	103	31
1	84	106	(22)
2	106	109	(3)

Once we have identified the seasonal variation we can use it to forecast the future value of the time series.

In this example, the trend appears to be going up in by 3 each quarter.

So the next quarter 3 the underlying trend would be 112.

The seasonal variation is -6, so the forecast for the upcoming qtr 3 would be: 112 – 6 = 106.

4.3 Seasonal variations and the multiplicative model

In the assessment you may be given the trend figures and seasonal variations but, instead of the seasonal variations being given in absolute figures as in the additive model that we have used so far, the seasonal variations may be given as percentage figures. This is the case if the multiplicative model is used for the time series analysis.

In order to find the forecast figures in this case, simply multiply the trend figure by the seasonal variation percentage and either add it to the trend or deduct it from the trend.

Example

Given below are the estimated trend figures for a company's revenue for the next four quarters:

20X3	**Trend**
	£
Quarter 1	560,000
Quarter 2	580,000
Quarter 3	605,000
Quarter 4	632,000

The seasonal variations have been calculated as:

Quarter 1	+ 15%
Quarter 2	+ 10%
Quarter 3	– 5%
Quarter 4	– 20%

Calculate the forecast revenue figures for each of the next four quarters.

Solution

Quarter 1	£560,000 + (560,000 × 0.15) =	£644,000
Quarter 2	£580,000 + (580,000 × 0.10) =	£638,000
Quarter 3	£605,000 – (605,000 × 0.05) =	£574,750
Quarter 4	£632,000 – (632,000 × 0.20) =	£505,600

5 Forecasting with time series analysis

5.1 Introduction

Earlier we noted that the analysis of a time series into its component parts would make extrapolation easier for forecasting future values for planning purposes.

In general, for short-term forecasts, only the trend and seasonal variations will be used; the cyclical variations will only have a significant effect over quite a long period of time and the random variations are, by their very nature, unpredictable.

Thus the approach to forecasting will be to:

- extrapolate the trend to the appropriate future time; and
- adjust the extrapolated trend value by the appropriate seasonal variation.

5.2 Extrapolating the trend

There is no unique method for extrapolation of the basic trend, as it will very much depend upon its particular shape (if, indeed, it has a discernible shape).

In practice, computers will be of great help in producing various possible equations for the trend, which can be rapidly tested against the data available to determine which fits best.

If the moving averages method has been used, a certain amount of judgement will be necessary. Possible approaches include the following:

- Plot the trend values on a graph and extrapolate by eye. (In fact, an initial sketch graph can be useful anyway to get a visual impression of the trend, before using one of the following methods to predict it.)
- Look at the increments between each trend value for any approximate pattern (e.g. roughly equal, which makes the trend approximately linear or steadily increasing) and continue this pattern to the future time required.

5.3 Problems with forecasting

There are a number of problems with using time series analysis in order to estimate or forecast future results.

- The main problem is the inherent weakness of extrapolation. In order to estimate the trend for the future the trend line is extended on the graph and the figures read off. However, although the time series has moved in that particular manner in the past, it does not necessarily mean that it will continue to do so in the future.
- The seasonal adjustments used to find the forecast for the future are again based upon historic figures that may well be out of date. There is no guarantee that the seasonal variations will remain the same in the future. If the time series has a large cyclical or random variation element, then this will make any forecasts even less reliable.

Test your understanding 3

Eastoft Feeds and Fertilisers Ltd uses a number of standard raw materials for its product range. Product F4's main raw material is 'EF1'. The average price per tonne for this material, which is subject to seasonal change, for each quarter during 20X1, was as below. The material is in short supply.

20X1	**Q1**	**Q2**	**Q3**	**Q4**
Average price per tonne	£40	£44	£64	£76
Seasonal variation	–£4	–£8	+£4	+£8

Task

(a) Determine the seasonally adjusted price per tonne for raw material 'EF1' for each of the four quarters of 20X1.

(b) If a similar pattern of price movements were to continue, determine the likely purchase price per tonne for each of the four quarters of 20X2.

Solution

(a) **20X1**

	Q1	**Q2**	**Q3**	**Q4**
Actual price per tonne				
Seasonal variation				
Trend				

(b) **20X2**

Trend				
Seasonal variation				
Forecast price per tonne				

6 Linear regression

6.1 Equation of the regression line

Only a broad understanding of linear regression is required in the context of producing a trend for a time series.

Regression analysis is a technique for estimating the line of best fit, given a series of data. It is essentially a statistical technique, and the description that follows is only a working guide for applying the technique.

Regression analysis is based on the concept of 'drawing the line that minimises the sum of the squares of the deviations of the line from the observed data' (so it is sometimes referred to as the least squares method). The regression line of y on x is used when an estimate of y (the **dependent** variable) is required for a given value of x (the **independent** variable).

The general equation for the regression line is given as:

$$y = a + bx$$

Where:

x is the independent variable

y is the dependent variable

a is the fixed element

b is the variable element

You do not have to understand how this equation is calculated, but you do need to be able to use it.

In particular, you must understand that the independent variable (x) in some way causes the dependent variable (y) to have the value given by the equation.

Thus, if we were calculating the value of umbrellas sold for given amounts of monthly rainfall, the rainfall would be the independent variable (x) and the sales value would be the dependent variable (y) (rainfall causes umbrella sales and not vice versa).

Example

X Ltd is forecasting its sales for the four quarters of 20X5. It has carried out a linear regression exercise on its past revenue data and established the following:

a = 20

b = 0.7

The equation of the regression line is therefore:

y = 20 + 0.7x

Where x is number of the quarter and y is revenue in £000s.

Calculate the revenue for each of the quarters in 20X5.

Solution

		£000
Quarter 1	y = 20 + (0.7 × 1) =	20.7
Quarter 2	y = 20 + (0.7 × 2) =	21.4
Quarter 3	y = 20 + (0.7 × 3) =	22.1
Quarter 4	y = 20 + (0.7 × 4) =	22.8

Test your understanding 4

Regression line

A regression line has been calculated as y = 192 + 2.40x, where x is the output and y is the total cost. You are required to:

(a) Fill in the blanks:

In the formula y = a + bx, y represents total cost (the ____________ variable), x represents the units of activity (the ____________ variable), 192 represents the ____________ cost element (£), 2.40 represents the ____________ cost per unit (£).

(Choose from: variable, fixed, dependent, independent)

The formula is estimating a linear relationship between activity level and total cost.

(b) Use it to predict the total cost for (i) 500 units and (ii) 1,500 units.

(i) x = 500

y =

= £ ___________

(ii) x = 1,500

y =

= £ ___________

6.2 The assumptions of regression analysis

Regression analysis is based on sample data and if we selected a different sample it is probable that a different regression line would be constructed. For this reason, regression analysis is most suited to conditions where there is a relatively stable relationship between variables.

Assumptions we are making:

- The relationship is a linear one
- The data used is representative of future trends.

7 Index numbers

7.1 Use of index numbers

A time series of figures for costs or income can be easily converted into an index. This is done firstly by choosing a base period and allocating to this period's figure an index of 100. Each subsequent period's figure is then converted into an index number using the formula:

$$\text{Index} = \frac{\text{Current period figure}}{\text{Base period figure}} \times 100$$

Example

The materials costs for a business for the last six months were:

	£
March	427,000
April	442,000
May	460,000
June	433,000
July	447,000
August	470,000

If the index for March is 100, what are the index numbers of the costs for each of the subsequent months and what do these index numbers tell us?

Solution

Month		**Index**
March	Base year	100.0
April	$\frac{442,000}{427,000} \times 100$	103.5
May	$\frac{460,000}{427,000} \times 100$	107.7
June	$\frac{433,000}{427,000} \times 100$	101.4
July	$\frac{447,000}{427,000} \times 100$	104.7
August	$\frac{470,000}{427,000} \times 100$	110.1

The index shows that the materials costs are generally rising although there is a fall back in June which has been made up for by the highest level yet in August.

7.2 Indices to measure inflation

Published indices that can be useful to the management accountant are the Consumer Price Index (CPI) and the Retail Price Index (RPI). These indices are published on a monthly basis by the Government and are used as measures of general price changes and inflation.

If we have a series of cost or revenue figures measured over a fairly long time period then they could have been distorted by price changes over the period and may not necessarily show the correct position.

We can use the RPI to adjust all of the figures in the time series into current day prices by using the formula:

$$\text{Current price adjusted figure} = \text{Actual revenue} \times \frac{\text{RPI in current year}}{\text{RPI in year of sales}}$$

Example

Suppose that a company has recorded annual revenue over the last six years as follows:

	£
20X0	735,000
20X1	764,000
20X2	791,000
20X3	811,000
20X4	833,000
20X5	856,000

The average RPI for each of those years was as follows:

	RPI
20X0	144.3
20X1	149.8
20X2	153.0
20X3	157.2
20X4	161.9
20X5	170.0

Show the revenue for the last six years in terms of current year (20X5) prices to the nearest £ and explain what this shows.

Solution

	Actual revenue	RPI adjustment	Price adjusted revenue
	£		£
20X0	735,000	× 170.0/144.3	865,904
20X1	764,000	× 170.0/149.8	867,023
20X2	791,000	× 170.0/153.0	878,889
20X3	811,000	× 170.0/157.2	877,036
20X4	833,000	× 170.0/161.9	874,676
20X5	856,000		856,000

The original, unadjusted figures indicated a fairly substantial increase in revenue over the period, but once the revenues are adjusted to current prices, a different picture appears. In fact the revenue increased very gradually until 20X2 and has been in decline for the last three years.

When comparing costs or revenue over time the accountant should consider the effects of either general inflation by using the RPI or more specific price changes that affect the cost or revenue by using a price index specifically related to that cost or revenue.

Test your understanding 5

Price indices

A product which cost £12.50 in 20X0, cost £13.65 in 20X1. Calculate the simple price index for 20X1 based on 20X0.

Simple price index = $\frac{P_1}{P_0} \times 100$

= ____________

This means that the price has increased by ____________% of its base year price of £12.50.

Test your understanding 6

If a machine costs £2,000 on 1 January 20X2 and the relevant cost index has risen from 125.0 to 133.4 from January to April 20X2, how much would the machine be expected to cost in April 20X2?

Test your understanding 7

Restating revenue figures

Given below are the revenue figures of an organisation and the Retail Price Index for a number of years.

	Revenues	**Retail Price**
	£000	Index
20X1	500	131
20X2	510	139
20X3	540	149
20X4	580	154
20X5	650	164

Restate the revenue figures for each year on the following bases:

(a) deflating each year's revenue in order to take out the effect of inflation

(b) restating each year's figures in terms of 20X5 prices.

Comment on your findings.

Restating revenue figures

(a) **Deflation of figures**

20X1 £500,000 × $\frac{131}{131}$ = £500,000

20X2 £510,000 × ______ =

20X3 £540,000 × ______ =

20X4 £580,000 × ______ =

20X5 £650,000 × ______ =

(b) **Inflation to current year prices**

20X1 £500,000 × =

20X2 £510,000 × =

20X3 £540,000 × =

20X4 £580,000 × =

20X5 £650,000 × =

Comment

Test your understanding 8

Index numbers

Complete the table below by converting the cost per kilogram for each of the months to index numbers using January X2 as the base month. The price per kilogram at January X2 was £96.00. Round your answers to two decimal places.

	June X2	July X2	August X2
	£	£	£
Cost per kg	99.00	99.40	99.80
Index			

7.3 Contracts

Indices can be used as a method of securing contracts to reduce the risk of rising prices. Particularly in the building industry, where some building contracts may span several years. For example the building of the Olympic village for the 2012 Olympic Games in London took several years. The price of the contract will probably have been agreed up front. If there is inflation then the final receipt will be worth less than when the contract price was agreed years earlier. It is for this reason that often inflation is built into the contract, whereby the final price paid will be increased according to an agreed change in an index.

 **Test your understanding 9**

Eastoft Feeds and Fertilisers uses a system of standard costing as a basis for its monthly management reporting.

Costs are revised on a quarterly basis to account for changes in price based on an index for specific categories of cost. The following information relates to current costs.

Category of cost	Standard
Direct labour rate per hour	£7.00
Raw material cost per tonne	£55.00
Fixed overhead recovery rate per hour	£12.50

The price index for these categories and the index for each quarter were:

	Current	Q1	Q2	Q3	Q4
Direct labour	105.00	108.15	108.15	108.15	108.15
Raw material	110.00	112.75	113.87	114.45	114.45
Fixed overhead	108.00	109.08	109.62	110.17	110.50

Task

Revise the standards for each quarter on the basis of the changes in the index for each category of cost shown above.

Revision of standards based on changes in the index

Category of cost	Current standard	Revised standards			
		Q1	Q2	Q3	Q4
Direct labour hour rate					
Raw material cost/tonne					
Fixed overhead recovery rate per hour					

8 Expected values

8.1 What is an expected value?

An expected value is a weighted average of all possible outcomes. It calculates the average return that will be made if a decision is repeated again and again. In other words, it is obtained by multiplying the value of each possible outcome (x), by the probability of that outcome (p), and summing the results.

The formula for the expected value is **EV = Σpx**

Example

An organisation is considering launching a new product. It will do so if the expected value of the total revenue is in excess of £1,000. It is decided to set the selling price at £10. After some investigation a number of probabilities for different levels of sales revenue are predicted; these are shown in the following table:

Units sold	Revenue	Probability	Pay-off
	£		£
80	800	0.15	120
100	1,000	0.50	500
120	1,200	0.35	420
		1.00	EV = 1,040

The expected sales revenue at a selling price of £10 per unit is £1,040, that is [800 × 0.15] + [1,000 × 0.50] + [1,200 × 0.35]. In preparing forecasts and making decisions management may proceed on the assumption that it can expect sales revenue of £1,040 if it sets a selling price of £10 per unit. The actual outcome of adopting this selling price may be sales revenue that is higher or lower than £1,040. And £1,040 is not even the most likely outcome; the most likely outcome is £1,000, since this has the highest probability.

8.2 Advantages and disadvantages of EVs

Advantages:

- Takes uncertainty into account by considering the probability of each possible outcome and using this information to calculate an expected value.
- The information is reduced to a single number resulting in easier decisions.
- Calculations are relatively simple.

Disadvantages:

- The probabilities used are usually very subjective.
- The EV is merely a weighted average and therefore has little meaning for a one-off project.
- The EV gives no indication of the dispersion of possible outcomes about the EV, i.e. the risk.
- The EV may not correspond to any of the actual possible outcomes.

9 Calculating forecasts questions

9.1 Exam style questions

This chapter is the final chapter covering the statistical techniques relevant to the AMAC syllabus. The tasks in the exam usually incorporate aspects of each of the three chapters on statistical techniques.

Test your understanding 10

Bex-Index-Perplex Co have been purchasing a valuable material for use in the manufacture of their products for many years, in 20X2 they started to look at the price index for the product. The price in 20X2 (the base year) was £320 per kg. It is now 20X8, following a computer error they have incomplete records regarding the prices paid and the price index for the material over the years.

(a) Complete the table below:

Give index numbers and prices to the nearest whole number.

Year	Index	Price per kg £
20X4	108	
20X5		350
20X6		380
20X7	116	

T-Rex-Pex Ltd have a table showing the index of prices for a certain commodity over the last five years (base 20X1):

Year	20X3	20X4	20X5	20X6	20X7
Index	102	120	110	125	115

The price was £52 per kg in 20X5.

(b) Complete the following sentences (to 2 decimal places):

The percentage increase in price from 20X3 to 20X5 is________%.

The price in 20X7 is £_______ per kg.

Reggie Quackton Co has found that total production costs (y) vary linearly according to the regression equation y = a + bx, where x = production volume. Total production costs of 500 units and 4,000 units are £17,500 and £35,000 respectively.

(c) Calculate the values of a and b.

Value of a	
Value of b	

(d) Complete the below sentences:

A down-turn in the size of the population is an example of __________________.

long term trend / cyclical variation / seasonal variation / random variation.

If the regression equation linking sales (Y) to advertising expenditure (X) is given by Y = 4,000 + 12X, the sales when £150 is spent on advertising, to the nearest £ is £________.

(e) Insert the appropriate three month moving averages into the table below:

Month	Sales (units)	Three month moving average (units)
February	12,003	
March	12,204	
April	12,306	
May	12,603	
June	13,209	

10 Summary

Forecasts of future events are normally based on historical information. Information may be available from a wide variety of sources, both internal and external to the business.

Time series analysis helps with the isolation of trends, although these still may not be easy to extrapolate into the future. Remember that you are using historic data which will not necessarily reflect future economic and environmental changes.

Also, you must be able to calculate the seasonal variations and be able to deseasonalise data if required.

Linear regression is a way of using historic information to help understand what may happen in the future and therefore help an organisation make decisions such as how many units should be made. While it is a very useful tool, it is not without its limitations.

Index numbers measure how a group of related commercial quantities vary, usually over time.

As with trend analysis, they can be very useful to help use historic information to extrapolate future economic and environmental changes.

We also briefly looked at expected values, but an awareness is all that is required and there will be no calculations on this topic.

Test your understanding answers

Test your understanding 1

Month	Value £000	Moving average order 3	Moving average order 4
1	10		
2	12	12.0	
			13.25
3	14	14.3	
			16.00
4	17	17.3	
			17.75
5	21	19.0	
			18.50
6	19	19.0	
			18.50
7	17	17.6	
8	17		

Test your understanding 2

Ski Fun Ltd

Quarter		Numbers	Four-period moving total Step 1	Four-period moving average Step 2	Trend Step 3
20X1 –	3	92			
	4	195			
			1,044	261	
20X2 –	1	433			262
			1,047	262	
	2	324			263
			1,054	264	
	3	95			271
			1,107	277	
	4	202			280
			1,130	283	

20X3 –	1	486			283
			1,133	283	
	2	347			285
			1,149	287	
	3	98			289
			1,162	291	
	4	218			293
			1,175	294	
20X4 –	1	499			295
			1,181	295	
	2	360			298
			1,199	300	
	3	104			
	4	236			

Test your understanding 3

(a) 20X1

	Q1	Q2	Q3	Q4
Actual price per tonne	£40	£44	£64	£76
Seasonal variation	– £4	– £8	+ £4	+ £8
Trend	£44	£52	£60	£68

(b) 20X2

Trend (+ £8 per quarter)	£76	£84	£92	£100
Seasonal variation	– £4	– £8	+ £4	+ £8
Forecast price per tonne	£72	£76	£96	£108

Test your understanding 4

Regression line

(a) In the formula y represents total cost (the **dependent** variable), x represents the units of activity (the **independent** variable), 192 represents the **fixed** cost element (£), 2.40 represents the **variable** cost per unit (£).

The formula is estimating a linear relationship between activity level and total cost.

(b) (i) x = 500

y = 192 + 2.40 (500)

= £1,392

(ii) x = 1,500

y = 192 + 2.40 (1,500)

= £3,792

Test your understanding 5

Price indices

$$\text{Simple price index} = \frac{P_1}{P_0} \times 100$$

$$= \frac{13.65}{12.50} \times 100$$

$$= 1.092 \times 100$$

$$= 109.2$$

This means that the price has increased by 9.2% of its base year price of £12.50.

Test your understanding 6

$$£2{,}000 \times \frac{133.4}{125.0} = £2{,}134.40$$

Test your understanding 7

Restating revenue figures

(a) **Deflation of figures**

20X1 £500,000 × $\frac{131}{131}$ = £500,000

20X2 £510,000 × $\frac{131}{139}$ = £480,647

20X3 £540,000 × $\frac{131}{149}$ = £474,765

20X4 £580,000 × $\frac{131}{154}$ = £493,377

20X5 £650,000 × $\frac{131}{164}$ = £519,207

(b) **Inflation to current year prices**

20X1 £500,000 × $\frac{164}{131}$ = £625,954

20X2 £510,000 × $\frac{164}{139}$ = £601,727

20X3 £540,000 × $\frac{164}{149}$ = £594,362

20X4 £580,000 × $\frac{164}{154}$ = £617,662

20X5 £650,000 × $\frac{164}{164}$ = £650,000

Comment

The revenue figures alone show increases year after year. However, once inflation is taken into account the result is different.

Both sets of figures, once deflated by one method or the other, show that in real terms revenues decreased in 20X2 and 20X3 and increased again in 20X4 and 20X5. By 20X5, even in real terms, revenues were higher than in 20X1.

Test your understanding 8

Index numbers

	June X2	July X2	August X2
	£	£	£
Cost per kg	99.00	99.40	99.80
Index	103.13	103.54 (W1)	103.96

Working:

(W1) $\frac{£99.40}{£96.00} \times 100 = 103.54$

The other numbers are obtained in a similar manner.

Test your understanding 9

Revision of standards based on changes in the index.

Category of cost	Current standard	Revised standards			
		Q1	Q2	Q3	Q4
Direct labour hour rate	£7.00	£7.21 (W1)	£7.21	£7.21	£7.21
Raw material cost/tonne	£55.00	£56.38	£56.94	£57.23	£57.23
Fixed overhead recovery rate per hour	£12.50	£12.63	£12.69	£12.75	£12.79

Working:

(W1) $£7 \times \frac{108.15}{105.00} = £7.21$

The other numbers are obtained in a similar manner.

Test your understanding 10

(a)

Year	**Index**	**Price per kg £**
20X4	108	**346**
20X5	**109**	350
20X6	**119**	380
20X7	116	**371**

108/100 × 320 = 345.6

350/320 × 100 = 109.375

380/320 × 100 = 118.75

116/100 × 320 = 371.2

(b) The percentage increase in price from 20X3 to 20X5 is **7.84**%.

110/102 = 1.0784

The price in 20X7 is £**54.36** per kg.

52/110 × 115 = 54.3636

(c)

Value of a	**£15,000**
Value of b	**£5**

Var cost (b) = (35,000 – 17,500)/(4,000 – 500) = 17,500/3,500 = 5

Fixed cost = 35,000 – (5 × 4,000) = 15,000

(d) A down-turn in the size of the population is an example of **long term trend.**

If the regression equation linking sales (Y) to advertising expenditure (X) is given by Y = 4,000 + 12X, the sales when £150 is spent on advertising, to the nearest £ is £**5,800**.

Y = £4,000 + (12 × £150) = £4,000 + £1,800 = £5,800

(e)

Month	Sales (units)	Three month moving average (units)
February	12,003	
March	12,204	**12,171**
April	12,306	**12,371**
May	12,603	**12,706**
June	13,209	

March = (12,003 + 12,204 + 12,306)/3 = 12,171

April = (12,204 + 12,306 + 12,603)/3 = 12,371

May = (12,306 + 12,603 + 13,209)/3 = 12,706

7 Introduction to budgeting

Introduction

As the title suggests, this chapter provides basic information about the concept of budgeting, a key element of management accounting. It is essential background knowledge and should be useful in answering tasks in the assessment.

Budget data is drawn from a variety of sources, both within the organisation and externally. This chapter highlights the importance of appropriate, reliable sources for each piece of information required in budget construction.

The external environment has a direct impact on sales demand, prices, availability of resources and costs. Some costs, including taxes, are not within the organisation's control. Even material and labour costs are subject to economic pressures that may not be quantifiable when budgets are constructed; realistic budgets have to be prepared in this context.

ASSESSMENT CRITERIA

- The budgetary process (LO 1.1)
- Budgetary responsibilities and accountabilities (LO 1.2)
- Impact of internal and external factors on forecasts (LO 1.5)
- Budget revision to reflect the changing circumstances (LO 1.7)

CONTENTS

1 Planning, budgeting and forecasting

1.1 Introduction

Given the increasing complexity of business and the ever-changing environment faced by firms, it is doubtful whether any firm can survive by simply continuing to do what it has always done in the past. If the firm wishes to earn satisfactory levels of profit in the future, it must plan its course of action in order to attempt to improve its performance.

In a management accounting context, the budgeting process is part of the overall planning process.

1.2 The concept of corporate planning

Planning is an important concept in all walks of life, including your own preparation for examinations. A **plan** is a series of actions to be carried out if objectives and goals are to be met.

In a business context, the term corporate planning is often used. **Corporate planning** is a long run, on-going activity which seeks to determine the direction in which the firm should be moving in the future:

'Where do we see ourselves in ten years?'

Frequently asked questions in formulating the corporate plan are:

(a) the reason why the company exists (its **mission**)

(b) what it wants to achieve (its corporate **objectives**)

(c) how it intends to get there (its business **strategy**)

(d) what resources will be required (its **operating plans**)

(e) how well it does in comparison to the plan (**control**).

Mission is a broad statement of the overall aims of the organisation.

A clearly defined mission, which is widely publicised within and outside the organisation, will guide it in its decision making. A lot of organisations prepare and publish their mission in a document known as a 'mission statement'.

Examples of real world mission statements are:

- 'Bring inspiration and innovation to every athlete* in the world. *If you have a body, you are an athlete.' (Nike)
- 'To inspire and nurture the human spirit – one person, one cup and one neighbourhood at a time.' (Starbucks).

- 'To transform the accounting profession by making leading-edge technologies accessible to all. We do this by providing flexible digital solutions and knowledge all while supporting advisors to add value to their clients in new and innovative ways.' (Inflo)

Note that mission statements give an overall aim or goal which is not time specific and not quantified. You should contrast this with the concept of objectives dealt with below.

Corporate objectives are quantified, time-limited statements of what a firm wishes to achieve. Traditionally it was assumed that all firms were only interested in the maximisation of profit (or the wealth of their shareholders). Nowadays it is recognised that for many firms profit is only one of many objectives pursued.

Examples of other objectives include:

(a) maximisation of sales (whilst earning a 'reasonable' level of profit)

(b) growth (in sales, asset value, number of employees, etc.)

(c) survival

(d) research and development leadership

(e) quality of service

(f) contented workforce

(g) respect for the environment.

For corporate planning purposes it is essential that the objectives chosen are quantified and have a timescale attached to them. It has been suggested that objectives should be **SMART**:

- **S**pecific
- **M**easurable
- **A**chievable
- **R**elevant
- **T**ime limited

A statement such as 'maximise profits and increase sales' would be of little use in corporate planning terms. The following would be far more helpful:

(a) achieve a growth in profit of 5% per annum over the coming ten-year period

(b) obtain a revenue of £X million within six years

(c) launch at least two new products per year, etc.

Some objectives may be difficult to quantify (e.g. contented workforce) but if no attempt is made there will be no yardstick against which to compare actual performance.

Strategy is the course of action, including the specification of resources required, that the company will adopt to achieve its specific objective.

Strategy formulation usually involves:

(a) an analysis of the environment in which the firm operates, a review of the strengths and weaknesses of the company and a consideration of the threats and opportunities facing it

(b) the results of the firm's existing operations being projected forward and compared with stated objectives

(c) any differences between projected performance and objectives ('gaps') being identified.

To bridge these gaps the firm will either change its objectives (because they are too optimistic) or attempt to change the firm's direction to improve performance. This change of direction is **strategy formulation**.

Formulation of strategy is largely a creative process, whereby the firm will consider the products it makes and the markets it serves. Typical strategies include:

- market penetration (sell more of existing products to existing customers)
- product development (new products sold to existing customers)
- market development (continue in existing markets, develop new ones)
- diversification (develop new products and sell them to new customers).

These strategies might be followed either:

- internally – for example, the company develops its own products
- by acquisition – the company buys another company which already has the product range it wants.

Operating plans are the short-term tactics of the organisation.

A strategic plan might call for expansion in a particular market; whereas the operating plan will detail how the extra products are to be made and how much is to be spent on advertising. Military analogy is useful here – strategy is how to organise to win the war, operating plans (or tactics) are how to fight individual battles.

Control is the comparison of the results of the plans and the stated objectives to assess the firm's performance, and the taking of action to remedy any differences in performance.

This is an essential activity as it highlights any weakness in the firm's corporate plan or its execution. Plans must be continually reviewed because as the environment changes so plans and objectives will need revising. Corporate planning is not a once-in-every-ten-years activity, but an 'on-going' process which must react quickly to the changing circumstances of the firm.

Overview of the planning process

The overall planning and control process is summarised in the diagram that follows.

You will note that the bottom section of the diagram introduces the word 'budget'.

We saw earlier the concept of a plan and mentioned the example of students having a plan to help them to achieve their objective of passing examinations. You, as an individual, might take the view that you can afford to buy this (essential and invaluable) textbook, but you may not be able to afford to attend a series of expensive seminars held in upmarket hotels where leading experts discuss management accounting topics in great detail. By taking this view, you are, in effect turning your plan to pass the examination into a budget.

The classic concept of a budget is that it takes a plan, which might be in terms of say, hours, number of units of sales etc. and turns it into money terms.

A budget is a plan in monetary terms.

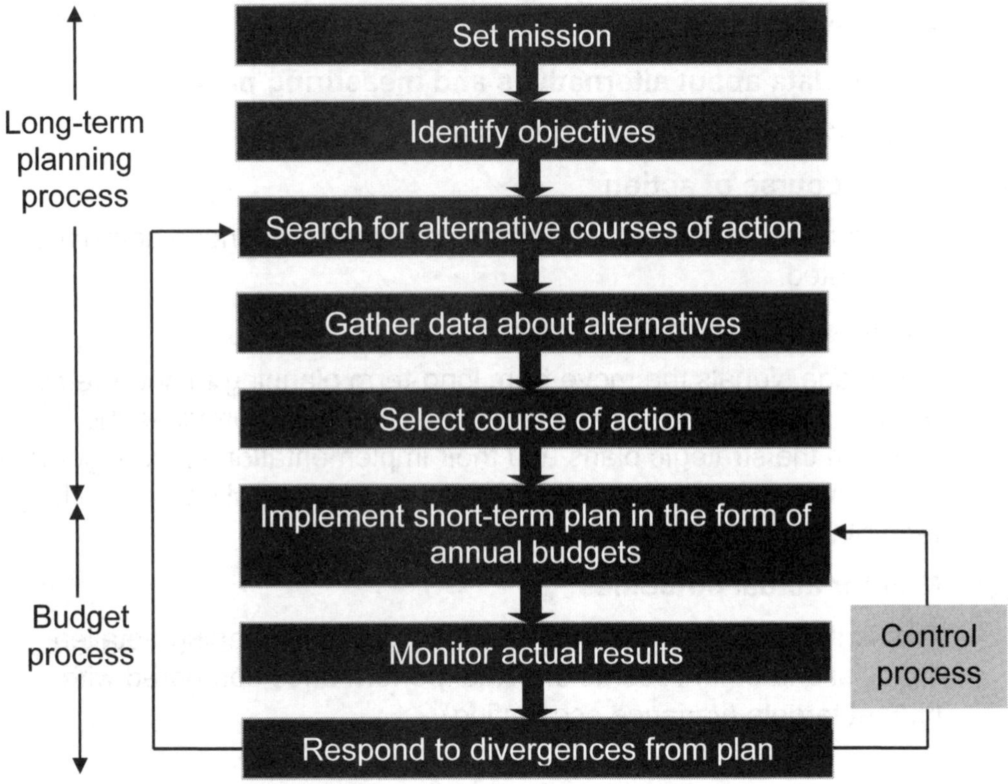

The eight stages are explained below:

(a) **Set mission**

This involves establishing the broad overall aims and goals of the organisation – these may be both economic and social.

(b) **Identify objectives**

This requires the company to specify objectives towards which it is working. These objectives may be in terms of:

- economic targets
- type of business
- goods/services to be sold
- markets to be served
- market share
- profit objectives
- required growth rates of sales, profits, assets.

(c) **Search for possible courses of action**

A series of specific strategies should be developed dealing particularly with:

- developing new markets for existing products
- developing new products for existing markets
- developing new products for new markets.

(d) **Gather data about alternatives and measuring pay-offs**

This is an information-gathering stage.

(e) **Select course of action**

Having made decisions, long-term plans based on those decisions are created.

(f) **Implement of short-term plans**

This stage signals the move from long-term planning to short-term plans in the form of annual budgeting. The budget provides the link between the strategic plans and their implementation in management decisions. The budget should be seen as an integral part of the long-term planning process.

(g) **Monitor actual outcomes**

This is the particular role of the cost accountant, keeping detailed financial and other records of actual performance compared with budget targets (variance accounting).

(h) **Respond to divergences from plan**

This is the control process in budgeting, responding to divergences from plan either through budget modifications or through identifying new courses of action.

Before we leave this section we should link together some of the most important features of management accounting, and of your examination syllabus, which we have now seen:

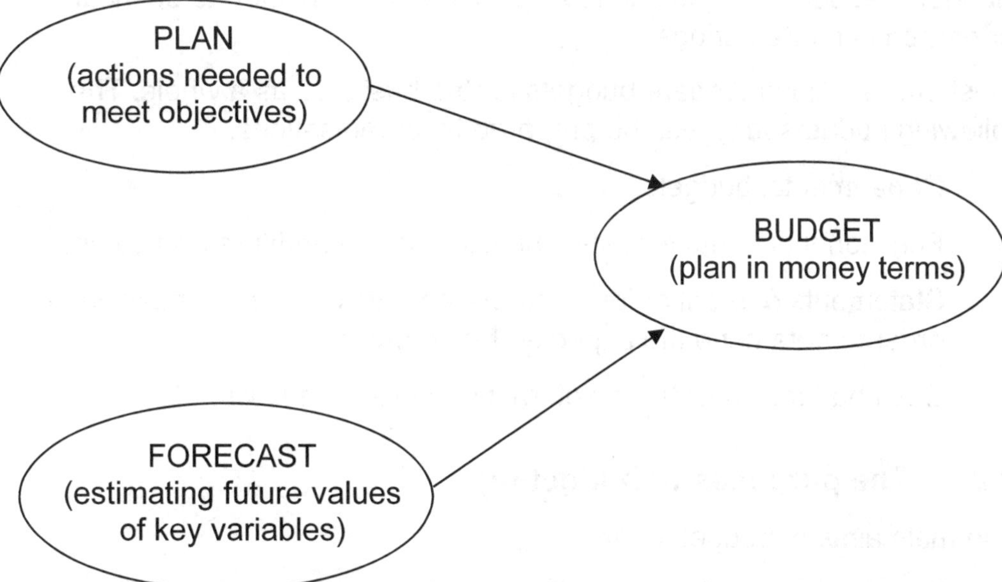

This indicates that the preparation of a budget, the subject matter of this and the next few chapters in this book needs a plan to be in place AND requires relevant forecast information to be available. Planning and forecasting are seen to be essential preliminary steps in the budgetary process.

1.3 Influences on planning and control systems

The planning and control system in all organisations should follow the general structure set out in the previous section. However, the detail of the process will be influenced by a number of factors and therefore will vary from one organisation to another.

The principal factors which will influence the process in a given organisation will include:

- organisational structure
- corporate objectives
- administrative procedures
- the nature of the activities of the business.

2 Budgeting

2.1 The basics of budgeting

A budget is a quantitative expression of a plan of action prepared in advance of the period to which it relates.

Budgets set out the costs and revenues that are expected to be incurred or earned in future periods.

Most organisations prepare budgets for the business as a whole. The following budgets may also be prepared by organisations:

- Departmental budgets.
- Functional budgets for sales, production, expenditure and so on.
- Statements of profit or loss and Statements of financial position in order to determine the expected future profits.
- Cash budgets in order to determine future cash flows.

2.2 The purposes of budgeting

The main aims of budgeting are:

- **Planning** for the future – in line with the objectives of the organisation.
- **Controlling** costs – by comparing the plan or the budget with the actual results and investigating significant differences between the two.
- **Co-ordination** of the different activities of the business by ensuring that managers are working towards the same common goal (as stated in the budget).
- **Communication** – budgets communicate the targets of the organisation to individual managers.
- **Motivation** – budgets can motivate managers by encouraging them to beat targets or budgets set at the beginning of the budget period. Bonuses are often based on 'beating budgets'. Budgets, if badly set, can also demotivate employees.
- **Evaluation** – the performance of managers is often judged by looking at how well the manager has performed 'against budget'.
- **Authorisation** – budgets act as a form of authorisation of expenditure.

In a management accounting context, the budgeting process is part of the overall planning process.

2.3 How are budgets prepared?

Before any budgets can be prepared, the long-term objectives of an organisation must be defined so that the budgets prepared are working towards the goals of the business.

Once this has been done, the budget committee can be formed, the budget manual can be produced and the limiting factor can be identified.

- **Budget committee is formed** – a typical budget committee is made up of the chief executive, budget officer (management accountant) and departmental or functional heads (sales manager, purchasing manager, production manager and so on). The budget committee is responsible for communicating policy guidelines to the people who prepare the budgets and for setting and approving budgets.
- **Budget manual is produced** – an organisation's budget manual sets out instructions relating to the preparation and use of budgets. It also gives details of the responsibilities of those involved in the budgeting process, including an organisation chart and a list of budget holders.
- **Limiting factor is identified** – in budgeting, the limiting factor is known as the principal budget factor. Generally there will be one factor that will limit the activity of an organisation in a given period. It is usually sales that limit an organisation's performance, but it could be anything else, for example, the availability of special labour skills.

If sales are the principal budget factor, then the sales budget must be produced first. If there is something else limiting the business, i.e. a resource such as material or labour hours, then this would become the principal budget factor that other budgets are based on. There is a lot more focus on making the best use of the limiting factor in other chapters.

- **Final steps in the budget process** – once the budget relating to the limiting factor has been produced then the managers responsible for the other budgets can produce them. The entire budget preparation process may take several weeks or months to complete.

The final stages are as follows.

1 Initial budgets are prepared.

2 Initial budgets are reviewed and integrated into the complete budget system.

3 After any necessary adjustments are made to initial budgets, they are accepted and the master budget is prepared (budgeted statement of profit or loss, statement of financial position and cash flow). This master budget is then shown to higher management for final approval.

4 Budgets are reviewed regularly. Comparisons between budgets and actual results are carried out and any differences arising are known as variances.

Test your understanding 1

Complete the following statement about budgets.

____**Gap 1**____ and ____**Gap 2**____ are two of the primary reasons why an organisation prepares a budget. Before the budgeting process can start the ____**Gap 3**____ of the organisation should be defined, then the ____**Gap 4**____ formed.

Gap 1		**Gap 2**	
A	Planning	E	profit
B	Risk taking	F	losses
C	Money	G	controlling
D	Achieving	H	market penetration

Gap 3		**Gap 4**	
I	shareholders	M	board of directors
J	long term objectives	N	long term objectives
K	profit	O	profit
L	budget committee	P	budget committee

2.4 More on the budget committee

A **budget committee** is a group of managers and employees drawn from a range of departments within the organisation with responsibility for the budgetary process.

A typical budget committee comprises the chief executive, the management accountant (acting as budget officer) and functional heads. Its role is to agree planning assumptions for budget preparations, so the functions of the committee are to:

(a) agree policy with regard to budgets

(b) co-ordinate budgets

(c) suggest amendments to budgets (e.g. because there is inadequate profit)

(d) approve budgets after amendment, as necessary

(e) examine comparisons of budgeted and actual results and recommend corrective action if this has not already been taken

(f) agree planning assumptions.

More generally, the budget committee oversee the budget preparation process.

The budget officer (usually a management accountant) is secretary to the committee and is responsible for seeing that the timetables are adhered to and for providing the necessary specialist assistance to the functional managers in drawing up their budgets and analysing results.

Management accountants may have specific responsibility for budgets and could be referred to as budget accountants, these would assist in the budget preparation along with senior managers.

2.5 More on the budget manual

A budget manual is a document which sets out standing instructions governing the responsibilities of persons, and the procedures, forms and records relating to the preparation and use of budgets. It sets out the procedures to be observed in budgeting, the responsibilities of each person concerned, and the timetable to be observed.

Nowadays much of the budget manual is likely to be distributed as blank computer files (particularly spreadsheet files) for managers to complete. In this way the management accountant or the finance director can ensure that information is received from the various sources in a form that is easy to consolidate into a master budget.

3 Responsibility accounting

3.1 Introduction to responsibility accounting

Examinations frequently require a discussion on whether the budgeting procedures used within an organisation are likely to achieve their aims.

These aims, and the methods used to achieve them, can be broadly categorised as follows:

- efficient management – management by exception
- motivation of workforce – responsibility accounting.

3.2 Management by exception

The features of this method of reporting are that:

(a) attention is drawn only to areas where operations are seen to be 'out of control'

(b) this may be achieved by identifying those variances that are deemed to be 'exceptional'

(c) only these variances will be investigated and (where possible) corrected

(d) management time and expertise are utilised where it can be most effective in improving the efficiency of future operations.

For it to be effective, it is important that:

- exceptional variances are correctly isolated
- only such variances owing to factors capable of correction be considered for investigation
- costs and benefits of investigation are assessed.

3.3 Responsibility accounting

The aim of a responsibility accounting system is to motivate management at all levels to work towards the company's objectives with the minimum of direction.

What is involved?

(a) The use of budgets as 'targets' against which management performance may be measured and (often) rewarded.

(b) The presentation of 'performance reports' relating to particular responsibility centres. These centres fall into four categories as follows.

(i) **Cost centre** or **expense centre** where a manager is held responsible for control of expenditure only.

(ii) A **revenue centre** is a part of the organisation that earns sales revenue. It is similar to a cost centre, but only accountable for revenues, and not expenditure.

(iii) **Profit centre** where a manager is held responsible for control of sales revenue and expenditure.

(iv) **Investment centre** where a manager is held responsible for investment decisions as well as the control of sales revenue and expenditure.

(c) The requirement is that the person deemed responsible for that area should give explanations of significant variances shown therein.

Examinations on this subject tend to concentrate on a practical application of the principles necessary for a system of responsibility accounting to work effectively, and often require the preparation of a draft performance report, or the criticism of such a report. An in-depth theoretical knowledge of the work carried out in this field is not needed; a common sense approach to a practical problem suffices.

3.4 Budgets and motivation

Motivation is the drive or urge to achieve an end result. Motivation can be seen as a force operating within an individual which drives that individual on to attain some goals or objectives. The word motivation comes from the Latin word meaning to move – this shows the key idea involved. An individual is motivated if they are moving forward to achieving goals or objectives.

Motivation may affect many aspects of the life of an individual. You have to be motivated to pass your examinations and to gain a recognised accounting qualification. At work you might be motivated to achieve promotion and to gain a position of greater authority and responsibility within the organisation.

In a business context, if employees and managers are not motivated, they will lack the drive or urge to improve their performance and to help the organisation to achieve its goals and move forward. This is the importance of motivation in a business.

Three main areas need to be examined in relation to the use of budgets in responsibility accounting:

(a) participation in budget setting

(b) budgets as motivational targets

(c) performance evaluation and reward.

The conclusions under each of these headings are largely common sense – you should try to think up practical examples in relation to your own position in study or at work to help you remember them.

4 Participation in budget setting

4.1 Why use participation?

Conventional wisdom suggests that managers should be encouraged to participate in the budget setting process and that the budget should be built up from the lower rungs of management ('bottom up' budgeting) rather than imposed from above ('top down' budgeting).

These are the **advantages**:

- Managers will then feel that they 'own' the budget and will therefore be more committed to the targets and motivated to achieve them.
- Operating managers are often the only people with sufficient detailed knowledge to develop a meaningful budget.

4.2 Disadvantages of participation

However, there are disadvantages to participation.

- The objectives of the managers and the objectives of the organisation may not be the same. 'Goal congruence' does not automatically result from empowering managers to develop their own budgets.
- Operating management may use their knowledge to manipulate the budget. They may deliberately set targets that they cannot fail to achieve, particularly if bonuses are awarded for meeting the budget.
- Managers may not wish to participate in the budget setting process. This may be because:
  - (i) they simply want to know what their targets are
  - (ii) they do not have the technical expertise to participate in budget setting
  - (iii) they do not have the necessary commitment to the organisation
  - (iv) they feel that the budget will be 'used against them'.

4.3 Budgets as motivational targets

In general, it is accepted that corporate objectives are more likely to be met if they are expressed as quantified targets, often in the form of budgets.

If a target is to have any influence on performance:

- the recipient must be aware of its existence and feel committed to achieving it
- it must be set at the right level of difficulty to act as a motivator; both unrealistic and over-generous targets will be demotivational.

Test your understanding 2

Complete the following statement about budgets.

One of the advantages of _____**Gap 1**____ in budgeting is that manager feel like they ____**Gap 2**____ the budget and are more likely to work hard to achieve the targets. A disadvantage is that ____**Gap 3**____ may manipulate the budget so that the targets are ____**Gap 4**____ to achieve.

Gap 1		**Gap 2**
A participation		E can achieve
B imposing		F don't know
C thinking		G have lost
D trying		H own

Gap 3		**Gap 4**
I customers		M impossible
J the budget committee		N easier
K operational managers		O tough
L the government		P hard

In theory, there may be a need for two budgets to be prepared for the same area.

- One should be a challenging (aspirations) budget to motivate the manager.
- The second should be a lower, and more realistic, expectations budget for planning and decision purposes.

Care should be taken to reward success as well as penalising failure, in order that a benefit is perceived in bettering rather than just achieving the target.

Budgets become stronger motivators as they become tighter up to a point, but thereafter motivation declines. The optimal degree of tightness depends on both the situation and the personality of the individuals concerned.

Empirical evidence suggests that if a budget target is set that is too easy, then actual performance will be a little better than the budget but it will not be optimised. In other words, managers do not usually work to their full potential if they know that a lower level of performance will still meet the budget – human behaviour will tend to lead to individuals putting in the minimum possible effort to achieve a set target. If greater effort were applied, a higher target may be achieved.

On the other hand, if the budget is too difficult, because it is based on ideal levels of performance, managers become discouraged at what they regard as an unattainable standard. This may de-motivate and as a result, actual performance falls short of what might reasonably have been expected.

You can apply these points to your own position in the context of examinations. If the pass mark for an examination is very low – say 10% – you know you can pass with little effort and you will (perhaps) not work to your full potential. On the other hand, if the pass mark were 99% you would, probably, view that as impossible to achieve and decide not to try at all!

The aim should be to agree a budget that falls between these two extremes and therefore incorporates just the right degree of difficulty which will lead to the optimal level of performance. At this level the budget should be challenging enough to motivate a manager to optimise his performance without being too ambitious. Authors writing on this subject have used the phrase 'tough but attainable' for the targets to be set.

The right level of difficulty is that which is acceptable to the individual manager. This level of acceptability will differ from manager to manager, as each individual behaves and reacts in a different way in similar circumstances.

This concept of budget difficulty can be demonstrated diagrammatically as follows:

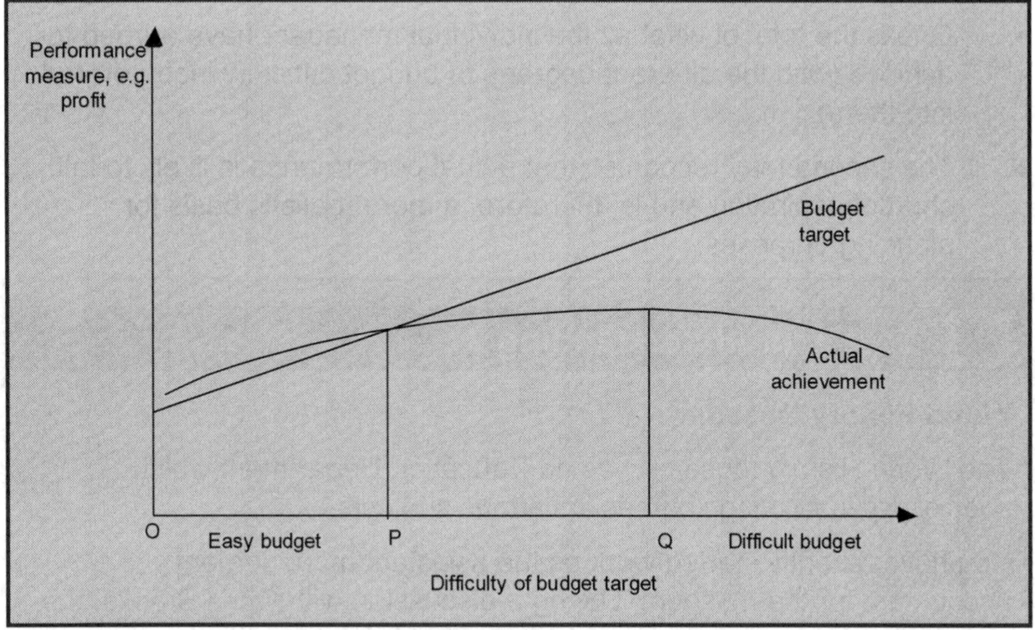

- A budget set at the degree of difficulty represented by point P is referred to as an 'expectations budget' as budget target and actual achievement are likely to coincide. The target level of performance has been met.
- However, a relatively easy-to-achieve budget, (set to the left of point P), is likely to lead to sub-optimal actual performance in that, although the budget has been met, the ACTUAL performance is at a relatively low level.
- In order to achieve a higher actual performance a more difficult budget needs to be set (an 'aspirations budget') at some point between P and Q. A budget set where point Q represents the degree of difficulty should lead to optimal performance (highest point on the 'actual' performance curve). However, it should be noted that this would give rise to an adverse variance compared with budget. If this target is set, senior management should not penalise the manager for the adverse variance, which may be unavoidable.

The diagram brings out one of the most fundamental points in budgeting:

How the degree of difficulty, represented by point Q, is determined is not at all easy in practice because it involves a knowledge of how each individual manager will react and behave. Attempts to quantify the degree of difficulty using work study assessments are a highly simplified approach to a very complex problem.

Furthermore, attempts to use the budget as a motivating tool in the manner described may in fact lead to the need for two budgets.

- One is the total of what all the individual managers have agreed to achieve (with the different degrees of budget difficulty incorporated into them).
- The second may recognise that actual performance is likely to fall short of aspiration and is, therefore, a more realistic basis for planning purposes.

Test your understanding 3

World History Museum

The World History Museum has an Education Department which specialises in running courses in various subjects.

You have recently started work as the assistant management accountant for the museum. During a discussion with Chris Brooks, the general manager, she expresses to you that her interest in the control aspects of budgeting has been sparked by her attendance on a course entitled 'Budgetary control for managers'. She has shown you the following extract from the course notes she was given:

> 'A system of participative budgeting involves managers in the process of setting their own budgets. Participative systems are likely to be more successful in planning and controlling the activities of an organisation.'

Write a brief memo to Chris Brooks which explains the advantages and disadvantages of participative budgeting as a part of the budgetary planning and control process.

4.4 Performance evaluation and reward

Managers should only be held accountable for items over which they have control, and measures of performance should be devised that promote decisions in line with corporate objectives.

Thus a manager of a profit centre may be judged by variances affecting sales and direct costs (before allocated fixed costs); the performance of the centre itself will be measured by direct controllable contribution (having accounted for costs that are directly attributable to that centre, but not necessarily all controlled by the manager).

There are three main styles of management in the use of budget performance reports:

(a) The budget-constrained style, which lays particular emphasis on results being closely in accordance with the budget plan.

(b) The profit-conscious style, which is less concerned with current deviations from budget than with a manager's ability to achieve a trend of results which is acceptable in relation to changing conditions.

(c) The non-accounting style, which tends to disregard accounting reports as a means of measuring management performance and instead looks at factors such as:

- the number of customer complaints or substandard items produced
- staff turnover
- morale in the department
- other qualitative measures.

Of the three styles, the middle is probably the most successful in achieving the company's long-term goals. The first creates good cost consciousness but also a great deal of tension between a manager and his subordinates, and manipulation of accounting information. The last promotes general good morale, but managers have a low involvement with costs.

Managers may receive financial rewards (for example, bonuses) and non-financial rewards (for example, promotion or greater responsibility) based on their ability to meet budget targets.

In the previous section the motivating effect of budgets was considered, but it should be remembered that the budgets by themselves have a limited motivational effect. It is the reward structure that is linked to achieving the budget requirements, or lack of reward for non-achievement, which provides the real underlying motivational potential of budgets.

A manager will need to regard the reward as being worthwhile if his or her behaviour is to be influenced so that he/she strives actively towards the achievement of the budget.

It is a common practice to attempt to assess the performance of a manager by a comparison of budgeted and actual results for his or her area of responsibility in the organisation. The choice of which particular measures to use is important to ensure that the individual manager sees the attainment of his or her targets as worthwhile for himself or herself and at the same time in the best interests of the organisation as a whole – this is the concept of goal congruence which we saw in the section on responsibility accounting. In practice, conflicts can and often do arise between individual managers' personal objectives and those of the organisation as a whole.

The way in which the information in budget reports is used in the assessment of managerial performance has to be considered. Different degrees of emphasis on the results of budget versus actual comparisons can lead to different attitudes and feelings among managers. There is a need to achieve the correct balance between on the one extreme, an over-emphasis on results leading to pressure and feelings of injustice from the system; and on the other, too little stress on results leading to a budget irrelevancy attitude and low morale.

In general, we can summarise the characteristics of a sound employee reward system as follows:

- **Fairness** – the system should reward effort which helps the organisation achieve its objectives.
- **Motivational** – it should motivate the managers and employees to behave congruently i.e. in a way which assists the organisation to achieve its objectives.
- **Understandability** – the system should be such that it is clear to managers what they need to do to achieve the rewards. Unduly complex reward systems, perhaps based on complex bonus formulae, are unlikely to be effective in generating improved performance.
- **Consistently applied** – the system should operate in the same way for all employees or, if not possible, for all employees at a given level in the organisation.
- **Objective** – the system should be based on measurable criteria with a minimum of subjectivity. It should also be such that it is not open to manipulation by managers in their own interests.
- **Universal** – all employees and managers at all levels in the organisation should be subject to an appraisal and reward system.

'Performance-related pay' is a method of rewarding employees in the form of bonuses, options to buy shares or other incentives, with a view to motivating them to improve their own performance or, in the case of managers, the performance of the part of the organisation which they manage.

Linking remuneration to budget achievement like this has its benefits: it can be a successful method of motivating managers to meet their budgetary targets. However, this only works when there is a short timescale between the target being met and the reward; and the risk is that managers start to focus on meeting short-term goals, rather than looking at the strategic, long-term objectives of the company.

4.5 The top down approach to budgeting

The top down approach is where budgets are set by higher levels of management and then communicated to the lower levels of management to whose areas of responsibility they relate. This is also known as an imposed budget.

In this approach lower-level managers are not allowed to participate in the budget-setting process.

The main problem with this approach is that those responsible for operating the budget will see it as something in which they have had no say. They lack ownership of the budget and as such they will be reluctant to take responsibility for it. It is unlikely to motivate the employees to achieve the budgetary targets set for them.

However, it can be argued that this top down approach may be the only approach to budgeting which is feasible if:

- lower level employees have no interest in participating in the process
- they are not technically capable of participating in budget setting
- only top level management have access to information which is necessary for budgeting purposes – perhaps information which is commercially sensitive.

4.6 The bottom up approach to budgeting

The bottom approach to budgeting is where lower level managers are involved in setting budget targets. This is known as a participative budget.

The more that individual managers are involved in setting budget targets, the more likely it is that they will accept those targets and strive actively towards the attainment of them. Employees are more likely to internalise the budget – accept it as part of themselves.

In this way actual performances should be improved by the motivational impact of budgets.

The main problem is:

- If budgets are used both in a motivational role and for the evaluation of managerial performance, then the problem of budgetary bias may arise.

Budgetary bias is where a manager deliberately sets a lower revenue target or a higher cost target.

By lowering the standard in the budget the target will be easier to achieve and performance will appear to be better. There is evidence to show that this tends to occur where a manager is actively seeking progression within an organisation or where financial rewards are based on ability to beat the budget. The effects of this sort of bias can be minimised by careful control, at the budget setting stage, and over any changes in the budget from one year to the next which are not due to external factors.

- Some people in organisations, by the very nature of their personality, do not wish to participate in the wider aspects of their jobs. They prefer an authoritarian style of leadership and do not strive for independence. Participative approaches to budget-setting will be very limited in their effect in such circumstances.
- Participation will be less effective in organisational situations where a manager or employee feels that he has little scope to influence the actual results for the budgeted area of responsibility. The lower down in the organisation structure the budget holder is, the more constrained is he by factors imposed from above. For example, objectives, strategies and policies, as well as the sales forecast and budget, limit the extent that a subordinate manager in the production function has for real participation in the setting of the budget for his area of responsibility.
- An important point to recognise is the difference between actual and perceived participation. It is the extent to which an individual manager perceives that he has influenced the budget that is crucial in that manager's acceptance of it.

An extension of this bottom up approach is the concept of budget challenging – employees are given the chance to question a budget presented to them (in a positive way!) before it is finalised.

4.7 Goal congruence

The principle of goal congruence involves ensuring that all members of the organisation pull in the same direction towards helping the organisation to achieve its overall goals and objectives.

If individuals in an organisation fail to demonstrate congruent behaviour, decisions taken may benefit that individual personally or the division which that individual works for, but may not benefit the organisation as a whole – this is known as dysfunctional behaviour.

An appropriate choice of performance evaluation methods is important in this context. The way the budgetary control system is operated can also be significant.

There may be a general fear and misunderstanding about the purpose of budgetary control. It is often regarded as a penny-pinching exercise by top management rather than recognised as a tool of management at all levels in an organisation structure. If this tends to be the attitude, a carefully planned campaign of education and training should be undertaken. Managers should be encouraged to discover how the budgetary control system can be of benefit to them personally as well as how it may benefit the organisation.

Employees may become united against management and devote their energies to finding excuses for not meeting targets. Targets that are realistic, and are seen by the employees as being realistic, are what is required. Good communications involving consultation and participation should help to minimise this problem.

One of the key roles in any organisation is at the supervisor level where the continual interface between management and employees exists. The leadership and motivational function of a supervisor is very important if the work is to be done and targets are to be achieved.

Conclusion

The main point to appreciate is that a budgetary control system should have the effect of motivating employees to work in the best interests of the organisation as a whole – the concept of goal congruence.

Participation (the 'bottom-up' approach) and education play important roles in encouraging a positive approach to budgeting in the mind of employees.

5 Sources of information

5.1 Budgetary information

When producing a budget in accordance with guidelines drawn up by the senior management of an organisation, the usual starting point is the previous year's actual results. In some cases the budgeting process merely takes the form of adding to last year's income statement a general allowance for changes in volume and prices. This 'incremental' approach to budgeting is not regarded as an effective means of providing useful information for planning and control. Any inefficiency that has occurred in the previous year will be perpetuated in future years. Nevertheless, the previous years' income statement provides useful information.

In addition to previous year information, figures in budgets can come from three other sources.

Other internal sources

Information about the state of repair of non-current assets, training needs of staff, long-term requirements of individual large customers, etc. can be obtained by talking to individual junior managers. Likely costs of new products or services can be estimated using work study techniques or the services of the research and development team, quantity surveyors or the sales team.

Statistical techniques

Figures such as sales forecasts or estimates of the fixed and variable elements of semi-variable costs can be produced with the aid of techniques such as linear regression. Other techniques can help determine optimal inventory levels and optimal ways of organising large construction projects.

External sources

The obvious external source of budgetary information will be suppliers' price lists both for materials and for services. It is important for a firm to try to establish how long those prices are likely to last and the size of any expected price rises. In addition, external market rates of pay should be established to determine a sensible level of wage rises.

The production of an annual budget is not a precise science. Figures are always subject to uncertainty. It is said that a budget is more than just a forecast of future costs and revenues that may be incurred or received, it is a statement of what management feels should be paid or received. Nevertheless, firms operate in an uncertain economic climate.

5.2 Internal sources

Internal information may come from various sources, this section considers some of the commonly used sources.

5.3 Accounting system

The accounting system will collect data from source documents such as invoices, timesheets and journal entries. The data will be sorted and analysed by the coding system by type of expense, department, manager and job. Reports of direct and indirect costs compared to budgets may be produced at regular intervals to help managers plan and control costs. Ad hoc reports may be produced to help managers make specific decisions.

Consider the examples listed below – you can probably think of many others from your own experience.

- Sales analysed by product will help management to assess the patterns of demand for each product.
- This same information will help plan production and inventory levels.
- In turn, production information will enable the organisation to plan its requirements for raw materials, labour and machine hours.
- Information on material, labour and other costs will allow the organisation to set estimated costs for its products. This will be the basis for a budgetary control and standard costing system, as we shall see in a later chapter.
- In the context of long-term, strategic decision making, the sales analysis given above may help management to assess future product strategies – expand output of those for which demand is increasing, reduce output of those for which demand is falling.
- An aged receivables report would provide the basis for debt collection decisions taken by a credit control manager.
- Figures for wastage rates or product reject rates may allow management to reach decisions on the product quality aspect of the organisation's operations.

5.4 Payroll system

The payroll system may provide information concerning detailed labour costs. Hours paid may be analysed into productive work and non-productive time such as training, sick, holiday and idle time. Labour turnover by department or manager may be analysed and may help management to assess the employment and motivation policies.

5.5 Strategic planning system

The strategic planning system may provide information relating to the organisation's objectives and targets. Assumptions relating to the external environment may be detailed. Details of the organisation's capital investment programme and product launch programme may also be recorded here. Some of this information will be very commercially sensitive and only accessed by very senior managers in the organisation.

A Customer Relationship Management System (CRMS) will provide information on customers, and its objective is to increase customer loyalty (in order to increase profitability).

5.6 External sources

Businesses will find it increasingly difficult to succeed if they ignore the external environment which will influence their activities. The process known as environmental scanning or environmental monitoring is becoming a more important part of the role of the management accountant. These terms are used to describe the process whereby data is collected from outside, as well as from inside, of the organisation and used in the decision-making process.

The main sources of external information which we shall consider here are:

- government sources
- business contacts – customers and suppliers
- trade associations and trade journals
- the financial and business press and other media.

These are dealt with in more detail below. A word of warning first, however. Internal information is produced by the company itself and so managers are aware of any limitations in its quality or reliability. External information is not under the control of the organisation – staff may not be aware of any limitations in its quality – this point should always be considered. Even government-produced statistics have been known to contain inaccuracies!

5.7 Government sources

There is a wealth of published statistical data covering many aspects of the nation's economy: population, manpower, trade, agriculture, price levels, capital issues and similar matters. Most, but not all of this is produced by national governments.

The primary purpose of this data is to provide information for economic planning at the national level. The data serves the secondary purpose of providing industry with useful background information for deciding on future policies such as raising new finance or recruiting specialised labour. The data is only published in general terms (e.g. for a particular industry or geographical area).

The following list shows some (there are many others) of the main sources of this type of information in the UK. Other countries will usually have similar information available. Copies are generally available in reference libraries and on government websites – have a look to see the type of data published.

Title	Frequency of publication	Main topics covered
Employment Gazette	Monthly	Earnings, basic wage rates, unemployment, indices of wholesale and retail prices.
British Business	Weekly	Wholesale and retail prices, production for specific sectors of industry, capital expenditure.
National Income and Expenditure Blue Book	Annually	Personal income and expenditure, gross national product.
Financial Statistics	Monthly	Money supply, interest rates, hire purchase liabilities, building societies.
Bank of England Quarterly Bulletin	Quarterly	Both summarise many of the above statistics.
Monthly Digest of Statistics	Monthly	
Economic Trends	Monthly	Similar coverage to Monthly Digest, but given information stretching back over a long period.
Annual Abstract of Statistics	Annually	
Price Indices for Current Cost Accounting	Annually, but updated by monthly supplement	Retail price index, also industry specific and asset specific price indices.

All the above publications relate to the UK. Publications concerned with statistics relating to the European Union include 'European Economy Annual Statistical Yearbook', 'Eurostat' (monthly) and 'OECD Main Economic Indicators' (monthly). Information on the World Economy is available from the United Nations ('Demographic Yearbook' and 'Statistical Yearbook'), the International Labour Organisation ('Yearbook of Labour Statistics') and UNESCO ('Statistical Yearbook').

5.8 Business contacts

Government produced information will be broadly based and general, dealing with the economy as a whole or particular sectors or industries. An organisation may be looking for information more focused on its own position. Its day-to-day business contacts, customers and suppliers, can be a useful source of this information – and often it is available free.

Customers can provide information on such matters as:

- the product specification which they require
- their quality requirements
- requirements for delivery periods
- their preference for packaging and distribution methods
- feedback on the above and on general aspects of customer service.

Suppliers may be able to provide information on:

- quantity discounts and volume rebates which may help the organisation to decide on order size
- availability of products and services
- alternative products or services which may be available or may become available
- technical specifications of their product.

5.9 Trade associations and trade journals

Most major industries have their own trade association. The role of these organisations includes:

- representing their member firms in legal and other disputes
- providing quality assurance schemes for customers of member organisations
- laying down codes of practice to be followed by their member organisations
- publishing trade journals and other information useful for the management and development of their businesses.

There are hundreds more of trade associations operating in the UK. For example: The International Air Transport Association.

These types of organisations often publish their own industry or trade journals which will contain useful news and other information for organisations operating in that industry. Trade journals are also published by many publishing organisations. In the UK one of the best known of these journals is 'The Grocer' aimed at the food and drink retail sector. Again, many others exist.

5.10 The financial press, business press and other media

In the UK, 'The Financial Times', the 'Guardian', 'The Times' and the 'Daily Telegraph', together with some regional newspapers, provide statistics and financial reviews as well as business and economic news and commentary. These include:

- the FTSE 100 Index, the stock market index of the 100 leading shares
- the FT Actuaries All-share Index – an index of all share prices quoted on the stock exchange.

Such information is now also widely available via electronic media. Digital television services available on satellite or cable systems carry specialist business and financial channels and programmes (such as Bloomberg TV) which give both national and world-wide coverage. There is also the internet as a widely available source of up-to-date financial information.

Test your understanding 4

Match the data in the first column with the appropriate source in the second column (only 1 source possible):

Data	**Source**
Currency exchange rates	A website for a leading business news and information organisation (e.g. The Financial Times' website)
TV licence fee cost	Office for National Statistics
Cost of electricity generated by wind power	BBC Website
Inflation trends in the UK	HMRC publications
	Gross National Product
	The Environment Agency

Test your understanding 5

Who would you contact in each of the following situations?

- You want to identify the production capacity of the firm.
- You want to forecast the price of raw materials.
- The draft budget has been reviewed by the Budget Committee and is ready to be submitted for final approval.

Choose from:

- Trade union representative
- Managing Director
- Buyer
- Board of Directors
- Production Planning Manager.

6 Basic methods of budgeting

There are a few basic methods of budgeting we need to know for the assessment.

6.1 Incremental budgeting

An incremental budget starts with the previous period's budget or actual results and adds (or subtracts) an incremental amount to cover inflation and other known changes.

It is suitable for stable businesses, where costs are not expected to change significantly. There should be good cost control and limited discretionary costs.

Advantages of incremental budgeting	Disadvantages of incremental budgeting
(1) Quickest and easiest method.	(1) Builds in previous problems and inefficiencies.
(2) Suitable if the organisation is stable and historic figures are acceptable since only the increment needs to be justified.	(2) Uneconomic activities may be continued. For example, the company may continue to make a component in house, when it may be cheaper to outsource.
	(3) Managers may spend unnecessarily to use up their budgeted expenditure allowance this year, thus ensuring they get the same, or a larger, budget next year.

6.2 Zero-based budgeting (ZBB)

A method of budgeting that requires each cost element to be specifically justified, as though the activities to which the budget relates were being undertaken for the first time. Without approval, the budget allowance is zero.

It is suitable for allocating resources in areas were spend is discretionary, i.e. non-essential. For example, research and development, advertising and training. ZBB is often practised in public sector organisations such as local authorities.

There are four distinct stages in the implementation of ZBB:

(1) Managers should specify, for their responsibility centres, those activities that can be individually evaluated.

(2) Each of the individual activities is then described in a decision package. The decision package should state the costs and revenues expected from the given activity. It should be drawn up in such a way that the package can be evaluated and ranked against other packages.

(3) Each decision package is evaluated and ranked, usually using cost/benefit analysis.

(4) The resources are then allocated to the various packages.

Advantages of ZBB

(1) Inefficient or obsolete operations can be identified and discontinued.

(2) ZBB leads to increased staff involvement at all levels since a lot more information and work is required to complete the budget.

(3) It responds to changes in the business environment.

(4) Knowledge and understanding of the cost behaviour patterns of the organisation will be enhanced.

(5) Resources should be allocated efficiently and economically.

Disadvantages of ZBB

(1) It emphasises short-term benefits to the detriment of long-term goals.

(2) The budgeting process may become too rigid and the organisation may not be able to react to unforeseen opportunities or threats.

(3) The management skills required may not be present.

(4) Managers may feel demotivated due to the large amount of time spent on the budgeting process.

(5) Ranking can be difficult for different types of activities or where the benefits are qualitative in nature.

Decision packages

A decision package was defined by Peter Pyhrr (who first formulated the ZBB approach at Texas Instruments) as:

A document that identifies and describes a specific activity in such a manner that senior management can:

(a) evaluate and rank it against other activities competing for limited resources, and

(b) decide whether to approve or disapprove it.

A decision package is a document that: analyses the cost of the activity (costs may be built up from a zero base, but costing information can be obtained from historical records or last year's budget); states the purpose of the activity; identifies alternative methods of achieving the same purpose; assesses the consequence of not doing the activity at all, or performing the activity at a different level; and finally, establishes measures of performance for the activity.

Pyhrr identifies two types of package.

(i) **Mutually exclusive packages**: these contain different methods of obtaining the same objective.

(ii) **Incremental packages**: these divide the activity into a number of different levels of activity. The base package describes the minimum effort and cost needed to carry out the activity. The other packages describe the incremental costs and benefits when added to the base.

For example, suppose a company is conducting a ZBB exercise, and a decision package is being prepared for its materials handling operations.

The manager responsible has identified a base package for the minimum resources needed to perform the materials handling function. This is to have a team of five workers and a supervisor, operating without any labour-saving machinery. The estimated annual cost of wages and salaries, with overtime, would be £375,000.

In addition to the base package, the manager has identified an incremental package. The company could lease two fork lift trucks at a cost of £20,000 each year. This would provide a better system because materials could be stacked higher and moved more quickly. Health and safety risks for the workers would be reduced, and there would be savings of £5,000 each year in overtime payments.

Another incremental package has been prepared, in which the company introduces new computer software to plan materials handling schedules. The cost of buying and implementing the system would be £60,000, but the benefits are expected to be improvements in efficiency that reduce production downtime and result in savings of £10,000 each year in overtime payments.

The base package would be considered essential, and so given a high priority. The two incremental packages should be evaluated and ranked. Here, the fork lift trucks option might be ranked more highly than the computer software.

In the budget that is eventually decided by senior management, the fork lift truck package might be approved, but the computer software package rejected on the grounds that there are other demands for resources with a higher priority.

6.3 Priority-based budgeting

Priority-based budgeting is designed to produce a competitively ranked listing of high to low priority discrete bids for resources which are called "decision packages".

- It is a method of budgeting whereby all activities are re-evaluated each time a budget is set.
- Discrete levels of each activity are valued from a minimum level of service upwards and an optimum combination chosen to match the level of resources available and the level of service required.
- The concept of ranking bids for capital expenditure is well known; priority-based budgeting applies a similar process to more routine expenditure.

It is similar to zero-based budgeting but does not require a zero assumption, as a result it also has similar advantages and disadvantages, although, without the zero assumption it should be slightly less time consuming.

6.4 Activity-based budgeting

ABB is defined as: 'a method of budgeting based on an activity framework and utilising cost driver data in the budget-setting and variance feedback processes'.

Or, put more simply, preparing budgets using overhead costs from activity based costing methodology.

Advantages of ABB

(1) It draws attention to the costs of 'overhead activities' which can be a large proportion of total operating costs.

(2) It recognises that it is activities which drive costs. If we can control the causes (drivers) of costs, then costs should be better managed and understood.

Disadvantages of ABB

(1) A considerable amount of time and effort might be needed to establish the key activities and their cost drivers.

(2) It may be difficult to identify clear individual responsibilities for activities.

(3) ABB can provide useful information in a total quality management (TQM) environment, by relating the cost of an activity to the level of service provided.

(3) It could be argued that in the short-term many overhead costs are not controllable and do not vary directly with changes in the volume of activity for the cost driver. The only cost variances to report would be fixed overhead expenditure variances for each activity.

6.5 Rolling budgets

A budget (usually annual) kept continuously up to date by adding another accounting period (e.g. month or quarter) when the earliest accounting period has expired. The remaining budget is re-forecast, as well as the new period being added.

Rolling budgets are suitable if accurate forecasts cannot be made (for example, in a fast moving environment), or for any area of business that needs tight control, for example a cash budget.

Example 1

A typical rolling budget might be prepared as follows:

(1) A budget is prepared for the coming year (say January – December), broken down into suitable, say quarterly, control periods.

(2) At the end of the first control period (31 March) a comparison is made of that period's results against the budget. The conclusions drawn from this analysis are used to update the budgets for the remaining control periods and to add a budget for a further three months, so that the company once again has budgets available for the coming year (this time April – March).

(3) The planning process is repeated at the end of each three-month control period.

Advantages of rolling budgets

(1) Planning and control will be based on a more accurate budget.

(2) Rolling budgets reduce the element of uncertainty in budgeting since they concentrate on the short-term when the degree of uncertainty is much smaller.

(3) There is always a budget that extends into the future (normally 12 months).

(4) It forces management to reassess the budget regularly and to produce budgets which are more up to date.

Disadvantages of rolling budgets

(1) Rolling budgets are more costly and time consuming than incremental budgets.

(2) May demotivate employees if they feel that they spend a large proportion of their time budgeting or if they feel that the budgetary targets are constantly changing.

(3) There is a danger that the budget may become the last budget 'plus or minus a bit'.

(4) An increase in budgeting work may lead to less control of the actual results.

(5) Issues with version control, as each month the full year numbers will change.

(6) Confusion in meetings as to which numbers the business is working towards; this can distract from the key issues as managers discuss which numbers to achieve.

6.6 Contingency budgets

The definition of a contingency is 'a future event or circumstance which is possible but cannot be predicted with certainty'. Generally, we see contingency planning as considering things that could go wrong.

This means that a contingency budget is where an organisation plans to set money aside, which can then be used to cover unexpected costs during the period. The money in a contingency budget is not allocated to one specific area of a project or the organisation, it is essentially a form of internal insurance against additional and unexpected costs.

Advantages of contingency budgets	Disadvantages of contingency budgets
(1) Better risk assessment by considering uncertainties like price fluctuations.	(1) Managers may use the contingencies to ensure they hit their targets/performance goals.
(2) Helps an organisation keep its operations running smoothly in the face of unexpected changes in the business environment.	(2) Managers may unintentionally or deliberately underestimate sales or overestimate costs.
(3) Forces managers to look ahead.	(3) If a business has a shortage of resources, the contingencies may reduce the availability cash, labour or materials for other parts of the business.
(4) Could help avoid high finance charges associated short-term borrowing, such as overdrafts.	

7 Summary

Budgeting is a fundamental part of management accounting. This chapter considers some of the aspects that underpin the budgeting process, and some of the general aspects of the budgeting process itself. This knowledge will be developed in further chapters as we look at the different types of budget, how it can be compiled and how we can use it for control.

This chapter also considers internal and external information which affects forecasts.

Forecasts of future events are normally based on historical information. Information may be available from a wide variety of sources both internal and external to the business.

We have also considered some of the different methods of budgeting and the advantages and disadvantages they provide.

Test your understanding answers

Test your understanding 1

Gap 1 the correct answer is A – planning.

Gap 2 the correct answer is H – controlling.

Gap 3 the correct answer is K – long term objectives

Gap 4 the correct answer is N – budget committee

Meaning the statement should read as follows:

Planning and **controlling** are two of the primary reasons why an organisation prepares a budget. Before the budgeting process can start the **long term objectives** of the organisation should be defined, then the **budget committee** formed.

Test your understanding 2

Gap 1 the correct answer is A – participation

Gap 2 the correct answer is H – own

Gap 3 the correct answer is K – operational managers

Gap 4 the correct answer is N – easier

Meaning the statement should read as follows:

One of the advantages of **participation** in budgeting is that managers feel like they **own** the budget and are more likely to work hard to achieve the targets. A disadvantage is that **operational managers** may manipulate the budget so that the targets are **easier** to achieve.

Test your understanding 3

World History Museum

MEMORANDUM

To: Chris Brooks

From: Accounting technician

Date: 13 June 20X4

Subject: Participative budgeting

As requested, I enclose brief explanations of the advantages and disadvantages of participative budgeting.

Advantages

(i) Managers are likely to be demotivated if budgets are imposed on them without any prior consultation. If they are consulted, they are more likely to accept the budgets as realistic targets.

(ii) If managers are consulted, then the budgets are more likely to take account of their own aspiration levels. Aspiration levels are personal targets which individuals or departments set for themselves. If budget targets exceed aspiration levels, then the budgets can have a negative motivational impact because they will be perceived as unachievable. However, if the targets fall too far below aspiration levels, then the performance of the individuals or departments may be lower than might otherwise have been achieved.

(iii) Managers who are consulted may be motivated by the feeling that their views are valuable to senior management.

(iv) Managers who are closely involved with the day to day running of operations may be able to give very valuable input to the forecasting and planning process.

Disadvantages

(i) If too many people are involved in budgetary planning, it can make the process very slow and difficult to manage.

(ii) Senior managers may need to overrule decisions made by local managers. This can be demotivating if it is not dealt with correctly.

(iii) The participative process may not be genuine. Managers must feel that their participation is really valued by senior management. A false attempt to appear to be interested in their views can be even more demotivating than a system of imposed budgets.

(iv) Managers may attempt to include excess expenditure in their budgets, due to 'empire-building' or to a desire to guard against unforeseen circumstances.

Signed: Accounting technician

Test your understanding 4

Data	**Source**
Currency exchange rates	A website for a leading business news and information organisation (e.g. The Financial Times' website)
TV Licence fee	BBC website
Cost of electricity (wind power)	The Environment agency
Inflation trend in the UK	Office for National Statistics

Test your understanding 5

Who would you contact in each of the following situations?

- You want to identify the production capacity of the firm
- You want to forecast the price of raw materials
- The draft budget is ready for final approval

- Production Planning Manager
- Buyer
- Board of Directors

Budgeting processes

8

Introduction

Having considered the ways in which cost, revenue and other business data may be collected, processed and analysed, we now turn to the task of putting this information to use in the future planning of the business.

The planning process starts with the identification of long term corporate objectives, based upon which a strategy is designed, resource utilisation and capital expenditure planned and ultimately short-term, quantified budgets are prepared. This chapter looks at this overall process.

In AMAC assessments you may be required to prepare budgets. You should also be prepared to discuss the budget preparation process and to suggest improvements to budget presentation.

For cash budgets, the closing cash balance may be taken as the balancing figure on the Statement of Financial Position, but at some stage this should be validated by building up a cash budget, itemised from the other budgets.

Again in the assessments you may be required to prepare a cash forecast. You will need to prepare cash flow forecasts from budget data to facilitate the achievement of organisational objectives, making due allowance for time lags or assumptions about changes in receivable, payable and inventory balances.

You could also be asked to analyse a cash flow forecast into shorter control periods, allowing for time lags.

ASSESSMENT CRITERIA

- Budgetary responsibilities and accountabilities (LO 1.2)
- Types of budgets and recommendations for their use (LO 1.3)
- Budget revision to reflect changing circumstances (LO 1.7)

CONTENTS

1 Functional budgets

1.1 Budgets to be produced

The budgets that a business produces will generally be a standard set of budgets that starts with the sales budget and progresses through budgets for the costs associated with those sales.

You will typically be asked to produce the following budgets for a manufacturing business. Note that generally you will produce the budgets for the number of units bought and sold before translating those into revenues and costs.

(a) The sales budget.

(b) The production budget of finished goods. This will follow on from the sales budget. It will be for the same number of units as the sales budget unless there are changes in the inventories held of finished goods.

(c) The raw materials purchases budget. This will follow on from the production budget. **A business needs a production budget as a quantitative expression of its operational plan.**

The raw materials purchased will, in general terms, be the number of finished goods produced × the raw material per unit (after adjustments for changes in inventories of materials and process losses).

(d) The labour budget, and

(e) The overheads budget.

1.2 Sales, production, materials, labour and overheads budgets

Preparing resource budgets for materials, labour and machine time in line with the projected operations of a business is a very important skill. You could be tested on this in the Applied Management Accounting assessment.

The most important aspect is to be sure of how to use the information given to you. In this chapter, we will learn to prepare those budgets.

We shall first of all look at a simple budget example.

Example 1

Toys Ltd budgets to sell 10,000 play cubes at £10 per cube in the month of July 20X8.

Inventory of finished cubes was 3,000 cubes at the start of the month and was budgeted to be 4,000 cubes at the end of the month.

Each cube requires 0.5 kg of material that costs £1 per kg. Opening inventory of material was 1,000 kg at the start of the month and is budgeted to be 750 kg at the end of the month.

Each cube requires 0.25 hours of direct labour. The labour rate is £12 per hour.

Production overheads are absorbed into production at the rate of £15 per hour.

Task

Produce the budgets for sales, production, materials, labour and overheads.

Solution

Step 1 – the sales budget

Number of cubes budgeted to be sold = 10,000 cubes

Budgeted sales revenue 10,000 × £10 = £100,000

Step 2 – the production budget

The standard layout for this is as follows – always work in units (cubes) first.

	Cubes
Sales budget	10,000
Closing inventory	4,000
	14,000
Less: opening inventory	(3,000)
Production of finished goods	11,000

Tutorial note. There are no costs associated with the finished goods because the company manufactures them. The cost of the goods will be found when we deal with the budgets and costs of raw materials, labour and overheads. However we have to prepare the production budget in order to be able to prepare the raw materials budget.

Step 3 – the raw materials budget

The standard layout for this is as follows – always work in units (kg) first. In this case remember that 1 cube requires 0.5 kg of raw material.

	Kg
For production budget 11,000 × 0.5 kg	5,500
Closing inventory	750
	6,250
Less: opening inventory	(1,000)
Purchases of raw material	5,250 kg

Budgeted purchases of raw materials = 5,250 kg × £1 = £5,250

Step 4 – the labour budget

To calculate the cost of labour we have to return to the production budget because the cost of labour is determined by the level of production.

Number of labour hours budgeted for month =
11,000 cubes × 0.25 hours = 2,750 hrs

Cost of direct labour = 2,750 hrs × £12 = £33,000

Step 5 – the overhead budget

To calculate the cost of overheads we have to return to the labour budget because the cost of the overhead is based on the number of hours worked.

Number of labour hours budgeted for month = 2,750 hrs

Cost of overhead = 2,750 hrs × £15 = £41,250

1.3 Calculating the sales budget and inventories of finished goods

Exam questions will frequently present information regarding sales and inventories as follows.

Example 2

XYZ has 13 accounting periods of four weeks during the year. It had sales of £40,000 in accounting period 5 and budgets for sales to increase by 3% for each accounting period.

The company budgets to have closing inventory at the end of an accounting period equal to two weeks sales of the following period.

Produce the budget for sales and inventories for accounting periods 6, 7 and 8.

Solution

		Period 6	Period 7	Period 8	Period 9
		£	£	£	£
Sales	40,000.00 × 1.03	41,200.00			
	41,200.00 × 1.03		42,436.00		
	42,436.00 × 1.03			43,709.08	
	43,709.08 × 1.03				45,020.35
Opening inventory		20,600.00 (W1)	21,218.00	21,854.50	
Closing inventory		21,218.00 (W2)	21,854.50 (W3)	22,510.00 (W4)	

Workings

1. £41,200 × 0.5 (i.e. two weeks sales of a 4 week period) = £20,600
2. £42,436 × 0.5 = £21,218.00
3. £43,709 × 0.5 = £21,854.50
4. £45,020 × 0.5 = £22,510.00

The example below illustrates the preparation of the functional budgets, starting with projected sales information.

Example 3

Hash Ltd makes two products – PS and TG. Sales for next year are budgeted at 5,000 units of PS and 1,000 units of TG. Planned selling prices are £100 and £140 respectively.

Hash Ltd has the following opening inventory and required closing inventory.

	PS units	**TG units**
Opening inventory	100	50
Projected closing inventory	1,100	50

You are also given the following data about the materials required to produce PS and TG and the machining and finishing processes involved in production.

	PS	**TG**
Finished products:		
Kg of raw material X, per unit of finished product	12	12
Kg of raw material Y, per unit of finished product	6	8
Direct labour hours per unit of finished product	8	12

Standard rates and prices:

Direct labour	£6.00 per hour
Raw material X	£0.72 per kg
Raw material Y	£1.56 per kg

Production overheads:

Variable	£1.54 per labour hour
Fixed	£0.54 per labour hour
	£2.08 per labour hour

You are required to prepare the functional budgets. Hash Ltd does not carry inventories of raw material.

Solution

(a) **The sales budget**

The sales budget represents the plan in terms of the quantity and value of sales, for sales management. In practice this is often the most difficult budget to calculate.

What is next year's sales budget?

The sales budget would be:

	Total	PS	TG
Sales units	6,000	5,000	1,000
Sales value	£640,000	£500,000	£140,000

In practice a business would market many more than two products. Moreover, the sales budget would probably be supported by subsidiary budgets to show analysis according to:

(i) responsibility e.g. Northern area, Western area, etc.

(ii) type of customer e.g. wholesale, retail, government, etc.

(b) **The production budget**

The production budget is usually expressed in quantity and represents the sales budget adjusted for opening/closing finished inventories and work in progress.

The production budget would be:

	PS units	TG units
Sales budget	5,000	1,000
Add projected closing inventory	1,100	50
	6,100	1,050
Less opening inventory	100	50
Production in units	6,000	1,000

The production budget needs to be translated into requirements for:

(i) raw materials

(ii) direct labour

(iii) factory overheads

(iv) closing inventory levels.

(c) **The raw materials and purchases budget**

(Remember that Hash Ltd is going to produce 6,000 units of PS and 1,000 units of TG.)

		PS		**TG**
		kg		**kg**
Raw material usage				
X	6,000 × 12 kg	72,000	1,000 × 12 kg	12,000
Y	6,000 × 6 kg	36,000	1,000 × 8 kg	8,000

		PS		**TG**
		£		£
Budgeted purchases:				
X	72,000 × £0.72	51,840	12,000 × £0.72	8,640
Y	36,000 × £1.56	56,160	8,000 × £1.56	12,480
		108,000		21,120

(d) **The direct labour budget**

		PS		**TG**
Usage	6,000 × 8 hrs	48,000 hrs	1,000 × 12 hrs	12,000 hrs
Cost	48,000 × £6	£288,000	12,000 × £6	£72,000

(e) **Production overheads**

		PS		**TG**
Variable costs	48,000 hours × £1.54	73,920	12,000 × £1.54	18,480
Fixed costs	48,000 hours × £0.54	25,920	12,000 × £0.54	6,480
		99,840		24,960

One of the most important points illustrated by this example is how the budgets are inter-related.

It is a simple example and you should be aware that in practice budgeting can be more than simply an arithmetical exercise. The practical problems are discussed later.

Test your understanding 1

PQR Ltd has a sales budget of 30,000, 31,000 and 32,000 for a particular product XYZ over the next three months. The inventory at the start of the first month is 3,600 units. The closing inventory at the end of each month should be 12% of the following months forecast sales volumes.

Required:

The production volume for month 1 will be ________.

The production volume for month 2 will be ________.

2 Practical aspects of functional budgets

2.1 Sales budgets

The sales income budget is uniquely difficult to prepare because it involves forecasting the actions of people outside the business (the potential customers).

The extent to which sales forecasting is necessary will depend on the period covered by the outstanding order book and on the consistency of the conversion rate from enquiries to orders. If there is a well-filled order book for some months ahead then less reliance will need to be placed on forecasting techniques.

Forecasts may be made in a variety of ways. The method used will depend on the nature of the business and the amount of information available, but a generalised formal procedure might be as follows:

- Review past years' sales for whatever period is appropriate to the company's business cycle.
- Analyse the time series to identify seasonal, cyclical and random fluctuations.
- Extrapolate from past years' figures, assuming no changes in products or prices. Adjust the extrapolation for proposed changes which are controllable by the company, such as price alterations, changes in marketing effort, the introduction of new products and the discontinuance of existing products (depending on the products' life cycles).

- Adjust for market changes due to external factors, such as government controls, action of competitors or social changes affecting demand. In particular, appropriate adjustments should be made for changing price levels or seasonal trends.
- Check that the resultant quantities are compatible with the quantities that can be purchased or produced.
- Check acceptability of forecast to sectional sales managers. In addition, other personnel who might contribute towards making realistic forecasts of trends should be consulted.
- Check consistency of forecast with long-term corporate plans.

The forecasting method outlined above depends on the existence of a 'time series' of figures from which extrapolation can be made and is mainly applicable to items in continuous demand. For other types of business, the sales forecast will be based on some form of market survey or on subjective estimates by people familiar with the market concerned.

Whichever forecasting method is used, the forecast should take account of significant anticipated changes in circumstances which would affect the validity of any statistically derived calculations.

2.2 Cost budgets

Budgeting for costs, in the same way as budgeting for sales, begins with facts. What facts they are will depend on the nature of the business; but every business will employ people, and most businesses will use materials of some kind. A manufacturing business will use tools and probably machinery. Floor space will be needed, also office equipment and perhaps motor vehicles.

All of these requirements will be related in some way to the output of the business – its sales and any changes in inventory or work in progress.

In practice there are a wide range of different ways to budget for costs, as follows:

- If standards for cost units are available, then there may be computer programs to identify the material and labour standards relative to a given output. It then remains for departmental managers to budget for material wastage or spoilage, labour efficiency and idle time.
- In a business carrying out long-term contracts, cost units (contracts) may be identical with cost centres (each contract having its own controller).
- In some businesses it may be sufficiently accurate for the budget for direct materials cost to be an extrapolation from past total figures, without any attempt at detailed justification or analysis.

2.3 Use of standards in budgeting

Budgeting will inevitably make use of standard costs, as in the worked example above, and you should ensure you are familiar with the techniques and principles involved in their determination.

However, budgeting will generally extend beyond the simple multiplication of planned production levels by the standard usages and costs for each product for the following reasons:

- Different ranges of output levels will often lead to changes in unit variable costs (e.g. materials discounts, learning effects, etc).
- Some variable costs will not vary neatly with production and will need to be estimated for each particular activity level (e.g. wastage, idle time, production set-up costs).
- Fixed costs are independent of production levels, although they may be stepped.
- A large proportion of a business's costs will not be directly involved in the production process (e.g. administration, marketing, capital expenditure, etc).

The following sections describe the common problems encountered in budgeting for the most common cost elements: labour, materials and over-heads.

2.4 Budgeting for numbers and costs of employees

When budgeting for the number and costs of people to be employed, the starting point must be to assess the work to be done by people with various skills and this is equally necessary for manual, clerical and managerial activities.

Having defined what work is to be done, the establishment of budgets for the employment of people falls into two main stages:

- planning the number of people needed
- calculating the relevant costs.

In defining the productive workload for the budget year it will be necessary to balance the requirements of the sales budget against the productive capacity available. If there is excess capacity over the year as a whole then a decision will be needed on whether to operate below full capacity or to use the excess capacity in making goods for inventory or getting ahead with work in progress for the following year.

If the sales budget does not provide a steady workload month by month, then in phasing the budgets it may be decided to keep productive output constant and to balance out the short-term differences by fluctuations in work in progress or finished inventory.

The degree of precision possible in budgeting for numbers of people employed will depend on the type of work involved and the extent to which work measurement is possible.

2.5 Budgeting for the cost of materials

Considerable effort can be involved in preparing detailed budgets of quantities and purchase prices of materials. Whether this effort is justified will depend on the significance of materials in relation to total costs, and the extent to which effective control can be exercised.

The starting point for materials budgeting is the quantity of material to be used during the budget year, whether in retail sales or in production or for indirect use.

The form of the materials usage budget will depend on the nature of the business. Where repetitive operations are carried out it will be possible, and worth the effort, to set standards for the usage of the various items of material, and these standards can be associated with the production forecast to build up the total material requirements.

The purchase prices to be applied to the usage of the various items may be obtained from inventory ledger records or recent purchase invoices, subject to adjustment for forecast price changes, using index numbers as necessary.

In budgeting for indirect materials (such as small tools, machine coolants and lubricants, fuel, cleaning materials and office stationery) the common practice is to budget merely for a total cost extrapolated from past experience. It will be important for control purposes, however, that the budget working papers contain as much detail as possible about anticipated usage, even though the individual items may not be evaluated separately.

2.6 Budgeting for overheads

The nature of overheads will depend on the type of business, but common categories are as follows:

(a) Premises charges

(b) Costs of plant, motor vehicles and other non-current assets

(c) Communication expenses

(d) Travelling and entertaining

(e) Insurances

(f) Discretionary costs

(g) Financial policy costs

(h) Random costs.

2.7 Calculating budget and actual overheads

In earlier studies we saw how budgeted overhead absorption rates (OARs) were calculated. You may be required to use overhead absorption rates to deduce budgeted and actual activity levels.

2.8 Budgeted activity level

If we know the overhead absorption rate and the budgeted fixed overhead then the budgeted activity level can be found.

$$\text{OAR} = \frac{\text{Budgeted fixed overhead}}{\text{Budgeted activity level}}$$

Therefore:

$$\text{Budgeted activity level} = \frac{\text{Budgeted fixed overhead}}{\text{OAR}}$$

Example 4

A business has an overhead absorption rate of £2 per unit produced. The budgeted fixed overhead was £400,000. What was the budgeted activity level?

Solution

$$\text{Budgeted activity level} = \frac{\text{Budgeted fixed overhead}}{\text{OAR}}$$

$$= \frac{£400{,}000}{£2}$$

$$= 200{,}000 \text{ units}$$

2.9 Actual activity level

When overheads are absorbed, this is done on the basis of the actual production level using the budgeted overhead absorption rate. Any under or over absorption is due to the difference between the overhead absorbed and the overhead actually incurred.

Under/over absorption = Overhead absorbed – overhead incurred

Example 5

You are given the following information:

Budgeted fixed overhead	£250,000
Actual fixed overhead	£280,000
Budgeted activity level	100,000 units
Under absorption	£5,000

What was the actual activity level for the period?

Solution

$$\text{OAR} = \frac{£250{,}000}{100{,}000}$$

$$= £2.50 \text{ per unit}$$

$$\text{Overhead absorbed} = £280{,}000 - £5{,}000$$

$$= £275{,}000$$

$$\text{Actual activity level} = \frac{\text{Fixed overhead absorbed}}{\text{OAR}}$$

$$= \frac{£275{,}000}{£2.50}$$

$$= 110{,}000 \text{ units}$$

2.10 Permanent budget record

For every type of revenue or cost it is highly desirable that a permanent budget record be prepared, giving the detailed calculations from which the budgeted amount has been derived. In particular, the data relevant to projecting forecasts of income and expenditure must be identified. This will not only impose a discipline on the budget preparation but will also:

- facilitate the eventual explanation of any differences between budgeted and actual results
- provide a starting point for budget revisions or for the preparation of budgets in future years.

The important features of such a record are as follows:

- details of the budget calculation
- comparison with the actual figures for the previous year
- basis of variability, noting how the amount is related to such factors as levels of output or numbers of people employed.

2.11 Capital expenditure budget

All short-term operating budgets are in effect abstracts from a continuously developing long-term plan. This, however, is particularly true of the capital expenditure budget because the major items included in it will not be completed within the bounds of any one budget year.

The main purpose of the capital expenditure budget, therefore, is to provide a forecast of the amount of cash likely to be needed for investment projects during the year ahead. It also indicates what items of plant, equipment, vehicles and so on will be needed for the purpose of implementing the profit and loss (or operating) budget; and therefore it must be submitted for approval at an early stage in the budgeting timetable.

Any capital expenditure budget would include the following:

- a brief descriptive title for the project
- the total required expenditure
- an analysis of the costs over various time periods
- where appropriate, expenditure to date on the project
- estimates of future benefits from the project
- investment appraisal calculations including details of assumptions made
- intangible benefits from the expenditure.

3 Problems in exam questions

3.1 The raw materials budget with losses

A question may be set where the there is a percentage loss of raw materials in the production process. In practice this 'wastage' may be due to such things as evaporation, faulty materials supplied or materials damaged in the process.

Example 6

The quarterly production requirements for product Omega are shown below. 4% of production fails the quality checks and must be scrapped. How many Omegas must be manufactured to allow for waste?

	Month 1	Month 2	Month 3
Required units	99,000 units	108,000 units	96,000 units
Manufactured units			

Solution

	Month 1	Month 2	Month 3
Required units	99,000 units	108,000 units	96,000 units
Manufactured units	$\frac{99,000}{96\%}$ = 103,125 units	$\frac{108,000}{96\%}$ = 112,500 units	$\frac{96,000}{96\%}$ = 100,000 units

Example 7

Each unit of a product called 'The Cube' requires 0.5 kg of material that costs £1 per kg. The business expects to produce 11,000 cubes in the month of March.

Opening inventory of material was 1,000 kg at the start of the month and is budgeted to be 750 kg at the end of the month. 5% of materials are lost during the manufacturing process.

The completed resource budget for materials looks as follows:

Resource budget – material for 'The Cube'		**March**	**Note**
Needed for production	kg	5,500	(1)
Wastage	kg	289	(2)
Total requirement	kg	5,789	(3)
Closing inventory	kg	750	(4)
Opening inventory	kg	1,000	(5)
Purchases in month	kg	5,539	(6)
Cost per kg	£	1	(7)
Purchase cost of material	£	5,539	(8)

Notes:

(1) Multiply the production quantity of cubes for the month (11,000 units) by the amount of kilograms used for each unit (0.5 kgs) to get 11,000 × 0.5 = 5,500 kgs.

(2) You are told that 5% of material is wasted in the production process, so (100% – 5%) = 95% of it is **not** wasted. In this cell, we write 5,500 × (5/95) = 289 kgs.

(3) The total number of kilograms required, taking wastage into account, is therefore 5,500 kgs + 289 kgs = 5,789 kgs.

(4) You will be told in the exam how much closing inventory is needed.

(5) You will be told in the exam how much opening inventory of material is at hand. Remember to deduct this figure when calculating purchases in the month. Opening inventory is available at the start of the month and used during the month, so purchases are reduced accordingly.

(6) Purchases in the month, in kgs, are calculated as follows:

Production + Wastage + Closing inventory – Opening inventory = 5,500 + 289 + 750 – 1,000 = 5,539 kgs.

(7) You will be told in the exam what the cost of material per kg is (£1 here).

(8) Purchases for the month, in £, is 5,539 × £1 = £5,539.

3.2 The production budget with losses

A question may be set where the there is a percentage loss of finished goods. In practice this may be due to such things as items rejected as inferior by quality control, items damaged in the warehouse or theft.

Example 8

This month, the Production Manager has informed you that 4% of all units produced are faulty. You all agree that you must produce enough units in total each month, to cater for this.

Complete the budgeted spreadsheet, identifying good production required, faulty production and total production required for the months of June and July.

Production budget spreadsheet		
	June	**July**
Opening inventory at the start of the month	3,200	
Good/fault-free production in month		
Sub-total	9,500	8,100
Sales in month (units)	7,000	5,400
Closing inventory at the end of the month	2,500	2,700
Good/fault-free production required		
Faulty production/wastage		
Total production		

Solution

Production budget spreadsheet		
	June	**July**
Opening inventory at the start of the month	3,200	**2,500**
Good/fault-free production in month	**6,300**	**5,600**
Sub-total	9,500	8,100
Sales in month (unit)	7,000	5,400
Closing inventory at the end of the month	2,500	2,700
Good/fault-free production required	**6,300**	**5,600**
Faulty production/wastage	**263**	**233**
Total production	**6,563**	**5,833**

The good/fault-free production in the month is the balancing figure to get from the opening inventory to the sub-total.

4% of all units produced are faulty, so the good/fault-free production will be 96% of all units produced.

	Units	%
Good/fault-free production in month	6,300	96
Faulty production/wastage = 6300/96 × 4 = 262.5	263	4
Total production = 6,300/96 × 100	6563	100

Test your understanding 2

A business needs 5,400 finished goods that are appropriate for resale to be produced in a period. Unfortunately, 10% of all units made fail quality control checks and must be sold as scrap.

Required:

How many units must be produced to ensure they have enough meeting the quality standard?

_______ units will be required.

Test your understanding 3

Schick Ltd operate a 30 day period. Closing inventory should be the equivalent of 6 days' sales volumes of the following period. Sales in period 4 are forecast to be 29,000 units

Required:

Complete the following production forecast:

	Period 1 Units	**Period 2** Units	**Period 3** Units
Opening inventory	5,520		
Production			
Subtotal			
Sales	27,600	28,000	28,800
Closing inventory			

Test your understanding 4

A business requires 34,000 items to be manufactured in July. Each unit requires 2.5 kgs of material, and the raw material is priced at £15 per kg, however, 15% of the input to the manufacturing process is lost. The business operates a just in time inventory management system, so opening and closing inventory levels will be zero.

Required:

How much material should be purchased? _______ kgs

How much will the purchases cost? £_________

Test your understanding 5

A business requires 25,000 items to be manufactured in August. Each unit requires 1.8 kgs of material, and the raw material is priced at £7.50 per kg, however, 10% of the input to the manufacturing process is lost. The opening inventory is 10,000 kgs and the business requires there to be 9,000 kgs of closing inventory.

Required:

How much material is required to fulfil production requirements? _______ kgs

How much material should be purchased? _______ kgs

How much will the purchases cost? £_________

3.3 Labour budgets and overtime requirements

Now we can look at the basic resource budget for labour and overtime requirements by looking at the following example:

Example 9

This month, the business expects to produce 1,200 units of its product called 'The Cube'. The month is a five-week month. Each cube requires 6 hours of labour but, due to renovation work, the workers are unable to operate to their usual efficiency and it has been estimated that they will be 5% less efficient as a result of the renovation work. Normally, 38 members of staff each work 38 basic hours per week, at £10 per hour.

Hours in excess of this are paid at a time and a half.

Resource budget – labour		Month A	Note
Needed for production	hours	7,200	(1)
Inefficiency	hours	379	(2)
Hours to be worked	hours	7,579	(3)
Basic hours available	hours	7,220	(4)
Hours of overtime needed	hours	359	(5)
Cost of basic hours	£	£72,200	(6)
Cost of overtime hours	£	£5,385	(7)

The completed resource budget for labour would look as follows:

Notes

(1) To arrive at the hours needed for production, you multiply the production quantity of units for the month by the number of hours each one takes to produce: 1,200 units × 6 hours = 7,200 hours.

(2) The workers are 5% less efficient this month, so only 95% of their time will be working, so in this cell we put 7,200 × (5%/95%) = 379 hours.

(3) The total hours that will need to be worked are therefore the sum of the first two cells: 7,200 + 379 = 7,579. You can check this result by multiplying 7,579 by 95% = 7,200, the number of hours needed for production.

(4) You are told 38 staff each work 38 hours for each of the five weeks, so total hours available amount to 38 × 38 × 5 = 7,220 hours.

(5) As more hours are needed than are available as basic hours, overtime is required. This is calculated as required hours less basic hours: 7,579 – 7,220 hours = 359 hours.

(6) Basic hours are paid at the basic rate of £10 per hour, so the basic wage bill is £10 × 7,220 hours = £72,200.

(7) Overtime hours are paid at £10 × 1.5 × 359 hours = £5,385.

Test your understanding 6

Wilmslow Ltd makes two products, the Alpha and the Beta. Both products use the same material and labour but in different amounts. The company divides its year into four quarters, each of 12 weeks. Each week consists of five days and each day comprises seven hours.

You are employed as the management accountant to Wilmslow Ltd and you originally prepared a budget for quarter 3, the 12 weeks to 17 September 2016. The basic data for that budget is reproduced below.

Original budgetary data: quarter 3
12 weeks to 17 September 2016

Product	**Alpha**	**Beta**
Estimated demand	1,800 units	2,100 units
Material per unit	8 kilograms	12 kilograms
Labour per unit	3 hours	6 hours

Since the budget was prepared, three developments have taken place:

1 The company has begun to use linear regression and seasonal variations to forecast sales demand. Because of this, the estimated demand for quarter 3 has been revised to 2,000 Alphas and 2,400 Betas.

2 As a result of the revised sales forecasting, you have developed more precise estimates of sales and closing inventory levels:

- The sales volume of both the Alpha and Beta in quarter 4 (the 12 weeks ending 10 December 2016) will be 20% more than in the revised budget for quarter 3 as a result of seasonal variations.
- The closing inventory of finished Alphas at the end of quarter 3 should represent five days' sales for quarter 4.
- The closing inventory of finished Betas at the end of quarter 3 should represent 10 days' sales for quarter 4.
- Production in quarter 4 of both Alpha and Beta is planned to be 20% more than in the revised budget for quarter 3. The closing inventory of materials at the end of quarter 3 should be sufficient for 20 days production in quarter 4.

3 New equipment has been installed. The workforce is not familiar with the equipment. Because of this, for quarter 3, they will only be working at 80% of the efficiency assumed in the original budgetary data.

Other data from your original budget which has not changed is reproduced below:

- 50 production employees work a 35-hour week and are each paid £210 per week.
- Overtime is paid for at £9 per hour.
- The cost of material is £10 per kilogram.
- Opening inventories at the beginning of quarter 3 are as follows:
  - Finished Alphas 500 units
  - Finished Betas 600 units
  - Material 12,000 kilograms
- There will not be any work in progress at any time.

Required:

The production director of Wilmslow Ltd wants to schedule production for quarter 3 (the 12 weeks ending 17 September 2016) and asks you to use the revised information to prepare the following:

(a) The revised production budget for Alphas and Betas.

(b) The material purchases budget in kilograms.

(c) A statement showing the cost of the material purchases.

(d) The labour budget in hours.

(e) A statement showing the cost of labour.

Test your understanding 7

The production budget for the next month is 4,608 units. Each unit requires 1.25 hours of actual work from the labour force, and staff are paid £14 per hour. Due to machine requirements, 10% of hours paid are non-productive.

Required:

What is the budgeted labour time to meet the production budget?

_______ hours will be required.

What is the budgeted cost to meet budgeted production? £_________

3.4 Machine time budgets

Extra machines may need to be hired to meet production requirements. Consider the following example:

Example 10

We are told that the business expects to produce 1,000 units of product A in a given month, and each unit of product A requires 5 hours of machine time.

In addition, the business will produce 1,200 units of product B (3 hours of machine time each) and 800 units of product C (5 hours of machine time each).

There are 45 machines in the factory, but more may be hired. Each machine (owned or hired) can be used for 250 hours in the month. The factory works at 100% efficiency with respect to machines.

The completed resource budget for **machine time** would look as follows:

Resource budget – machine time	**Units**	**Hours per unit**	**Hours required**
Product A	1,000	5	5,000
Product B	1,200	3	3,600
Product C	800	5	4,000
Total machine hours required			12,600
Factory machine hours available (45 × 250)			11,250
Additional machine hours required			1,350
Number of machines to hire (1,350/250)			6

4 The master budget

4.1 Introduction

The master budget for approval by the board will take the form of a budgeted statement of profit or loss, a forecast statement of financial position as at the year-end and a cash budget. These will be supported by such summaries of the various functional budgets as may be required, and by calculations of the key ratios which indicate conformity with the objectives for the year.

Cash budgets will be assessed in Budgeting, so you should be aware of their existence.

4.2 The budgeted statement of profit or loss

The budgeted income statement shows the net profit by deducting the budgeted costs from the budgeted sales revenue.

Example 11

In the earlier example of Hash Ltd. which made the two products ('PS' and 'TG'), we had gathered and calculated the following budgetary information:

	PS	**TG**
Sales units	5,000	1,000
Sales value	£500,000	£140,000
Opening inventory	100 units	50 units
Closing inventory	1,100 units	50 units
Production	6,000 units	1,000 units
Purchases costs	£108,000	£21,120
Direct labour costs	£288,000	£72,000
Production overheads	£99,840	£24,960

Using this information, the budgeted profit and loss account would be as follows:

	£	£
Sales	500,000	140,000
Materials	108,000	21,120
Labour	288,000	72,000
Production overheads	99,840	24,960
Production cost	495,840	118,080
add opening inventory (working)	8,264	5,904
less closing inventory (working)	90,904	5,904
Cost of sales	413,200	118,080
Profit	86,800	21,920

Working

Inventory values = (production cost/units produced) × units of inventory.

1 Opening inventory of PS = (495,840/6,000) × 100 = £8,264

2 Closing inventory of PS = (495,840/6,000) × 1,100 = £90,904

3 Opening inventory of TG = (118,080/1,000) × 50 = £5,904

4 Closing inventory of TG = (118,080/1,000) × 50 = £5,904

4.3 The forecast statement of financial position

In arriving at the forecast Statement of Financial Position, it will be necessary to take account of the following:

- The capital expenditure budget.
- Changes in inventory levels and work in progress (as calculated in connection with the budgeting of material and labour costs). If work in progress and finished inventories are valued on a total absorption cost basis, then it will be necessary to calculate overhead recovery rates.
- Changes in receivables balances. Subject to any special delays in collection, the closing receivables balances will be calculated by applying the company's normal credit terms to the phased budget of sales.

- Changes in payables balances. In theory, the closing payables will be calculated by applying a normal credit period to the phased budgets of material purchases, subcontracted work and any other relevant items. In practice, it may be necessary to review the budgeted cash flow before finalising a decision on the credit to be taken.
- Changes in the cash balance. Initially, the closing cash balance may be taken as the balancing figure on the Statement of Financial Position, but at some stage this should be validated by building up a cash budget itemised from the other budgets. This is discussed in the following section.

5 Cash budgeting: purposes

5.1 The purposes of cash budgets

The purposes of the cash budget are as follows:

- To ensure that the various items of income and expenditure budgeted departmentally, and subject to the normal credit policy of the business, will result in cash flows which enable the company to pay its way at all times. In other words, to ensure that there is a practical plan for how to deal with cash surpluses or shortages.
- Where the cash flow over the year as a whole is satisfactory but there are intermediate periods of difficulty in financing operations, to give a basis from which the timing of particular items can be re-planned. For example delay the purchase of non-current assets where there is an expected cash shortage.
- Where cash proves inadequate to finance the plan as originally envisaged, to give the financial controller an opportunity to seek sources of additional capital. For example an overdraft if the shortage is expected to be short-lived or a bank loan if it's expected for a prolonged period. (If the budget cannot be financed as it stands, then a revised budget will have to be prepared.)
- Like any other budget, to provide a basis for control during the forth-coming year.

In the exam, you will have to prepare a cash flow forecast from the operating budget and statement of financial position assumptions, considering time lags and changes in receivables.

Example 12

Prepare the forecast from the operating budget and Statement of Financial Position (SFP) assumptions. The SFP assumptions are as follows:

1 Receivables will increase by £4,000.

2 Materials payables will reduce by £4,500.

3 Labour costs are paid in the period in which they are incurred.

4 Other payables will increase by £3,000.

Operating budget	£	£
Sales revenue		172,000
Expenditure		
Materials	34,200	
Labour	38,500	
Other costs	16,400	89,100
Operating profit		82,900

Enter receipts and payments as positive figures:

Cash flow forecast	£	£
Sales receipts		
Payments		
Materials		
Labour		
Other costs		
Cash flow forecast		

Solution

Cash flow forecast	£	£
Sales receipts (172,000 – 4,000)		168,000
Payments		
Materials (34,200 + 4,500)	38,700	
Labour	38,500	
Other costs (16,400 – 3,000)	13,400	90,600
Cash flow forecast		77,400

6 Cash budgeting: components

6.1 Sales on credit and discounts

In some businesses a cash or settlement discount is offered to customers for payment within a certain time period. This means that although the cash is received sooner, a lower amount is received than was invoiced. This must be taken into account when preparing the cash budget.

Example 13

A business offers a 3% discount for payment received from credit customers in the month of sale. The business has found that 40% of customers take advantage of this by paying in the month of sale, 50% of customers pay in the month after the sale and 10% of customers pay two months after the month of sale.

Credit sales for the business are as follows:

	Actual		Budgeted		
	February	**March**	**April**	**May**	**June**
	£	£	£	£	£
Credit sales	20,000	22,000	24,000	18,000	21,000

What are the cash receipts from receivables for the three months ending 30 June?

Solution

Cash inflow

			April	**May**	**June**
			£	£	£
February sales	–	20,000 × 10%	2,000		
March sales	–	22,000 × 50%	11,000		
		22,000 × 10%		2,200	
April sales	–	24,000 × 40% × 97%	9,312		
		24,000 × 50%		12,000	
		24,000 × 10%			2,400
May sales	–	18,000 × 40% × 97%		6,984	
		18,000 × 50%			9,000
June sales	–	21,000 × 40% × 97%			8,148
Cash inflow			22,312	21,184	19,548

Note that the cash received in the month of sale is 97% of the amount invoiced as these customers have taken advantage of the settlement discount.

6.2 Sales quantities and prices

In the examples so far you have been given the monetary amount of the sales in each month in order to calculate the receipts from receivables. However, you may be given information about the sales quantity in units each month and the selling price per unit. From this, the total monetary amount of the sales for the month can be calculated.

6.3 Payments to payables

The determination of the cash payments that are to be made to payables each month can be a little more complicated than the calculation of the receipts from receivables, as the information can be expressed in a variety of different ways. The simplest form in which you might come across payments to payables' information is similar to that for receipts from receivables – you will be told the amount of credit purchases and the payment pattern to payables.

Example 14

A business estimates that its credit purchases for February and March will be £14,000 but will increase by 10% each month thereafter. Its payment pattern to payables is that 60% are paid in the month following the purchases and the remaining 40% two months after the purchase.

What are the payments to payables for April, May and June?

Solution

	February	**March**	**April**	**May**	**June**
	£	£	£	£	£
Purchases (increasing by 10% each month)	14,000	14,000	15,400	16,940	18,634
Payments to payables					
– February purchases					
14,000 × 40%			5,600		
– March purchases					
14,000 × 60%			8,400		
14,000 × 40%				5,600	
– April purchases					
15,400 × 60%				9,240	
15,400 × 40%					6,160
– May purchases					
16,940 × 60%					10,164
Cash payments			14,000	14,840	16,324

Test your understanding 8

The following data and estimates are available for ABC Ltd for June, July and August:

	June	July	August
Sales	£45,000	£50,000	£60,000
Wages	£12,000	£13,000	£14,500
Overheads	£8,500	£9,500	£9,000

The following information is available regarding direct materials:

	June	July	August	September
Opening inventory	£5,000	£3,500	£6,000	£4,000
Material usage	£8,000	£9,000	£10,000	
Closing inventory	£3,500	£6,000	£4,000	

Notes:

(1) 10% of sales are for cash, the balance is received the following month.

The amount to be received in June for May's sales is £29,500.

(2) Wages are paid in the month they are incurred.

(3) Overheads include £1,500 per month for depreciation. Overheads are settled in the month following. £6,500 is to be paid in June for May's overheads.

(4) Purchases of direct materials are paid for in the month purchased.

(5) The opening cash balance in June is £11,750.

(6) A tax bill of £25,000 is to be paid in July.

Required:

(a) Calculate the amount of direct material purchases in EACH of the months of June, July and August.

(b) Prepare cash budgets for June, July and August.

Test your understanding 9

XYZ Ltd has the following forecast sales at list price for the nine months to 29 February 20X2:

June	£40,000	September	£48,000	December	£44,000
July	£44,000	October	£40,000	January	£42,000
August	£50,000	November	£45,000	February	£50,000

- 60% of the company's sales are on credit, payable in the month after sale. Cash sales attract a 5% discount off list price.
- Material costs amount to 40% of selling price, and purchases are paid for two months after delivery.
- Inventory is maintained at a level equal to 50% of the following month's sales, except that in November inventory is to be increased by £2,000 (at cost prices) to ensure that XYZ Ltd has a buffer during the period when its major supplier shuts down. This safety inventory will be released in March.
- Wages comprise a fixed sum of £2,000 per month plus a variable element equal to 10% of sales; these are payable in the month they are incurred.
- Fixed costs amount to £7,500 per month, payable one month in arrears, of which £1,500 is depreciation.
- XYZ Ltd has capital expenditure/receipts scheduled as follows:

Acquisitions:	£
September	15,000
November	10,000
February	4,000
Disposal:	
October	8,000

- Corporation tax, payable in November, amounts to £44,000.
- The bank balance on 1 September 20X1 is expected to be £5,000.

Task

Prepare a cash flow forecast for XYZ Ltd for EACH of the six months from September 20X1 to February 20X2, using a row and column format.

Test your understanding 10

Prepare a cash forecast for May from the following budget data

Budget data	March	April	May	June
	£	£	£	£
Invoiced sales	2,500	3,000	2,800	4,000
Purchases	900	1,300	1,250	1,200
Wages	500	510	520	480
Other overheads	600	660	620	630
Capital expenditure	–	1,200	–	–

Cash forecast	May
	£
Opening cash balance	(500)
Customer receipts	
Payments	
For purchases	
For wages	
For overheads	
For capital expenditure	
Total	
Closing cash balance	

Average terms

Half of customers pay after 1 month.
Half pay after 2 months.

Purchases paid for after 2 months.

Wages paid in the current month.

Other overheads paid after one month.

Capital expenditure paid in the current month.

7 Summary

The budget must be prepared in a logical and orderly manner, ensuring co-ordination and co-operation between departments and different levels of management. Final proposals must be fully understood and accepted by all involved via a clear set of instructions and detailed discussions where necessary.

You should be prepared to discuss the types of budgets that may be required for a particular business and how they might be prepared, probably with numerical illustrations.

Similarly, you should be prepared to construct a cash budget for a particular business.

Test your understanding answers

Test your understanding 1

Using a proforma like this can help. The numbers in **bold** were originally given in the question:

	Month 1 units	Month 2 units	Month 3 units
Sales budget	**30,000**	**31,000**	**32,000**
Closing inventory (W1)	3,720	3,840	
	33,720	34,840	
Less: opening inventory	(**3,600**)	(3,720)	
Production of finished goods	30,120	31,120	

The production volume for month 1 will be **30,120** units.

The production volume for month 2 will be **31,120** units.

Workings:

(W1) –

Month 1 closing inventory = 31,000 × 12% = 3,720

Month 2 closing inventory = 32,000 × 12% = 3,840

Test your understanding 2

90% of the output passes the quality checks, the business need 5,400 to pass the quality checks.

	Units	%
Produced		100
Pass quality checks	5,400	90
Fail checks		10

5,400 is 90% of the units produced in total, so the number of units required to achieve this output is 5,400/0.9 = **6,000**.

	Units	%
Produced	**6,000**	100
Pass quality checks	5,400	90
Fail checks	600	10

Test your understanding 3

	Period 1	**Period 2**	**Period 3**
	Units	Units	Units
Opening Inventory	5,520	**5,600**	**5,760**
Production (W3)	**27,680**	**28,160**	**28,840**
Subtotal (W2)	**33,200**	**33,760**	**34,600**
Sales	27,600	28,000	28,800
Closing Inventory (W1)	**5,600**	**5,760**	**5,800**

Workings:

(W1) The start point for each period is the closing inventory requirement.

For period 1 it is 6/30 × 28,000 = 5,600

For period 2 it is 6/30 × 28,800 = 5,760

For period 3 it is 6/30 × 29,000 = 5,800

This closing inventory is then the opening inventory for the next period.

(W2) Next we work backwards to identify the subtotal:

For period 1 it is 27,600 + 5,600 = 33,200

For period 2 it is 28,000 + 5,760 = 33,760

For period 3 it is 28,800 + 5,800 = 34,600

(W3) Finally, working backwards again, we work out the production for each period, this is the balancing figure between the opening inventory and the subtotal.

For period 1 it is 33,200 – 5,520 = 27,680

For period 2 it is 33,760 – 5,600 = 28,160

For period 3 it is 34,600 – 5,760 = 28,840

Test your understanding 4

First of all work how much material we need to fulfil the production requirement: 34,000 units × 2.5 kgs = 85,000 kgs

We know that 15% of the input is lost/wasted, so the output is 85% of the input.

Material input required = 85,000 kgs / 0.85 = **100,000 kgs**

The cost will be 100,000 kgs × £15 = **£1,500,000**

Test your understanding 5

First of all work how much material we need to fulfil the production requirement: 25,000 units × 1.8 kgs = 45,000 kgs

We know that 10% of the input is lost/wasted, so the output is 90% of the input.

Material input required = 45,000 kgs / 0.9 = **50,000 kgs**

In terms of how many kgs should be purchased:

	kgs
Material required in production	50,000
Closing inventory	9,000
	59,000
Less: Opening inventory	10,000
Purchases	**49,000**

And the cost = 49,000 kgs × £7.50 = **£367,500**

Test your understanding 6

(a) **Production budget – quarter ended 17 September 2016**

	Alphas (units)	**Betas (units)**
Budgeted sales	2,000	2,400
Add: Closing inventory (see Note 1)	200	480
Less: Opening inventory	(500)	(600)
Production (finished units)	1,700	2,280

Note 1	**Alphas**	**Betas**
Sales this quarter 3	2,000	2,400
Add 20% seasonal variation	400	480
Budgeted sales next quarter 4	2,400	2,880
Closing inventory (5/60 × 2,400 = 200) (10/60 × 2,880 = 480)	200	480

(b) **Material purchases budget – quarter ended 17 September 2016**

	Kilograms
Usage – Alpha production (8 kg × 1,700)	13,600
Usage – Beta production (12 kg × 2,280)	27,360
	40,960
Add Closing material stock (see Note 2)	16,384
Less Opening material stock	(12,000)
Purchases of material	45,344

Note 2

Closing inventory of materials:	
Usage this period	40,960
Add 20%	8,192
Material required for production next period	49,152
Stock required (20/60 × 49,152)	16,384

(c) **Cost of purchases**

(45,344 kg × £10) £453,440

(d) **Labour budget – quarter ended 17 September 2016**

	Hours
Labour hours required for Alpha production (3 hours × 1,700)	5,100
Labour hours required for Beta production (6 hours × 2,280)	13,680
Total hours required before efficiency adjustment	18,780
Efficiency adjustment (20%/80%)	4,695
Gross labour hours	23,475
Normal hours (50 employees × 35 hours × 12 weeks)	21,000
Overtime hours required	2,475

(e)

Normal hours (50 employees × 12 weeks × £210)	£126,000
Overtime (2,475 hours × £9)	£22,275
Direct labour cost	£148,275

Test your understanding 7

The first step is to work out how many hours of work are needed:

The production plan is for 4,608 units which require 1.25 hours of labour time each:

Labour hours work required = 4,608 × 1.25 hours = 5,760 hours.

Next we need to adjust for the non-productive time. This is 10% of the total time, so that means the labour force are working for 90% of the hours paid.

Hours paid = 5,760/0.9 = **6,400 hours**

Now we have the hours paid, we multiply it by the rate of pay per hour:

Labour cost = 6,400 × £14 per hour = **£89,600**

Test your understanding 8

Tutorial note: Inventory is used up by material usage, and by closing inventory. This usage is made up partly from opening inventory. The balance must be made up from purchases.

	June	**July**	**August**
	£	£	£
Material usage	8,000	9,000	10,000
Closing inventory	3,500	6,000	4,000
	11,500	15,000	14,000
Less: Opening inventory	(5,000)	(3,500)	(6,000)
Purchases	6,500	11,500	8,000

Tutorial note: The main points to watch out for are sales receipts and overheads. Tackle sales receipts by calculating separate figures for cash sales (10% of total sales, received in the month of sale) and credit sales (90% of last month's sales). For overheads, remember that depreciation is not a cash expense and must therefore be stripped out of the overheads total cost.

Cash budgets, June – August

	June	**July**	**August**
	£	£	£
Receipts of cash			
Cash sales	4,500	5,000	6,000
Credit sales	29,500	40,500	45,000
	34,000	45,500	51,000
Cash payments			
Wages	12,000	13,000	14,500
Overheads	6,500	7,000	8,000
Direct materials	6,500	11,500	8,000
Taxation	–	25,000	–
	25,000	56,500	30,500
Surplus/(deficit) for month	9,000	(11,000)	20,500
Opening balance	11,750	20,750	9,750
Closing balance	20,750	9,750	30,250

Test your understanding 9

	Sept	Oct	Nov	Dec	Jan	Feb
Receipts	£	£	£	£	£	£
Cash sales (W1)	18,240	15,200	17,100	16,720	15,960	19,000
Credit sales (W2)	30,000	28,800	24,000	27,000	26,400	25,200
Capital		8,000				
	48,240	52,000	41,100	43,720	42,360	44,200
Payments						
Materials (W3)	18,800	19,600	17,600	17,000	19,800	17,200
Wages (W4)	6,800	6,000	6,500	6,400	6,200	7,000
Fixed costs (W5)	6,000	6,000	6,000	6,000	6,000	6,000
Capital	15,000		10,000			4,000
Corporation tax			44,000			
	46,600	31,600	84,100	29,400	32,000	34,200
Surplus/(Deficit)	1,640	20,400	(43,000)	14,320	10,360	10,000
Balance b/f	5,000	6,640	27,040	(15,960)	(1,640)	8,720
Balance c/f	6,640	27,040	(15,960)	(1,640)	8,720	18,720

Workings

(W1) Since 60% of sales are credit sales, 40% are cash sales, e.g.

	£
September cash sales = £48,000 × 40% =	19,200
5% discount on £19,200	(960)
Net cash receipt	18,240

(W2) August credit sales are paid in September, and so on.

Credit sales = 60% so the September receipt = 60% × £50,000 = £30,000

(W3)

	July	**Aug**	**Sept**	**Oct**	**Nov**	**Dec**
Sales:						
Inventory used (40% of sales)	17,600	20,000	19,200	16,000	18,000	17,600
Opening inventory (50% of 40% of sales)	(8,800)	(10,000)	(9,600)	(8,000)	(9,000)	(8,800)
Closing inventory (50% of 40% of next month's sales)	10,000	9,600	8,000	9,000	8,800	8,400
Extra stock					2,000	
PURCHASES	18,800	19,600	17,600	17,000	19,800	17,200
Paid in	Sept	Oct	Nov	Dec	Jan	Feb

(W4) 10% of sales + £2,000

e.g., September:

(10% × £48,000) + £2,000 = £6,800

(W5) £7,500 – £1,500 Depreciation: £6,000

Test your understanding 10

Prepare a cash forecast for May from the following budget data.

Budget data	March	April	May	June	Cash forecast	May
	£	£	£	£		£
Invoiced sales	2,500	3,000	2,800	4,000	Opening Cash balance	(500)
Purchases	900	1,300	1,250	1,200	Customer receipts (W1)	2,750
Wages	500	510	520	480		
Other overheads	600	660	620	630	**Payments**	
Capital expenditure	–	1,200	–	–	For purchases	900
					For wages	520
Average terms					For overheads	660
					For capital expenditure	0
Half of customers take 1 month to pay. Half take 2 months.					Total	2,080
Purchases paid for after 2 months.						
Wages paid in the current month.					Closing cash balance	170
Other overheads paid after one month.						
Capital expenditure paid in the current month.						

Working 1

April £3,000 × 0.5 = £1,500

March £2,000 × 0.5 = £1,250

Total = £1,500 + £1,250 = £2,750

Further aspects of budgeting

Introduction

In our third chapter on budgeting we are going to consider some other issues relating to the production of the budget and the uses of the budget. First of all, we must be able to deal with the situation when demand for an organisation's products is likely to outstrip its capacity to supply; this happens when it was originally planned to make a number of different products, but a shortage of some resource now makes the plan impossible. The resource that is preventing normal output is known as the limiting factor. The most common limiting factors are either materials or labour.

Then, as a reminder from earlier studies some costs change when activity levels change, whilst others do not. The ability to isolate cost elements by behaviour is essential to management who are concerned with predicting future costs as part of the planning and decision making processes.

In order to be able to compare actual figures with budgeted figures to give a meaningful analysis, a **flexible** or flexed budget must be prepared. This will lead to budget variances and the broad principles are similar to those already studied in the chapters on variance analysis.

A further important aspect of budgeting that appears in examinations is the effect of the budgeting process and the final budget on the motivation of managers and employees.

ASSESSMENT CRITERIA

- Budgetary responsibilities and accountabilities (LO 1.2)
- Budgeting where resource constraints exist (LO 1.4)
- Impact of internal and external factors on forecasts (LO 1.5)
- Uncertainty in the budget setting process (LO 1.6)
- Budgetary control (LO 2.1)

CONTENTS

1 Preparing production budgets with limiting factors

1.1 Limiting factors

The level of activity at which a business can operate will very seldom be unlimited. Limitations may be imposed, for example, by:

- market demand for its products or services
- the number of skilled employees available
- the availability of material supplies
- the space available either as a working area or for the storage of goods
- the amount of cash or credit facilities available to finance the business.

1.2 Production budget limited by sales

Most businesses gear their production to their expected sales, so this is the usual limiting factor – they would make more units if they could sell them.

1.3 Analysing limitations on production

When presented with an upper limit on production capacity, production adjustments may be necessary so that the maximum does no longer represent a problem.

Example 1

Here is an extract from our basic production budget spreadsheet for months 1 and 2. The business can only produce a maximum of 2,500 units each month, but the production budget currently plans for production of 3,000 units in Month 2:

Production budget spreadsheet	**Quantity in units**	
	Month 1	*Month 2*
Good/fault-free production required	900	2,700
Faulty production/wastage	100	300
Total revised production in month	1,000	3,000

We need to adjust the production as follows:

Production budget spreadsheet	**Quantity in units**	
	Month 1	Month 2
Good/fault-free production required	900	2,700
Faulty production/wastage	100	300
Total production for the month	1,000	3,000
Capacity adjustment		**–500**
Total revised production in month		2,500

We have changed the production for Month 2 to the maximum possible, and made a reduction adjustment of 500 units.

This, in turn, increased the production in Month 1 by 500 units:

Production budget spreadsheet	**Quantity in units**	
	Month 1	Month 2
Good/fault-free production required	900	2,700
Faulty production/wastage	100	300
Total production for the month	1,000	3,000
Capacity adjustment	**+500**	**–500**
Total revised production in month	1,500	2,500

The total revised production for Month 1, taking into account the adjustment, is 1,000 + 500 = 1,500 units.

If a business has limited resources of materials, labour or machine time, but still wants to achieve its production/sales budget, it must work out how many items it can make using these limited resources, and how many will require extra resources to be found, – usually at greater than standard cost.

Example 2

In this example, the business expects to sell 1,200 units in the month and keeps no inventory of finished goods. You are also given data on the standard cost and current availability of materials, labour and machine time at this cost.

Production budget	Required to produce 1,200 units	Current availability	Units to be made from current availability	Extra resource needed
Materials: 0.75 kgs per unit	900 kgs	720 kgs	960 units	180 kgs
Labour: 1.25 hours per unit	1,500 hours	1,350 hours	1,080	150 hours
Machine time: 0.5 hours per unit	600 hours	667 hours	1,334 units	0 hours

1.4 Identifying the limiting factor

When a manager starts to prepare a budget he or she should review the elements in it and identify where limiting factors (or governing factors) exist.

They will not all be equally significant; but where one particular limitation is of major importance it may be necessary to budget for that item first and to construct the rest of the budget around it. This can happen not merely in one department but for the company as a whole, when the item concerned may be referred to as the principal budget factor or key factor.

Quite commonly, the rate of growth in sales is the principal budget factor and this would have to be forecast before any other budget plans were made.

It is essential to identify the principal budget factor and any other limiting factors at an early stage in the budgeting process so that management may consider whether:

- it is possible to overcome the limitation which they impose (e.g. by finding new markets for sales or by obtaining alternative supplies or substitute raw materials)
- the limitations imposed must be accepted and the business's budgets must be produced within those limitations.

Example 3

In this example, the business expects to sell 500 units in the month and has identified the availability of its resources as given in this table.

Resource	Usage		Maximum availability
Materials	2	litres per unit	890 litres
Labour	1	hours per unit	600 hours
Machine time	0.1	hours per unit	50 hours

No more resources are available.

Which resource is the limiting factor for production in the month, and how many units can be produced and sold?

Solution

Materials is the limiting factor, and only 445 units can be made and sold.

890 litres of material will produce 890/2 = 445 units, so production is limited to this quantity. The maximum labour will produce 600 units, and so does not limit production. The maximum machine time will be enough to produce 500 units if and when more material becomes available.

1.5 Changing the production mix because of a limiting factor

If a business makes more than one product and does not have enough resources to make all it can sell of all products, it must decide which one(s) to produce and in what quantity. This is done based on the contribution per unit of the limiting factor as we saw in chapter 3.

Example 4

Barbecue Limited manufactures two products for which the following details are available.

	Product X		Product Y
Selling price	£38		£38
Direct materials 8 units @ £1	£8	4 units @ £1	£4
Labour 4 hours @ £2	£8	6 hours @ £2	£12
Variable overhead 4 machine hours @ £3	£12	3 machine hours @ £3	£9
Fixed overheads	£5		£7

Maximum demand for X is 2,500 units.

Maximum demand for Y is 2,000 units.

Calculate the optimum production plan for Barbecue in each of the following two situations:

(a) Labour in the next period is limited to *16,000* hours, with no limit on machine hours.

(b) Machine hours in the next period are limited to *12,000* hours, with no limit on labour hours.

Solution

We would like to produce Xs and Ys up to the point where maximum demand is reached. (There is no point producing beyond this, because customers do not want any more.) So ideally we would like to produce 2,500 X and 2,000 Y. To do this we would require the following resources.

	Labour hours	**Machine hours**
2,500 X	10,000	10,000
2,000 Y	12,000	6,000
	22,000	16,000

If labour is limited to 16,000 hours we will not have enough labour hours to achieve this. Similarly, if machine hours are limited to 12,000 our production will be restricted.

To tackle this problem we begin by calculating the contribution earned per unit of each product.

Contribution for each unit of X = £ (38 – 8 – 8 – 12) = £10 per unit
Contribution for each unit of Y = £ (38 – 4 – 12 – 9) = £13 per unit

(a) Labour is limited so we calculate the contribution earned per labour hour for each product.

X = £10/4 = £2.50 per labour hour

Y = £13/6 = £2.17 per labour hour

You get more contribution per labour hour for X than for Y so make as many Xs as possible.

Available hours = 16,000, and 2,500 Xs require 10,000 hrs

The remaining hours are all used to make as many Ys as possible.

Remaining Ys will take six hours each to make so produce 6,000/6 = 1,000 Ys.

Contribution = (2,500 × £10) + (1,000 × £13) = £38,000

(b) In this case, machine hours are the scarce resource so we calculate contribution per machine hour.

X = £10/4 = £2.50 per machine hour

Y = £13/3 = £4.33 per machine hour

Now it is better to make Ys. Making 2,000 Ys requires 2,000 × 3 = 6,000 machine hours. That leaves us a further 6,000 machine hours for making Xs.

6,000 remaining hours for X means making 6,000/4 = 1,500 Xs

Contribution = (1,500 × £10) + (2,000 × £13) = £41,000

Note that in the examination, if you are told the maximum demand for a product it is a big hint that this method should be used.

1.6 Revising the budget because of a limitation

Sometimes it may not be a complete adjustment to our production plan, it could be slight changes to a policy or outsourcing aspects that cannot be completed by the business because of the limitations.

Example 5

A manufacturing business has made a budget that involves making and selling 20,000 units for the upcoming financial year.

Each item needs to be tested and they can only test 1,000 units a month internally.

They business hold no opening or closing inventory. Any units that cannot be tested internally must be tested by a third party.

How many units will need to be tested by a third party?

Solution

In total 20,000 units need to be tested.

There is internal capacity to do 12 months × 1,000 units = 12,000 units.

Meaning they will need to outsource testing of 8,000 units.

Example 6

A manufacturing business makes two products the *** and the ***. Both products use the same raw materials. The supply of these raw materials is limited to 10,000 kg per month.

The business has always used a just in time approach and held no inventory of raw materials.

Raw material requirements are in the table below.

Complete the table below to schedule purchases in order to achieve maximum production while holding the lowest inventory possible.

	June	July	August	September
	kg	kg	kg	kg
Material required	7,500	11,000	9,800	11,200
Potential shortage				
Purchases				
Closing inventory				
Used in production				

Solution

In June the materials requirements are ok, but because of the future months, they can buy excess material now to achieve future month requirements.

There is a shortage in July of 1,000kg and September of 1,200kg.

In August there is only capacity to buy 200kg more than required so we need to buy more in June to compensate for this.

	June	July	August	September
	kg	kg	kg	kg
Material required	7,500	11,000	9,800	11,200
Potential shortage	0	1,000	0	1,200
Purchases	9,500	10,000	10,000	10,000
Closing inventory	2,000	1,000	1,200	0
Used in production	7,500	11,000	9,800	11,200

Test your understanding 1

A manufacturing business has made a budget that involves making and selling 125,000 units for the upcoming financial year.

Due to some specification changes and increased legislation the quality control department have highlighted a concern over their ability to meet the testing capacity to allow this to happen. They can test 9,000 units each month.

All units must be tested before they can be sold. They business hold no opening or closing inventory.

Required:

Complete the following table

	Units
Units that require testing	
Units that can be tested internally	
Units to be tested by an alternative source	

Test your understanding 2

A manufacturer makes a single product, this product is unique and requires 6kg of a very rare ingredient. Due to its rarity, there will only be 150,000kg available in the coming year.

The manufacturer is planning to make and sell 32,000 units in the coming year.

Required:

Complete the following table

The number of units that can be produced in total is		units
There is a shortfall of		kg
This is equivalent to		units

Test your understanding 3

A manufacturer makes a single product. In the upcoming period, they have a maximum demand of 30,000 units.

Each unit of the product requires the following:

1.75 hours of labour

1 hour of machine time

0.75kg of material

The manufacturer has a workforce of 217 staff, and each staff member is contracted to work for 40 hours (maximum) a week. They have 15 machines that can work for a maximum of 800 hours each. Finally, they have 8,400kg of material available in the period.

Required:

Complete the following table

How many labour hours are available in the period?		hours
How many machine hours are available in the period?		hours
What is the requirement of each of the following to meet the demand?		
Labour hours		hours
Machine hours		hours
Material		kg
Budgeted production level for the period will be:		units

Test your understanding 4

Your organisation is about to commence work on the preparation of the forthcoming year's annual budget.

As assistant management accountant, you have been asked to assist budget-holders and to respond to any queries which they may raise in the course of submitting their budget proposals.

The following notes are extracts taken from your organisation's budget manual.

'The key or principal budget factor in our organisation's budgetary process is sales volume ... The need for co-ordination in the budgetary process is paramount ...'

The marketing manager is a budget holder and she has approached you with a number of queries concerning the above extract.

Required:

Prepare a memo for the marketing manager which provides brief answers to the following queries:

(a) What is meant by the term key factor and why is the determination of this factor so important in the budgetary process?

(b) How can co-ordination be achieved?

Test your understanding 5

You are a management accountant employed by Aspen Ltd and you report to Adriana Jonas, the managing director. One of your responsibilities is the production of budgets. Aspen Ltd only has one customer, Advanced Industries plc, for whom it makes the Omega, a specialist product. Advanced Industries demands that Aspen keeps a minimum closing inventory of Omegas in case there is an error in the forecast requirements. There is no work-in-progress at any time.

- Both companies divide the year into four-week periods. Each week consists of five days and each day comprises eight hours.
- Advanced Industries plc has recently informed Aspen Ltd of its Omega requirements for the five periods ending Friday 25 May 2001. The details are reproduced below.

Forecast demand for Omegas					
Four weeks ending:	2 February Period 1	2 March Period 2	30 March Period 3	27 April Period 4	25 May Period 5
Number of Omegas required	5,700	5,700	6,840	6,460	6,080
Closing inventory of Omegas					
Closing inventories are to equal 3 days of the next period's demand for Omegas.					

The production director gives you the following information:

- The actual opening inventories for period 1, the four weeks ending 2 February, will be 1,330 Omegas.
- Each Omega requires 6 litres of material.

- The material is currently supplied under a long-term contract at a cost of £8.00 per litre and is made exclusively for Aspen by Contrax plc.
- Contrax only has sufficient production capacity to make a maximum of 34,000 litres in any four-week period. Aspen normally purchases the material in the same four-week period it is used.
- Should Aspen require more than 34,000 litres in a four-week period, Contrax would be willing to supply additional material in the preceding period, providing it had spare capacity.
- There is a readily available alternative source for the material but the cost is £12.00 per litre.
- Before buying from the alternative source, any shortage of material in a period should be overcome, where possible, by first purchasing extra material from Contrax in the immediately preceding period.
- There are 78 production employees who are paid a guaranteed basic wage of £160 per 40-hour week.
- Each Omega should take 2 labour hours to make but, due to temporary technical difficulties, the workforce is only able to operate at 95% efficiency in periods 1 to 4.
- Any overtime incurred is payable at a rate of £6.00 per hour.

Required:

Adriana Jonas asks you to prepare the following budgets for each of the periods 1 to 4:

(a) The production budget in Omegas using the inventory levels given in the data.

(b) The material purchases budget in litres.

(c) The cost of the material purchases.

(d) The labour budget in hours including any overtime hours.

(e) The cost of the labour budget including the cost of any overtime.

Data

On receiving your budgets, Adriana Jonas, the managing director, tells you that:

- She is concerned about the cost of the planned overtime and the extra cost of purchasing materials from the alternative supplier.
- The minimum demand in any four week period is forecast to be 5,700 Omegas.

- It is not possible to reduce costs by Advanced Industries plc improving its current method of forecasting.

However, she believes that some immediate and longer-term cost savings are possible.

Required:

Write a memo to Adriana Jonas. In your memo you should:

(a) Use the budget information prepared above to identify ONE immediate possible cost saving proposal other than renegotiating the conditions imposed by Advanced Industries plc.

(b) Calculate the value of the cost savings in the proposal identified in part (a).

(c) Use the forecast minimum demand for Omegas to show whether or not:

(i) the need to obtain material supplies from the alternative source is a short-term problem, and

(ii) the need for overtime payments is also a short-term problem.

(d) Suggest TWO cost savings which may be possible in the longer term.

Test your understanding 6

You have recently been promoted to the post of management accountant with Northern Products Ltd, a company formed four years ago. The company has always used budgets to help plan its production of two products, the Exe and the Wye. Both products use the same material and labour but in different proportions.

You have been asked to prepare the budget for quarter 1, the 12 weeks ending 24 March 2000. In previous budgets the closing inventories of both raw materials and finished products were the same as opening inventories. You questioned whether or not this was the most efficient policy for the company.

As a result, you have carried out an investigation into the inventory levels required to meet the maximum likely sales demand for finished goods and production demand for raw materials. You conclude that closing inventories of finished goods should be expressed in terms of days sales for the next quarter and closing inventories of raw materials in terms of days production for the next quarter.

Your findings are included in the data below which also shows data provided by the sales and production directors of Northern Products Ltd.

Product data

	Exe	Wye
• Budgeted sales in units, quarter 1	930 units	1,320 units
• Budgeted sales in units, quarter 2	930 units	1,320 units
• Budgeted material per unit (litres)	6 litres	9 litres
• Budgeted labour hours per unit	12 hours	7 hours
• Opening units of finished inventory	172 units	257 units
• Closing units of finished inventories (days sales next quarter)	8 days	9 days
• Failure rate of finished production*	2%	3%
• Finance and other costs of keeping a unit in inventory per quarter	£4.00	£5.00

* Failed products are only discovered on completion of production and have no residual value.

Other accounting data

• Weeks in accounting period	12 weeks
• Days per week for production and sales	5 days
• Hours per week	35 hours
• Number of employees	46 employees
• Budgeted labour rate per hour	£6.00
• Overtime premium for hours worked in excess of 35 hours per week	30%
• Budgeted cost of material per litre	£15.00
• Opening raw material inventories (litres)	1,878 litres
• Closing raw material inventories (days production current quarter)	5 days
• Financing and other costs of keeping a litre of raw material in inventory per quarter	£1.00

Required:

(a) Calculate the following information for *quarter 1*, the 12 weeks ending 24 March 2000:

(i) The number of production days.

(ii) The closing finished inventory for Exe and Wye in units.

(iii) The labour hours available before overtime has to be paid.

(b) Prepare the following budgets for quarter 1, the 12 weeks ending 24 March 2000:

(i) The production budget in units for Exe and Wye including any faulty production.

(ii) The material purchases budget in litres and value.

(iii) The production labour budget in hours and value including any overtime payments.

(c) Calculate the savings arising from the change in the required inventory levels for the 12 weeks ending 24 March 2000.

2 Cost centres

2.1 Introduction

Definition

A cost centre is a location, function or item(s) of equipment in respect of which costs may be accumulated and related to cost units for control purposes.

A cost centre therefore is used as an initial collection point for costs; once the total cost of operating the cost centre for a period has been ascertained, it can be related to the cost units that have passed through the cost centre.

The location, function or item of equipment referred to in the definition can be directly related to production, to a service department or to a business.

2.2 Examples of cost centres

Production	Assembly line Packing machine
Service department	Stores Canteen Quality control
Service	Tax department (accountants) Ward (hospital) Faculty (college)

2.3 Responsibility for cost centres

Control can only be exercised by people, and for every cost somebody must be responsible; so whether a cost centre is impersonal or personal there must always be a manager in whose sphere of responsibility that cost centre is included.

2.4 Profit centres

Definition

A profit centre is a location, function or item(s) of equipment in respect of which costs and revenues may be ascertained for the purposes of controlling the resulting profit.

Thus, while the paint shop in a factory might be treated as a cost centre (to monitor the costs incurred there), a large company might treat its French operations as a profit centre (since they generate both costs and revenues).

3 Cost classification

3.1 Types of cost classification

Costs can be classified (collected into logical groups) in many ways. The particular classification selected will depend upon the purpose for which the resulting analysed data will be used.

Purpose	Classification
Cost control	By nature – materials, labour, overheads, etc.
Cost accounts	By relationship to cost units – direct/ indirect costs, etc.
Budgeting, contribution analysis	By behaviour – fixed/variable costs.
Decision-making	Relevant and non-relevant costs.
Responsibility accounting	Controllable and uncontrollable costs.

You will come across these classifications in more detail as you work through this study text. At this stage, we will revise the basic classification terms used in cost accounting.

3.2 Direct and indirect costs

For cost accounting purposes, the costs of the business will be classified in quite a different way from the analysis required by a financial accountant for the income statement in published accounts.

The basic classification of costs in cost accounting may be illustrated as follows.

Example 7

	£	£
Direct costs		
Direct materials		250,000
Direct labour		120,000
Direct expenses		10,000
Prime cost (= total of direct costs)		380,000
Indirect production costs		25,000
Production cost		405,000
Indirect non-production costs		
Administration overhead	20,000	
Selling and distribution overhead	25,000	
		45,000
Total cost		450,000

3.3 Direct costs

Definition

Direct costs are costs which can be related directly to one cost unit. Direct costs comprise direct materials, direct labour and direct expenses.

For example, considering a cost unit of a chair, direct costs will include the cost of wood and screws used (direct material cost) and the cost of manufacturing labour hours per chair (direct labour cost).

In a service context, the direct costs relating to, say, a student enrolled at a college would include the costs of books provided, individual tuition and marking costs.

3.4 Indirect costs

Definition

Indirect costs cannot be identified directly with a cost unit and are often referred to as *overheads.*

For inventory valuation purposes a distinction needs to be made between overheads incurred in the production process (factory costs, e.g. factory rent and rates, power etc) and non-production costs.

Non-production costs are indirect costs involved in converting finished goods into revenue, comprising:

(a) administrative overhead costs (e.g. executive salaries and office costs) and

(b) marketing, selling and distribution overhead costs.

Non-production costs are not included in inventory valuation since they are not costs of making a product, but costs of selling it. Inventory on hand at the end of a period is valued at total production cost only, including production overheads (in a total absorption costing system). We shall return to this point in the next chapter.

Considering the cost unit of a chair, the salaries of the sales representatives who promote and sell the chairs to retail outlets would be a selling overhead.

Indirect costs associated with a college would include premises running costs, lecturers' salaries and administrative staff costs.

Overhead costs can always be identified with cost centres. Because cost centres are the responsibility of particular functional managers one will usually find overheads classified according to the main functional divisions of the business.

4 Cost behaviour

4.1 The nature of costs

We mentioned earlier the need for cost classification by behaviour for budgeting purposes. In order to make predictions of future cost levels, we must determine the basis of the charge.

As an example, consider the cost of direct materials expected next month. The charge would depend on the amount used and the cost per unit. The amount used would depend, in turn, on the production anticipated for the period.

In order to derive this cost therefore we must make an estimate such as the following:

(a)	Production levels	10,000 units
(b)	Usage of materials per unit:	
	Material A	2 kg
	Material B	1 kg
	Material C	0.2 kg
(c)	Costs of materials:	
	Material A	30 pence per kg
	Material B	25 pence per kg
	Material C	50 pence per kg

Estimate of next month's material cost

		£
Material A	20,000 kg @ 30p/kg	6,000
Material B	10,000 kg @ 25p/kg	2,500
Material C	2,000 kg @ 50p/kg	1,000
Total estimated material cost		9,500

4.2 Variable costs

Once we can identify the factors affecting material cost we can set up a simple mathematical model which will, for any level of production, usage and cost of materials, enable the total level of cost in a future period to be predicted. In practice, we may wish to build in other variables which affect the cost such as wastage rates thus producing a slightly more complex model.

Direct labour costs may tend to vary due to changes in productivity and other factors in addition to the more obvious variables such as grade and rate of payment. A certain amount of estimation will be required; if payment is on a production related basis we would expect a cost which, like materials, will vary in line with the volume of production.

As a rule-of-thumb guide, therefore direct material, labour and expenses will vary roughly in line with anticipated production levels or the level of activity. We call such costs **variable** costs.

4.3 Fixed costs

This will not be the case with all costs. If we take the cost of rent and rates, for example, the charge is not determined on the basis of the intensity of usage of the premises but rather on the basis of time. Costs that are unaffected by the volume of production are called **fixed costs**. Rent and rates are an example. Labour paid on a time basis (for example, a monthly salary) would also fall under this heading. How then can we predict the cost of such expenses for next month? Well, there is no difficulty in doing this as all we have to do is consult our rental agreement and the rates notice and we can forecast with complete certainty what these costs will be for the month.

4.4 Classification of costs by behaviour

The above example illustrates the need for cost behaviour classification. For cost prediction purposes, we must make a distinction between costs which vary with production or activity levels (variable costs) and those which do not (fixed costs). There also exists a type of cost which moves in sympathy with production levels but contains an element which does not, such as an electricity charge which contains a minimum standing charge plus an element which relates to the usage of the period. Such a cost would be described as semi-variable or mixed.

Definition

Variable costs are those that vary (usually assumed in direct proportion) with changes in level of activity of the cost centre to which they relate (e.g. output volume). An example would be the raw material used in a product. It should be noted that the variable cost per unit may not remain constant over a wide range. It may be possible, for example, to obtain discounts for large purchases of material, reducing the cost per unit.

Fixed costs are those that accrue with the passage of time and are not affected by changes in activity level; they are therefore also known as period costs, for example rent of premises.

Stepped costs are fixed over a range of output and then suddenly increase in one big jump, for example a staffing level of up to 20 people may only require one supervisor but, if the staff level is more than 20, an extra supervisor will be needed.

Semi-variable (mixed) costs contain both a fixed and a variable element. When output is nil, the fixed element is incurred, but costs also increase, like variable costs, as output increases. An example is telephone charges where there is a fixed rental to which is added the charge for calls made. These are also sometimes known as semi-fixed costs.

4.5 Graphical illustrations

Various cost behaviour patterns are illustrated in the graphs below.

(a) **Variable cost:** direct materials, the purchase price per unit being constant

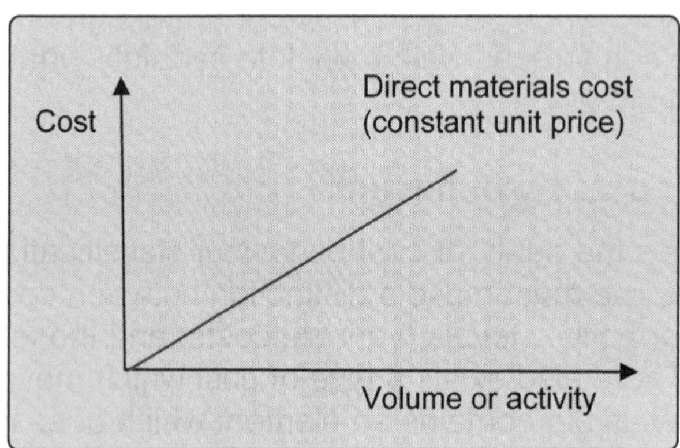

(b) **Fixed cost:** rent of factory payable under a long-term lease

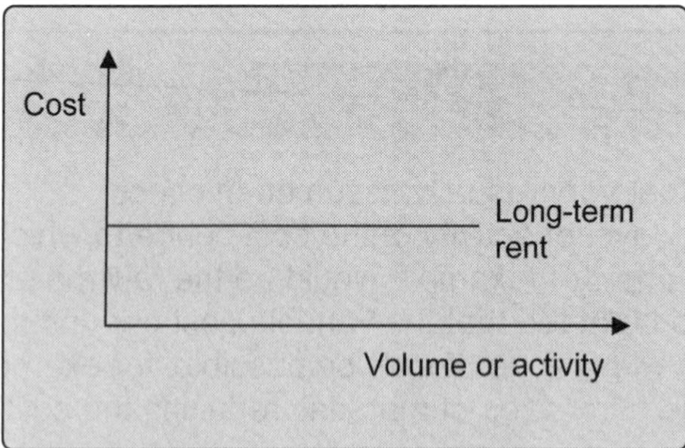

(c) **Stepped costs**

(i) Canteen cost where additional assistants are required as increases in activity result in larger numbers of factory personnel.

(ii) Rent of premises, additional accommodation eventually being required.

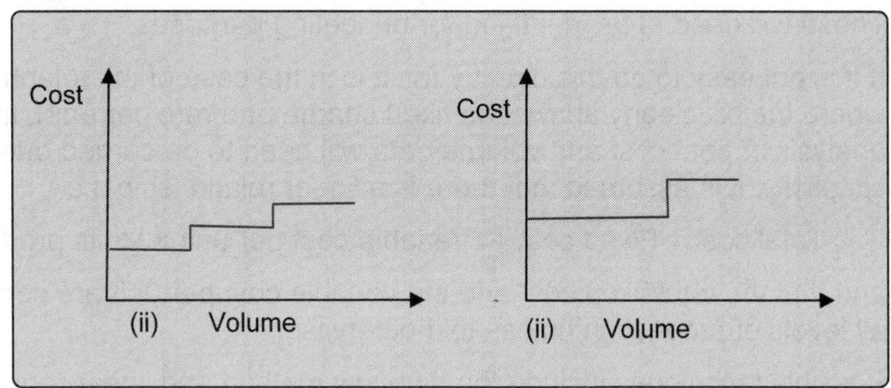

(d) **Semi-variable costs**

(i) Direct materials cost (trade discount at higher levels of activity).

(ii) Salesmen's remuneration (salary with added commission from a certain level of activity).

(iii) Electricity charges comprising a fixed standing charge and variable unit charge.

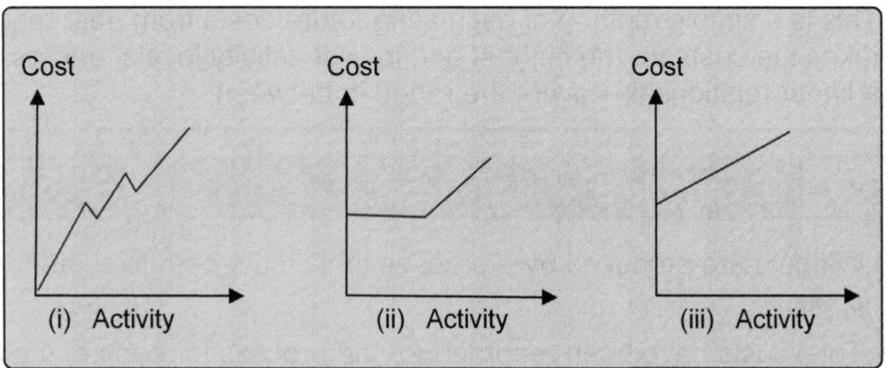

The common approach is as follows:

(a) Treat as variable those costs which change by regular steps.

(b) Treat as fixed those costs which only change at wide intervals of activity; this recognises that review will be required if there is a permanent change in the normal level of activity.

5 Cost estimation

5.1 Introduction

As we have seen, some costs may have both fixed and variable elements. These will need to be identified for budgeting purposes.

If it is not easy to do this directly (as it is in the case of the telephone cost, where the bill clearly shows the fixed charge and rate per unit), then an analysis of past cost and volume data will need to be carried out. For simplicity, it is assumed that there is a linear relationship, i.e.:

Total cost = Fixed cost + (Variable cost per unit × Units produced)

and that the total fixed cost and the variable cost per unit are constant at all levels of production unless told otherwise.

Possible techniques include the high/low method and linear regression. Linear regression (which we referred to in Chapter 6) is a statistical technique which estimates a line of best fit for the observed costs at various activity levels and derives a total cost equation to identify variable and fixed costs at any activity level within the normal range. You will not be expected to apply this method in the exam. A simpler method is the high/low method.

5.2 The high/low method

This is a simple method of estimating future costs from past results. It takes the costs for the highest and lowest activity levels, and assumes that a linear relationship covers the range in between.

Example 8

Widgets are produced by a process that incurs both fixed and variable costs.

Total costs have been recorded for the process for each of the last six months as follows.

Month	Output (units)	Total cost £
1	4,500	33,750
2	3,500	30,500
3	5,100	34,130
4	6,200	38,600
5	5,700	38,000
6	4,100	31,900

As a check on the accuracy of the calculations, at the 6,200 units level:

	£
Total costs	38,600
Variable cost (6,200 × £3)	(18,600)
Fixed costs	20,000

(a) Therefore the estimated fixed cost element is £20,000 and the estimated variable cost is £3 per unit.

(b) At an output level of 6,000 units the total estimated cost would be:

	£
Variable cost (6,000 × £3)	18,000
Fixed cost	20,000
Total cost	38,000

5.3 Advantages of high-low method

- Simple to operate.
- Easy to understand.

5.4 Disadvantages of high-low method

The problem with the high-low method is that it could give a completely inaccurate result. This is because we are only considering two sets of data, and ignoring all of the others.

It is possible that the points we have chosen are completely unrepresentative of the rest of the data. This is a distinct possibility since we have chosen the two points at the extreme ends of the activity range.

At these levels it is more likely that operating conditions will be atypical compared with more normal output. One way around this problem is to choose the 'next to highest' and 'next to lowest' figures, but this destroys some of the simplicity of the model.

6 Dealing with uncertainty

6.1 Introduction

Inherent in any attempt to predict what will happen in the future is the issue that, the future is very difficult to predict because there is so much uncertainty. There are tools that an organisation can use to help understand and deal with that uncertainty. The following are some of the methods an organisation can use:

- Rolling budgets
- Sensitivity analysis
- Simulation
- Expected values.

Rolling budgets and expected values are covered in more detail in other chapters. We will briefly look at sensitivity analysis and simulation now

6.2 Sensitivity analysis

Sensitivity analysis considers the impact of using different forecasts. It takes each uncertain factor in turn, and calculates the change that would be necessary in that factor before the organisation would be concerned by it changing. Typically, it involves posing 'what-if' questions. By using this technique it is possible to establish which estimates (variables) are more critical than others in affecting a decision.

This is closely allied to the scenario planning or 'what-if analysis' technique. For example, if the employees pay level is not yet determined for the budget period, then alternative budgets based on (say) current pay levels, increases of 2%, or increases of 4% could be drafted to evaluate the impact.

Strengths of sensitivity analysis:

- There is no complicated theory to understand.
- Information will be presented to management in a form which facilitates subjective judgement to decide the likelihood of the various possible outcomes considered.
- It identifies areas which are crucial to the success of the project. If the project is chosen, those areas can be carefully monitored.

Weaknesses of sensitivity analysis

- It assumes that changes to variables can be made independently, e.g. material prices will change independently of other variables. Simulation allows us to change more than one variable at a time.
- It only identifies how far a variable needs to change; it does not look at the probability of such a change.
- It provides information on the basis of which decisions can be made but it does not point to the correct decision directly.

6.3 Simulation

Simulation is a modelling technique that shows the effect of more than one variable changing at the same time.

It is often used in capital investment appraisal.

The Monte Carlo simulation method uses random numbers and probability statistics. It can include all random events that might affect the success or failure of a proposed project – for example, changes in material prices, labour rates, market size, selling price, investment costs or inflation.

The model identifies key variables in a decision: costs and revenues, say. Random numbers are then assigned to each variable in a proportion in accordance with the underlying probability distribution. For example, if the most likely outcomes are thought to have a 50% probability, optimistic outcomes a 30% probability and pessimistic outcomes a 20% probability, random numbers, representing those attributes, can be assigned to costs and revenues in those proportions.

A powerful computer is then used to repeat the decision many times and give management a view of the likely range and level of outcomes. Depending on the management's attitude to risk, a more informed decision can be taken.

This helps to model what is essentially a one-off decision using many possible repetitions. It is only of any real value, however, if the underlying probability distribution can be estimated with some degree of confidence.

There are major **drawbacks** of simulation:

- It is not a technique for making a decision, only for obtaining more information about the possible outcomes.
- Models can become extremely complex.
- The time and costs involved in their construction can be more than is gained from the improved decisions.
- Probability distributions may be difficult to formulate.

Example 9

Simulation for a chain of betting shops would be particularly useful on an operational level for analysing the possible implications of a single event, such as a major horse race or football match:

- Possible outcomes are easy to identify (e.g. win, lose, draw, 2–1, 3–0, etc)
- Quoted odds can help estimate probabilities
- The outcomes of the simulation could be used to assess impact on cash flow, whether bets should be laid off with other betting agents to reduces risk, etc.

Simulation could also be used for wider strategic analysis such as for assessing the possibility and implications of stricter anti-gambling legislation.

6.4 Regular reforecasting

Another method could be to update forecasts regularly to ensure that recent events are taken into account. As the initial forecasts may be completed well in advance of the budget period, it would make sense to see if they are still valid as the budget period approaches. For example a sales forecast based on trend analysis may initially be developed using historical data that ceases a year before the budget period.

By reforecasting using more recent sales data as it becomes available, the managers can reassure themselves that the forecast being used is still valid, or if not they can make appropriate changes to their plans.

7 Flexing budgets

7.1 Variable and fixed costs

In connection with expense budgeting, the budget working sheets should include some indication of the 'basis of variability' of each item of cost.

The most common general bases of variability of costs are in line with sales or the volume of productive output. In some systems of budgetary control, therefore, costs are divided between those which tend to vary with the output or sales achieved, and those which tend to remain fixed regardless of sales or the volume of output over an expected range of volumes.

7.2 Flexed budgets

This distinction having been established then, for variable costs, it is possible to establish in any period an allowable level of cost appropriate to the output actually achieved. This new level is known as the budget allowance for that volume of output. This is also known as a flexed budget. The total variance from the original budget figure will then be divided into two parts:

- The difference between the original budget and the budget allowance, assumed to arise from the nature of the business. This is sometimes referred to as an 'activity variance' and may be excluded from sectional control reports.
- The difference between the budget allowance and the actual cost incurred. This, by definition, should not have occurred and might be thought of as the 'controllable variance' of the manager concerned.

Example 10

	Budget	Actual
Sales volume	100 units	90 units
Sales value	£1,000	£990
Variable costs	£500	£495
Fixed costs	£200	£210
Profit	£300	£285

The Finance Director wishes to blame someone for the fact that profit is down by £15: "It is obvious who is to blame. Sales are below target and fixed costs have not been controlled."

In the example above, it is futile to compare the actual variable costs with the budget. To do so suggests that the manager is doing better than budget, but actual volume is below budget, so costs should be lower. It is vital to produce a revised budget to use for comparison.

This does not mean that the original budget is useless. It merely means that in order to analyse the £15 difference, it is important to **start by removing the impact of volume changes** on the various headings which are affected by it.

	Budget	Revised budget	Actual
Sales volume	100 units	90 units	90 units
Sales value	£1,000	£900	£990
Variable costs	£500	£450	£495
Fixed costs	£200	£200	£210
Profit	£300	£250	£285

This recalculates the budget using **actual volume, but budget prices** and shows that the expected profit for 90 units is £250. Thus the impact on profit of the fall in sales is a reduction of £50 and this can be identified as sales volume variance £(50). Now, the other variances can be calculated.

8 Flexible budgets

8.1 Uses

A system incorporating budget allowances is referred to as flexible budgetary control.

This idea has been seized on by writers of textbooks and setters of examination questions and converted into the concept of 'flexible budgets'. In other words, at the beginning of the year there should be a schedule showing what the various cost allowances would be at various levels of output. The use of spreadsheets makes this very simple.

Example 11

You are the budget officer of Majestic Limited, which produces a single product. The following forecasts have been prepared from the best information available for the production costs to be incurred at the highest and lowest production levels likely to be encountered in any particular period.

	Production level	
	10,000 units	**20,000 units**
	£	£
Direct materials	2,000	4,000
Direct labour	15,000	30,000
Warehouse rental	8,000	13,000
Machine maintenance	2,400	3,000
Factory rent, rates, etc	4,000	4,000
Factory power	4,500	6,300

Machine maintenance is under contract with the machine supplier. The period cost is based upon the production level and is charged at £15 per 100 units, with a minimum charge payable of £2,400 per period.

Warehouse rent is fixed per warehouse per period. One warehouse is sufficient to cope with the storage demands up to 12,500 units. Should production exceed this level, a further warehouse will need to be rented for the period, at an additional cost of £5,000. This will give sufficient space to cover the highest production level.

All other variable costs and the variable part of semi-variable costs follow constant linear patterns.

Required:

Prepare a set of flexible budgets which show the budget allowance for the period for the following activity levels: 10,000 units; 12,500 units; 15,000 units; 17,500 units; 20,000 units.

Solution

The following steps illustrate a good approach to such a question. You may like to try preparing your own answer as we go through before looking at our solution at the end.

1 **Draw up a proforma statement**

This will have the cost headings listed down the left-hand side and columns headed up with each production level; in this case, five columns will be needed. It is also a good idea to have an additional column next to the cost headings in which to insert references to workings (e.g. 'Note 2' etc).

The statement should also have a heading.

2 **Insert known figures**

You have already been given the costs for the lowest and highest production levels, so put these in.

3 **Deal with the particular costs you have further information about (in this case, machine maintenance and warehouse rental)**

Machine maintenance

This cost will be fixed up to a certain production level (to cover the minimum charge) and will then rise linearly (at £15 per 100 units or £0.15 per unit).

The level up to which the minimum charge is applicable is £2,400/£0.15 = 16,000 units. So the charge for the 12,500 and 15,000 unit levels will also be £2,400.

For 17,500 units the charge will be 17,500 × £0.15 = £2,625 and for 20,000 units it will reach 20,000 × £0.15 = £3,000 (as given).

These can now be inserted in your statement.

Warehouse rental

This is an example of a 'stepped' fixed cost. It will remain at £8,000 for all levels up to (and including) 12,500 units, and will rise to £13,000 for all levels above this.

These can now be inserted in your statement.

4 **Deal with remaining costs**

These will be strictly fixed, strictly variable or semi-variable.

Strictly fixed costs

These will be obvious – here, factory rent and rates must be fixed within the range, as the costs for the lowest and highest production levels are the same.

Insert this fixed cost across all levels on your statement.

Strictly variable costs

Usually direct materials and direct labour costs will be strictly variable. You can see here that, as the production level doubles, so does the cost. Use either level to determine the cost per unit.

Direct materials: £2,000/10,000 = £0.20 per unit

Direct labour: £15,000/10,000 = £1.50 per unit

Use these to calculate the appropriate cost for the other levels and insert them on the statement.

Semi-variable costs

These costs will not be the same for the two extreme levels, but they will not increase proportionately from one to the other either. If you are not sure, calculate a cost per unit at the two levels; these will not be the same, as they would be if the cost were strictly variable.

In this example, the power cost is semi-variable. It can be split between the fixed and variable elements by the 'high-low' method which we saw in a previous chapter.

	Production level (units)	**Cost £**
Highest	20,000	6,300
Lowest	10,000	4,500
Change	+10,000	+1,800

Variable cost = £1,800/10,000 = £0.18 per unit

Using the lowest level to determine the fixed cost element:

	£
Total cost	4,500
Less: Variable element (10,000 × £0.18)	(1,800)
Fixed element	2,700

So for each level, the total power cost can be calculated as follows.

£2,700 + (£0.18 × Production level)

For example, the cost for 15,000 units will be as follows.

£2,700 + (£0.18 × 15,000) = £5,400

The remaining costs can be calculated in this way and the statement completed, as below.

Budget allowance for activity levels between 10,000 and 20,000

	Production level				
	10,000 units	12,500 units	15,000 units	17,500 units	20,000 units
	£	£	£	£	£
Direct materials	2,000	2,500	3,000	3,500	4,000
Direct labour	15,000	18,750	22,500	26,250	30,000
Warehouse rental	8,000	8,000	13,000	13,000	13,000
Machine maintenance	2,400	2,400	2,400	2,625	3,000
Factory rent, rates	4,000	4,000	4,000	4,000	4,000
Factory power	4,500	4,950	5,400	5,850	6,300
Total	35,900	40,600	50,300	55,225	60,300

8.2 Budgetary control statement

A typical continuation to the above example would be the requirement to produce a budgetary control statement (or budget report) given some actual data for the period.

Example 12

In period 3 Majestic Limited produced 17,500 units and incurred the following costs.

	£
Direct materials	3,200
Direct labour	29,750
Warehouse rental	13,000
Machine maintenance	3,150
Factory rent, rates, etc	3,800
Factory power	4,720

Produce a budgetary control statement to compare these actual costs with the flexed costs that would be budgeted for.

Solution

The budgetary control statement will compare the actual costs with the relevant budget allowances from the flexible budget to highlight variances.

In this case, the relevant flexed budget is that for 17,500 units.

We have also included the original budget (for 20,000 units). This is good practice, as it is probable that a lot of managers who see the budgetary control statement will have had access to the original budget. If they don't see those figures on the statement, they will think they were given the wrong information before, or else they will think they are being given the wrong information now!

	20,000 units original budget (£)	17,500 units flexed budget (£)	17,500 units actual (£)	Flexed to actual variance (£)
Direct materials	4,000	3,500	3,200	300 F
Direct labour	30,000	26,250	29,750	3,500 A
Warehouse rental	13,000	13,000	13,000	–
Machine maintenance	3,000	2,625	3,150	525 A
Factory rent, rates, etc	4,000	4,000	3,800	200 F
Factory power	6,300	5,850	4,720	1,130 F
	60,300	55,225	57,620	2,395 A

You may then be asked to comment on the variances, suggesting any further investigations or action that might be required.

Note that if the actual costs for output of 17,500 units were compared to the original budget of 20,000 units of output, the resulting variances would be meaningless.

Test your understanding 7

Visiguard Ltd is a division of Alton Products plc. It makes a single product, the Raider. Just over a year ago, the chief executive of Alton Products, Michaela Green, was concerned to find that Visiguard was budgeting to make only £20,000 profit in the year to 31 May 20X0. As a result, she imposed her own budget on the division. Her revised budget assumed:

- increased sales volume of the Raider
- increased selling prices and
- that suppliers would agree to reduce the cost of the material used in the Raider by 10%.

The only other changes to the original budget arose solely as a result of the increased volume in the revised budget.

The original budget and the revised budget imposed by Michaela Green are reproduced below, together with the actual results for the year to 31 May 2000.

Visiguard Limited

Budgeted and actual operating statements for one year ended 31 May 20X0

	Original budget	Revised budget	Actual results
	£	£	£
Sales and production volume	10,000	11,000	11,600
	£	£	£
Revenue	1,400,000	1,760,000	1,844,400
Variable materials	400,000	396,000	440,800
Production and administrative labour	580,000	630,000	677,600
Light, heat and power	160,000	164,000	136,400
Fixed overheads	240,000	240,000	259,600
Budgeted profit	20,000	330,000	330,000

Required:

Using the information provided in the two budgets, calculate the following:

(a) The unit selling price of the Raider in the revised budget.

(b) The material cost per Raider in the revised budget.

(c) The variable cost of production and administrative labour per Raider.

(d) The fixed cost of production and administrative labour.

(e) The variable cost of light, heat and power per Raider.

(f) The fixed cost of light, heat and power.

Data

On receiving the actual results for the year, Michaela Green states that they prove that her revised budget motivated managers to produce better results.

Required:

Write a memo to Michaela Green. Your memo should:

(a) Use the information calculated before to prepare a flexed budget statement for Visiguard including any variances.

(b) Identify TWO situations where an imposed budget might be preferable to one prepared with the participation of managers.

(c) Briefly discuss whether or not her requirement that material costs be reduced would have motivated the managers of Visiguard.

(d) Identify TWO ways in which profit could have increased without additional effort by the managers of Visiguard.

Test your understanding 8

Rivermede Ltd makes a single product called the Fasta. Last year, Stephanie Jones, the managing director of Rivermede Ltd, attended a course on budgetary control. As a result, she agreed to revise the way budgets were prepared in the company. Rather than imposing targets for managers, she encouraged participation by senior managers in the preparation of budgets.

An initial budget was prepared but Mike Fisher, the sales director, felt that the budgeted sales volume was set too high. He explained that setting too high a budgeted sales volume would mean his sales staff would be demotivated because they would not be able to achieve that sales volume. Stephanie Jones agreed to use the revised sales volume suggested by Mike Fisher.

Both the initial and revised budgets are reproduced below complete with the actual results for the year ended 31 May 20X3.

Rivermede Ltd – Budgeted and actual costs for the year ended 31 May 20X3

	Original budget	Revised budget	Actual results	Variances from revised budget
Fasta production and sales (units)	24,000	20,000	22,000	2,000 (F)
	£	£	£	£
Variable costs				
Material	216,000	180,000	206,800	26,800 (A)
Labour	288,000	240,000	255,200	15,200 (A)
Semi-variable costs				
Heat, light and power	31,000	27,000	33,400	6,400 (A)
Fixed costs				
Rent, rates and depreciation	40,000	40,000	38,000	2,000 (F)
	575,000	487,000	533,400	46,400 (A)

Assumptions in the two budgets

1 No change in input prices.

2 No change in the quantity of variable inputs per Fasta.

As the management accountant at Rivermede Ltd, one of your tasks is to check that invoices have been properly coded. On checking the actual invoices for heat, light and power for the year to 31 May 20X3, you find that one invoice for £7,520 had been incorrectly coded. The invoice should have been coded to materials.

Required:

(a) Using the information in the original and revised budgets, identify:

- the variable cost of material and labour per Fasta
- the fixed and unit variable cost within heat, light and power.

(b) Prepare a flexed budget, including variances, for Rivermede Ltd after correcting for the miscoding of the invoice.

Data

On receiving your flexed budget statement, Stephanie Jones states that the total adverse variance is much less than the £46,400 shown in the original statement. She also draws your attention to the actual sales volume being greater than in the revised budget. She believes these results show that a participative approach to budgeting is better for the company and wants to discuss this belief at the next board meeting. Before doing so, Stephanie Jones asks for your comments.

Required:

Write a memo to Stephanie Jones. Your memo should:

(a) **Briefly** explain why the flexed budgeting variances differ from those in the original statement given.

(b) Give TWO reasons why a favourable cost variance may have arisen other than through the introduction of participative budgeting.

(c) Give TWO reasons why the actual sales volume compared with the revised budget's sales volume may not be a measure of improved motivation following the introduction of participative budgeting.

Test your understanding 9

You are an accounting technician employed by Telford plc. Telford has a subsidiary, Shifnal Ltd that makes one product, the Omega. Bart Ceglowski, the Finance Director of Telford, has asked you to prepare a statement analysing the performance of Shifnal Ltd. He gives you a copy of the company's latest operating statement and tells you the assumptions made about costs when preparing the statement.

Shifnal Ltd: operating statement – 12 months ended 30 November 2003

	Budget	**Actual**
Number of Omegas produced and sold	120,000	95,000
	£000	£000
Revenue	4,800	3,990
Variable expenses		
Material A	480	456
Material B	840	665
Material C	360	266

Semi-variable expenses		
Light, heat and power	290	249
Water	212	182
Stepped expenses		
Labour	200	168
Maintenance	60	54
Fixed expenses		
Rent and rates	360	355
Distribution expenses	600	620
Administrative expenses	300	280
Operating profit	1,098	695

Assumptions made

- Budgeted semi-variable expenses
  - The variable cost of light, heat and power was £2.00 per Omega.
  - The fixed cost of water was £20,000 per year.
- Budgeted stepped expenses
  - For every £5,000 spent on labour, Shifnal could produce up to 3,000 Omegas.
  - For every £10,000 spent on maintenance, Shifnal could produce up to 20,000 Omegas.
- The budgeted selling price per Omega was the same throughout the year.
- There were no inventories of any kind.

Required:

(a) Calculate the budgeted selling price per Omega.

(b) Calculate the budgeted variable cost per Omega of:

(c) (i) material A

(ii) material B

(iii) material C.

(c) Calculate the:

(i) budgeted fixed cost of light, heat and power

(ii) budgeted variable cost of water per Omega.

(d) Prepare a statement showing Shifnal's actual results, the flexible budget and any variances.

Test your understanding 10

Excelsior Manufacturing Company

Excelsior Manufacturing Company produces a single product on an assembly line. As budget officer you have prepared the following production budgets from the best information available, to represent the extremes of high and low volume of production likely to be encountered by the company over a three month period.

	Production of 4,000 units	**Production of 8,000 units**
	£	£
Direct materials	80,000	160,000
Indirect materials	12,000	20,000
Direct labour	50,000	100,000
Power	18,000	24,000
Repairs	20,000	30,000
Supervision	20,000	36,000
Rent, insurance and rates	9,000	9,000

Supervision is a 'step function'. One supervisor is employed for all production levels up to and including 5,000 units. For higher levels of production, an assistant supervisor (£16,000) is also required. For power, a minimum charge is payable on all production up to and including 6,000 units. For production above this level, there is an additional variable charge based on the power consumed.

Other variable and semi-variable costs are incurred evenly over the production range.

Required:

(a) Prepare a set of flexible budgets for presentation to the production manager to cover the following levels of production over a period of three months:

(i) 4,000 units

(ii) 5,000 units

(iii) 6,000 units

(iv) 7,000 units

(v) 8,000 units

(b) During the three months July to September (covering most of the summer holiday period) 5,000 units were produced. Costs incurred during the three-month period were as follows:

	£
Direct materials	110,000
Indirect materials	14,000
Direct labour	70,000
Power	18,000
Repairs	30,000
Supervision	20,000
Rent, insurance and rates	8,000

Note that **price variances** have been eliminated from the figures for direct and indirect materials and **rate variances** have been eliminated from the labour and supervision costs.

Required:

You are preparing a budget report for presentation to the production manager. For each variance suggest any further investigations which might be required and any action which might be taken by the production manager.

9 Control

9.1 Feedback control

The budgetary control statement in the previous section is an example of feedback control.

Feedback control is defined as 'the measurement of differences between planned outputs and actual outputs achieved, and the modification of subsequent action and/or plans to achieve future required results'. This is the most common type of control system.

Positive feedback is feedback taken to reinforce a deviation from standard. The inputs or processes would not be altered.

Negative feedback is feedback taken to reverse a deviation from standard. This could be by amending the inputs or process, so that the system reverts to a steady state. For example, a machine may need to be reset over time to its original settings.

Example 13

A sales manager receives monthly control reports about sales values. The budgeted sales for the year to 31 December are £600,000 in total. At the end of April the manager might receive the following feedback control report.

Sales report for April

	Month			**Cumulative**		
	Budget	**Actual**	**Variance**	**Budget**	**Actual**	**Variance**
Product	£000	£000	£000	£000	£000	£000
P1	35	38	3 (F)	90	94	4 (F)
P2	20	14	6 (A)	50	39	11 (A)
P3	25	23	2 (A)	50	45	5 (A)
Total	80	75	5 (A)	190	178	12 (A)

9.2 Feedforward control

A feedforward control system operates by comparing budgeted results against a forecast. Control action is triggered by differences between budgeted and forecast results.

Feedforward control is control based on forecast results. In other words, if forecast is bad, control action is taken before the actual results come through

Example 14

An alternative to the feedback control report in the previous example would be the sales manager might be presented with a feedforward control report, as follows:

Sales report for April

	Budget	**Latest forecast for the year**	**Expected variance**
Product	£000	£000	£000
P1	240	250	10 (F)
P2	150	120	30 (A)
P3	210	194	16 (A)
Total	600	564	36 (A)

Notice the second column is now a forecast for the year, so is forward looking, and the variance has now become an expected variance. This would be the latest forecast and expected variance if no action was taken.

The use of a feed-forward control system means that corrective action can be taken to avoid expected adverse variances.

Feedforward control may be particularly appropriate for the capital expenditure budget because capital expenditure is often long-term in nature. It is more useful to compare actual costs to forecast completion costs so that action can be taken when a project is in progress rather than waiting for completion.

It is also often associated with cash budgets as the cash budget may highlight an expected future shortfall or surplus, so corrective action may be taken to avoid the issue.

10 Summary

In this chapter, we have taken a specific look at how limiting factors impact the budgets produced. We have also considered some of the core aspects of budgeting from cost behaviour and the high low method to classification of costs.

We also considered how uncertainty can be dealt with in the budget setting process, discussing topics such as simulation and sensitivity analysis as well as reforecasting.

Finally, we introduced the key concept of using a budget for control by looking at variances based on flexed or flexible budget. We will take this control aspect further in the coming chapters, so it is important to make sure you are comfortable with what we have introduced here.

Test your understanding answers

Test your understanding 1

	Workings	Units
Units that require testing	given	**125,000**
Units that can be tested internally	9,000 × 12 =	**108,000**
Units to be tested by an alternative source	125,000 – 108,000 =	**17,000**

Test your understanding 2

The number of units that can be produced in total is	150,000/6 =	**25,000**	units
There is a shortfall of	Kgs required = 32,000 × 6 = 192,000 192,000 – 150,000 =	**42,000**	kgs
This is equivalent to	42,000/6 =	**7,000**	units

Test your understanding 3

How many labour hours are available in the period?	217 × 40	**8,680**	hours
How many machine hours are available in the period?	15 × 800	**12,000**	hours
What is the requirement of each of the following to meet the demand?			
Labour hours	30,000 × 1.75	**52,500**	hours
Machine hours	30,000 × 1	**30,000**	hours
Material	30,000 × 0.75	**22,500**	kg
The budgeted production level for the period will be:	Working 1	**4,960**	units

Working 1

There is the least amount of labour hours and that is the resource each unit requires the most of.

The maximum amount that can be produced in the period is therefore: 8,680 labour hours divided by 1.75 labour hours per unit = 4,960 units.

Test your understanding 4

Your organisation

MEMORANDUM

To: Marketing Manager

From: Assistant Management Accountant

Date: 12 July 2016

Subject: Budgetary planning process

As requested, I provide below answers to your queries about the budgetary planning process.

(a) **The key factor**

Otherwise known as the principal budget factor or limiting factor, the key factor is the factor which limits the activity of an organisation. In our organisation it is sales volume, since there is a limit to how much we can sell. However, it is possible for other factors to be key factors, especially in the short term. Examples could be cash, machine capacity or skilled labour.

The determination of the key factor is important in the budgetary process because this is the budget which must be prepared first. Then all other budgets can be co-ordinated with this budget.

For example, once the sales budget has been determined, this will provide the basis for the production budget and for other budgets such as the materials purchasing budget and the cash budget.

(b) A number of steps can be taken to achieve co-ordination in the budgetary planning process, including the following:

(i) Set up a budget committee which consists of representatives from all parts of the organisation. Regular meetings of this committee should ensure that each part of the organisation is aware of what all other parts are doing.

(ii) Give one person the overall responsibility for ensuring that budgets are prepared on time and that they take into account all relevant factors. This person is often called the budget officer and will usually chair the budget committee.

(iii) Provide a timetable to all those involved in the budgetary process, detailing who is responsible for preparing each budget and when it must be prepared. This should reduce the risk of bottlenecks in the budgetary process and will co-ordinate the order of budget preparation.

(iv) Ensure that all those involved in the budgetary process have access to the budget manual which include the budget timetable mentioned above, instructions on completing the budget planning forms and proforma budgets, details on key assumptions to be made in the planning process (such as the inflation rate and exchange rate), links to the other budgets being drawn up and so on.

(v) Provide regular feedback on the progress of budget preparation.

The key to co-ordinated budget preparation is communication.

Test your understanding 5

(a) **Production budget in units**

	Period 1	Period 2	Period 3	Period 4	Period 5
Demand	5,700	5,700	6,840	6,460	6,080
Less Opening inventory	(1,330)	(855)	(1,026)	(969)	(912)
Add Closing inventory	855	1,026	969	912	
Production	5,225	5,871	6,783	6,403	

(b) **Material purchases budget (litres)**

		Period 1	Period 2	Period 3	Period 4
Production (units)		5,225	5,871	6,783	6,403
Material required (production × 6 litres)	(i)	31,350	35,226	40,698	38,418
Maximum material available	(ii)		34,000	34,000	34,000
Shortfall of material available (i – ii)			1,226	6,698	4,418
Reschedule purchases		1,226	–1,226		
Material purchases from Contrax plc	(iii)	32,576	34,000	34,000	34,000
Material purchases from outside supplier	(iv)			6,698	4,418

(c) **Material purchases budget (£)**

	Period 1	**Period 2**	**Period 3**	**Period 4**
	£	£	£	£
Material purchases from Contrax plc (c) × £8	260,608	272,000	272,000	272,000
Material purchases from outside supplier (d) × £12			80,376	53,016
	260,608	272,000	352,376	325,016

(d) **Labour hours budget**

	Period 1	**Period 2**	**Period 3**	**Period 4**
Production (units of Omega)	5,225	5,871	6,783	6,403
Standard hours required (units × 2 hours)	10,450	11,742	13,566	12,806
Inefficiency (5/95 × standard hours)	550	618	714	674
Total labour hours required	11,000	12,360	14,280	13,480
Basic hours (78 employees × 4 weeks × 40 hours)	12,480	12,480	12,480	12,480
Overtime	Nil	Nil	1,800	1,000

(e) **Labour budget (£)**

	Period 1	**Period 2**	**Period 3**	**Period 4**
Basic wage (£160 × 78 employees × 4 weeks)	49,920	49,920	49,920	49,920
Overtime (Overtime hours × £6)			10,800	6,000
	49,920	49,920	60,720	55,920

MEMO

To: Adriana Jonas

From: Management Accountant

Date: X-X-XX

Subject: Cost savings

Following our recent discussions and your observations regarding the level of overtime and the material supplier, I list my comments below.

(a) **Immediate cost savings**

The material available in period 1 is 34,000 litres, whereas our requirement is 32,576 litres. A further 1,424 litres is available from Contrax and could result in a saving in one of two ways.

(b) By bringing production forward to period 1, there would be a saving of £5,696 because of the reduction in purchases, at a later date, from the alternative supplier – 1,424 litres × £4 = £5,696.

The same saving is possible by simply buying the 1,424 litres in advance to be used in a later period.

(c) **Continuing difficulties**

If minimum demand for the product continues at 5,700 per four-week period, the material requirements will be 34,200 litres per period, which suggests that the material constraint is a longer term problem.

The planned labour hours for minimum demand would be 12,000 per period, even if the inefficiency problem continues. However, with 12,480 hours available each period, this constraint is considered short-term.

(d) **Possible long-term cost savings**

In the longer term it may be possible to renegotiate the stock requirements with Advanced Industries. This would allow a lower investment in finished stocks.

However, we would need to satisfy them that we could supply them on time if their forecast requirement were inaccurate. One way of dealing with this would be flexible working, whereby excess demand was met by working unpaid overtime and allowing time off, paid in lieu, when demand was low.

Test your understanding 6

(a) (i) Number of production days in quarter 1:

12 weeks × 5 days = 60 days

(ii) Units of closing finished stock:

Exe 930 × $\frac{8}{60}$ = 124 units

Wye 1,320 × $\frac{9}{60}$ = 198 units

(iii) Labour hours in the period before overtime:

12 weeks × 35 hours × 46 employees = 19,320 hours

(b) (i) **Production budget for the 12 weeks ending 24 March 20X0**

	Exe	**Wye**
Budgeted sales (units)	930	1,320
Add Closing inventories	124	198
Less Opening inventories	(172)	(257)
Production of good units	882	1,261
Faulty production (Exe = 2/98 × 882, Wye = 3/97 × 1,261)	18	39
Gross production before faults	900	1,300

(ii) **Material purchases budget for the 12 weeks ending 24 March 20X0**

	Litres
Material requirement for Exe production (6 litres × 900 Exe)	5,400
Material requirement for Wye production (9 litres × 1,300 Wye)	11,700
Total material required for production	17,100
Add Closing raw material stock (5 days/60 days × 17,100 litres)	1,425
Less Opening raw material stock	(1,878)
Material purchases (litres)	16,647
Total material cost (16,647 × £15)	£249,705

(iii) **Production labour budget for the 12 weeks ending 24 March 20X0**

	Hours
Budgeted hours required for Exe production (12 hours × 900)	10,800
Budgeted hours required for Wye production (7 hours × 1,300)	9,100
Total planned labour hours	19,900
Hours available before overtime	19,320
Overtime hours	580
Cost of normal hours (19,320 × £6)	£115,920
Cost of overtime (580 × £6 × 130%)	£4,524
Total labour cost	£120,444

(c) Finance and other savings per quarter

Finance and other savings per quarter		£192
Exe	([172 – 124] × £4)	
Wye	([257 – 198] × £5)	£295
Raw material	([1,878 – 1,425] × £1)	£453
		£940

Test your understanding 7

(a) Revised budgeted selling price:

(£1,760,000/11,000)	£160

(b) Material cost per unit in revised budget:

(£396,000/11,000)	£36

(c) Variable cost of production and administrative labour – high/low method:

Increase in budgeted labour cost (£630,000 – £580,000)	£50,000
Increase in budgeted volume (11,000 – 10,000)	1,000
Variable cost of labour per unit (£50,000/1,000)	£50

(d) Fixed cost of production and administrative labour:

Total budgeted cost of labour for 11,000 units	£630,000
Variable cost of labour (11,000 × £50)	£550,000
Budgeted fixed cost of labour	£80,000

(e) Variable cost of light, heat and power – high/low method:

Increase in budgeted light, heat and power (£164,000 – £160,000)	£4,000
Increase in budgeted volume	1,000
Budgeted variable cost of light, heat and power per unit (£4,000/1,000)	£4

(f) Fixed cost of light, heat and power:

Total budgeted cost of light, heat and power for 11,000 units	£164,000
Variable cost of light, heat and power (11,000 × £4)	£44,000
Budgeted fixed cost of light, heat and power	£120,000

MEMO

To: Michela Green

From: Management Accountant

Date: 22 June 20X0

Subject: Motivation and performance

I attach a budgetary control statement for Visiguard based on the flexible budget technique and wish to make the following observations.

(a) **Visiguard Ltd – Flexible budgetary control statement for the year ended 31 May 20X0**

	Flexed budget	Actual results	Variances
Sales and production volume (units)	11,600	11,600	Nil
	£	£	£
Revenue (£160 × 11,600)	1,856,000	1,844,400	11,600 (A)
Variable materials (£36 × 11,600)	417,600	440,800	23,200 (A)
Production and administrative labour (£80,000 + [£50 × 11,600])	660,000	677,600	17,600 (A)
Light, heat and power 120,000 + [4 × 11,600]	166,400	136,400	30,000 (F)
Fixed overheads	240,000	259,600	19,600 (A)
Profit	372,000	330,000	42,000 (A)

(b) There is an assumption that a participative approach to budgets and budgetary control will improve management motivation and results. However, there are a number of situations where imposed budgets may be more effective than participative budgets. These include:

- Managers' objectives may not be those of the organisation as a whole.
- Managers do not have the training, skill or technical knowledge to set budgets.
- Managers would prefer not to set their own targets.
- Time constraint whereby full participation is not practicable.

(c) Setting of budgetary targets that are not achievable can be demotivating. If managers recognise this they are likely not even to attempt to achieve the target. Impossible targets can also bring into disrepute the whole planning process; and managers may question the validity and usefulness of the budgetary process.

This might have been the case in terms of the request to reduce material costs. If Visiguard do not have an alternative supplier, the managers may have little control over material prices.

(d) It does not always follow that improved performance compared to the original budget is because managers were motivated by the budget revision.

- Actual activity was greater than the agreed revision. This may have been due to the increased energy and motivation of managers. However, there may have been, outside the control of managers, a general increase in demand for the product.
- The only cost less than planned in the budget is light, heat and power. This may have been an inaccurate forecast or because weather conditions have been milder, thus reducing heating costs. It is unlikely that the power supplier has reduced costs.

Test your understanding 8

(a) **Calculation of unit variable costs – high/low method**

	High original budget	**Low Revised budget**	**Range**	**Variable unit cost**
Fasta units	24,000	20,000	4,000	
Variable costs	£	£	£	
Material	216,000	180,000	36,000	£9
Labour	288,000	240,000	48,000	£12
Semi-variable costs				
Heat, light and power	31,000	27,000	£4,000	£1

Analysis of heat, light and power

Variable cost (£1/unit)	£24,000	£20,000
Total cost	£31,000	£27,000
Fixed cost	£7,000	£7,000

(b) **Rivermede Ltd**

Flexible budgetary control statement for the year ended 31 May 20X3

	Flexed budget	**Actual results**	**Adjustment**	**Revised actual**	**Variance**
Production and sales (units)	22,000	22,000		22,000	
	£	£	£	£	£
Variable costs					
Material (W1)	198,000	206,800	7,520	214,320	16,320 (A)
Labour (W2)	264,000	255,200		255,200	8,800 (F)
Semi-variable costs					
Heat, light and power (W3)	29,000	33,400	(7,520)	25,880	3,120 (F)
Fixed costs					
Rent, rates and depreciation	40,000	38,000		38,000	2,000 (F)
	531,000	533,400		533,400	2,400 (A)

Workings for flexed budget:

(W1) Material	22,000 × £9
(W2) Labour	22,000 × £12
(W3) Heat, light and power	(22,000 × £1) + £7,000

MEMO

To: Stephanie Jones

From: Management Accountant

Date: 16 June 20X3

Subject: Flexible budgetary control

(a) The original operating statement compares an actual level of activity of 22,000 units with a revised forecast of 20,000 units. This is not a 'like with like' comparison and is of little use for management control purposes.

The flexible budget, however, informs on a 'like with like' comparison by giving an allowance for costs and revenue in relation to the actual level of activity achieved. The variances reported are therefore smaller and also are more meaningful. The reduction in these variances is not attributable to participative budgeting.

(b) There are a number of reasons why favourable cost variances may arise other than with the introduction of participative budgeting.

- A favourable variance may arise for a reason outside management's span of control.

  The variance on fixed expenditure relates to rent, rates and depreciation which are costs that are not controllable.

  A further example is that the fixed charge for heat, light and power may be different from planned.

- Managers may have deliberately inflated costs in the budget to improve their reported performance and potentially increase any performance related rewards payable.

(c) Similar reasons could be argued for the increase in sales volume.

- There could have been a general increase in demand without extra sales effort.

- The revision to the budget may have been too low. This may have been a genuine concern that the original target was not achievable. However, it may have been intentional, since by understating forecast demand, the actual performance looks better.

We should continue with participative budgeting but based on the flexible budgetary control technique.

Test your understanding 9

(a)	**Budgeted unit selling price:** £4,800,000/120,000		£40.00
(b)	**Budgeted variable cost of material**		
	(i)	**A:** £480,000/120,000	£4.00
	(ii)	**B:** £840,000/120,000	£7.00
	(iii)	**C:** £360,000/120,000	£3.00
(c)	(i)	**Budgeted fixed cost of light, heat and power**	
		Total budgeted cost	£290,000
		Variable cost: £2 × 120,000	£240,000
			£50,000

(ii) Budgeted variable cost of water

Budgeted total cost	£212,000
Budgeted fixed cost	£20,000
Total variable cost	£192,000
Unit variable cost (£192,000/120,000)	£1.60

(d) **Shifnal Ltd: Flexible budget statement year ended 30 November 20X3**

Omegas produced and sold	**Flexed budget**	**Actual**	**Variance**	
	95,000	95,000		
	£000	£000	£000	
Revenue (95,000 × £40)	3,800	3,990	190	(F)
Material A (95,000 × £4)	380	456	76	(A)
Material B (95,000 × £7)	665	665	–	(A)
Material C (95,000 × £3)	285	266	19	(F)
Light, heat and power (W1)	240	249	9	(A)
Water (W2)	172	182	10	(A)
Labour (W3)	160	168	8	(A)
Maintenance (W4)	50	54	4	(A)
Rent and rates	360	355	5	(F)
Distribution expenses	600	620	20	(A)
Administrative expenses	300	280	20	(F)
Operating profit	588	695	107	(F)

Workings

(W1) £50,000 + (£2.00 × 95,000) = £240,000

(W2) £20,000 + (£1.60 × 95,000) = £172,000

(W3) Up to 3,000 units cost £5,000 of labour

95,000 units require $\frac{95,000}{3,000}$ = 31.67 'groups' of labour 3,000

This is rounded to 32 as it is a stepped cost and you cannot employ part of a 'group'. Cost of labour = 32 × £5,000 = £160,000

(W4) 95,000/20,000 = 4.75. Round up, therefore cost is 5 × £10,000 = £50,000

Test your understanding 10

Excelsior Manufacturing Company

(a)

	Production level (units)				
	4,000	5,000	6,000	7,000	8,000
	£	£	£	£	£
Direct materials (W1)	80,000	100,000	120,000	140,000	160,000
Indirect materials (W2)	12,000	14,000	16,000	18,000	20,000
Direct labour (W3)	50,000	62,500	75,000	87,500	100,000
Power (W4)	18,000	18,000	18,000	21,000	24,000
Repairs (W5)	20,000	22,500	25,000	27,500	30,000
Supervision (W6)	20,000	20,000	36,000	36,000	36,000
Rent, insurance and rates	9,000	9,000	9,000	9,000	9,000
Total cost	209,000	246,000	299,000	339,000	379,000

Workings:

(W1) **Direct materials**

£80,000/4,000 units = £20 per unit

So at 5,000 units for example £20 × 5,000 = £100,000

(W2) **Indirect materials**

At 4,000 units the cost is £12,000 or £3 per unit but at 8,000 units the cost is £20,000 or £2.5 per unit. Since the costs are not rising linearly, the cost must be semi-variable.

For semi-variable costs use the high low method

Increase in cost (£20,000 – £12,000) = £8,000

Increase in volume (8,000 – 4,000) = 4,000

Cost per unit – £8,000/4,000 = £2

Fixed element at 4000 units = £12,000 – (4,000 × £2) = £4,000

So at 5,000 units for example £4,000 + (5,000 × £2) = £14,000

(W3) **Direct labour**

£50,000/4,000 units = £12.50 per unit

So at 5,000 units for example £12.50 × 5,000 = £62,500

(W4) **Power**

Minimum charge payable up to 6,000 units, therefore minimum charge is £18,000

At 8,000 units cost is £24,000, an increase of £6,000 for 2,000 units over minimum level or £6,000/2,000 = £3 per unit

So at 7,000 units for example £18,000 + £3 × (7,000 – 6,000) = £21,000

(W5) **Repairs**

At 4,000 units the cost is £20,000 or £5 per unit but at 8,000 units the cost is £30,000 or £3.75 per unit. Since the costs are not rising linearly, the cost must be semi-variable.

For semi-variable costs use the high low method

Increase in cost (£30,000 – £20,000) = £10,000

Increase in volume (8,000 – 4,000) = 4,000

Cost per unit – £10,000/4,000 = £2.50

Fixed element at 4000 units = £20,000 – (4,000 × £2.5) = £10,000

So at 5,000 units for example £10,000 + (5,000 × £2.5) = £22,500

(W6) **Supervision**

A stepped fixed cost, for 6,000 units and above cost is £20,000 = £16,000 = £36,000

(b)

	Budget	**Actual**	**Variance**
	£	**£**	**£**
Direct materials	100,000	110,000	10,000 (A)
Indirect materials	14,000	14,000	–
Direct labour	62,500	70,000	7,500 (A)
Power	18,000	18,000	–
Repairs	22,500	30,000	7,500 (A)
Supervision	20,000	20,000	–
Rent, insurance and rates	9,000	8,000	1,000 (F)
Total cost	246,000	270,000	24,000 (A)

Comments on variances

- Direct materials: more was used than expected. Possibly waste in production, poor quality materials, operatives need more training. Is a particular department or machine at fault?
- Direct labour: again more was used than expected. Investigate reasons. Excessive overtime (should not be needed at a low level of production)?
- Repairs: needs investigation. Possible exceptional item. Do some pieces of capital equipment need replacing?
- Rent, insurance and rates: this is probably a price variance. Is this a one-off item or does the budget need to be altered in future?

Standard costing and variances

10

Introduction

In this chapter, we examine how standard costs are set for the various inputs that go into production. This is called 'standard costing'.

We will also examine how and why the actual results may vary from the standard.

Assessments will tend to concentrate on the calculation of variances for sales, materials, labour, variable and fixed overheads and the intelligent interpretation of these variances.

ASSESSMENT CRITERIA

Standard costing (LO 2.2)

CONTENTS

1 Standard costing

1.1 Introduction

Standard costing provides detailed information to management as to why actual performance differs from expected performance.

Standard costing systems are widely used because they provide cost data which can be used for many different purposes, including the following:

(a) To assist in budget setting and evaluating performance.

(b) To act as a control device by highlighting those activities that do not conform to plan and thus alerting managers to those situations which may be 'out of control' and hence in need of corrective action.

(c) To provide a prediction of future costs to be used in decision-making.

(d) To simplify the task of tracing costs to products for inventory valuation.

(e) To provide a challenging target that individuals are motivated to achieve.

An effective standard costing system relies on standard cost reports, with variances clearly identified, presented in an intelligible form to management as part of the overall cost reporting cycle.

Definitions

A **standard cost** is a predetermined cost which is calculated from management's standards of efficient operation and the relevant necessary expenditure. It may be used as a basis for fixing selling prices, for valuing inventory and work in progress, and to provide control over actual costs through the process of variance analysis.

Standard costing is the preparation and use of standard costs, their comparison with actual costs, and the analysis of variances to their causes.

2 Methods of developing standards

2.1 The nature of standards

Whenever identical operations are performed, or identical products are manufactured time and time again, it should be possible to decide in advance not only what they are likely to cost but also what they ought to cost. In other words, it is possible to set a standard cost for each operation or product unit, taking account of:

(a) technical standards for the quantities of material to be used and the working time required

(b) cost standards for the material prices and hourly rates that should be paid.

2.2 Standards from past records

Past data can be used to predict future costs if operating conditions are fairly constant between past and future time periods. This method may not be appropriate for newly introduced operations.

The main disadvantage with this method is that past data may contain inefficiencies which would then be built into the standards.

2.3 Engineering standards

This involves engineers developing standards for materials, direct labour and variable overheads by studying the product and the production process, possibly with the help of time and motion studies. This method is particularly useful when managers are evaluating new products.

The main disadvantage is that engineering standards may be too tight as they may not allow for the behaviour of the workers.

3 Setting standards

3.1 Standard material usage

In setting material usage standards, the first stage is to define what quantity of material input is theoretically required to achieve one unit of measured output.

In most manufacturing operations the quantity or volume of product emerging will be less than the quantity of materials introduced. This type of waste is normal to most operations and the usage figure would be increased by an allowance for this normal waste.

3.2 Standard time allowed

The standard or allowed time for an operation is a realistic estimate of the amount of productive time required to perform that operation based on work study methods. It is normally expressed in standard hours.

Various allowances may be added to the theoretical operating time, to take account of operator fatigue and personal needs, and periodic activities such as machine setting, clearing up, regrinding tools and on-line quality inspection. An allowance may also be made for spoilt work, or for rectification of defects appearing in the course of processing.

3.3 Basic approach to price standards

When setting cost standards, there are two basic approaches:

(a) **To use the prices or rates which are current at the time the standards are set.**

This has the advantage that each standard is a clearly known fact. On the other hand, if prices are likely to change then the standards based on these prices will have limited value for planning purposes.

The standards would have to be revised in detail from time to time to ensure that they are up to date. If this is not done, then any differences between standard and actual costs are likely to be largely due to invalid standards.

(b) **To use a forecast of average prices or rates over the period for which the standard is to be used.**

This can postpone the need for revision, but has the disadvantages that the standard may never correspond with observed fact (so there will be a price variance on all transactions) and the forecast may be subject to significant error.

3.4 Material price standards

In setting material price standards, a particular item of material may be purchased from several suppliers at slightly different prices; which price should be adopted as standard? There are three possible approaches:

(a) **To identify the major supplier and to use their price as the standard**

This is particularly appropriate where there is no intention of buying large quantities from the alternative suppliers, but merely to use them as a means of ensuring continuity of supply should there be any delay or failure by the principal supplier.

(b) **To use the lowest quoted price as the standard**

This method can be used if it is desirable to put pressure on the buyer to obtain price reductions from other suppliers.

(c) **To forecast the proportion of supplies to be bought from each supplier and to calculate a weighted average price as the costing standard**

This is the most satisfactory method for control purposes if the required forecast can be made with reasonable accuracy.

Another question in relation to material price standards is whether to include the cost of carriage inwards and other costs such as non-returnable packing and transit insurance.

The objective always will be to price incoming goods at their total delivered cost, so these costs should be included in the standards.

3.5 Standard labour rates

When setting standard labour rates, one can either use basic pay rates only, or incorporate overtime premiums as well. The nature of the overtime work and the approach to cost control adopted by management will decide this issue.

(a) If a normal level of overtime work can be identified and is accepted as necessary, or if overtime is planned for the company's convenience, then the relative overtime premium payments will normally be included in the standard labour rate.

(b) If it is a management objective to reduce or eliminate overtime working, the standard rate may be restricted to basic pay.

4 Standard cost card

A standard cost card is built up using the appropriate standards for one unit.

A simple standard cost card is as follows:

Standard cost card – absorption costing

For one unit of output:	£
Direct material: 1.5 sq m @ £28 per sq m	42.00
Direct labour: 4 hours @ £5.25 per hour	21.00
Variable overheads: 4 hours @ £3 per hour	12.00
Fixed overheads:	28.00
Total standard cost	103.00

You can see that:

(a) Standard direct material cost

= Standard quantity of material × standard material price.

(b) Standard direct labour cost

= Standard direct labour hours × standard labour rate.

(c) Standard variable overhead cost

= Standard direct labour hours × standard variable overhead rate.

Note: this assumes that variable overheads are absorbed by labour hour, but they can be on machines hours, depending on the guidance given in the scenario.

(d) Standard fixed overhead cost

are absorbed on a unit bases.

Test your understanding 1

North manufactures a single product which has the following specification:

- Raw materials – 1 tonne @ £75 per tonne
- Direct labour – 3 hours @ £10 per hour
- Variable overheads – 3 hours @ £5 per hour
- Fixed overheads – £6

Complete the standard cost card using absorption costing principles.

	Workings:	£
Raw material		
Labour		
Variable overhead		
Fixed overhead		
Standard cost for one unit		

Test your understanding 2

South manufactures a single product which has the following specification:

- Raw materials – 5 kg @ £7.50 per kg
- Direct labour – 2 hours @ £7.50 per hour
- Variable overheads – 2 hours @ £2 per hour
- Fixed overheads – £10

Complete the standard cost card using absorption costing principles.

	Workings:	£
Raw material		
Labour		
Variable overhead		
Fixed overhead		
Standard cost for one unit		

5 Types of standard

5.1 Introduction

The way in which control is exercised, and the interpretation and use of variances from standards, will depend on which type of standard is used.

5.2 Basic standards

A basic standard is one which, having been fixed, is not revised with changing conditions, but remains in force for a long period of time. It may be set originally having regard to either ideal or expected conditions. Under circumstances of rapid technological change or of significant price changes, basic standards are of limited value in relation to the achievement of the benefits outlined above since they will be out of date.

5.3 Normal standards

Normal standards are those which give consideration to the usual level of activity managed by the company. They are more recent than the basic standard and are usually based on what the company manages to achieve on a regular basis.

These standards are sometimes referred to as **current standards**.

5.4 Target standards

In other cases the standards set will be those which give consideration to the state of efficiency which can be achieved from the existing facilities. The target set will be 'stretching' and a positive effort will made to achieve a high level of efficiency, but there is no question of going beyond what is attainable. These standards are often referred to as **attainable standards**.

The aim should be to set the standard cost which is likely to be the most realistic for the business concerned. It should be remembered that standards are the yardstick against which efficiency is measured and therefore, if they are unrealistic then any variances calculated will be of little meaning. Management and staff are usually motivated using this method.

5.5 Ideal standards

In some cases standards are established on the assumption that machines and employees will work with optimal efficiency at all times, and that there will be no stoppages and no losses of material or services. Such standards would represent an ideal state of affairs and therefore the objectives they set are never achieved.

Managers who are responsible for the costs can hardly approve of targets which they can never reach and which, therefore, result in large adverse variances from the standards. This is demotivating for managers (and their staff), particularly if there is an element of performance-related pay in their remuneration. Managers and staff have often been found to 'give up' when faced with these standards.

Test your understanding 3

The setting of ideal standards is motivational to employees.

True ☐

False ☐

6 Advantages and disadvantages of standard costing

6.1 Advantages

The advantages of standard costing fall into two broad categories: planning and control.

Planning

Predetermined standards make the preparation of forecasts and budgets much easier. If the standards are to be used for these operational decisions then they must obviously be as accurate as possible. This again means that standards should be revised on a frequent basis.

Control

Control is primarily exercised through the comparison of standard and actual results, and the isolation of variances. This is done by breaking down the simple variance identified in a budgetary control system into components based upon an expected outcome. This will highlight areas of apparent efficiency and inefficiency, and as necessary investigations as to the causes of the variance can be made. If these investigations discover the causes of the variances, then corrective action can be taken to improve efficiency in the future or alter the standards if necessary.

In addition to the above, there are some other advantages such as:

(a) if the standards are perceived to be attainable, then they will serve to motivate the employees concerned

(b) a standard costing bookkeeping system can be set up that will fulfil all requirements, for both internal and external reporting

(c) recording of inventory issues is simplified, as it is done at the standard price.

6.2 Disadvantages

A standard costing system is costly to set up and maintain, and standards must be revised on a regular basis to maintain effectiveness. It is for this reason that standard costing is most effective for well-established and repetitive processes, so that the revisions of standards are kept to a minimum.

7 Sales variances

7.1 Variance analysis

As well as being the basis for preparing budgets, standard costs are also used for calculating and analysing variances.

Basic variance analysis has been seen in the Budgeting chapter when comparing the flexed budget with the actual results.

The following variance analysis produces more detailed results as to the causes of the differences between what the costs and revenues should have been and what they actually were.

The variances that will be looked at here are:

- Sales variances

Then in the next section we'll look at the following cost variances:

- Raw material variances
- Labour variances
- Variable overhead variances
- Fixed overhead variances.

Two of the variances discussed in the following sections are calculated differently depending on the costing system a business uses:

- The sales volume variance will be calculated using standard contribution under marginal costing systems and using standard profit under absorption costing systems.
- The fixed overhead variance under marginal costing only consists of the fixed overhead expenditure variance, whereas under absorption costing the total fixed overhead variance is split into expenditure and volume.

7.2 Sales variances

There are two causes of sales variances

- a difference in selling price
- a difference in sales volume

7.3 A common sense approach

The important thing to remember is that variances are quite easy if you understand what you are calculating.

All you are calculating is the difference between what something **should have cost or sold for** and what it **actually did cost or sell for**.

We shall see this time and time again as we work through the variances.

7.4 Sales price variance

The sales price variance shows the effect on profit of selling at a different price from that expected.

The following proforma can be used

Sales price variance		£
Actual sales units DID sell for	Actual sales units @ the actual sales price	X
They SHOULD have sold for	Actuals sales units @ the standard sales price	Y
Sales price variance		X – Y

This variance is favourable if actual sales revenue is higher than actual sales at the standard selling price, and adverse if actual sales revenue is lower than standard

7.5 Sales volume variance

The sales volume variance calculates the effect on profit of the actual sales volume being different from that budgeted. The effect on profit will differ depending upon whether a marginal or absorption costing system is being used.

- Under absorption costing any difference in units is valued at the standard profit per unit.
- Under marginal costing any difference in units is valued at the standard contribution per unit.

Sales volume variance		**Units of sale**
Actual sales volume	The company DID sell	X
Budgeted sales volume	The amount they SHOULD have sold	Y
Sales volume variance (in units)		X – Y
@ standard profit/ contribution		£
Sales volume variance (in monetary terms)		£(X – Y)

The variance in units can be valued in one of two ways:

- at the **standard profit per unit** – if using absorption costing
- at the **standard contribution per unit** – if using marginal costing

This variance is favourable if actual sales volumes are greater than budgeted and adverse if actual sales volumes are lower than budgeted.

Example

The following data relates to 20X8:

Actual sales:	1,000 units @ £650 each
Budgeted output and sales for the year:	900 units
Standard selling price:	£700 per unit
Budgeted contribution per unit:	£245
Budgeted profit per unit:	£205

Required:

Calculate the following:

(a) sales price variance

(b) sales volume variance (under absorption costing)

(c) sales volume variance (under marginal costing

Solution

(a) **Sales price variance**

This is calculated using the actual sales.

			£	
Actual sales units DID sell for Actual sales @ the actual price	1,000 × £650	=	650,000	
They SHOULD have sold for Actual sales @ the standard selling price	1,000 × £700	=	700,000	
Sales price variance			50,000	(A)

(b) **Sales volume variance – absorption costing**

This is calculated using the budgeted profit per unit.

		Units	
Actual sales volume	DID	1,000	
Budgeted sales volume	SHOULD	900	
Sales volume variance (in units)		100	(F)
@ standard profit		£205	
Sales volume variance (in monetary terms)		£20,500	(F)

(c) **Sales volume variance – marginal costing**

This is calculated using the budgeted contribution per unit.

		Units	
Actual sales volume	DID	1,000	
Budgeted sales volume	SHOULD	900	
Sales volume variance (in units)		100	(F)
@ standard contribution		£245	
Sales volume variance (in monetary terms)		£24,500	(F)

There are many ways to calculate variances and the following tabulation method is another method that we can use to do the same thing.

Thus, what we have really done is the following:

Actual sales units × Actual selling price	Sales price variance
Actual sales units × Standard selling price	
Actual sales units × Standard margin per unit	Sales volume variance
Budgeted sales units × Standard margin per unit	

Test your understanding 4

WD Ltd has budgeted sales of 400 units at £25 each. The variable costs are expected to be £18 per unit, and there are no fixed costs.

The actual sales were 500 units at £20 each and costs were as expected.

Required:

Calculate the sales price variance and the sales volume contribution variance.

Sales Price variance

			£
Actual sales units DID sell for Actual sales @ the actual price		=	
They SHOULD have sold for Actual sales @ the standard selling price		=	
Sales price variance			

Sales volume contribution variance

		Units
Standard contribution per unit =		
Actual sales volume	DID	
Budgeted sales volume	SHOULD	
Sales volume variance (in units)		
@ standard contribution		
Sales volume variance (in monetary terms)		

Test your understanding 5

The following data is available for the most recent month of sales:

	Budget	Actual
Sales units	320	380
Selling price per unit	£45	£42
Total cost per unit	£23	£22
Variable cost per unit	£17	£15

Required:

Calculate the sales variances, calculating the sales volume variance using absorption costing and marginal costing.

Sales Price variance

			£
Actual sales units DID sell for Actual sales @ the actual price		=	
They SHOULD have sold for Actual sales @ the standard selling price		=	
Sales price variance			

Sales volume variance (absorption costing)

		Units
Standard profit per unit =		
Actual sales volume	DID	
Budgeted sales volume	SHOULD	
Sales volume variance (in units)		
@ standard profit		
Sales volume variance (in monetary terms)		

Sales volume variance (marginal costing)

		Units
Standard contribution per unit =		
Actual sales volume	DID	
Budgeted sales volume	SHOULD	
Sales volume variance (in units)		
@ standard contribution		
Sales volume variance (in monetary terms)		

8 Cost variances

8.1 Introduction

Definition

A **cost variance** is the difference between the standard cost of a product and its actual cost.

Cost variances are usually calculated for each element of cost separately, e.g. material, labour, variable overheads and fixed overheads.

We have seen how management will develop standard costs in advance of the period under review. During the course of that period actual costs will then be compared with standard costs, and any differences isolated for investigation as to their causes. This will then enable any corrective action to be taken as soon as possible.

If we consider top level management within the firm, perhaps the board of directors, then they will want to see a clear and succinct summary of the results for a given period. In particular they will wish to see a reconciliation between budgeted profit and actual profit that highlights the factors causing the difference.

8.2 Diagrammatic view of cost variances

Consider the cost of materials for producing 1,000 units of product X.

The standard cost of one unit is calculated as 2 kg of material at £2 per kg = £4 per unit.

To produce 1,000 units in period 1, the process actually uses 2,200 kg which cost £2.30 per kg.

The actual and standard costs for materials can be calculated as follows:

Standard cost of 1,000 units = 2,000 kg × £2 = £4,000

Actual cost of 1,000 units = 2,200 kg × £2.30 = £5,060

Total cost variance £1,060 (adverse)

This can be shown in a diagram as follows:

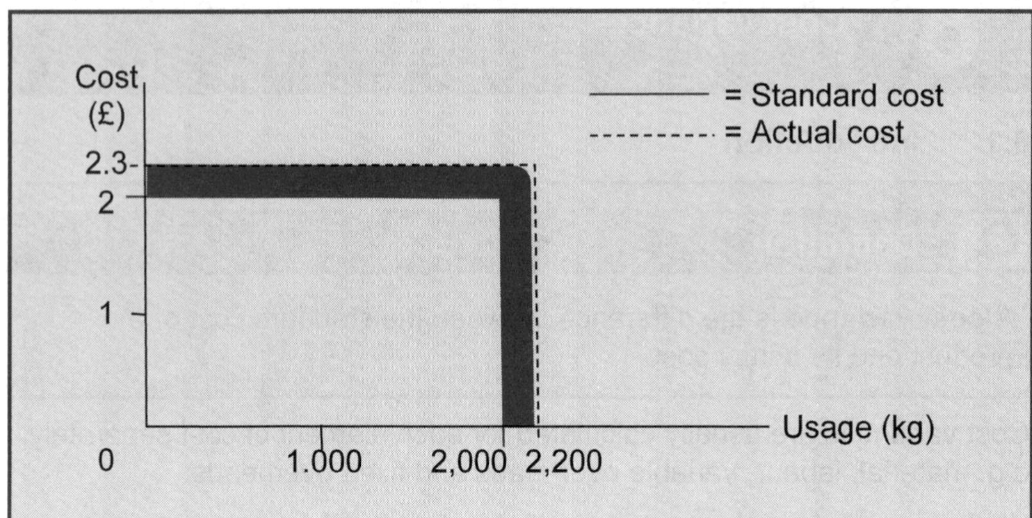

The shaded area shows the excess of the total actual cost over the total standard cost.

We need to analyse this into two parts:

(a) the price variance, i.e. the amount of the excess cost caused by actually paying £2.30 rather than standard £2.00 per unit

(b) the usage variance, i.e. the amount of the excess cost caused by actually using 2,200 kg rather than the standard 2,000 kg.

This is shown in the diagram by dividing the shaded area of total excess cost into two parts as shown below:

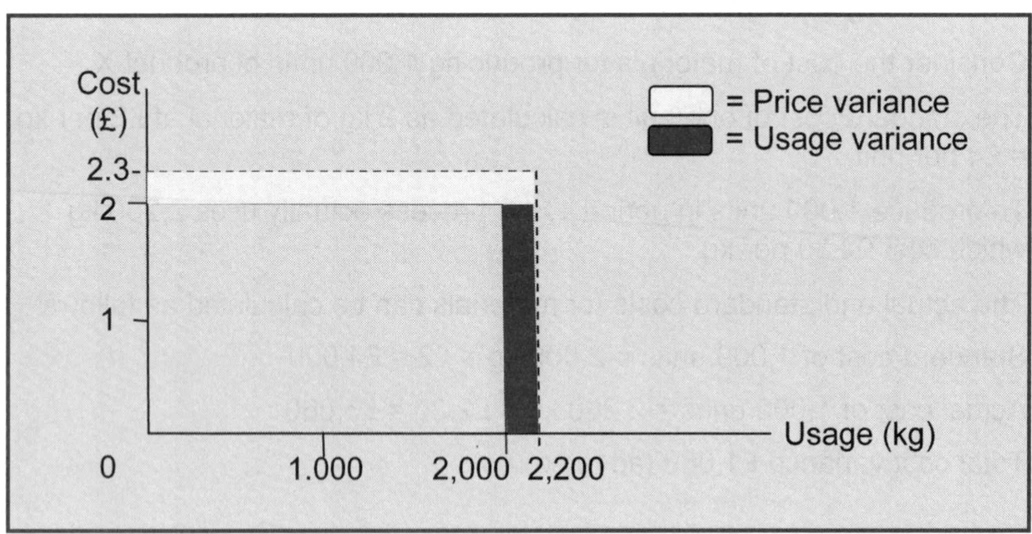

(a) The price variance is calculated as:

Quantity actually purchased × Actual price

Compared to:

Quantity actually purchased × Standard price

2,200 kg × £2.30 = £5,060

Compared to:

2,200 kg × £2.00 = £4,400

This is an adverse variance of £660 as we actually paid more than we should have paid.

(b) The usage variance is calculated as:

Quantity actually purchased × Standard price

Compared to:

Quantity that should have been used × Standard price

2,200 kg × £2.00 = £4,400

Compared to:

1,000 units × 2 kg × £2.00 = £4,000

This is an adverse variance of £400 as we actually used more than we should have used.

The two variances give the total variance as follows:

	£
Price variance	660 (adverse)
Usage variance	400 (adverse)
Total material variance	£1,060 (adverse)

9 Raw material variances

9.1 Introduction

This section has three variances. The direct material total variance, which shows the total difference in the amount spent on materials, and this can also be split into two further components – the materials price and materials usage variances.

9.2 Total material cost variance

The difference between:

(a) the standard direct material cost of the actual production and

(b) the actual direct material cost.

The following proforma can be used

Total material cost variance		£
Actual quantity of output	SHOULD cost (standard)	X
	DID cost	Y
Total cost variance		X – Y

This variance is favourable if actual cost is lower than standard cost, and adverse if actual cost is higher than standard

We'll use the following numbers to illustrate the process.

Drumbo makes drums, to produce 7,800 drums they should have used (7,800 × 100 kg)

= 780,000 kg. The material should have cost £2 per kg.

		£
Therefore, 7,800 drums SHOULD have cost	780,000 kg × £2 =	1,560,000
To produce 7,800 drums we DID actually used 900,000 kg.	This actually cost	1,755,000
Total cost variance (adverse)		195,000A

The budgeted level of 7,500 drums is irrelevant here, since we must compute the standard cost for **actual** production.

A total material variance actually conveys very little useful information. It needs to be analysed further. It can be analysed into two sub-variances:

(1) a direct material price variance, i.e. paying more or less than expected for materials and

(2) a direct material usage variance, i.e. using more or less material than expected for the actual output.

9.3 Materials price variance

The material price variance is defined as the difference between the actual price paid for purchased materials and their standard cost.

The materials price variance shows the effect on profit of buying materials at a different price from that expected.

The following proforma can be used

Material price variance		£
Actual quantity of materials	SHOULD cost (standard)	X
	DID cost	Y
Direct materials price variance		X – Y

Continuing the Drumbo illustration, we actually purchased 900,000 kg.

The price variance is simply the difference between what 900,000 kg should have cost and what they did actually cost.

	£
At actual price per kg, they DID cost	1,755,000
Actual quantity × Standard price, they SHOULD cost 900,000 kg × £2	1,800,000
Price variance (favourable)	45,000F

Therefore, there is a favourable price variance of £45,000.

This means that the actual price per kg purchased must have been less than standard. We can compute the actual price as follows:

$$\frac{\text{Actual cost}}{\text{quantity purchased}} = \frac{£1,755,000}{900,000} = £1.95/\text{kg}$$

Thus, for every kg we purchased, we actually paid £0.05 less than the standard price. This is a cost saving and gives rise to a favourable variance.

9.4 Materials usage variance

The materials usage variance shows the effect on profit of using a different amount of materials than expected

It is the difference between:

(a) the standard quantity of material specified for the actual production and

(b) the actual quantity used

multiplied by the standard purchase price.

The following proforma can be used

Material usage variance		
Actual output produced	SHOULD use (standard quantity)	X
	DID use (actual quantity)	Y
Direct materials usage variance	(in material quantity)	X – Y
× standard prices	(per unit of material)	£P
Direct materials usage variance		£P × (X – Y)

Continuing with Drumbo, we actually produced 7,800 drums.

	kg
Standard quantity × Standard price 7,800 units × 100 kg × £2	= 780,000
Actual quantity × Standard price 900,000 kg × £2	= 900,000
Usage variance (adverse)	120,000 A
× standard price per kg	× £2
Direct materials usage variance	£240,000 A

This over-usage is valued at the standard price per kg.

Clearly, the variance is adverse, since the additional usage above standard incurs extra cost.

Test your understanding 6

The standard direct material usage per unit of product K is 0.4 tonnes. The standard price of the material is £30/tonne.

During April, 500 units of K were produced using 223 tonnes of material costing £6,913. Calculate the direct material usage variance.

Standard usage of 500 units of K:

Actual usage

_____

Excess usage tonnes

_____

Valued at standard price of £30/tonne:

Direct material usage variance is:

£______________

Reconciliation

We can summarise the above computations as follows:

	Calculations		£	
Step 1	Actual quantity purchased at actual cost	900,000 kg	1,755,000	Price variance £45,000 F
Step 2	Actual quantity purchased at standard cost	900,000 kg × £2	1,800,000	Usage variance £240,000 A
Step 3	Standard quantity that should have been used at standard cost	780,000 kg × £2	1,560,000	Total variance £195,000 A

There are different ways of calculating the variances This tabulation is the method that we will use to compute the variances in this chapter.

Thus, what we have really done is the following:

Actual quantity × Actual price

AQ × AP

Actual quantity × Standard price

AQ × StdP

} Price variance

Standard quantity for actual production × Standard price

StdQ × AProd × StdP

} Usage variance

9.5 Assessment style question – materials

A typical example is shown below for materials.

Example

Materials Ltd makes boxes and the budget and actual results for June 20X8 were as follows.

		Budget		**Actual**
Production (units)		1,000		1,200
Direct materials	500 kg	£5,000	530 kg	£5,700

Calculate the following variances:

Variance	£	A/F
Direct material price		
Direct material usage		

Workings:

Standard price of materials per kilogram £5,000/500 kg = £10/kg

Standard usage for one unit = 500 kg/1,000 = 0.5 kg

Standard usage for actual production = 0.5 × 1,200 = 600 kg

(a) **Direct materials price variance**

530 kg did cost	£5,700
530 kg should have cost 530 × £10	£5,300
Price variance	400 (A)

(b) **Direct materials usage variance**

1,200 units did use 530 kg	
which should have cost at standard price 530 × £10	£5,300
1,200 units should have used 600 kg	
which should have cost at standard price 600 × £10	£6,000
Usage variance	£700 (F)

Variance	£	A/F
Direct material price	400	A
Direct material usage	700	F

Tutorial note:

You are not asked to reconcile the total materials variance, but you could do this as follows.

Total material budget cost of 1,200 units from data in question =

(£5,000/1,000 units) × 1,200 units =	£6,000
Total actual cost from data in question	£5,700
Total variance	£300 (F)
Variances per answer	
Price	£400 (A)
Usage	£700 (F)
	£300 (F)

9.6 Interpretation of the variances

The variances computed in 9.5 above act as error signals to management. They in no way explain why we have used more material than the standard allowed, or why we have succeeded in purchasing material more cheaply than the standard price.

If management decided that these exceptional performances (compared to budget) demanded explanation, then investigations would have to be carried out as to their causes. This would enable responsibility for the variance to be identified, and management could then take any preventative action considered necessary.

Some possible causes of the variances in 9.5 above are listed below.

Price variance

- Purchase of a cheaper substitute than the material per the standard cost and specification. Such an action may be a deliberate policy of the buying department (and therefore controllable), or may result from uncontrollable external factors such as market shortages.
- Bulk buying leading to discounts that the standard had not envisaged. This is sometimes referred to as economies of scale.
- Market factors leading to a lower price than anticipated (this would apply for example where raw materials depend upon random factors such as the weather affecting harvests).
- Using different suppliers from normal.
- The standard may have been set at a 'mid-year' price, anticipating future price rises. Thus we would expect favourable variances initially.

Usage variance

- Sub-standard raw materials. Notice the possibility here of interdependence between the variances. If the favourable price variance is due to buying a cheaper substitute, this may well cause operating inefficiencies leading to an adverse usage variance. Thus, in allocating responsibility for the variances, after investigation we may hold the purchasing manager responsible for the usage variance!
- Mechanical breakdown leading to spoilage of raw materials.
- The standard itself could be too tight (is it an ideal standard that is unattainable in practice?).
- Measurement errors. For example, if there are raw materials closing inventories that have not been recorded, this would overstate actual usage for the current period, but underestimate usage in the next period. Widely fluctuating variances from period to period may be indicative of such errors.
- Operating inefficiencies could lead to increased wastage of materials.
- The learning effect, as workers become more familiar with a material or a process they may make fewer mistakes leading to reduced wastage of material.

Test your understanding 7

Total material variance

The standard direct material cost of product A is £5. During August 600 units of product A were made (standard usage of material is 1 kg per unit) and the actual direct material cost was £3,200. Calculate the direct material total cost variance for the period.

Variance	£	F/A
Direct material total cost		

Test your understanding 8

Materials price and usage variance

A raw material, used in the manufacture of product F, has a standard price of £1.30 per litre. During May, 2,300 litres were bought and used at a cost of £3,128. The 600 units made should have used 4 litres per unit. Calculate the direct material price and usage variances for May.

Variance	£	F/A
Direct material price		
Direct material usage		

Test your understanding 9

A company bought 112,000 kilograms of material paying £4 per kilogram. It managed to make 2,100 units whilst the budget had been for 1,900 units. The standard quantity of material allowed for in the budget was 56 kilograms per unit, and the budgeted price per kilogram was £4.50.

Complete the following table.

			£
Budgeted/Standard cost of materials for actual production			
Variances	**F**	**A**	
Direct materials price			
Direct materials usage			
Total variance			
Actual cost of materials for actual production			

Test your understanding 10

A company bought 2,000 kilograms of material paying £5 per kilogram. It managed to make 400 units whilst the budget had been for 420 units. The standard quantity of material allowed for in the budget was 6 kilograms per unit, and the budgeted price per kilogram was £5.50.

Complete the following table.

			£
Budgeted/Standard cost of materials for actual production			
Variances	**F**	**A**	
Direct materials price			
Direct materials usage			
Total variance			
Actual cost of materials for actual production			

9.7 Materials variances with inventory

So far we have only considered an example where all of the materials purchased were used in production and so that there is no inventory at the end of the period.

We also need to consider cases where all of the materials purchased are not used and inventory therefore remains at the end of the period.

9.8 Materials price variance calculated on purchases

The most important thing to understand is that the materials price variance is calculated on the total of all the materials purchased in the period, whether they are used or not.

This means that any inventory carried to the next period is carried at its standard cost.

Note that the materials usage variance is based on the quantity of materials used as before.

Example

X Ltd purchases 4,000 kg of material at a cost of £8,400. It uses 3,300 kg to produce 600 of product A. Product A's standard cost card for material is as follows:

	Standard cost per unit
	£
Material – 5 kg at £2 per kg	10.00

Calculate:

(a) the price variance

(b) the usage variance

(c) the value of closing inventory in the cost records.

Solution

(a) **Price variance**

This is calculated on all the materials purchased whether they are used in production or not.

			£	
Actual cost of 4,000 kg		=	8,400	
Actual quantity purchased × Standard price	= 4,000 × £2	=	8,000	
			——	
Price variance (adverse)			400	(A)
			——	

(b) **Usage variance**

			£	
Actual quantity used × Standard price	= 3,300 kg × £2	=	6,600	
Standard cost of producing 600 units	= 600 × 5 kg × £2	=	6,000	
			———	
Usage variance (adverse)			600	(A)
			———	

(c) **Closing inventory**

Closing inventory will be valued at standard cost

Purchased	4,000 kg
Used	3,300 kg
Closing inventory	700 kg

Value per cost accounts = 700 × £2 = £1,400.

Test your understanding 11

Y Ltd

Y Ltd produces a product B which has the following standard cost for materials.

	Standard cost per unit
	£
Material – 5 kg at £3 per kg	15.00

Y Ltd produces 100 units of B in a period. It purchased 750 kg of material at a cost of £2,500 and used 600 kg for production.

Calculate:

(a) the price variance

(b) the value of closing inventory of material in the cost records

(c) the usage variance.

Solution

(a)

	£
Actual cost of materials purchased	
Standard cost of materials purchased	
Price variance	

(b) Closing inventory (kg) = Purchase quantity – quantity used

= ____________

Valued at standard cost, this gives a closing inventory valuation of £ __________.

(c)

	£
Actual materials used at standard price	
Standard cost of producing 100 B	
Usage variance	

10 Labour variances

10.1 Introduction

This section has four variances. The direct labour total cost variance, which shows the impact of any overall change in the amount spent on labour, and this can also be split into two further components – the labour rate and labour efficiency variances. In some scenarios we might also see a labour idle time variance.

10.2 Total labour cost variance

The difference between:

(a) the standard direct labour cost of the actual production and

(b) the actual cost of direct labour.

Total labour cost variance		£
Actual quantity of output	SHOULD cost (standard)	X
	DID cost	Y
Total cost variance		X – Y

This variance is favourable if actual cost is lower than standard cost, and adverse if actual cost is higher than standard

Referring back to the original example, you will see that the standard for labour per drum of soap is 12 hours at £3 per hour.

The actual results were:

Hours paid	110,000	costing £341,000
Actual production	7,800 drums	

Total labour cost variance

To produce 7,800 drums we should have taken (7,800 × 12 hours) = 93,600 hours.

	£
This did cost	341,000
This should have cost, at the standard rate, (93,600 × £3)	280,800
Total cost variance (adverse)	60,200 A

Note that, just as for materials variances:

- the variance is adverse because the actual labour cost exceeds the standard cost for actual production
- the budgeted production level of 7,500 drums is again irrelevant
- again, we would obtain more useful management information if we could analyse the total cost variance further into the rate of pay and efficiency variances.

A total labour variance can also be analysed further. It can be analysed into two sub-variances:

(1) a direct labour rate variance, i.e. paying more or less than expected per hour for labour and

(2) a direct labour efficiency variance, i.e. using more or less labour hours per unit than expected.

10.3 Labour rate variance

The direct labour rate variance is defined as one which indicates the actual cost of any change from the standard labour rate of remuneration.

The difference between:

(a) standard rate per hour and the

(b) actual rate per hour

multiplied by the actual hours that were paid for.

The following proforma can be used

Labour rate variance		£
Number of hours paid	SHOULD cost (standard rate per hour)	X
	DID cost (actual rate per hour)	Y
Direct labour rate variance		X – Y

Referring back to the Drumbo illustration, we actually paid for 110,000 hours.

	£
This did cost	341,000
At standard rate per hour, this should have cost (110,000 × £3)	330,000
Rate variance (adverse)	11,000 A

This means that the actual rate of pay per hour must have been more than the standard.

The actual rate is $\frac{\text{Actual cost}}{\text{Hours paid}} = \frac{£341{,}000}{110{,}000} = £3.10\text{/hour}$

Thus, for every hour paid for, we have actually paid £0.10 more than the standard price, and so the labour rate of pay variance is adverse.

10.4 Labour efficiency variance

The direct labour efficiency variance is defined as standard labour cost of any change from the standard level of labour efficiency.

The difference between:

(a) the standard hours specified for the actual production and

(b) the actual hours worked

multiplied by the standard hourly rate.

Labour efficiency variance		
Actual output produced	DID take (actual hours)	X
	SHOULD take (standard hours)	Y
Direct labour efficiency variance	(in hours)	X – Y
× standard rate per hour		£P
Direct labour efficiency variance		£P × (X – Y)

Considering our illustration, Drumbo, we actually produced 7,800 drums.

This did take 110,000 hrs	=	110,000
At standard efficiency, this should have taken (7,800 drums × 12 hours per unit)	=	93,600
Efficiency variance in hours (adverse)		16,400 A
		× £3
Efficiency variance (adverse)		£49,200 A

This variance is adverse, because we have taken more hours, and therefore incurred more cost, to produce 7,800 drums than the standard allowed.

Reconciliation

We can summarise the above computations as follows:

			£	£
Step 1	Actual hours paid at actual rate (actual cost)	110,000 hrs	341,000	11,000 A Rate of pay variance
Step 2	Actual hours paid at standard rate	110,000 hrs × £3	330,000	
Step 3	Standard hours that should have been paid at standard rate (standard cost)	93,600 hrs × £3	280,800	49,200 A Efficiency variance
				Total variance 60,200 A

Again, we can show the above in 'shorthand' as:

Actual hours paid	×	Actual rate	Rate variance
Actual hours paid	×	Standard rate	
Standard hours for actual production	×	Standard rate	Efficiency variance

Test your understanding 12

The standard direct labour cost of product H is £7. During January 450 units of product H were made and the actual direct labour cost was £3,450.

Calculate the direct labour total cost variance of the period.

	£
Standard direct labour cost of 450 units:	
Actual direct labour cost	
Direct labour total cost variance	

10.5 Assessment style question – labour

Example

Labour Ltd makes boxes and the budget and actual results for June 20X8 were as follows.

		Budget		Actual
Production (units)		1,000		1,200
Direct labour	300 hrs	£4,500	340 hrs	£5,440

Calculate the following

(a) Direct labour rate variance

(b) Direct labour efficiency variance.

Variance	£	A/F
Direct labour rate		
Direct labour efficiency		

Solution

Standard labour rate per hour

£4,500/300 hr = £15 per hr

Standard labour hours for one unit = 300/1,000 = 0.3 hrs

Standard labour hours for actual production = 0.3 × 1,200 units = 360 hrs

(a) **Direct labour rate variance**

340 hrs did cost	£5,440
340 hrs should have cost 340 × £15 =	£5,100
Labour rate variance	£340 (A)

(b) **Direct labour efficiency variance**

1,200 units did use 340 hrs which should have cost at standard price 340 × £15	£5,100
1,200 units should have used 360 hrs which should have cost at standard rate 360 × £15	£5,400
Labour efficiency variance	£300 (F)

Variance	£	A/F
Direct labour rate	340	A
Direct labour efficiency	300	F

Tutorial note:

Reconciliation:

Total labour budget cost of 1,200 units from data in question

= (£4,500/1,000 units) × 1,200 units = £5,400
Total actual cost from data in question £5,440

Total variance £40 (A)

Variances per answer:

£340A + £300F = £40A

10.6 Idle time

The labour force can be paid for a greater number of hours than they actually work. This may be due to a late delivery of raw materials preventing production and causing the workers to stand idle. If this is the case, then this idle time affects the labour efficiency variance and needs to be separated from it.

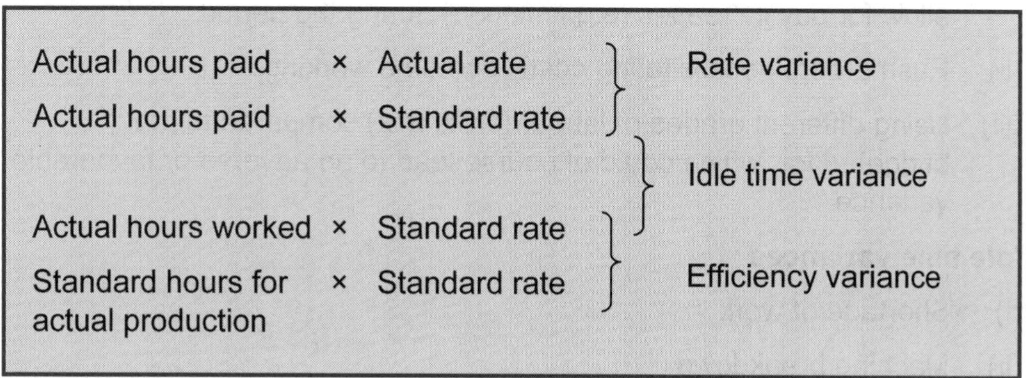

For example, if the labour force were paid a standard rate of £10 per hour and in January they were paid for 6,500 hours, but only worked 6,000 hours. During the month 620 units were made that take 10 hours each.

Calculate the idle time and efficiency variances.

Actual hours paid	×	Standard rate	
6,500 hours	×	£10 per hour	£65,000
			Idle time variance = £5,000 A
Actual hours worked	×	Standard rate	
6,000 hours		£10 per hour	£60,000
			Efficiency variance = £2,000 F
Standard hours for actual production	×	Standard rate	
10 hours × 620 units	×	£10 per hour	£62,000

In the assessment all idle time variances will be adverse.

10.7 Interpretation of labour variances

Some possible causes of labour variances may be:

Rate of pay variances

(i) Failure to include overtime premiums in the standard, or failure to allow for pay increases (e.g. inflation) during the period.

(ii) Rush orders necessitating costly overtime working.

(iii) Using different grades of labour (skills mix) compared to that budgeted for, which could of course lead to an adverse or favourable variance.

Idle time variances

(i) Shortage of work

(ii) Machine breakdown

(iii) Shortage of material.

Efficiency variances

(i) Better quality raw materials could lead to favourable labour efficiency, or of course sub-standard materials could cause inefficiencies. Time could be lost in setting up machines after breakdowns, or rectifying poor quality output.

(ii) The learning effect, as the workers become more familiar with a process this could lead to reductions in the time taken to do the work.

(iii) Random fluctuations such as high morale due to the local football team's winning streak.

Although this last example is somewhat flippant, it does illustrate an important point. We are dealing here with labour – a human asset. As such its efficiency will depend greatly upon behavioural factors.

The plan itself could be wrong! Remember that to compute the variance we compare standard labour time with actual labour time. If the standard represents an ideal time, then adverse variances are inevitable. Alternatively, if the standard is outdated due to technical innovations or revised working practices, then again we would expect to see variances.

Test your understanding 13

The following data relates to product C:

Actual production of C (units)	700
Standard wage rate/hour	£4
Standard time allowance per unit of C (hours)	1.50
Actual hours worked	1,000
Actual hours paid	1,050
Actual wage cost	£4,200

Calculate the following from the above data:

(a) the direct labour rate variance

(b) the idle time variance

(c) the efficiency variance

(a) Rate variance

	£
Actual hours paid did cost	
Actual hours paid should cost	
Rate variance	

(b) Idle time:

	£
Hours paid	
Hours worked	
Idle time variance	

(c) Efficiency variance:

	£
Standard hours for actual production at standard rate	
Actual hours worked at standard rate	
Efficiency variance	

Test your understanding 14

Compute labour variances for the following examples:

(a)

Standard	2 hours per unit at £3 per hour
Labour hours	5,000 hours, cost £14,000
Units produced	2,800 units

Variances	£	A/F
Direct labour rate		
Direct labour efficiency		

(b)

Standard	3 hours per unit, £12 per unit
Original budget	20,000 units
Production	18,000 units
Hours worked	48,000 hours
Hours paid	50,000 hours, cost £210,000

Variances	£	A/F
Direct labour rate		
Idle time		
Direct labour efficiency		

Test your understanding 15

A company used 2,000 hours of labour paying £10 per hour. During this time the company made 2,050 units whilst the budget had been for 2,500 units. The standard number of hours allowed was one hour per unit, and the budgeted rate per hour was £9.80.

Complete the following table.

			£
Budgeted/Standard cost of labour for actual production			
Variances	**F**	**A**	
Direct labour rate			
Direct labour efficiency			
Total variance			
Actual cost of labour for actual production			

Test your understanding 16

A company used 24,000 hours of labour paying £8 per hour. During this time it managed to make 400 units whilst the budget had been for only 190 units. The standard number of hours allowed was 50 per unit, and the budgeted rate per hour was £8.50.

Complete the following table.

			£
Budgeted/Standard cost of labour for actual production			
Variances	**F**	**A**	
Direct labour rate			
Direct labour efficiency			
Total variance			
Actual cost of labour for actual production			

10.8 Labour variances – ratios

Three control ratios can be used to measure productivity, as follows:

Labour Activity ratio:

$$\text{Labour activity ratio} = \frac{\text{Standard hours for actual production}}{\text{budgeted hours}} \times 100$$

Labour Efficiency ratio:

$$\text{Labour efficiency ratio} = \frac{\text{standard hours for actual production}}{\text{actual hours worked}} \times 100$$

Idle time ratio:

$$\text{Idle time ratio} = \frac{\text{idle hours}}{\text{total hours}} \times 100$$

Example

	Budget	Actual
Output (units)	10,000	9,000
Hours worked	200	190
Hours paid	200	195

Calculate:

(a) the labour activity ratio

(b) the labour efficiency ratio

(c) the idle time ratio

Solution

(a) Standard time for one unit: $\frac{200}{10,000}$ = 0.02 hours per unit

Actual output in standard hours: 9,000 × 0.02 = 180 hours

Labour activity ratio: $\frac{180}{200}$ = 90%

In other words, the production level was only 90% of the budgeted level.

(b) Labour efficiency ratio: $\frac{180}{190}$ = 94.74%

According to the budget, 50 units should have been produced in an hour and therefore in the 190 hours that were actually worked, 9,500 units should have been produced. Only 94.74% of that quantity (9,000) were actually produced.

(c) Idle time ratio: $\frac{195-190}{195}$ = 2.56%

Only 2.56% of hours paid were idle.

11 Variable overhead variances

11.1 Introduction

Variable overhead variances are similar to direct labour variances.

- In standard product costing, a variable production overhead total variance can be calculated, and this can be analysed into an expenditure variance and an efficiency variance.
- With service costing, a variable overhead total variance can be calculated, but this might not be analysed any further.

Since variable production overheads are normally assumed to vary with labour hours worked, labour hours are used in calculations. This means, for example, that the variable production overhead efficiency variance uses exactly the same hours as the direct labour efficiency variance.

11.2 Total variable overhead variance

The difference between:

(a) the standard variable overhead cost of the actual production and

(b) the actual cost of variable production overheads.

Total variable overhead variance		£
Actual quantity of output	SHOULD cost (standard)	X
	DID cost	Y
Total cost variance		X – Y

Referring back to the original example, you will see that the standard for variable overheads per drum of soap is 12 hours at £2 per hour.

Total variable overhead variance

To produce 7,800 drums we should have taken (7,800 × 12 hours) = 93,600 hours.

	£
This did cost	176,500
This should have cost, at the standard rate, (93,600 × £2)	187,200
Total variable cost variance (favourable)	10,700

Note that, just as for materials or labour variances:

- the variance is favourable because the actual variable overhead cost is less than the standard cost for actual production
- the budgeted production level of 7,500 drums is again irrelevant
- again, we would obtain more useful management information if we could analyse the total cost variance further into expenditure and efficiency variances.

Variable overhead variances are usually calculated on the **labour hours worked**.

A total variable production overhead variance can also be analysed further. It can be analysed into two sub-variances:

(1) a variable production overhead expenditure variance, i.e. paying more or less than expected per hour for variable overheads and

(2) a variable production overhead efficiency variance, i.e. using more or less variable overheads per unit than expected.

11.3 Variable overhead expenditure variance

The variable production overhead expenditure variance is defined as one which indicates the actual cost of any change from the standard rate per hour. Hours refer to either labour or machine hours depending on the recovery base chosen for variable production overhead.

Variable production overhead expenditure variance		£
Actual number of hours worked	DID cost (actual)	X
	SHOULD cost/hr (standard)	Y
Variable production overhead expenditure variance		X – Y

Continuing the illustration:

	£
This did cost	176,500
At standard rate per hour, this should have cost (110,000 hrs × £2)	220,000
Expenditure variance (favourable)	43,500 F

This variance is favourable because we incurred less cost, to produce 7,800 drums, than the standard allowed.

11.4 Variable overhead efficiency variance

The variable production overhead efficiency variance is defined as the standard variable overhead cost of any change from the standard level of efficiency.

Variable overhead efficiency variance

Actual output produced	DID take (actual hours)	X
	SHOULD take (standard hours)	Y
Variable overhead efficiency variance	(in hours)	X – Y
× standard variable overhead rate per hour		£P
Variable overhead efficiency variance		£P × (X – Y)

We actually produced 7,800 drums.

		hours
This did take 110,000 hrs which should have cost £2/hr	=	110,000
At standard efficiency, this should have taken (7,800 × 12)		93,600
Efficiency variance in hours (adverse)		16,400 A
		× £2
Variable overhead efficiency variance (adverse)		£32,800

This variance is adverse because we have taken more hours (as per the labour efficiency variance) and therefore incurred more cost to produce 7,800 drums, than the standard allowed.

Reconciliation

We can summarise the above computations as follows:

			£	£
Step 1	Actual hours paid at actual rate (actual cost)	110,000 hrs	176,500	43,500 F Expenditure variance
Step 2	Actual hours paid at standard rate	110,000 hrs × £2	220,000	32,800 A Efficiency variance
Step 3	Standard hours that should have been paid at standard rate (standard cost)	93,600 hrs × £2	187,200	

Again, we can show the above in 'shorthand' as:

Actual hours worked	×	Actual rate	Expenditure variance
Actual hours worked	×	Standard rate	Efficiency variance
Standard hours for actual production	×	Standard rate	

11.5 Assessment style question – variable overheads

Example

Skill Ltd makes bags and the budget and actual results for June 20X2 were as follows.

		Budget		Actual
Production (units)		1,000		1,200
Variable overheads	3,000 hrs	£4,500	3,400 hrs	£5,440

Calculate the following:

(a) Variable overhead expenditure variance

(b) Variable overhead efficiency variance

Solution

Variance	£	A/F
Variable overhead expenditure	340	A
Variable overhead efficiency	300	F

Standard labour rate per hour

£4,500/3,000 hr = £1.50 per hr

Standard labour hours for one unit = 3,000/1,000 = 3 hrs

Standard labour hours for actual production = 3 × 1,200 = 3,600 hrs

(a) **Variable overhead expenditure variance**

3,400 hrs did cost	£5,440
3,400 hrs should have cost 3,400 × £1.50 =	£5,100
Variable overhead expenditure variance	£340 (A)

(b) **Variable overhead efficiency variance**

1,200 units did use 3,400 hrs	
which should have cost at standard rate 3,400 × £1.50	£5,100
1,200 units should have used 3,600 hrs	
which should have cost at standard rate 3,600 × £1.50	£5,400
Variable overhead efficiency variance	£300 (F)

11.6 Interpretation of variable overhead variances

Some possible causes of variable overhead variances may be:

Expenditure variances

(i) Failure to allow for rate increases during the period.

Efficiency variances

(i) Better quality raw materials could lead to favourable labour and variable overhead efficiency, or of course sub-standard materials could cause inefficiencies. Time could be lost in setting up machines after breakdowns, or rectifying poor quality output, all affecting labour hours and therefore the labour and variable overhead efficiency variances.

(ii) The plan itself could be wrong! Remember that to compute the variance we compare standard labour hours with actual labour hours. If the standard represents an ideal time, then adverse variances are inevitable. Alternatively, if the standard is outdated due to technical innovations or revised working practices, then again we would expect to see variances.

You should see from the above that many of the factors affecting the labour efficiency variances are the same for the variable overhead efficiency variance.

Test your understanding 17

Compute the variable overhead variances for the following examples:

(a)

Standard	2 hours per unit at £4 per hour
Hours worked	3,000 hours, cost £12,000
Units produced	1,400 units

Variances	£	A/F
Variable overhead expenditure		
Variable overhead efficiency		

(b)

Standard	5 hours per unit, £10 per unit
Original budget	10,000 units
Production	9,500 units
Hours worked	48,000 hours, cost £90,000

Variances	£	A/F
Variable overhead expenditure		
Variable overhead efficiency		

12 Fixed overheads

12.1 Introduction

Remember that, in order to set a fixed overhead absorption rate per unit, we had to make an estimate of the activity level, as well as of the fixed cost itself.

The relevant information from the example is:

Budgeted fixed production costs	=	£90,000
Standard hours per drum	=	12 hours
Budgeted production	=	7,500 drums
The actual results were:		
Labour	=	110,000 hours paid
Fixed production costs	=	£86,000
Production	=	7,800 drums

From these estimates we obtained the standard fixed overhead absorption rate per drum:

$$\frac{\text{Budgeted cost}}{\text{Budgeted drums}} = \frac{£90,000}{7,500} = £12/\text{drum}$$

This means that, as units are produced, we will absorb £12 (12 hours at the standard of £1) per drum. Thus, there may be a variance due to the over or under absorption of fixed overheads.

For example, if actual fixed costs were exactly as per budget of £90,000, but we actually produced 8,000 units, then we would absorb 8,000 × £12 = £96,000.

Thus we would have over-absorbed £6,000, due to the increased production compared to budget. Finished goods will therefore be valued at £6,000 more than the actual cost, and so a favourable variance would be needed to reduce this standard cost back to the actual cost. This variance is called the volume variance, and only arises because we have chosen to absorb fixed overheads into production.

12.2 Fixed overheads – total cost variance

The amount of overhead absorbed for each unit of output is the standard fixed overhead cost per unit. The total cost variance is therefore calculated as follows:

The difference between:

(a) the standard fixed production overhead cost absorbed by the actual production (i.e. the amount of fixed overhead actually absorbed into production using the standard absorption rate), and

(b) the actual fixed production overheads incurred.

Total fixed overhead variance	£
Actual fixed overhead incurred	X
Overheads absorbed (actual output × standard fixed production over head absorption rate)	Y
Fixed overhead total variance	(X – Y)

Referring back to the Drumbo illustration:

	£
The actual cost was	86,000
In producing 7,800 drums we have absorbed (7,800 × £12)	93,600
Total cost variance (favourable)	7,600 F

12.3 Fixed overhead expenditure variance

Since fixed costs do not vary with the level of production, the expenditure variance is simply a comparison of budgeted and actual fixed costs.

Fixed overhead expenditure variance	£
Actual total cost	X
Budgeted cost	Y
Fixed overhead expenditure variance	(X – Y)

Referring back to the Drumbo illustration:

	£
Actual total cost	86,000
Budgeted cost	90,000
Expenditure variance (favourable)	4,000 F

Thus we have actually incurred, regardless of activity level, £4,000 less fixed costs than budgeted. The variance is therefore favourable.

12.4 Fixed overhead volume variance

The volume variance is calculated as the difference between:

(a) Budgeted output in units and

(b) Actual output in units multiplied by the standard fixed overhead cost (FOAR) per unit.

The fixed overhead volume variance does not occur in a marginal costing system.

Fixed overhead volume variance	£
Budgeted output at the OAR per unit	X
Actual output at the OAR per unit	Y
Fixed overhead volume variance	(X – Y)

In Drumbo we actually produced 7,800 drums.

	£
Budgeted absorption (7,500 × £12)	90,000
Actual absorption (7,800 × £12)	93,600
Volume variance (favourable)	3,600 F

Remember that the variance is favourable because we have over absorbed fixed overheads. We thus require a favourable variance to compensate for this over-absorption.

We have produced 300 units more than budget, thus over-absorbing fixed overheads by 300 × the standard rate of £12 per unit i.e. £3,600 favourable volume variance.

12.5 Assessment style question – fixed overheads

Example

Fixed Ltd makes boxes and the budget and actual results for June 20X8 were as follows

	Budget		Actual
Production (units)	1,000		1,200
Fixed overheads	£2,000		£2,500

Calculate the following

(a) Budgeted overhead absorption rate per unit

(b) Fixed overheads absorbed into actual production

(c) Fixed overhead expenditure variance

(d) Fixed overhead volume variance.

Solution

(a) Budgeted overhead absorption rate per unit

£2,000/1,000 = £2 per unit

(b) Fixed overheads absorbed into actual production

Units actually produced = 1,200 units

Overheads absorbed into actual production = 1,200 × £2 = £2,400

(c) Fixed overhead expenditure variance

£2,000 – £2,500 = £500 (A)

(d) Fixed overhead volume variance

Actual overhead absorbed =	£2,400
Budgeted overhead =	£2,000
Variance	£400 (F)

Tutorial note:

You are not asked to reconcile the fixed overhead variance, but you could do this as follows.

Overhead absorbed	2,400	
Actual overhead	2,500	
Total variance	£100	(A)

Variances per answer

Expenditure variance	£500	(A)
Volume variance	£400	(F)
	£100	(A)

12.6 Usefulness of fixed overhead variances

We must be clear throughout the above analysis that we are dealing with a fixed cost. Referring back to the earlier sections on materials and labour and you will see that there are no volume variances for these items. The volume variance arises for fixed overheads purely because of our desire to absorb fixed costs into production, and the consequent setting up of an arbitrary absorption basis such as labour hours.

Conflict

Thus we are really seeing a conflict between the use of standard costing for control purposes, and the use of standards for product costing. We may for example base our selling price on cost plus a fixed mark-up, in which case a production cost inclusive of fixed costs may be desired. However, for control purposes the only variance of any real significance is the expenditure variance. Since we are dealing with a fixed cost, then the cost will not change simply because we are operating at something other than budgeted output level.

Thus the volume variance is really uncontrollable, and arises due to our failure to operate at the budgeted activity level.

Test your understanding 18

PD has the following data concerning its fixed production overheads:

Budget cost	£50,000
Budget production	10,000 units
Budget labour hours	20,000
Actual cost	£47,500
Actual production	8,450 units
Actual labour hours	16,600

Calculate the fixed overhead total variance assuming an absorption system based upon labour hours.

Absorption rate = £____________ per labour? hour

Actual output in standard hours = ______________ standard hours

	£
Overhead cost	
Overhead absorbed	
Variance	

Test your understanding 19

A company has budgeted fixed overheads of £40,000 and budgeted output is 20,000 units.

Actual output was 19,000 units and actual overheads were £39,000.

Complete the following table.

			£
Budgeted/Standard fixed cost for actual production			
Variances	**F**	**A**	
Fixed overhead expenditure			
Fixed overhead volume			
Total variance			
Actual fixed cost for actual production			

Test your understanding 20

A company has budgeted fixed overheads of £1,250,000 and budgeted output is 25,000 units.

Actual output was 24,100 units and actual overheads were £1,245,000.

Complete the following table.

			£
Budgeted/Standard fixed cost for actual production			
Variances	**F**	**A**	
Fixed overhead expenditure			
Fixed overhead volume			
Total variance			
Actual fixed cost for actual production			

Test your understanding 21

From the information below calculate (a) the fixed overhead variance and (b) all the sub-variances, using absorption costing (based on absorbing by unit).

TP has the following data concerning its fixed production overheads:

Budget fixed overhead	£44,000
Budget production	8,000 units
Budget labour hours	16,000
Actual fixed overhead	£47,500
Actual production	8,450 units
Actual labour hours	16,600

Calculate:

Fixed overhead recovery rate =

(a) **Fixed overhead total variance**

(b) **Sub-variances**

(i) Fixed overhead expenditure variance:

(ii) Fixed overhead volume variance:

Test your understanding 22

Brown Ltd manufactures and sells office furniture. The company operates an integrated standard cost system in which:

purchases of materials are recorded at standard cost

finished goods are recorded at standard cost

direct materials and direct labour costs are both variable costs

fixed production overheads are absorbed on a per unit basis.

You are an accounting technician at Brown Ltd. You report to Ximena Thomas, the Finance Director.

The company's most popular product is an executive desk. Its standard cost is as follows:

Product: Executive desk

Inputs	**Quantity**	**Unit price**	**Total cost**
		£	£
Direct materials	30 kg	5.00	150.00
Direct labour	5 hours	6.00	30.00
Fixed production overheads			20.00
Standard cost			200.00

Actual and budgeted data for the manufacture of executive desks for May 20X4 are shown below:

- 27,500 kg of direct materials were purchased for £143,000.
- Issues from stores to production totalled 27,500 kg.
- The actual output for the month was 900 desks.
- The budgeted output for the month was 1,000 desks.
- 4,200 direct labour hours were worked at a cost of £26,040.
- Actual fixed production overheads were £23,000.

Task

Calculate the following variances for the production of executive desks for May:

(i)	Material price variance	
(ii)	Material usage variance	
(iii)	Labour rate variance	
(iv)	Labour efficiency variance	
(v)	Fixed overhead expenditure variance	
(vi)	Fixed overhead volume variance	

13 Reporting variances

13.1 Reconciling budgeted and actual performance

We have seen that standard costs are developed in advance of the period under review. During the course of that period, actual costs are compared with standard costs. Any variances are isolated for investigation as to their cause, enabling corrective action to be taken as soon as possible.

Management will wish to see a clear and succinct summary of the results for the period and in particular will want any unusual or unexpected items to be brought to their attention (exception reporting). In general, this will take the form of a reconciliation between budgeted and actual profits which highlights the variances between them. To be useful as a management tool, the reconciliation should be part of an overall report to management.

Example

The calculation of basic cost variances is covered in previous AAT units.

The following budgeted and actual data for TJB Limited for 20X1 will be used to revise the principles and computations, and lead on to reporting these variances.

TJB Limited – Budgeted profit for the year ending 31 December 20X1

Produce and sell 10,000 units

	Produce and sell 10,000 units		
		£	£
Budgeted sales units	10,000		100,000
Production cost	£/unit		
Direct materials – 10,000 tons @ £1 per ton (1 ton per unit)	1.00	10,000	
Direct labour – 20,000 hours @ 50p per hour (2 hours per unit)	1.00	10,000	
Fixed production overhead – £1.50 per unit	1.50	15,000	
Total budgeted production cost	3.50		35,000
Budgeted profit for the period			65,000

During the year to 31 December 20X1, the following actual results were obtained.

TJB Limited – Actual profit for the year ending 31 December 20X1

Production and sales 8,000 units

	£	£
Sales		96,000
Production cost		
Direct materials – 7,750 tons purchased and used (£1.0968 per ton)	8,500	
Direct labour – 16,500 hours paid (£0.4545 per hour)	7,500	
Fixed production overhead incurred	15,500	
Total actual production cost		31,500
Total profit		64,500

The purpose of a cost analysis is to reconcile the budgeted costs of £35,000 to the actual costs of £31,500.

This reconciliation is the budgetary control statement or budgetary control report.

Solution

Cost variances

	Flexed budget cost of producing 8,000 units *	**Actual cost of producing 8,000 units**	**Difference (variance)**	
	£	£	£	
Direct materials	8,000	8,500	500	A
Direct labour	8,000	7,500	500	F
Fixed production overhead	12,000	15,500	3,500	A
Total	28,000	31,500	3,500	A

*In a total absorption costing system such as the one used here by TJB Ltd., the initial flexed budget will flex every line of the costs recorded by the actual activity level. This leads to a fixed cost figure of £1.50 × 8,000 = £12,000 and it is this figure the company will have absorbed. We will see below how this is dealt with in the control statement.

All these total variances can be analysed into at least two further types of variance:

(a) a price variance

(b) a usage or utilisation variance, which in some cases can be broken down further.

Total direct material cost variance

		£	
(a)	The actual amount of material used at the actual price	8,500	
(b)	The standard amount of material that should have been used for the actual production at the standard price – 8,000 tons × £1	8,000	
	Total variance	500	A

To analyse this further we need first to calculate the actual amount of material used at the standard price: the direct materials price variance.

Direct materials price variance

	Tons	£	
Actual materials purchased, at actual price	7,750	8,500	
Actual materials purchased, at standard price per ton (£1)	7,750	7,750	
Materials price variance	–	750	A

TJB Ltd. has paid more than they had hoped for the materials they bought, reducing profits by £750.

We next need to compare this with the standard materials that should have been used for that level of production: the direct materials usage variance.

Direct materials usage variance

	Tons	£	
Actual materials used at standard price	7,750	7,750	
Standard materials allowed for production achieved at standard price	8,000	8,000	
Materials usage variance (@ £1 per ton)	250	250	F

TJB Ltd. have used less material to make the goods than expected, improving profits by £250.

Total direct material cost variance = £750 A + £250 F
= £500 A

The reduced material usage, combined with the higher cost of the purchases has produced a £500 drop in profit overall.

Total direct labour cost variance

		£	
(a)	The actual hours paid at the actual rate per hour	7,500	
(b)	The standard time allowed to produce the output, priced at the standard rate per hour (16,000 × £0.50)	8,000	
	Total variance	500	F

The total variance can be analysed into rate and efficiency variances as with materials.

Labour rate variance

	Hours	£	
Actual hours paid at actual rate per hour	16,500	7,500	
Actual hours paid at standard rate per hour (50p/hour)	16,500	8,250	
Direct labour rate variance	–	750	F

TJB Ltd. has paid less than they expected for the labour they used, increasing profits by £750.

Total labour efficiency variance

	Hours	£	
Actual hours paid at standard rate per hour	16,500	8,250	
Standard hours allowed for production achieved at standard rate per hour (50p)	16,000	8,000	
Direct labour usage variance		250	A

TJB Ltd. have used more labour hours to make the goods than expected, reducing profits by £250.

Total direct labour cost variance = £750 F + £250 A
= £500 F

The cheaper cost of labour, combined with longer time taken to produce the goods has produced a £250 drop in profit overall.

Total fixed overhead cost variance

	£	
Actual fixed overhead cost	15,500	
Standard cost absorbed into actual production (8,000 × £1.50 per unit)	12,000	
Total fixed overhead cost variance	3,500	A

This is then analysed into price (expenditure) and volume variances. The volume variance is then sub-analysed into usage (efficiency) and capacity variances.

Fixed overhead expenditure variance

	£	
Actual fixed overhead cost	15,500	
Budgeted fixed overhead cost	15,000	
Fixed overhead expenditure variance	500	A

Fixed overhead volume variance

This is the under-absorption (at standard rates) due to the lower actual production level than that budgeted.

	Units	£	
Actual production	8,000		
Budgeted production	10,000		
Fixed overhead volume variance (in units)	2,000		
Valued at standard absorption rate (£1.50 per unit)		3,000	A

The variance is adverse because we have under-absorbed fixed overhead by 2,000 units' worth. We thus require an extra charge to the cost account to compensate for this under-absorption.

Having computed all the variances, we can now reconcile budgeted costs with actual costs.

		Adverse	Favourable	
		£	£	£
Total budgeted cost				28,000
Cost variances				
Materials	Price	750		
	Usage		250	
Labour	Rate		750	
	Efficiency	250		
Fixed overheads	Expenditure	500		
	Volume	3,000		
Total/net cost variances		4,500	1,000	3,500
Total actual cost				31,500

13.2 Marginal costing

The previous example of TJB Limited was based upon total absorption costing as the fixed production overhead was absorbed into the standard cost of the product. Under marginal costing the fixed overhead is charged to the income statement as a period cost and is not absorbed into the cost of the product.

For the purpose of variances this means that the only fixed overhead variance that exists is the fixed overhead price or expenditure variance. There is no volume variance.

13.3 Materials price variance and price changes

In some examination tasks you may be given information about specific price indices that have affected the materials prices during the period. In these circumstances it is then possible to split the materials price variance into that element that relates to the price increase and any other cause of the variance.

Example

The standard material cost for a business' single product is 4 kg at a price of £12.00 per kg. The standard price was set when the index for this material price stood at 120. During August, 10,000 units of the product were made using 42,000 kg at a total cost of £525,000. The August price index for this material is 122.

What is the total materials price variance, the element relating to the price increase and the element relating to other causes?

Solution

Total materials price variance

		£
Standard cost of actual materials	42,000 × £12.00	504,000
Actual cost		525,000
		21,000 Adverse

This adverse variance of £21,000 can then be split into the element relating to the price increase and the element relating to other factors:

Variance relating to price increase

		£
Standard cost of actual materials	42,000 × £12.00	504,000
Adjusted price for actual materials	42,000 × (£12.00 × 122/120)	512,400
		8,400 Adverse

Variance relating to other factors

		£
Adjusted price for actual materials	42,000 × (£12.00 × 122/120)	512,400
Actual cost		525,000
		12,600 Adverse

14 Measuring the significance of variances

14.1 Introduction

As we have seen, the key tool for management control within a standard costing system is some form of variance analysis report or budgetary control statement. The aim is to prepare a report to management on a routine basis in which variances are clearly identified and can be acted upon as appropriate.

In exercising control, it is generally impracticable to review every variance in detail at each accounting period and attention will usually be concentrated on those variances which have the greatest impact on the achievement of the budget plan.

14.2 Identifying significant variances

One method of identifying significant variances is to express each variance as a percentage of the related budget allowance or standard value. Those showing the highest percentage deviation would then be given the most urgent attention.

This method, however, could result in lack of attention to variances which, although representing a small percentage of the standard value, nevertheless involve significant sums of money. Both percentages and absolute values should be looked at in deciding where the priorities for control actually lie.

In practice, management will review the variance report presented to them and decide which variances should be investigated on the basis of whether the costs of investigation are outweighed by the benefits.

Management may request that a more detailed analysis and explanation of specific variances is produced.

14.3 Fluctuating variances – looking at trends

The variances in a particular period may not be representative of a general trend. Items like stationery costs can fluctuate widely from month to month, depending on the invoices received.

Sometimes, the accountant will make estimated adjustments to either the budget or the actual figures in an attempt to give a better picture of the underlying trend but this is not a completely satisfactory way of dealing with the matter.

The simplest way of getting the month's figures into context is to show also the accumulated cost for the year to date. High cost and low cost periods will then be revealed but will balance out in the cumulative figures.

A development of the above idea is also to report, each period, the manager's latest forecast compared with the annual budget. It will then be possible to see whether variances from budget currently being reported are likely to continue to accumulate during the remainder of the year, or whether they will be offset by later opposite variances.

Although this technique is dependent on managers' subjective assessments, it ensures that the correct control actions are taken based on the current figures.

Example

You might like to spend a few minutes considering what the report below tells you about the business.

Income statement – Seven periods cumulative to 31/12/20X2

	Current period		Var.	Seven months cumulative		Var.	Annual budget	Latest annual forecast
	Budget	Actual	Fav / (Adv)	Budget	Act.	Fav / (Adv)		
	£000	£000	£000	£000	£000	£000	£000	£000
Sales	500	600	100	3,500	3,420	(80)	6,000	6,200
Direct cost of sales	280	322	(42)	1,960	1,951	9	3,500	3,850
Factory overhead	58	69	(11)	420	400	20	700	750
Administration and selling costs	122	123	(1)	840	800	40	1,320	1,147
Total costs	460	514	(54)	3,220	3,151	69	5,520	5,747
Operating profit	40	86	46	280	269	(11)	480	453
Profit: sales %	8.0%	14.3%		8.0%	7.9%		8.0%	7.3%

Solution

(a) Sales, which had obviously been below budget for the first six periods of the year, are significantly in excess of budget for period 7 (reducing the cumulative shortfall to £80,000), and are now expected to exceed the budget for the year as a whole.

(b) Direct costs are naturally higher when sales are higher. The percentage of direct costs to sales value is not consistent, however, as the following calculations show:

	Budget	Actual
Period 7 (280/500 322/600)	56.0%	53.7%
Cumulative to date (1,960/3,500 1,951/3,420)	56.0%	57.0%
Forecast for whole year (3,500/6,000 3,850/6,200)	58.3%	62.1%

For the seven periods as a whole, direct costs have been in excess of the budgeted percentage and even though the budget for the twelve months provides for an increase in that percentage the forecast actual increase is still higher. Period 7 in isolation shows an anomalous result, perhaps due to some peculiarity in sales mix.

(c) The variance on factory overhead, which is favourable over the seven periods as a whole, has become adverse in period 7 and is forecast as adverse for the year as a whole (though not at the rate experienced in period 7).Failure to budget adequately for inflationary increases is one possibility.

(d) Administration and selling costs have a cumulative favourable variance to date of £40,000 against a budget of £840,000, i.e. 4.8%. By the end of the year a favourable variance of £173,000 (13.1% on budget) is expected. It would appear that considerable economies are planned, and have already commenced. The fact that period 7 above shows a small adverse variance is not significant. Such results can emerge in administration costs, which can be influenced by random occurrences like a large purchase of stationery or a major visit overseas by the managing director.

14.4 Comparing against forecasts

Some large organisations in the UK have taken the idea of comparing against forecasts a step further. Many companies employ the following comparisons.

	Comparison	**Information**
1	Budget v actual	What progress have we made towards achieving objectives?
2	Budget v forecast	Will we continue to progress towards achievement of objectives?
3	Budget v revised forecast	Will suggested corrective actions lead us back to achievement of objectives?
4	Latest forecast v previous	Why are the forecasts different? And are circumstances getting better or worse?
5	Actual v past forecast	Why were forecasts incorrect and can they be improved?

It may not be necessary to perform each of these control comparisons every month or quarter. The actual versus past forecast may only be necessary annually or less frequently.

It must be remembered that managers will need to be motivated to produce these forecasts and use them. They must be educated to recognise why and how they can use them to enable them to do a better job and not feel that they are just another means for higher level management to check on them and apply pressure.

Finally, this year's results are sometimes compared with those for the corresponding period last year. In some cases this may be helpful in establishing a trend, but it must never be forgotten that the budget is this year's plan, and it is against that plan that performance must be controlled.

15 Investigation of variances

15.1 Introduction

Variance analysis, if properly carried out, can be a useful cost-controlling and cost-saving tool. However, the traditional variance analysis seen so far is only a step towards the final goal of controlling and saving costs.

15.2 Generalised reasons for variances

The causes of variances can be classified under four headings:

- Planning errors
- Measurement errors
- Random factors
- Operational causes

Planning errors lead to the setting of inappropriate standards or budgets. This may be due to carelessness on the part of the standard setter (not taking account of known changes in the production process or expected price rises, for example) or due to unexpected external changes (a market shortage of a resource leading to increased price for example). These need to be isolated from hindsight information and a revision of the standard considered for future budgets.

Measurement errors include errors caused by inaccurate completion of timesheets or job cards, inaccurate measurement of quantities issued from stores, etc. The rectification of such errors or errors caused by random factors will probably not give rise to any cost savings (though this is a generalisation).

Random factors are by definition uncontrollable, although they need careful monitoring to ensure that they are not, in fact, one of the other types of variance. For example, a fire or flood causing excess wastage of inventory.

15.3 Operational causes of variances

Examples of some operational reasons for individual variances are shown below.

Variance		Possible causes
Materials:	Price	Bulk discounts Different suppliers/different materials Unexpected delivery costs Different buying procedures
	Usage	Different quality material Theft, obsolescence, deterioration Different quality of staff Different mix of material Different batch sizes and trim loss
Labour:	Rate	Different class of labour Excessive overtime Productivity bonuses National wage negotiations Union action
	Efficiency	Different levels of skill Different working conditions The learning effect Lack of supervision Works to rule Machine breakdowns Lack of material Lack of orders Strikes (if paid) Too long over coffee breaks
Overhead:	Price	Change in nature of overhead Unforeseen price changes
	Volume	Excessive idle time Increase in workforce

It will nearly always be useful to consult staff working in operational departments to resolve any queries in the data as they will have 'local' knowledge of the day-to-day operations.

Example

An adverse materials usage variance of £50,000 arose in a month as follows:

Standard cost per kg	£10
Actual cost per kg	£12
Units produced	2,000
Standard quantity per unit	25 kg
Actual quantity used	55,000 kg

	£
Standard cost of actual usage (55,000 kg × £10)	550,000
Standard cost of standard usage (2,000 × 25 kg × £10)	500,000
Adverse usage variance	50,000 A

On further investigation, the following is ascertained.

1 The actual quantity used was based on estimated inventory figures. An inventory count showed that 53,000 kg were in fact used.

2 3,000 kg is the best estimate for what might politely be called the monthly 'shrinkage' but, in less polite circles, theft.

3 2,000 kg of inventory was damaged by hoodlums who broke into the stores through some of the shaky panelling.

4 The supervisor feels that existing machinery is outmoded and more efficient machinery could save 1,000 kg a month.

Additional considerations

1 A security guard would cost £9,000 a year to employ and would stop 20% of all theft. Resultant dissatisfaction amongst works staff might cost £20,000 per annum.

2 Given the easy access to stores, vandals might be expected to break in every other month; £10,000 would make the stores vandal-proof.

3 New machinery would cost £720,000.

Analyse the usage variance in the light of this information and comment on your results.

Solution

The original £50,000 usage variance could be analysed as follows:

		Adverse/(favourable) variance
		£
(a)	Bad measurement (53,000 – 55,000) × £10	20,000
(b)	Theft (3,000 × £10)	30,000
(c)	Damage (2,000 × £10)	20,000
(d)	Obsolete machinery (1,000 × £10)	10,000
(e)	Other operational factors (balance)	(30,000)
		50,000

In each case, the variances should be studied and compared with the cost of rectification.

(a) **Bad measurement** – Assuming no costly decisions were made, or are likely to be made in the future, such as over-stocking, the component is of no future consequence.

(b) **Theft** – Annual cost due to theft is 12 × £30,000 or £360,000; 20% of this saved would amount to £72,000 at a cost of £9,000 + £20,000, thus the security guard is worth employing.

(c) **Damage** – Annual cost due to vandalism is 6 × £20,000 or £120,000; this would presumably be avoided by spending £10,000 now; again worthwhile.

(d) **Obsolete machinery** – Annual cost of using old machines is 12 × £10,000 or £120,000; the cost of making this saving (the saving would increase as purchase prices increased or if production increased) is £720,000; the decision over this investment would require further consideration such as discounted cash flow analysis.

(e) **Other factors** – We now see a favourable usage variance once all known factors above have been accounted for. This may need further investigation, particularly if it affects the quality of goods produced.

15.4 Fixed overhead variances

These are worth a special note, due to the particular nature of the fixed overhead volume variance.

We have seen that the volume variance is a product of the absorption costing system, and represents the adjustment for over-/under-absorption of fixed costs due to actual production being higher or lower than budgeted. Unlike the other variances, it does not actually represent a cost saving or overspend.

If this is the case, is it worth spending any time on the investigation of fixed overhead volume variances? Does it really matter if overheads are under-/over-absorbed, since it will all be adjusted for in the end?

The problem with having an inappropriate absorption rate is that decisions may have been taken on a unit cost that is too high or too low – for example, in setting the price of a product. If this is too high, sales may have been unnecessarily lost; if it is too low, profit margins may have been significantly eroded.

To minimise such effects of over-/under-absorption, regular reviews should be conducted of expenditure and activity levels arising throughout the period. The absorption rate can then be adjusted if it is felt necessary to reflect more recent estimates of expenditure and activity levels.

15.5 The cost of variance analysis

The provision of any information involves the costs of collecting the basic data, processing it, and reporting the results. Variance analysis is no exception and, as with other forms of management information, the benefits to which it gives rise must be commensurate with the costs incurred.

Benefits include:

(a) Variance analysis allows 'management by exception' and it is presumably for this purpose that a standard costing system has been introduced.

(b) When variances are known to exist, failure to make adequate investigations, even on a random basis, will weaken the control system and thus the motivation of managers.

(c) The amount of analysis required can sometimes be reduced by defining levels of significance below which detailed investigation is not required.

(d) The costs of clerical work can be over-estimated. In most working days there will be some spare capacity that can be utilised without extra cost.

What has to be considered, therefore, is the amount of detail that can be incorporated usefully in variance analysis. This will fall into two categories:

(a) **Including more detailed coding** in source documents indicating causes and responsibilities. Such coding is likely to involve people outside the accounts department, who may be unwilling to give time to the task. How useful the analysis will be, will depend on whether or not it is practicable to identify causes and responsibilities at the time the document is initiated.

(b) **Investigations and re-analysis of variances after the event**. This can involve the time of quite senior people, but the process of investigation may well be more useful from the point of view of the management of the business than any quantity of formal variance calculations.

Utilising variance information to improve budgeting practices means that budget planning and control has been used to create a cycle of **continuous improvement**. A continuous improvement culture will help ensure that the internal budget process is efficient and effective and remains relevant to the organisation's needs and priorities. Measuring budget accuracy (with variances) and timeliness on an ongoing basis and periodically conducting more formal reviews are two ways to identify areas for improvement.

We have seen that responsibility accounting is a system which recognises various decision centres within a business and traces costs (and possibly revenues) to the individual managers who are primarily responsible for making decisions about the items in question.

Example

An opportunity arises for a buying department to obtain a consignment of a particular material at an exceptionally low price. The purchase is made; a favourable price variance is recorded and the buying department is duly praised.

Subsequently, when products are being manufactured using this type of material, significant adverse material usage variances and labour efficiency variances are recorded, and are initially regarded as the responsibility of the department where the work is done.

Is it fair to blame the adverse variances on the operational departments?

Solution

Investigations may reveal a number of relevant facts, for example:

- The 'cheap' material was of poor quality, and in consequence much of it was wasted in the process of machining. The resultant material usage and labour efficiency variances should presumably be regarded as the responsibility of the buying department, to offset the favourable price variance.
- Due to an employee leaving it had been necessary to use an operator who was not familiar with the job. At least part of the excess usage of materials could be attributed to this cause; but whether it should be regarded as the responsibility of the operating department or of the personnel department (for failing to recruit a replacement) is still open to question. If the employee who left had been highly paid, his removal might cause a favourable wage rate variance in the period under review – an offset to the adverse efficiency variance.
- The tools used had been badly worn, thus causing excessive time on the job. It would be necessary to consider whether this condition was attributable to the operating department (failing to sharpen tools or to requisition replacements) or to the tools store-keeper or to the buying department (for failing to buy on time or for buying poor quality items again).

The important points to bear in mind are as follows:

- Different types of variance can be inter-linked by a common cause.
- In many cases, the responsibility for variances cannot be identified merely by reference to the cost centre where the variance has been reported. Responsibility may be shared by several managers or may lie completely outside the cost centre in which the variance has arisen.

16 Summary

In this chapter we have looked at the various ways of establishing standard costs within a standard cost reporting system.

We have examined the causes of variances and outlined techniques which may be used to decide whether to investigate them

We have reviewed the computation and interpretations of sales, material, labour, variable and fixed overhead variances.

We have also incorporated some full assessment style questions covering all the variances studied so far.

Test your understanding answers

Test your understanding 1

	Workings:	£
Raw material	1 tonne × £75 per tonne	75.00
Labour	3 hours × £10 per hour	30.00
Variable overhead	3 hours × £5 per hour	15.00
Fixed overhead		6.00
		–––––
Standard cost for one unit		126.00
		–––––

Test your understanding 2

	Workings:	£
Raw material	5 kg × £7.50 per kg	37.50
Labour	2 hours × £7.50 per hour	15.00
Variable overhead	2 hours × £2 per hour	4.00
Fixed overhead		10.00
		–––––
Standard cost for one unit		66.50
		–––––

Test your understanding 3

False. It is impossible to be 100% certain, since different managers will react in different ways, but generally ideal standards will demotivate since adverse variances will continually be reported.

Test your understanding 4

Sales Price variance

			£	
Actual sales units DID sell for Actual sales @ the actual price	500 × £20	=	10,000	
They SHOULD have sold for Actual sales @ the standard selling price	500 × £25	=	12,500	
Sales price variance			2,500	(A)

Sales volume contribution variance

Standard contribution per unit =	£25 – £18 =	£7	
		Units	
Actual sales volume	DID	500	
Budgeted sales volume	SHOULD	400	
Sales volume variance (in units)		100	(F)
@ standard contribution		£7	
Sales volume variance (in monetary terms)		£700	(F)

Test your understanding 5

Sales Price variance

			£	
Actual sales units DID sell for Actual sales @ the actual price	380 × £42	=	15,960	
They SHOULD have sold for Actual sales @ the standard selling price	380 × £45	=	17,100	
Sales price variance			1,140	(A)

Sales volume variance (absorption costing)

Standard profit per unit =	£45 – £23 =	£22	
		Units	
Actual sales volume	DID	380	
Budgeted sales volume	SHOULD	320	
Sales volume variance (in units)		60	(F)
@ standard profit		£22	
Sales volume variance (in monetary terms)		£1,320	(F)

Sales volume variance (marginal costing)

Standard contribution per unit =	£45 – £17 =	£28	
		Units	
Actual sales volume	DID	380	
Budgeted sales volume	SHOULD	320	
Sales volume variance (in units)		60	(F)
@ standard contribution		£28	
Sales volume variance (in monetary terms)		£1,680	(F)

Test your understanding 6

Standard usage of 500 units of K:

500 × 0.4 tonnes	200 tonnes
Actual usage	223 tonnes
Excess usage	23 tonnes

Valued at standard price of £30/tonne:

Direct material usage variance is:

23 tonnes × £30/tonne = £690 Adverse

i.e.: (Standard usage – actual usage) × standard price = (200 – 223) × £30 = £690 Adverse.

Test your understanding 7

Total material variance

	£
Actual direct material cost	3,200
Standard direct material cost of 600 units i.e. standard cost of actual production £5 × 600	3,000
Direct material total cost variance – Adverse	200A

Test your understanding 8

Material price variance

	£
Actual cost of 2,300 litres	3,128
Standard cost of 2,300 litres:	
2,300 litres × £1.30/litre	2,990
Direct material price variance – Adverse	138 A

Material usage variance

Actual usage 2,300 × £1.30	2,990
Standard usage 600 units × 4 × £1.30	3,120
Materials usage variance – Favourable	130 F

Test your understanding 9

AQ × AP

112,000 × £4 = £448,000

AQ × StdP Price variance = £56,000 F

112,000 kg × £4.50 = £504,000

StdQ × AProd × StdP Usage variance = £25,200 F

56 kg × 2,100 units × £4.50 = £529,200

			£
Budgeted/Standard cost of materials for actual production			529,200
Variances	**F**	**A**	
Direct materials price	56,000		
Direct materials usage	25,200		
Total variance	81,200		81,200
Actual cost of materials for actual production			448,000

Test your understanding 10

AQ × AP

2,000 × £5 = £10,000

AQ × StdP — Price variance = £1,000 F

2,000 × £5.50 = £11,000

StdQ × AProd × StdP — Usage variance = £2,200 F

6 × 400 × £5.50 = £13,200

			£
Budgeted/Standard cost of materials for actual production			13,200
Variances	**F**	**A**	
Direct materials price	1,000		
Direct materials usage	2,200		
Total variance	3,200		3,200
Actual cost of materials for actual production			10,000

Test your understanding 11

Y Ltd

(a)

	£	
Actual cost of materials purchased =	2,500	
Standard cost of materials purchased = 750 × £3 =	2,250	
Price variance	250	(A)

(b) Closing inventory (kg) = Purchase – quantity used

= 750 – 600

= 150 kg

Valued at standard cost, this gives a closing inventory valuation of 150 kg × £3 = £450

(c)

	£
Actual materials used at standard price 600 kg × £3	1,800
Standard cost of producing 100 units of B	1,500
100 × 5 kg × £3	
Usage variance	300 (A)

Test your understanding 12

	£
Standard direct labour cost of 450 units: £7 × 450	3,150
Actual direct labour cost	3,450
Direct labour total cost variance	300 A

Test your understanding 13

(a)

Actual hours paid did cost		£4,200
Actual hours paid should cost	1,050 × £4 =	£4,200
Rate variance		NIL

(b) Idle time:

Hours paid @ standard rate	1,050 × £4	£4,200
Hours worked @ standard rate	1,000 × £4	£4,000
		£200 A

(c)

	£
Hours worked @ standard rate 1,000 × £4 =	4,000
Standard hours produced @ standard rate 700 units × 1.50 standard hours × £4	4,200
Direct labour total cost variance	200 F

The hours worked were less than those allowed.

Test your understanding 14

(a)

	Hours	£
Actual hours paid at actual rate per hour	5,000	14,000
Actual hours paid at standard rate per hour 5,000 × £3	5,000	15,000
Direct labour rate variance	–	1,000 F

Actual hours worked at standard rate per hour	5,000	15,000
Standard hours for production achieved at standard rate per hour 2,800 × 2 hrs × £3	5,600	16,800
Direct labour efficiency variance	600	1,800 F

(b)

	Hours	£
Actual hours paid at actual rate per hour	50,000	210,000
Actual hours paid at standard rate per hour 50,000 × £4 per hour	50,000	200,000
Direct labour rate variance	–	10,000 A

Actual hours paid at standard rate per hour	200,000
Actual hours worked at standard rate per hour 48,000 × £4	192,000
Idle time variance	8,000 A

Actual hours worked at standard rate per hour	48,000	192,000
Standard hours for production achieved at standard rate per hour 18,000 × 3 hrs × £4	54,000	216,000
Direct labour efficiency variance	6,000	24,000 F

Test your understanding 15

AH × AR

2,000 × £10 = £20,000

AH × SR

2,000 × £9.80 = £19,600 Rate variance = £400 A

SH × SR

2,050 × 1 × £9.80 = £20,090 Efficiency variance = £490 F

			£
Budgeted/Standard cost of labour for actual production			20,090
Variances	**F**	**A**	
Direct labour rate		400	
Direct labour efficiency	490		
Total variance	490	400	90
Actual cost of labour for actual production			20,000

Test your understanding 16

AH × AR

24,000 × £8 = £192,000

AH × SR

24,000 × £8.50 = £204,000 Rate variance = £12,000 F

SH × SR

400 × 50 × £8.50 = £170,000 Efficiency variance £34,000A

			£
Standard cost of labour			170,000
Variances	**F**	**A**	
Direct labour rate	12,000		
Direct labour efficiency		34,000	
Total variance	12,000	34,000	22,000
Actual cost of labour for actual production			192,000

Test your understanding 17

(a)

	Hours	£
Actual hours at actual rate per hour	3,000	12,000
Actual hours at standard rate per hour		
3,000 × £4	3,000	12,000
Variable overhead expenditure variance	–	Nil
Actual hours at standard rate per hour	3,000	12,000
Standard hours for production achieved at standard rate per hour	2,800	11,200
1,400 × 2 hrs × £4		
Variable overhead efficiency variance	200	800 A

(b)

	Hours	£
Actual hours at actual rate per hour	48,000	90,000
Actual hours at standard rate per hour	48,000	96,000
48,000 × £2 per hour		
Variable overhead expenditure variance	–	6,000 F
Actual hours at standard rate per hour	48,000	96,000
Standard hours for production achieved at standard rate per hour	47,500	95,000
9,500 × 5 hrs × £2		
Variable overhead efficiency variance	500	1,000 A

Test your understanding 18

Absorption rate = $\frac{\text{Budgeted cost}}{\text{Budgeted hours}} = \frac{£50,000}{20,000}$ = £2.50/ labour hour

Actual output in standard hours = 8,450 × $\frac{20,000}{10,000}$ = 16,900 labour hours

Actual overheads	£47,500
Amount absorbed = 16,900 × £2.50 =	£42,250
Variance – under-recovery	£5,250 A

Test your understanding 19

Actual fixed overheads = £39,000

Expenditure variance = £1,000 F

Budgeted fixed overheads = £40,000

Volume variance = £2,000 A

AQ × SR

19,000 × £2 = £38,000

			£
Budgeted/Standard fixed cost for actual production			38,000
Variances	**F**	**A**	
Fixed overhead expenditure	1,000		
Fixed overhead volume		2,000	
Total variance	1,000	2,000	1,000
Actual cost for production			39,000

Test your understanding 20

Actual fixed overheads = £1,245,000

Expenditure variance = £5,000 F

Budgeted fixed overheads = £1,250,000

Volume variance = £45,000 A

AQ × SR

24,100 × £50 = £1,205,000

			£
Budgeted/Standard fixed cost for actual production			1,205,000
Variances	**F**	**A**	
Fixed overhead expenditure	5,000		
Fixed overhead volume		45,000	
Total variance	5,000	45,000	40,000
Actual fixed cost for actual production			1,245,000

Test your understanding 21

$$\text{Fixed overhead recovery rate} = \frac{\text{Budgeted overhead}}{\text{budgeted units}}$$

$$\text{Fixed overhead recovery rate} = \frac{£44,000}{8,000} = £5.50/\text{unit}$$

(a) **Fixed overhead variance**

	£
Fixed overhead recovered = 8,450 × £5.50/unit =	46,475
Actual fixed overhead incurred =	47,500
Variance (under-recovered)	1,025 (A)

(b) **Sub-variances**

(i) Fixed overhead expenditure variance:

	£
Actual cost	47,500
Budgeted overhead	44,000
	£3,500 A

£3,500 adverse, represents an overspend

(ii) Fixed overhead volume variance:

Budget overhead	44,000
Actual production 8,450 × £5.50/unit	46,475
Over-recovery	£2,475 F

Test your understanding 22

(i) The material price variance

Actual price paid for 27,500 kg	£143,000
Standard price 27,500 kg × £5	£137,500
Variance	£5,500 (A)

(ii) The material usage variance

Actual material used for 900 desks = 27,500 kg × £5	£137,500
Standard usage for 900 desks = 900 × 30 = 27,000 kg × £5	£135,000
Variance	£2,500 (A)

(iii) The labour rate variance

Actual price paid for 4,200 hours	£26,040
Standard price for 4,200 hours × £6	£25,200
Variance	840 (A)

(iv) The labour efficiency variance

Actual hours producing 900 desks	4,200 hours × £6
Standard hours = 900 × 5 hours	4,500 hours × £6
Variance	£1,800 (F)

(v) The fixed overhead expenditure variance

£23,000 – £20,000 (W) = £3,000 (A)

(W) Budgeted fixed overhead = 1,000 × £20 per unit

(vi) The fixed overhead volume variance

1,000 × £20 compared to 900 × £20 = £2,000 (A)

Performance indicators

11

Introduction

Variances, covered earlier, are ultimately a type of performance indicator – looking at how individual operational managers perform against pre-set budgets and standard cost targets.

Here we continue this theme, but look at measures for productivity and efficiency; ratios that assist in the assessment of resource utilisation; and overall profitability measures that may be applied to operating divisions and the business as a whole. We also look at the particular performance evaluation aspects of service industries, in particular the measurement of quality of service.

The objective will always be to highlight activities, processes, products and business units that need some attention in order to enhance their value to the business.

ASSESSMENT CRITERIA

Financial performance indicators (4.1)

Non-financial performance indicators (4.2)

CONTENTS

1 Types of performance indicator

1.1 Introduction

Performance indicators may be categorised as quantitative or qualitative.

1.2 Quantitative performance indicators

Quantitative measures are expressed in numerical terms which include the following:

(a) variances

(b) profit, sales, costs

(c) ratios and percentages

(d) indices.

1.3 Qualitative performance indicators

Qualitative indicators are far more subjective and cannot be expressed as an objective, numerical measure. Examples relevant to business and managerial performance would include the following:

(a) level of customer satisfaction: expressed as a subjective level, such as 'very satisfied' … to …'not at all satisfied'

(b) staff performance grades: 'excellent', 'average', 'poor'

(c) company performance: 'steady', 'volatile results', 'disappointing'.

1.4 Efficiency

Performance indicators can be used to measure the efficiency of organisations.

Definition

Efficiency can be defined as the relationship between inputs and outputs achieved. The fewer the inputs used by an organisation to achieve any given output, the more efficient the organisation is. In commercial organisations, efficiency is usually measured in terms of profitability, often in relation to assets employed.

2 Ratio analysis

2.1 Introduction

Ratio analysis is one of the main tools utilised in appraising the performance of a company, the main advantage being that the magnitude of the individual figures is eliminated, allowing the appraiser to concentrate on relative movements.

Ratio analysis is generally utilised in two ways as follows:

(a) comparison of performance year to year

(b) comparison with other companies.

It is important that you can calculate and interpret appropriate ratios.

2.2 Types of ratio

The main types of ratio used are:

(a) profitability ratios

(b) liquidity ratios

(c) gearing ratios

(d) investment ratios.

Of these, profitability and liquidity ratios are of the greatest significance to the management accountant, and are the only types of financial performance indicator included in the AMAC syllabus.

Example

In order to illustrate the most common ratios, let's look at some calculations based on the summarised accounts of Knotty plc. The information from Knotty plc's financial statements will be used in the following sections.

Statement of profit or loss and other comprehensive income for the year ended 31 July 20X9

	Notes	20X9		20X8	
		£000	£000	£000	£000
Revenue			37,589		30,209
Cost of sales			(28,380)		(22,808)
Gross profit			9,209		7,401
Distribution costs		(3,755)		(3,098)	
Administrative expenses		(2,291)		(2,030)	
			(6,046)		(5,128)
Profit from operations			3,163		2,273
Other operating income			108		279
Operating profit			3,271		2,552
Interest receivable			7		28
			3,278		2,580
Finance costs			(442)		(471)
Profit before taxation			2,836		2,109
Tax			(1,038)		(650)
Profit for the period from continuing operations			1,798		1,459

Statement of financial position as at 31 July 20X9

	Notes	20X9		20X8	
ASSETS		£000	£000	£000	£000
Non-current assets					
Tangible assets			8,687		5,669
Investments			15		15
			8,702		5,684
Current assets					
Inventories		8,486		6,519	
Receivables	1	8,836		6,261	
Cash and cash equivalents		479		250	
			17,801		13,030
Total assets			26,503		18,714
EQUITY AND LIABILITIES					
Called up share capital					
Ordinary shares of 20p each	2		2,003		1,762
4.2% cumulative preference shares of £1 each			150		150
			2,153		1,912
Share premium account			123		123
Other reserves			2,576		–
Retained earnings			8,704		6,670
			13,556		8,705
Non-current liabilities					
Debentures			2,840		2,853
Current liabilities					
Bank loans and overdrafts		929		511	
Payables		9,178		6,645	
			10,107		7,156
Total equity and liabilities			26,503		18,714

Notes:

1 Receivables at 31 July 20X9 include trade receivables of £8,233,000 (20X8 £5,735,000).

2 The number of ordinary shares in issue at 31 July 20X9 was 10,014,514 (20X8: 8,808,214).

3 Profitability

3.1 Return on capital employed (ROCE)

Return on capital employed (ROCE) expresses profit as a percentage of the assets in use (the capital employed in the business) and can be further subdivided into profit margin and asset turnover (use of assets):

Profit margin × Asset turnover = Return On Capital Employed (ROCE)

$$\frac{\text{Profit}}{\text{Revenue}} \times \frac{\text{Revenue}}{\text{Assets}} = \frac{\text{Profit}}{\text{Assets}}$$

The equation helps to demonstrate how management can influence the rate of return on capital employed:

(a) By increasing profit margins:

- (i) increase sales prices
- (ii) reduce costs.

(b) By increasing asset turnover (use of assets):

- (i) increase revenues
- (ii) reduce assets (capital employed).

3.2 Year-end or average capital employed

Ideally, the profits for the year ended 31 July 20X9 should be related to the assets in use throughout the year (the average capital employed). In practice, the ratio is usually computed using the assets at the year-end (the year-end capital employed). Using year-end figures of capital employed can distort trends and inter-company comparison; if new investment has been undertaken near to the year-end and financed (for example) by the issue of new shares, the capital employed will have risen by the total finance raised, whereas the profits will only have a month or two of the new investment's contribution.

A range of different acceptable measures of the assets in use is available; the matter of principle should be that the profit figure which is related to the capital employed should include all types of return on those assets.

The AAT have stipulated to use net assets as the capital employed figure for AMAC. And have stated that net assets are the same as total equity, in other words, the amount the organisation owes its owners'.

For Knotty plc, a suitable calculation would be as follows.

	20X9	**20X8**
	£000	£000
Non-current assets	8,702	5,684
Current assets	17,801	13,030
Less: Current liabilities	(10,107)	(7,156)
Less: Long term liabilities	(2,840)	(2,853)
Net assets	13,556	8,705

	20X9	**20X8**
	£000	£000
Operating profit	3,271	2,552
Interest receivable	7	28
Profit before finance costs and tax	3,278	2,580

So the return on capital employed is calculated as:

$$\frac{\text{Profit before finance costs and tax}}{\text{net assets}} \times 100$$

20X9 $\frac{3,278}{13,556} \times 100 = 24.2\%$

20X8 $\frac{2,580}{8,705} \times 100 = 29.6\%$

The capital employed figure includes the long-term debt, the debentures. Therefore, the profit used must be that available to these providers of capital, the profit before finance costs.

The rate of return on year-end capital employed has fallen in 20X9 compared with 20X8 and might indicate less effective management. To comment further, we need to sub-analyse the ratio into profit margin and asset turnover.

We also need to understand that the way in which business managers are assessed can have a great influence on the decisions that they make. The use of ratios such as ROCE can lead to a lack of goal congruence whereby managers improve the performance of certain ratios, but this may not be in the best interests of the organisation as a whole.

For example, a manager may not be prepared to invest in new machinery if the increase in the net asset position will reduce the ROCE. (Despite the investment reducing other costs, leading to zero defects or an increase in customer satisfaction.)

3.3 Profit margin

If the profitability ratios are to interlock perfectly, the profit margin will be calculated expressing the same profit before interest payable and tax as a percentage of revenue:

$$\frac{\text{Profit before finance costs and tax}}{\text{Revenue}} \times 100$$

A small problem with the approach in this example is that the profit includes interest receivable which is not represented in revenue; however, as the amount is small, this can be ignored.

In order that the profit can be related more fairly to revenue, profit margin is sometimes calculated using operating profit.

For Knotty plc: 20X9 $\frac{3,271}{37,589} \times 100 = 8.7\%$

20X8 $\frac{2,552}{30,209} \times 100 = 8.4\%$

Operating profit margins have improved slightly over the last year, possibly due to better cost control.

Low margins within a sector may arise from a policy designed to increase market share by cutting selling prices, or may be due to high development costs associated with new products, both of which may be positive factors for the future. However, low margins are often associated with inefficiency and poor quality management.

Conversely, high margins relative to competitors, or improving margins, are usually taken as indicators of efficiency and good management. High margins achieved by dominating a particular market may, however, attract competitors into that market and imply lower margins in the longer term.

3.4 Costs as a % of revenue

Specifically included in the specification for AMAC as a measure of efficiency is the expression of any cost as a % of revenue.

The calculation of any type of cost as a percentage of revenue is simply performed using the formula:

$$\frac{\text{Cost}}{\text{Revenue}} \times 100$$

For the distribution costs in our example:

$$\text{Distribution cost as a \% of revenue} = \frac{\text{Distribution cost}}{\text{Revenue}} \times 100$$

20X9 $\frac{3,755}{37,589} \times 100\% = 9.99\%$ 20X8 $\frac{3,098}{30,209} \times 100\% = 10.26\%$

Distribution costs as a percentage of revenue are falling which will improve profit.

3.5 Asset turnover

Another aspect of efficient management is to 'make the assets work'. This may involve disposing of those 'underperforming' assets which cannot be made to generate revenue, as well as developing and marketing the company's products or services.

Once again, the simplest method of computing the ratio is to relate revenue to the same figure of year-end capital employed used in calculating return on capital employed:

(again the AAT have stipulated to use net assets)

$$\text{Asset turnover} = \frac{\text{revenue}}{\text{net assets}}$$

20X9 37,589/13,556 = 2.8 times 20X8 30,209/8,705 = 3.5 times

Asset turnover has fallen which is bad for the business at this time. Revenue has not increased in line with investment. However this may improve in the future. The business has invested in assets which may not be generating increased turnover quite yet. Hopefully this will happen soon and the asset turnover ratio will improve.

However, as with profit margins, certain assets represented by capital employed have no turnover implications. One method of avoiding this illogicality is to exclude long and short-term investments from capital employed. For companies with substantial investments this will make a considerable difference.

Asset turnover will tend to be lower in capital-intensive manufacturing industries, which carry substantial tangible non-current assets, inventories and trade receivables, than in service industries where the principal resource is people rather than plant and machinery, and where inventories are low.

There are often trade-offs between asset turnover and profit margins in different sectors. For example, food retailers have relatively low profit margins compared to electronic equipment manufacturers, but asset turnover is higher. Typical numbers might be:

	Profit margin	**×**	**Asset turnover**	**=**	**ROCE**
	%				%
Food retailer	3.7	×	6.7	=	24.8
Electronic equipment manufacturer	10.3	×	2.3	=	23.7

3.6 Gross profit margin

The profit margin given above used a profit figure that included non-productive overheads and sundry items of income. The gross profit margin looks at the profitability of the pure trading activities of the business:

$$\frac{\text{Gross profit}}{\text{Revenue}} \times 100$$

For Knotty plc: 20X9 $\frac{9,209}{37,589} \times 100 = 24.5\%$

20X8 $\frac{7,401}{30,209} \times 100 = 24.5\%$

The company has maintained its gross profit margin; thus the slight rise in operating profit margin must be due to overhead costs being better controlled.

Test your understanding 1

WH Limited is a member of a trade association which operates an inter-company comparison scheme. The scheme is designed to help its member companies to monitor their own performance against that of other companies in the same industry.

At the end of each year, the member companies submit detailed annual accounts to the scheme organisers. The results are processed and a number of accounting ratios are published and circulated to members. The ratios indicate the average results for all member companies.

Your manager has given you the following extract, which shows the average profitability and asset turnover ratios for the latest year. For comparison purposes, WH Limited's accounts analyst has added the ratios for your company.

	Results for year 4	
	Trade association average	**WH Limited**
Return on capital employed	20.5%	18.4%
Net (operating) profit margin	5.4%	6.8%
Asset turnover	3.8 times	2.7 times
Gross margin	14.2%	12.9%

Required:

As assistant accountant for WH Limited, your manager has asked you to prepare a report for the senior management committee. The report should cover the following points:

(a) an explanation of what each ratio is designed to show

(b) an interpretation of WH Limited's profitability and asset turnover compared with the trade association average

(c) comments on any limitations of these ratios and of comparisons made on this basis.

Solution

WH Limited

REPORT

To:

From:

Date:

Subject:

We have received the Trade Association results for year 4 and this report looks in detail at the profitability and asset turnover ratios.

(a) **What each ratio is designed to show**

(i) Return on capital employed (ROCE)

(ii) Net operating profit margin

(iii) Asset turnover

(iv) Gross margin

(b) **WH Limited's profitability and asset turnover**

(c) **Limitations of the ratios and of inter-company comparisons**

4 Liquidity

4.1 Introduction

What follows would classically be referred to as liquidity ratios, for the AMAC syllabus specification they are included under the heading efficiency.

4.2 Working capital ratios

An analysis of the movement in the elements of working capital can be made with the help of the following ratios.

- Receivable period
- Payable period
- Inventory holding period

The result of these ratios can be combined to give the working capital cycle period.

4.3 Trade receivables collection period (trade receivable days)

This calculation is always made using revenue since trade receivables includes the profit element:

$$\frac{\text{Trade receivables}}{\text{Revenue}} \times 365 \text{ days}$$

20X9 $\frac{8,233}{37,589} \times 365 = 80$ days

20X8 $\frac{5,735}{30,209} \times 365 = 69$ days

The company is taking approximately 11 days longer, on average, to collect its debts.

As the year-end figures may be unrepresentative (due perhaps to seasonality of revenues), an average receivables figure for the year might be used if this were available.

4.4 Trade payables payment period (trade payable days)

A similar calculation can be made to determine the trade payables payment (settlement) period:

$$\frac{\text{Trade payables}}{\text{purchases}} \times 365 \text{ days}$$

If the figure for purchases is not given, an acceptable approximation to purchases would be cost of sales.

20X9 $\frac{9,178}{28,380} \times 365 = 118$ days

20X8 $\frac{6,645}{22,808} \times 365 = 106$ days

There has been a slight increase in the payables payment period, indicating Knotty is taking longer to pay suppliers. A review of payables may be necessary to determine whether invoices are in dispute. There may be a deliberate policy to increase the time taken to pay suppliers to reduce the working capital cycle and reduce the strain on the business.

4.5 Inventory holding period (inventory days)

Inventory holding periods can be calculated using:

$$\frac{\text{Inventories}}{\text{Cost of sales}} \times 365 \text{ days}$$

20X9 $\frac{8,486}{28,380} \times 365 = 109$ days

20X8 $\frac{6,519}{22,808} \times 365 = 104$ days

There has been a slight increase in the holding period, indicating inventory is taking longer to sell. A review of inventories may be necessary to determine whether levels of obsolete or damaged inventories are increasing. There may be a deliberate policy to increase inventories prior to a promotion or in response to a specific order.

4.6 Working capital cycle

Working capital cycle period = Receivable period + Inventory holding period – Payable period

20X9: 80 + 109 – 118 = 71 days

20X8: 69 + 104 – 106 = 67 days

There has been a slight increase in the working capital cycle, indicating cash is tied up in the business for longer, this could put a strain on the liquidity of the business.

Test your understanding 2

Two working capital ratios are:

Inventory turnover	☐
Receivables days	☐
Return on capital employed	☐
Gearing	☐

Test your understanding 3

Stately Hotels plc is considering making an offer to buy a small privately owned chain of hotels, Homely Limited. In order to carry out an initial appraisal, you have been provided with an abbreviated set of their accounts for 20X4.

Homely Limited – Statement of profit or loss for the year ended 31 December 20X4 (extract)

	£000
Revenue	820
Operating costs	754
Operating profit	66
Finance costs	4
Profit before tax	62
Taxation	18
Profit after tax	44
Dividends	22
Profit for the year	22

Homely Limited – Statement of financial position as at 31 December 20X4 (extract)

	£000
Non-current assets at carrying amount	230
Net current assets	70
Total assets less current liabilities	300
Long-term loans	50
Equity	250
Number of employees (full-time equivalents)	20
Number of rooms, each available for 365 nights	18
Number of room nights achieved in 20X4	5,900

Stately Hotels plc uses a number of key accounting ratios to monitor the performance of the group of hotels and of individual hotels in the chain. An extract from the target ratios for 20X4 is as follows:

Stately Hotels plc – target ratios for 20X4 (extract)

(i)	Return on capital employed, based on profit before finance costs and tax	27%
(ii)	Operating profit percentage	13%
(iii)	Asset turnover	2 times
(iv)	Working capital period = $\frac{\text{Working capital}}{\text{Operating costs}} \times 365$	20 days
(v)	Percentage room occupancy = $\frac{\text{Number of room nights let}}{\text{Number of room nights available}} \times 100\%$	85%
(vi)	Revenue per employee (full-time equivalent)	£30,000

Required:

(a) Calculate the six target ratios above based on Homely Limited's accounts and present them in a table which enables easy comparison with Stately Hotels' target ratios for 20X4.

(b) Prepare a memorandum for the management accountant of Stately Hotels plc, giving your initial assessment of Homely Limited based on a comparison of these ratios with Stately Hotels' target ratios. Your memorandum should provide the following information for each of the six ratios.

   (i) Comments on the performance of Homely Limited and suggestions about the management action which might be necessary to correct any apparent adverse performance.

   (ii) A discussion of any limitations in the use of the ratio for this performance comparison.

Solution

Homely Limited

(a) **Target ratios**

Return on capital employed =

Operating profit percentage =

Asset turnover =

Working capital period =

Percentage room occupancy =

Revenue per employee =

Key ratios for 20X4

	Stately Hotels plc target	Homely Limited actual
Return on capital employed	27%	
Operating profit percentage	13%	
Asset turnover	2.0 times	
Working capital period	20 days	
Percentage room occupancy	85%	
Revenue per employee	£30,000	

MEMORANDUM

To:

From:

Date:

Subject:

I have carried out an initial assessment of Homely Limited, based on an extract from their accounts for 20X4. I have calculated their key accounting ratios and compared them with our company's target ratios and my conclusions and recommendations are as follows.

Return on capital employed (ROCE)

Operating profit percentage

Asset turnover

Working capital period

Percentage room occupancy

Revenue per employee

4.7 Comparing entities using performance indicators

Comparing an entity with a similar one may come up as a very practical task in an examination. The likely situation is where you have two firms in competition with each other, and one of them sets itself a performance indicator as a target to help it achieve a competitive advantage. The other firm must try to match or better that target.

4.8 What if? analysis

'What if? analysis' is a technique used to test the effect on a set of figures of altering one of the variables that produced those figures. Flexible budgeting is a form of 'what if?' analysis – what if we produce 20,000 units rather than 15,000, say?

With 'what if? analysis' we need to understand that elements of the income statement and statement of financial position are linked. For example, a 10% increase in sales volume will lead to a 10% increase in variable costs, as more units are produced but no increase in fixed costs, assuming that capacity exists. A 10% increase in sales price, however, will not lead to any changes in costs. The increase in costs (caused by volume change) will change the profit and, if no dividends are paid, this will increase the net assets of the business. The change will therefore affect several ratios.

Example

Theo has cost of sales of £250,000 and inventories of £45,000.

Calculate Theo's inventory days.

$$\frac{45{,}000}{250{,}000} \times 365 = 65.7 \text{ days}$$

Theo would like to improve on his inventory days by setting a target of only 60 days.

If Theo intends to achieve this by lowering his inventory holding, inventory would need to be:

$$\frac{x}{250{,}000} \times 365 = 60 \text{ days}$$

x = £41,096

If Theo intends to achieve this by altering his cost of sales, cost of sales would need to be:

$$\frac{45{,}000}{x} \times 365 = 60 \text{ days}$$

x = £273,750

Test your understanding 4

Diamond Limited is a retail jeweller operating 30 branches in similar localities. Common accounting policies operate throughout all branches, including a policy of using straight-line depreciation for non-current assets.

All branches use rented premises. These are accounted for under 'other costs' in the operating statement. Non-current assets are predominantly fixtures and fittings.

Each branch is individually responsible for ordering inventory, the authorising of payments to trade payables and the control of trade receivables. Cash management, however, is managed by Diamond Limited's head office with any cash received by a branch being paid into a head office bank account twice daily.

You are employed in the head office of Diamond Limited as a financial analyst, monitoring the performance of all 30 branches. This involves calculating performance indicators for each branch and comparing each branch's performance with company standards. Financial data relating to Branch 24 is reproduced below.

Diamond Limited – Branch 24 – Year ended 31 December 20X9

Operating statement			**Operating net assets at year end**		
	£000	£000		£000	£000
Revenue		720.0	Non-current assets		
Opening inventory	80.0		Cost		225.0
Purchases	340.0		Accumulated depreciation		(90.0)
Closing inventory	(60.0)				
	–––––				–––––
		360.0	Carrying amount		135.0
		–––––			
Gross profit		360.0	**Working capital**		
Wages and salaries	220.6		Inventories	60.0	
Depreciation	45.0		Receivables	96.0	
Other costs	36.8		Payables	(51.0)	
	–––––			–––––	
					105.0
					–––––
		302.4	Net assets		240.0
		–––––			–––––
Operating profit		57.6			
		–––––			

Task 1

Prepare a statement showing the following performance indicators for Branch 24:

(a) the return on capital employed

(b) the gross profit margin as a percentage

(c) the asset turnover

(d) the net profit margin as a percentage

(e) the average age of receivables in months

(f) the average age of payables in months

(g) the average age of the closing inventory in months.

The financial director of Diamond Limited is Charlotte Walden. She is concerned that Branch 24 is not performing as well as the other branches. All other branches are able to meet or exceed most of the performance standards laid down by the company.

Charlotte is particularly concerned the branches should achieve the standards for return on capital employed and for asset turnover. She also feels that managers should try to achieve the standards laid down for working capital management.

The relevant standards are:

Return on capital employed	40%
Asset turnover	4 times per annum
Average age of receivables	0.5 months
Average age of payables	3 months
Average age of closing inventory	1 month

Charlotte Walden has recently attended a course on financial modelling and scenario planning. Charlotte explains that scenario planning shows the likely performance of a business under different assumed circumstances. It requires an understanding of the relationship between the different elements within the financial statements and how these change as the circumstances being modelled change. As an example, she tells you that if the volume of branch revenue was to increase then the cost of sales would also increase but that all other expenses would remain the same as they are fixed costs.

She believes scenario planning would be particularly helpful to the manager of Branch 24, Angela Newton. Charlotte had previously discussed the performance of the branch with Angela and emphasised the importance of improving the asset turnover and maintaining control of working capital. However, Angela raised the following objections:

- Turning over assets is not important; making profit should be the main objective.
- Branch 24 has been in existence for two years less than all the other branches.

Task 2

Show the return on capital employed that Branch 24 would have achieved had it been able to achieve the company's asset turnover during the year to 31 December 20X9 while maintaining prices and the existing capital employed.

Solution

Task 1

Diamond Ltd
Performance report – Branch 24
Year ended 31 December 20X9

(a)	Return on capital employed	
(b)	Gross profit margin	
(c)	Asset turnover	
(d)	Net profit margin	
(e)	Average age of receivables	
(f)	Average age of payables	
(g)	Average age of inventory	

Task 2

	£
Revised revenue	
Cost of sales = 50%	
	–––––
Gross profit	
Fixed costs	
	–––––
Operating profit	
	–––––
Revised return on capital employed	

5 Manufacturing industries

5.1 Introduction

The performance of a manufacturing business and its constituent activities will commonly be measured in quantitative terms, mainly monetary. However, we shall also consider relevant non-monetary and qualitative factors that can be useful.

5.2 Productivity

Productivity is a measure of the efficiency of resource usage and expresses the rate of output in relation to resource used, often in non-financial terms.

Examples include the following:

(a) units produced per labour or machine hour

(b) productive hours to total hours paid

(c) actual output to full capacity output

(d) number of operations undertaken per day

(e) number of passengers transported per month

(f) number of vehicles manufactured per week

(g) units produced per worker per day

(h) rooms cleaned per hour

(i) meals served per sitting.

Productivity is closely linked with resource utilisation (which is considered later).

5.3 Value added

Definition

Value added is the pool of wealth created, out of which a business provides for:

- payment of wages, salaries and other employee benefits
- reward for providers of capital, in the form of interest and dividends
- payment of government taxation
- maintenance and expansion of assets.

It is also defined as:

- the value of revenue less the cost of bought in materials and services.

Example

Value added statement

	£m
Revenue	1.35
Bought in materials and services	0.55
Value added	0.80

Number of employees = 20

- Value added per employee

$$\frac{£0.80}{20} = £0.04\text{m or } £40{,}000$$

Test your understanding 5

Task

(a) From the following information, draft the value added statement for the years 20X2 and 20X3.

Sandsend Engineering Ltd

Extract from Statements of profit or loss for the years ended 31 December 20X2 and 20X3

	20X2	**20X3**
	£m	£m
Revenue	6.1	6.5
*Costs	4.2	4.5
Operating profit	1.9	2.0
Finance costs	0.6	0.6
	1.3	1.4
Taxation	0.3	0.3
Profit	1.0	1.1

*Costs comprise:

	£m	£m
Wages and salaries	1.8	1.9
Depreciation	0.4	0.5
Other bought in items	2.0	2.1
Other information: Dividends	0.2	0.2

	20X2	*20X3*
Revenue	£m	£m
Less bought in materials and services		
	——	——
Value added		
	——	——

(b) Calculate for both years the value added per '£' of employee costs, and state why this measure is considered an indicator of labour productivity.

	20X2	20X3
Value added	£m	£m
Employee costs		
	——	——
Value added per '£' of employee costs		
	——	——

Why value added is considered to be a measure of productivity:

5.4 Unit costs

Unit costs are the actual average cost of production of each unit of product in the period. Management will attempt to drive down unit costs over time.

5.5 Resource utilisation

This is a measure of the extent to which resources were used in relation to maximum capacity. Examples of utilisation and related measures for different resources include the following:

Machines	–	utilisation (hours used : potential hours)
	–	down time (machine down hours : total hours)
Materials	–	wastage (normal/abnormal loss percentage)
	–	inventory turnover (linked to levels of slow-moving inventory)
Labour	–	utilisation (productive : total hours)
	–	absenteeism, lateness
	–	mix variances (where different grades are used)
	–	idle time (non-productive hours : total hours)
	–	labour turnover (leavers replaced : total employed)

5.6 Quality of service

For a manufacturing business, this can be categorised into quality of service to customers and quality of service from service departments. The latter is covered in the section on the service departments.

Quality of service to customers is essentially a subjective, qualitative measure, although some quantitative measures can be used in connection with it – for example, ratios such as customer returns to total sales and customer complaints per units sold. Speed of service can be measured in retail outlets by numbers of customers waiting at each checkout in a supermarket.

The main source of measure of customer satisfaction will generally be through some sort of questionnaire. This is all considered in more detail later in this chapter.

5.7 Other non-monetary measures

Quality is a particular area in which such indicators are required; two others that have recently been identified as important attributes of world-class manufacturing are innovation and flexibility.

5.8 Innovation

Innovation is concerned with the business's ability to beat their competitors in developing new products, improvements to existing ones or additional customer services.

Measurement of innovation must concentrate on its effectiveness as well as its existence – counting the number of new products developed is of little help without knowing the extent to which they have been accepted by the market. Possible measures include the following:

(a) research and development expenditure related to new revenues;

(b) viable new products to existing products;

(c) percentage of total profits relating to new products/ improvements.

5.9 Flexibility

Flexibility is concerned with the business's ability to respond to customers' needs, in terms of speed of delivery of existing products, speed of reaction to changes in demand patterns and ability to respond to particular customer requests or specifications.

In a manufacturing context, it is often the case that flexibility is connected with the amounts of products using common parts. If demand for one type of product falls, it is easier to switch stock and processing to another if there is a common base between them.

6 Service departments

6.1 Introduction

Many of the measures discussed above will be relevant in the assessment of the performance of service departments within a business. Unless an internal charge-out system operates (for example, the charging of user departments per hour of computer department time spent on their work), the emphasis will be on costs rather than profits.

6.2 Types of performance indicator

As well as the normal cost variances (with activity levels based on the departments' own cost unit, e.g. maintenance hours, meals served, data processing hours), other cost ratios will be appropriate, for example:

(a) meal cost per employee per period (canteen);

(b) running costs per van-mile (deliveries);

(c) cost per call-out (maintenance department).

Example

Consider a transport/distribution department. What type of cost performance indicators might be appropriate?

Solution

(a) **Standing costs** (ascertained as a rate per day), including:

- (i) Road tax
- (ii) Insurance
- (iii) Garage and administration costs
- (iv) Drivers' wages
- (v) Depreciation

(b) **Running costs** (ascertained as a rate per ton/mile), including:

(i) Fuel and lubricants

(ii) Tyres

(iii) Repairs

(iv) Maintenance

Standing costs will be incurred for vehicles owned whether or not they are in use and are in the nature of stepped fixed costs. Fixed because, for each vehicle, they do not vary in amount and 'stepped' because for each additional vehicle required, costs, on a graph, will rise by a further step and remain fixed for a further range of activity until another vehicle is required.

7 Service sectors

7.1 Introduction

Service organisations include the following:

(a) **Professional services**, such as firms of accountants, architects, surveyors, solicitors, whose main assets will be their employees and who provide individual, personalised services to their customers.

(b) **Mass services**, such as transport, which are highly capital asset based and provide a standard range of services to a wide range of customers.

(c) **Public sector services**, such as health, education and local authorities.

7.2 Types of performance indicator

Service sector measures can be considered under very similar headings as those for manufacturing organisations, although there will be a different emphasis on their relative importance.

The main difference between the two types of organisation is the nature of their output.

Output from manufacturing businesses comprises tangible, clearly identifiable products, usually of a standard design and quality which can be rejected by a customer if not required or unsuitable, and produced in advance of demand and stored until needed.

Think about a service provided to you – can it be said to have any of these characteristics? This leads to a different approach needed for performance measurement where costs per product or units per hour are of little relevance or meaning. However, in earlier chapters, we have seen that cost units do not have to be in terms of products and that measures may be activity rather than product based.

So, using similar headings as before, particular areas to be considered about the performance indicators of service organisations are productivity, unit costs, resource utilisation, profitability and quality of service.

In assessments the tasks will ask for performance indicators which are tailored to the scenario set. Make sure that you read the scenario information carefully and actually calculate the indicators that are asked for.

7.3 Productivity

Productivity can be difficult to measure, because services rarely have a standard unit of output. For example, it would be meaningless to measure a conveyancing solicitor's productivity on the basis of 'property purchase completions per month', as each will have a different degree of complexity and value to the business. Similarly, it would be inappropriate to assess a bus line on the basis of 'journeys per day', as the contribution to the company's profits would depend upon the number of people carried at each stage of the journey and how many buses were operating on the line.

Meaningful measures of productivity or efficiency for a service depend upon a clearly defined measure of activity and resources.

So, for example, the measure of activity for the bus line might be 'passenger miles' and of the resource might be 'driver hours'.

Professional firms, such as accountants and solicitors, will generally use 'chargeable hours' as a measure of activity and employees' productivity will be judged by 'chargeable hours per employee'.

7.4 Unit costs

Again, the difficulty here is in defining an appropriate unit for the activity being measured. Once this has been established, appropriate costs need to be attributed to it. So the cost of a professional chargeable hour would mainly consist of employee costs (salaries, NICs, benefits, etc.) but will also include a recovery of general overheads.

The cost of a 'passenger mile' for a transport company will include driver costs, vehicle running costs and overheads.

7.5 Resource utilisation

Resource utilisation is the extent to which available resources are used for productive service. Examples of suitable measures for various types of service businesses are illustrated by the following ratios:

Professional	Chargeable hours : Total hours available
Transport	Passenger miles : Total train miles available
Hotel	Rooms occupied : Rooms available
Car hire	Car-days hired : Car-days available

7.6 Profitability

Clearly, for the service business overall, the usual measures can apply – ROCE, profit margins, etc. Unit profitability measures will again depend upon the clear definition of the cost unit or unit of activity. The profit can then be determined by comparison of the cost per unit (as discussed above) with the income generated (e.g. the charge-out rate for a professional chargeable hour or the average fare per mile on a bus/train route).

Test your understanding 6

A transport company is reviewing the way in which it reports vehicle operating costs to the company management. In particular, it is interested in the use of performance ratios which will help to assess the efficiency and effectiveness of the use of its vehicles.

Information on the following items is available for each vehicle for the period as follows:

Costs

Variable costs

Fuel	Tyres
Oil	Other parts
Hydraulic fluid	Repairs and maintenance

Fixed costs

Road fund licence	Cleaning
Insurance	Depreciation
Drivers' wages	

Activity measures

Miles driven	Number of days available for use
Tonnes carried	Number of days vehicle actually used
Journeys made	

Required:

You are asked to indicate six suitable performance ratios which could be used to monitor the effectiveness and efficiency of the usage of each vehicle.

Three of your ratios should relate to the efficient control of costs and three should relate to the effective usage of vehicles.

Solution

Transport company

Performance ratios

(i) **Costs**

(ii) **Usage**

7.7 Quality of service

This has more significance in the service sector than in the manufacturing sector. Customers will make their buying decisions in the service sector on the basis of how well they expect the service to be provided.

The factors contributing to quality of service will vary according to the nature of the business. As an illustration, consider the service provided to trainee accountancy students by a private college. Possible factors that would influence a potential student in their choice of college and the ways in which these might be measured are as follows:

Factor	**Possible measures**
Technical expertise	Pass rates
Communication	Clarity of lectures, study material and administrative information
Access	Staff/student ratios
	Availability of tutorial help outside lecture hours
	Ease of finding department/member of staff required
	Location of college
Friendliness	Approachability of staff
Flexibility	Ability to tailor service to individual student's needs
Facilities	Availability and standard of canteen, library, phones
Aesthetics	Appearance of college
	Staff presentation
Comfort	Roominess of classrooms
	Heating/air-conditioning
	Comfort of seats, size of desks

You can no doubt think of some more factors and different ways in which those given could be measured. For example, it is perhaps a little glib to use pass rates as a measure of the college's technical expertise, as these are also likely to be significantly influenced by the abilities and commitment of the students themselves.

7.8 Quantitative and qualitative performance indicators

Having identified what needs to be measured, how can this be achieved? Some are a matter of fact or record – like pass rates or the existence of facilities; most of the rest are qualitative judgement and would need to be measured by the use of questionnaires completed by students.

An overall measure of the quality of service provided by the college could be the trend in the number of students enrolling for courses, although again this can be affected by other factors, such as the location of the college and students, the policy of the students' employers and the size of the market for trainee accountants.

8 Total quality management (TQM)

Definition

Total quality management (TQM) can be defined as 'a continuous improvement in quality, efficiency and effectiveness'.

There are several requirements and aims of TQM:

- It aims towards an environment of zero defects at a minimum cost – the principle of 'get it right first time'.
- It requires awareness by all personnel of the quality requirements with supplying the customer with products of the agreed design specification.
- It aims towards the elimination of waste where waste is defined as anything other than the minimum essential amount of equipment, materials, space and workers' time.
- It must embrace all aspects of operations from pre-production to post-production stages in the business cycle.

Total quality management will, therefore, seek method changes which will help in achieving such objectives. Examples include the use of Just-in-time (JIT) production procedures whereby each component or product is produced or purchased only when needed by production or by a customer, rather than for inventory.

8.1 Quality circles

An important element of TQM is that every employee is involved and anyone with an idea about how to improve quality should be heard. This is done by forming groups of employees known as quality circles. These groups normally consist of about 10 employees of differing levels of seniority and with different skills who meet regularly to discuss quality problems and put forward ideas.

8.2 Indicators measuring quality and the cost of quality

Indicators to measure quality of service may include:

- The number of defects
- Units returned
- Warranty claims
- Customer complaints
- The cost of inspection
- Repairs
- Reworking.

Traditionally failure rates, scrap and reworking were subsumed within the costs of production while other aspects of poor quality were accounted for in either production or marketing overheads. TQM does not accept the cost of poor quality as inevitable and requires that the cost of quality is highlighted in management reports. This enables alternative approaches (such as built-in quality at the design stage) to be developed.

Quality-related costs are the expenditure incurred in defect prevention and appraisal activities and the losses due to internal and external failure of a product or service through failure to meet agreed specifications.

8.3 Types of quality-related cost

Quality-related costs may be classified as follows:

(a) **Failure costs** (or non-conformance costs) are the costs required to evaluate, dispose of, and either correct or replace a defective or deficient product.

   (i) **Internal failure costs** are costs incurred before the product is delivered to the customer. Examples include the following:

   - Rework costs
   - Net cost of scrap
   - Disposal of defective products
   - Downtime due to quality problems.

(ii) **External failure costs** are costs incurred after the product is delivered to customers. Examples include the following:

- Complaint investigation and processing
- Warranty claims
- Cost of lost sales
- Product recalls.

(b) **Conformance costs** are further divided into prevention costs and appraisal costs.

(i) **Appraisal costs** are costs of monitoring and inspecting products in terms of specified standards before the products are released to the customer. Examples include the following:

- Measurement equipment
- Inspection and tests
- Product quality audits
- Process control monitoring
- Test equipment expense.

(ii) **Prevention costs** are designed to reduce the level of failure costs. Examples include the following:

- Quality education and training programmes
- Regular equipment maintenance
- Supplier reviews
- Investment in improved production equipment
- Quality circles.

Example

Carlton Limited makes and sells a single product.

The following information relates to its costs and revenues.

1 5% of incoming material from suppliers is scrapped due to poor receipt and storage organisation.

2 4% of material X input to the machine process is wasted due to processing problems.

3 Inspection of the storage facilities for material X costs 10 pence per square metre purchased.

4 Inspection during the production cycle, calibration checks on inspection equipment and other checks cost £25,000 per period.

5 Production quantity is increased to allow for the downgrading of 12.5% of product units at the final inspection stage. Downgraded units are sold as 'second quality' units at a discount of 30% on the standard selling price.

6 Production quantity is increased to allow for returns from customers which are replaced free of charge. Returns are due to specification failure and account for 5% of units initially delivered to customers. Replacement units incur a delivery cost of £8 per unit. 80% of the returns from customers are rectified using 0.2 hours of machine running time per unit and are re-sold as 'third quality' products at a discount of 50% on the standard selling price. The remaining returned units are sold as scrap for £5 per unit.

7 Product liability and other claims by customers are estimated at 3% of sales revenue from standard product sales.

8 Machine idle time is 20% of gross machine hours used (i.e. running hours = 80% of gross hours).

9 Sundry costs of administration, selling and distribution total £60,000 per period.

10 Carlton Limited is aware of the problem of excess costs and currently spends £20,000 per period on training staff in efforts to prevent a number of such problems from occurring.

Give examples of internal and external failure costs, appraisal costs and prevention costs borne by Carlton Limited.

Solution

Internal failure costs. The machine processing losses, downgrading of products, and materials which are scrapped due to poor receipt and storage.

External failure costs. Product liability claims and the costs of making free replacements, including delivery costs.

Appraisal costs. Inspection during the production process, inspection of materials in storage and calibration checks.

Prevention costs. Training costs.

It is generally accepted that an increased investment in prevention and appraisal is likely to result in a significant reduction in failure costs. As a result of the trade-off, there may be an optimum operating level in which the combined costs are at a minimum. In short, an investment in "prevention" inevitably results in a saving on total quality costs.

Test your understanding 7

An example of an external failure cost is:

A Customer survey

B Product recalls

C Inspection

D Rework

8.4 Successful implementation of TQM

An organisation should undertake to achieve each of the following to ensure TQM is successful:

- Total commitment throughout the organisation.
- Get close to their customers to fully understand their needs and expectations.
- Plan to do all jobs right first time.
- Agree expected performance standards with each employee and customer.
- Implement a company-wide improvement process.
- Continually measure performance levels achieved.
- Measure the cost of quality mismanagement and the level of firefighting.
- Demand continuous improvement in everything you and your employees do.
- Recognise achievements.
- Make quality a way of life.

9 Human behaviour

9.1 What gets measured gets done

In some respects the statement seems obvious – measuring something gives you the information you need in order to make sure you actually achieve what you set out to do. Without a standard, there is no logical basis for making a decision or taking action.

The statement assumes that staff have some motivation to deliver what is measured, whether due to the potential of positive feedback and/or rewards or the consequences of failure. The statement could thus be modified to say "What gets measured and fed back gets done well. What gets rewarded gets repeated."

If managers know they are being appraised on various aspects of performance, they will pay attention to these areas.

Careful attention must be paid to the choice of performance indicators. Selection of the wrong measure, would lead to individuals/departments trying to achieve that measure and it could detrimentally impact the overall business performance. Prioritising personal gains over business objectives is often referred to as dysfunctional behaviour and usually means a lack of goal congruence too.

Example

A salesperson paid a bonus for hitting a target based on number of sales transactions in a month could offer excessive discounts to customers to increase sales or could ask customers to place lots of smaller orders instead of one big order.

The excessive discounts would reduce revenue and margins, the smaller orders would increase administrative work and most likely increase costs.

9.2 Ethical code of practice

The AAT's 'Code of Professional Ethics' is based on the IFAC Code and takes a similar conceptual framework approach, listing an identical set of Fundamental Principles that must be followed.

- **Integrity** – This implies fair dealing and truthfulness. Accountants should not be associated with any false, misleading or recklessly provided statements.

- **Objectivity** – Accountants must ensure that their business or professional judgement is not compromised because of bias or conflict of interest.
- **Professional competence and due care** – Accountants are required to have the necessary professional knowledge and skills required to carry out work for clients and must follow all applicable technical and professional standards when carrying out that work.
- **Confidentiality** – Information obtained in a business relationship is not to be disclosed to third parties without specific authority being given to do so, unless there is a legal or professional reason to do so. This information should not be used for the personal advantage of the accountant.
- **Professional behaviour** – Accountants must comply with all relevant laws and regulations and must avoid any actions that would bring the profession into disrepute.

Example

A member of the AAT is a manager and receives a bonus based on net labour variances. The bonus is only paid if the net variance is favourable.

Explain any ethical conflicts or goal congruence issues that may arise.

Solution

1 Objectivity

The manager's judgement may be compromised by their desire to receive a personal bonus and put their preferences before the business.

2 Integrity

The manager may not be truthful about why they carried out their actions and may lay off staff and claim that laying off unskilled staff rather than take the time to train them up was the only option.

3 Professional behaviour

If the manager did lay off staff and their action was discovered to be motivated by personal gain they will have brought the profession into disrepute.

9.3 Ethics and performance indicators

When considering performance indicators and ethics it's important to think about how a target will influence the behaviour of an individual or a group. If you assign a measure and a target to a department they will try to achieve it, especially if there is an incentive for achieving that target.

This means that careful consideration of measures should be given to make sure it does not put staff under undue pressure. Any measures used should be controllable.

Example

YGT Inc manufactures and sells cutting edge, high technology gadgets. Peter Jones was appointed a year ago to run the division responsible for gaming products and was told that, if he could significantly improve the bottom line profit, then he would be promoted to the main board. Peter delivered the increase required by a combination of the following:

- outsourcing design and making older design staff redundant
- cutting back on marketing and research costs
- reducing staff training costs.

Peter has not behaved in an ethical manner. He has achieved short term targets at the expense of the division's long term competitive advantage. The negative consequences of the above were not realised within the period Peter was in control but will affect future periods. His successor will be penalised for decisions made by Peter.

Test your understanding 8

AV is a worker in the accounts department of a large multinational company and receives a bonus if profits for the company are above a certain level. The worker decides to manipulate some of the expenses, artificially increasing the profits and allowing them to get a bonus.

Which of the fundamental principles has the worker NOT breached?

A Confidentiality

B Professional behaviour

C Integrity

D Objectivity

10 The balanced scorecard

10.1 Introduction

The balanced scorecard approach to performance indicators recognises that historically too much emphasis has been placed on financial ratios in assessing an entity's performance. A successful business will only succeed in the long-term if it keeps its customers happy as well as making profits. The approach therefore combines financial measures with operational, organisational innovation and customer service measures. All of these perspectives must be managed by managers if the business is to prosper in the long-term.

The balanced scorecard becomes the manager's instrument panel for managing the complexity of the organisation within a dynamic external environment.

10.2 Four perspectives of the balanced scorecard

The table below is an example of a balanced scorecard performance management system which demonstrates the role of critical success factors (CSFs) and key performance indicators (KPIs) in this process.

The balanced scorecard

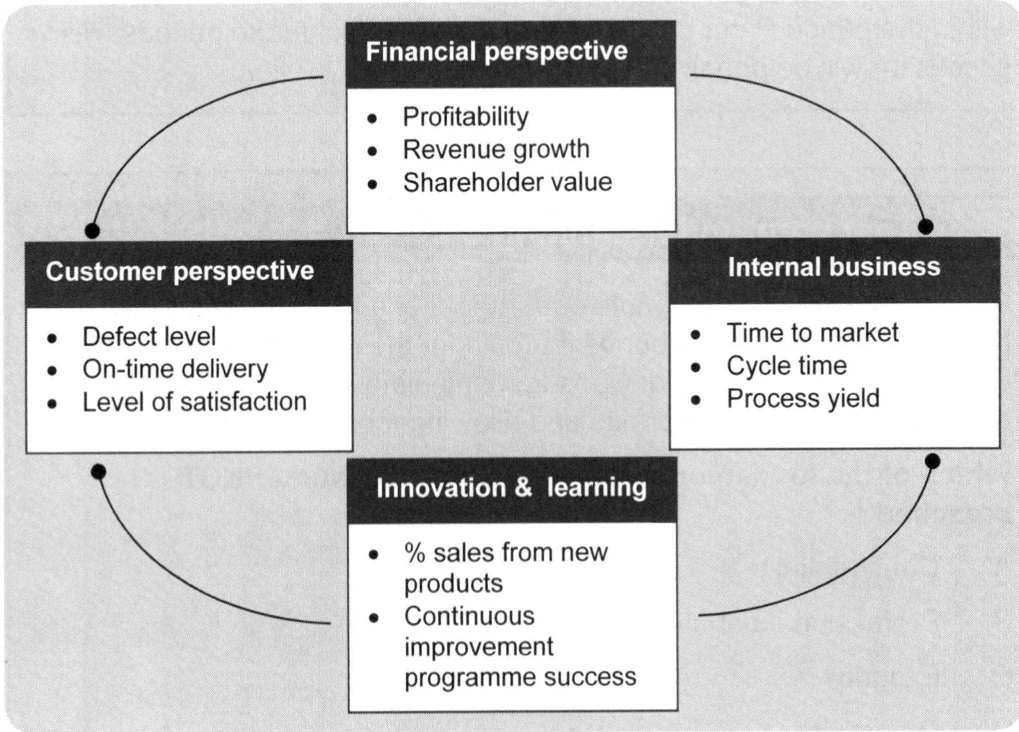

10.3 Key performance indicators

Typical key performance indicators for the balanced scorecard approach are illustrated below.

	Financial perspective	**Customer perspective**	**Internal business process perspective**	**Innovation and learning perspective**
Strategic objective	Shareholder satisfaction	Customer satisfaction	Manufacturing excellence	New product innovation
▼	▼	▼	▼	▼
Critical success factor	Grow shareholder wealth	Achieve preferred supplier status	State-of-the-art process plant	Successful new product development
▼	▼	▼	▼	▼
Key performance indicators	ROCE	Number of new customers	Cycle times Unit cost % yield	% of revenue represented by new products

Test your understanding 9

The four perspectives of the balanced scorecard include:

A Competitor

B Financial

C Economic

D Political

Test your understanding 10

Kaplan and Norton's concept of the 'balanced scorecard' is a way of viewing performance from four perspectives, namely:

- the financial perspective
- the customer perspective
- the internal business process perspective
- the innovation and learning perspective.

Task

(a) Explain what is meant by each of these perspectives.

The financial perspective

The customer perspective

The internal business process perspective

The innovation and learning perspective

(b) You work as an accounting technician in the business planning unit of a large company which has a number of subsidiaries. You use the balanced scorecard concept in appraising performance.

The following information relates to subsidiary A for the year ended 31 December 20X3.

	£m
Revenue	6.85
Cost of sales	5.71
Operating profit	1.14
Number of employees	75

Cost of sales includes training costs of £40,000 and quality assurance costs of £350,000. Assets employed by the subsidiary total £6.30m.

Analysis of revenue by products:

	£m
Existing products	4.85
New products	2.00

Analysis of revenue by customer:

	£m
Existing established customers	4.90
New customers	1.95

Task

Identify a performance indicator for each of the four perspectives for subsidiary A for the year ended 31 December 20X3.

Financial perspective:

Customer perspective:

Internal business process perspective:

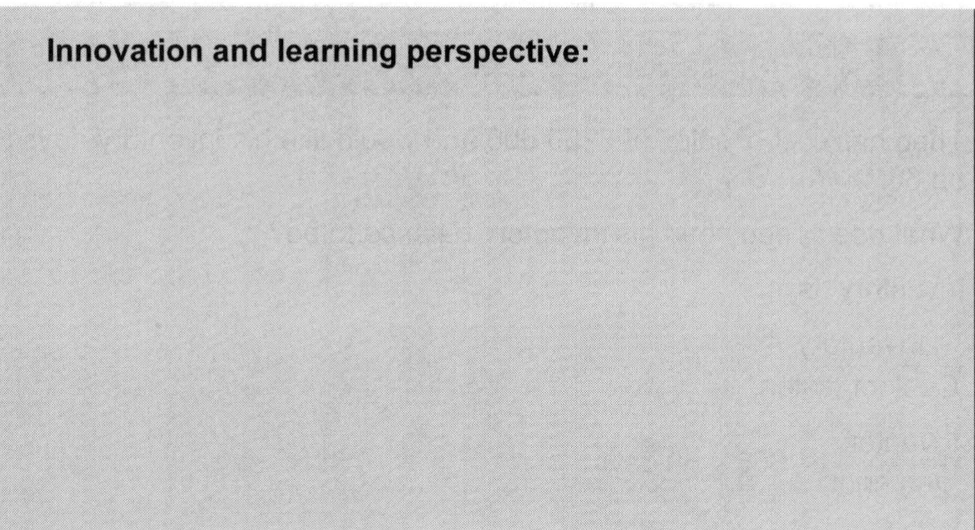

11 Other considerations

11.1 How to change a ratio

In the exam there may be questions about how a proposal may affect a performance indicator, so it is important to be comfortable with both the mechanics of the indicator, but also the impact of a proposal.

In terms of the mechanics, most ratios involve some kind of division, for example gross profit margin equals gross profit **divided** by revenue multiplied by 100 to give a percentage.

To improve this ratio, the end percentage needs to be higher. To make the end percentage higher, either increase the number on the top of the division (the numerator) in this case gross profit or reduce the number on the bottom of the division (the denominator), in this case revenue.

11.2 Working backwards

The examiners like to test that a formula has been learnt, but more importantly that it has been understood. The understanding can come from written questions or through working backwards. Similar to backwards variances, there could be questions where you are given the result of a ratio and are required to work back to calculate one of the inputs to that ratio.

Example

Theo has cost of sales of £250,000 and would like his inventory days to be 60.

What does Theo need his inventory balance to be?

Inventory days:

$$\frac{\text{Inventory}}{\text{Cost of sales}} \times 365$$

$$\frac{\text{Inventory}}{250{,}000} \times 365 = 60 \text{ days}$$

Rearranging:

Inventory = 60/365 × 250,000 = £41,096

Test your understanding 11

What would the revenue need to have been for the asset turnover to be 5 times if the total assets are £50,000?

[ ]

What would the operating profit need to have been for the ROCE to be 20% if the net assets are £400,000?

[ ]

What would the gross profit need to have been if sales revenue was £1,000,000 and the gross profit margin was 20%?

[ ]

What would sales revenue need to be (to the nearest £) if receivable days were 80 days and receivables were £400,000?

[ ]

What would be the 'value added' if sales revenue was £950,000, materials used were £400,000; labour employed was £150,000 and bought in services were £200,000?

What would payables need to be (to the nearest £) if sales were £1,200,000, cost of sales were £700,000 and the payables days were 30 days?

11.3 Influences on performances indicators

Another area to consider is how as a business evolves or as operations change a performance indicator may change.

When a business first sets up, or when it launches a new operation they are unlikely to be very efficient, but a number of factors could lead to efficiency improving and performance indicators improving

(i) **Economies of scale** – volume could grow which would mean more effective use of fixed costs, as the costs is spread over more units. It may also lead to buying larger quantities from suppliers and being offered a bulk buy discount.

(ii) **The learning effect** – as workers become more familiar with a process they will work more efficiently reducing the time they take to make a unit and potentially making savings on the amount of material used as less mistakes are made and material wastage reduces.

Test your understanding 12

You work as an accounting technician for Moran and Geoff, a firm of licensed accounting technicians.

One of your clients, Stonehill Quarries Ltd, has experienced an increase in revenue but a downturn in their overall financial performance in recent times. The company is owner managed by Rita Martine and a small management team.

The following is a summary of the Quarrying Trade Association's performance for the sector as a whole for the year 20X3.

Performance indicators

Return on capital employed	24%
Asset turnover	1.6
Net profit before finance costs and tax as a percentage of revenue	15%
Receivables collection period	60 days
Payables payment period	70 days
Finished goods inventory in days	38 days
Labour costs as % of revenue	18.1%
Operating costs as % of revenue	85.01%
Distribution costs as % of revenue	9.5%
Administrative costs as % of revenue	4.5%
Value added per '£' of employee costs	£1.95

An extract from the company's financial statements for the years 20X2 and 20X3 shows the following:

Income statements

	20X2	**20X3**
	£m	£m
Revenue	5.38	6.68
*Operating costs	4.43	5.82
	0.95	0.86
Finance costs	0.08	0.08
	0.87	0.78
Taxation	0.30	0.27
Profit for the year	0.57	0.51
Dividends	0.16	0.16
*Operating costs comprise:		
	£m	£m
Wages, salaries and other employee costs	0.98	1.25
Bought in materials and services	3.21	4.32
Depreciation	0.24	0.25
	4.43	5.82

Operating costs include the following:

	£m	£m
Distribution	0.49	0.61
Administration	0.22	0.27

Statements of financial position

	20X2	20X3
Assets	£m	£m
Non-current assets	3.77	3.88
Current assets:		
Inventories — Raw materials	0.12	0.15
Finished goods	0.43	0.45
Receivables	0.88	1.19
Cash and cash equivalents	0.04	0.05
	1.47	1.84
Total assets	5.24	5.72
Equity and liabilities		
Equity	3.12	3.47
Non-current liabilities:		
Debentures	1.00	1.00
Current liabilities:		
Trade payables	0.66	0.82
Taxation	0.30	0.27
Dividends	0.16	0.16
	5.24	5.72

Task

(a) Calculate the ratios listed in the trade association statistics for Stonehill Quarries for the years 20X2 and 20X3.

(b)

20X2	20X3
Return on capital employed	
Asset turnover	
Net profit before finance costs and tax as a % of revenue	
Receivables collection period	
Payables payment period	
Finished goods inventory days	
Labour cost % of revenue	
Operating costs % of revenue	

Distribution costs % of revenue	
Admin costs % of revenue	
Value added	
Value added per £ of employee costs	

(c) Comment on the performance of Stonehill Quarries compared with the sector as a whole.

Return on capital employed

Asset turnover

Profit margin

Receivables collection period

Payables payment period

Finished goods inventory in days

Labour costs % of revenue

Operating costs % of revenue

Distribution and admin costs to revenue

Value added per '£' of employee costs

Test your understanding 13

Smithex Ltd makes a single product, the Alpha, which is sold directly to domestic customers. Smithex is able to sell as many Alphas as it can produce.

Each Alpha contains a specialist part, the A10, which is in short supply. Smithex operates a just-in-time stock policy for the other material plus bought in services but not for the A10.

Smithex does not offer credit facilities to customers or hold any inventory of Alphas. The internal accounts of Smithex for the year to 31 May 20X1 are shown below.

Operating statement for the year ended 31 May 20X1

	Units	**£**	**£**
Revenue			6,480,000
Purchases A10	12,000	1,200,000	
Less returns	1,200	120,000	
Net purchases	10,800	1,080,000	
Add opening inventory	1,200	120,000	
Less closing inventory	(1,200)	(120,000)	
A10 issued to production	10,800	1,080,000	
Other material plus bought in services		108,000	
Production wages		1,296,000	
Variable cost of production and sales			2,484,000
Contribution			3,996,000
Production overhead		3,024,000	
Inspection cost of A10 goods received		69,600	
Cost of A10 returns		48,000	
Cost of remedial work		120,000	
Customer support for faulty products		194,400	
Administrative and distribution expenses		216,000	
Total fixed overheads			3,672,000
Net operating profit			324,000

Statement of financial position as at 31 May 20X1

	£	£
Net non-current assets		1,600,000
Inventories	120,000	
Cash	80,000	
Payables	(180,000)	
Net current assets		20,000
		1,620,000
Financed by:		
Equity		800,000
Loans		820,000
		1,620,000

- Number of production employees 140
- Maximum production capacity per year 12,000
- Closing inventory only consists of units of A10
- Payables only arise from purchases of A10

You are employed by Smithex as its management accountant. One of your duties is to prepare management accounting information for Janet Noble, the Managing Director of Smithex.

Task

Janet Noble asks you to prepare the following performance indicators for Smithex:

(a)	Net operating margin		
(b)	Return on capital employed		
(c)	Asset turnover		

(d)	Average age of inventory			
(e)	Average age of payables			
(f)	Added value per employee			
	Revenue			
	Less: Material A10			
	Less: Other material and bought in services			
			————	————
	Added value			
				————
	Added value per employee			
(g)	Wages per production employee			
(h)	Contribution per Alpha			
				————

Test your understanding 14

Travel Bus Ltd is a company owned by Travel Holdings plc. It operates in the town of Camford. Camford is an old town with few parking facilities for motorists. Several years ago the Town Council built a car park on the edge of the town and awarded Travel Bus the contract to carry motorists and their passengers between the car park and the centre of the town.

Originally, the Council charged motorists £4.00 per day for the use of the car park but, to encourage motorists not to take their cars into the town centre, parking has been free since 1 December 20X1.

The journey between the car park and the town centre is the only service operated by Travel Bus Ltd in Camford. A summary of the results for the first two years of operations, together with the net assets associated with the route and other operating data, is reproduced below.

Operating statement year ended 30 November

	20X1	**20X2**
	£	£
Revenue	432,000	633,600
Fuel	129,600	185,328
Wages	112,000	142,000
Other variable costs	86,720	84,512
Gross profit	103,680	221,760
Bus road tax and insurance	22,000	24,000
Depreciation of buses	12,000	12,000
Maintenance of buses	32,400	28,512
Fixed garaging costs	29,840	32,140
Administration	42,000	49,076
Net profit/(loss)	(34,560)	76,032

Extract from statement of financial position as at 30 November

	20X1	20X2
	£	£
Buses	240,000	240,000
Accumulated depreciation	168,000	180,000
Carrying amount	72,000	60,000
Net current assets	14,400	35,040
	86,400	95,040

Other operating data	**20X1**	**20X2**
Fare per passenger per journey	£0.80	£1.00
Miles per year	324,000	356,400
Miles per journey	18.0	18.0
Days per year	360	360
Wages per driver	£14,000	£14,200

Throughout the two years the drivers were paid a basic wage per week, no bonuses were paid and no overtime was incurred.

In two weeks there will be a meeting between officials of the Town Council and the Chief Executive of Travel Holdings to discuss the performance of Travel Bus for the year to 30 November 20X2. The previous year's performance indicators were as follows:

Gross profit margin	24%
Net profit margin	–8%
Return on capital employed	–40%
Asset turnover	5 times
Number of passengers in the year	540,000
Total cost per mile	£1.44
Number of journeys per day	50
Maintenance cost per mile	£0.10
Passengers per day	1,500
Passengers per journey	30
Number of drivers	8

Task

In preparation for the meeting, you have been asked to calculate the following performance indicators for the year to 30 November 20X2:

(a)	Gross profit margin:	
(b)	Net profit margin:	
(c)	Return on capital employed:	
(d)	Asset turnover:	
(e)	Number of passengers in the year:	
(f)	Total cost per mile:	
(g)	Number of journeys per day:	
(h)	Maintenance cost per mile:	
(i)	Passengers per day:	
(j)	Passengers per journey:	
(k)	Number of drivers:	

On receiving your performance indicators, the Chief Executive of Travel Holdings raises the following issues with you:

- The drivers are claiming that the improved profitability of Travel Bus reflects their increased productivity.
- The managers believe that the change in performance is due to improved motivation arising from the introduction of performance related pay for managers during the year to 30 November 20X2.
- The officials from the Town Council are concerned that Travel Bus is paying insufficient attention to satisfying passenger needs and safety.

The Chief Executive asks for your advice.

Task

Write a memo to the Chief Executive of Travel Holdings plc. Where relevant, you should make use of the data and answers to earlier Tasks to:

(a) **Briefly** discuss whether or not increased productivity always leads to increased profitability.

(b) Develop ONE possible measure of driver productivity and suggest whether or not the drivers' claim is valid.

(c) Suggest ONE reason, other than improved motivation, why the profitability of Travel Bus might have improved.

(d) Suggest:

   (i) ONE **existing** performance indicator which might measure the satisfaction of passenger needs; and

   (ii) ONE other possible performance indicator of passenger needs which cannot be measured from the existing performance data collected by Travel Bus.

(e) Suggest:

   (i) ONE **existing** performance indicator which might measure the safety aspect of Travel Bus's operations; and

   (ii) ONE other possible safety performance indicator which cannot be measured from the existing performance data collected by Travel Bus.

MEMO

To:

From:

Date:

Subject:

I refer to your observations relating to the performance of Travel Bus Ltd and detail my comments below.

(a) **Relationship between productivity and profitability**

(b) **Driver productivity**

(c) **Reasons for improved profitability**

(d) **Indicator of passenger satisfaction**

(e) **Possible safety indicators**

Test your understanding 15

LandAir and SeaAir are two small airlines operating flights to Waltonville. LandAir operates from an airport based at a town on the same island as Waltonville but SeaAir operates from an airport based on another island. In both cases, the flight to Waltonville is 150 air-miles. Each airline owns a single aircraft, an 80-seat commuter jet and both airlines operate flights for 360 days per year.

You are employed as the management accountant at SeaAir and report to Carol Jones, SeaAir's chief executive. Recently both airlines agreed to share each other's financial and operating data as a way of improving efficiency. The data for the year to 31 May 20X0 for both airlines is reproduced below. The performance indicators for LandAir are reproduced further below.

Operating statement year ended 31 May 20X0

	LandAir	**SeaAir**
	£000	£000
Revenue	51,840	29,700
Fuel and aircraft maintenance	29,160	14,580
Take-off and landing fees at Waltonville	4,320	2,160
Aircraft parking at Waltonville	720	2,880
Depreciation of aircraft	500	400
Salaries of flight crew	380	380
Home airport costs	15,464	8,112
Net profit	1,296	1,188

Extract from statement of financial position as at 31 May 20X0

	LandAir	SeaAir
	£000	£000
Non-current assets		
Aircraft	10,000	10,000
Accumulated depreciation	2,500	4,000
Carrying amount	7,500	6,000
Net current assets	3,300	5,880
	10,800	11,880

Other operating data		
Number of seats on aircraft	80	80
Return flights per day	12	6
Return fare	£200	£275
Air-miles per return flight	300	300

Performance indicators	**LandAir**
Return on capital employed	12.00%
Asset turnover per year	4.80
Revenue (or net profit) margin	2.50%
Actual number of return flights per year	4,320
Actual number of return passengers per year	259,200
Average seat occupancy[1]	75.00%
Actual number of passenger-miles[2]	77,760,000
Cost per passenger mile	£0.65

Notes:

1 Actual number of return passengers ÷ maximum possible number of return passengers from existing flights.

2 Actual number of passengers carried × number of miles flown.

Task

Carol Jones asks you to prepare the following performance indicators for SeaAir:

(a)	**Return on capital employed:**	
(b)	**Asset turnover:**	
(c)	**Revenue (or net profit) margin:**	
(d)	**Actual number of return flights per year:**	
(e)	**Actual number of return passengers per year:**	
(f)	**Average seat occupancy:**	
(g)	**Actual number of passenger-miles:**	
(h)	**Cost per passenger mile:**	

Carol Jones is concerned that the overall performance of SeaAir is below that of LandAir, despite both airlines operating to the same destination and over a similar distance. She finds it all the more difficult to understand as LandAir has to compete with road and rail transport. Carol Jones has recently attended a seminar on maintaining competitive advantage and is eager to apply the concepts to SeaAir. She explains that there are two ways to gain a competitive advantage:

- by being the lowest cost business; or
- by having a unique aspect to the product or service allowing a higher price to be charged.

This involves managers attempting to eliminate costs which do not enhance value, that is, costs for which customers are not prepared to pay either in the form of a higher price or increased demand.

She makes the following proposals for next year, the year ending 31 May 20X1:

- The number of return flights is increased to 9 per day.
- The estimated average seat occupancy will change to 55%.
- The price of a return fare will remain the same.

As a result of the proposals, there will be some changes in operating costs:

- Fuel and aircraft maintenance, and take-off and landing fees at Waltonville airport, will increase in proportion with the increase in flights.
- Aircraft parking at Waltonville will be halved.
- Aircraft depreciation will increase to £600,000 for the forthcoming year.
- Additional flight crew will cost an extra £58,000.
- There will be no other changes in costs.

Task

Carol Jones is interested in forecasting the performance of SeaAir for next year, the year to 31 May 20X1. Write a memo to Carol Jones. In your memo you should:

(a) Calculate the forecast number of passengers next year for SeaAir.

(b) Calculate SeaAir's forecast net profit for next year.

(c) Show SeaAir's forecast return on capital employed for next year assuming no change in its net assets other than any additional depreciation.

(d) Identify ONE competitive advantage SeaAir has over LandAir.

(e) Identify ONE expense in SeaAir's operating statement which does not add value.

MEMO

To:

From:

Date:

Subject:

I outline below the forecast performance for SeaAir for the year to 31 May 20X1.

(a)	Forecast number of passengers:	
(b)	Forecast net profit for the year to 31 May 20X1:	
		£000
	Revenue:	
		———
	Fuel and aircraft maintenance	
	Take off and landing fees at Waltonville	
	Aircraft parking at Waltonville	
	Depreciation of aircraft	
	Salaries of flight crew	
	Home airport costs	
		———
	Net profit	
		———
(c)	Revised return on capital employed:	

(d)

(e)

Test your understanding 16

You are employed as a financial analyst with Denton Management Consultants and report to Jamie Alexander, a local partner. Denton Management Consultants has recently been awarded the contract to implement accrual accounting in the St Nicolas Police Force and will shortly have to make a presentation to the Head of the Police Force. The presentation is concerned with showing how performance indicators are developed in 'for profit' organisations and how these can be adapted to help 'not for profit' organisations.

Jamie Alexander has asked for your help in preparing a draft of the presentation that Denton Management Consultants will make to the Head of the Police Force. Jamie suggests that a useful framework would be the balanced scorecard and examples of how this is used by private sector organisations.

The balanced scorecard views performance measurement in a 'for profit' organisation from four perspectives.

The financial perspective

This is concerned with satisfying shareholders and measures used include the return on capital employed and the profit margin.

The customer perspective

This attempts to measure how customers view the organisation and how they measure customer satisfaction. Examples include the speed of delivery and customer loyalty.

The internal business process perspective

This measures the quality of the organisation's output in terms of technical excellence and consumer needs. An example would be total quality measurement.

The innovation and learning perspective

This emphasises the need for continual improvement of existing products and the ability to develop new products to meet customers' changing needs. In a 'for profit' organisation, this might be measured by the percentage of revenue attributable to new products.

To help you demonstrate how performance indicators are developed in 'for profit' organisations, she gives you the following financial data relating to a manufacturing client of Denton Management Consultants.

Statement of profit or loss for the 12 months ended 30 November 20X0

	£000	£000
Revenue		240.0
Material	18.0	
Labour	26.0	
Production overheads	9.0	
Cost of production	53.0	
Opening finished inventory	12.0	
Closing finished inventory	(13.0)	
Cost of sales		52.0
Gross profit		188.0
Research & development	15.9	
Training	5.2	
Administration	118.9	
		140.0
Net profit		48.0

Extract from statement of financial position at 30 November 20X0

	Opening balance £000	Additions £000	Deletions £000	Closing balance £000
Non-current assets				
Cost	200.0	40.0	10.0	230.0
Depreciation	80.0	8.0	8.0	80.0
Carrying amount				150.0
Net current assets				
Inventory of finished goods			13.0	
Receivables			40.0	
Cash			6.0	
Payables			(9.0)	
				50.0
Net assets				200.0

Task

Jamie Alexander asks you to calculate the following performance indicators and, for each indicator, to identify ONE balanced scorecard perspective being measured:

(a)	Return on capital employed:	
	Scorecard:	
(b)	Net margin percentage	
	Scorecard:	
(c)	Asset turnover:	
	Scorecard:	
(d)	Research and development as percentage of production:	
	Scorecard:	

(e)	Training as percentage of labour costs:	
	Scorecard:	
(f)	Average age of finished inventory:	
	Scorecard:	

Test your understanding 17

You are employed by ALV Ltd as an accounting technician. Two companies owned by ALV Ltd are ALV (East) Ltd and ALV (West) Ltd. These two companies are located in the same town and make an identical electrical product which sells for £84.

Financial data relating to the two companies is reproduced below. In addition, performance indicators for ALV (East) Ltd are also enclosed. Both companies use the same straight-line depreciation policy and assume no residual value.

ALV (East) Ltd

Extract from statement of financial position as at 31 May 20X0

	Cost	**Accumulated depreciation**	**Net book value**
	£000	£000	£000
Non-current assets			
Buildings	1,000	700	300
Plant & machinery	300	240	60
	1,300	940	360
Net current assets			
Inventory		45	
Receivables		30	
Cash		5	
Payables		(40)	40
			400

ALV (East) Ltd
Operating statement – year to 31 May 20X0

	£000
Revenue	840
Material and bought-in services	340
Production labour	180
Other production expenses	52
Depreciation – buildings	20
Dep'n – plant and machinery	30
Admin and other expenses	50
Operating profit	168

Other data

Number of employees	18	Units produced	10,000

Performance indicators for ALV (East) Ltd

Asset turnover	2.1 times	Production labour cost per unit	£18.00
Net profit margin	20.00%	Output per employee	556
Return on capital employed	42.00%	Added value per employee	£27,778
Wages per employee	£10,000	Profit per employee	£9,333

ALV (West) Ltd
Extract from statement of financial position as at 31 May 20X0

	Cost	**Accumulated depreciation**	**Carrying amount**
	£000	£000	£000
Non-current assets			
Buildings	1,500	120	1,380
Plant & machinery	900	180	720
	2,400	300	2,100
Net current assets			
Inventory		20	
Receivables		30	
Cash		5	
Payables		(55)	Nil
			2,100

ALV (West) Ltd
Operating statement – year to 31 May 20X0

	£000
Revenue	2,520
Material and bought-in services	1,020
Production labour	260
Other production expenses	630
Depreciation – buildings	30
Dep'n – plant and machinery	90
Admin and other expenses	112
Operating profit	378

Other data

Number of employees	20	Units produced	30,000

ALV Ltd is considering closing one of the companies over the next two years. As a first step, the board of directors wish to hold a meeting to consider which is the more efficient and productive company.

Task

In preparation for the board meeting, calculate the following performance indicators for ALV (West) Ltd:

(a)	Asset turnover:	
(b)	Net profit margin:	
(c)	Return on capital employed:	
(d)	Wages per employee:	
(e)	Production labour cost per unit:	

(f)	Output per employee:	
(g)	Added value:	
	Added value per employee:	
(h)	Profit per employee:	

Test your understanding 18

You are the Management Accountant of Care4, a registered charity. You report to Salma Anahit, the Chief Executive. Care4 owns Highstone School, a residential school for children with special needs. One of your duties is to prepare performance indicators for Highstone School. The accounts for the year to 31 August 20X2 are shown below.

Operating statement – year to 31 August 20X2

	£	£
Fee income		1,760,000
Teacher salaries	600,000	
Nursing and support staff salaries	480,000	
Administrative expenses	120,000	
Power	128,000	
Housekeeping	160,000	
Depreciation	236,800	
Total expenses		1,724,800
Operating surplus		35,200

Statement of financial position extract at 31 August 20X2

	Land	Buildings and equipment	Total
	£	£	£
Non-current assets			
Cost	4,502,800	11,840,000	16,342,800
Depreciation to date		9,708,800	9,708,800
Carrying amount	4,502,800	2,131,200	6,634,000
Net current assets			
Receivables	440,000		
Cash	62,000		
Payables	(96,000)		406,000
Net assets			7,040,000

Local authorities refer children with special needs to the school and pay the school fees. There is a standard contract that states the number of children per teacher and the number of nursing and support staff required. You are provided with the following additional information:

- The school fee per child for the year ended 31 August 20X2 was £22,000.
- The contracts state there must be:
  - one teacher for every four children (The average salary per teacher is £30,000)
  - one member of the nursing and support staff for every two children. (The average salary per member of the nursing and support staff is £12,000).
- The school can accommodate a maximum of 100 children.
- The buildings and equipment are depreciated by equal amounts each year and are assumed to have no residual value.
- Payables entirely relate to power and housekeeping.

Task

Prepare the following school performance indicators for Salma Anahit:

(a)	Operating surplus/fee income	
(b)	Return on capital employed	
(c)	Average age of receivables	
(d)	Average age of payables	
(e)	Number of children in school	
(f)	Occupancy rate of school	
(g)	Number of teachers	
(h)	Number of nursing and support staff	
(i)	Total cash-based expenses = total expenses – depreciation	

Test your understanding 19

You are employed as an accounting technician by Aspex Technologies Ltd. One of your duties is to prepare performance indicators and other information for Marwa Eisha, the Financial Director.

Aspex Technologies make a single product, the Zeta. In the year to 30 November 20X3, the company has had problems with the quality of the material used to make Zetas and Marwa would like to know what the cost of quality has been for the year.

The cost of quality is defined as the total of all costs incurred in preventing faults plus those costs involved in correcting faults once they have occurred. It is a single figure measuring all the explicit costs of quality – that is, those costs collected within the accounting system.

Marwa provides you with the following financial statements and data.

Operating statement – year ended 30 November 20X3

	Units	£000	£000
Revenue	360,000		14,400
Purchases	400,000	6,400	
Less returns	(40,000)	(640)	
Net purchases	360,000	5,760	
Add opening inventory	90,000	1,440	
Less closing inventory	(90,000)	(1,440)	
Material issued to production	360,000	5,760	
Production labour		3,600	
Variable cost of production and sales			9,360
Contribution			5,040
Heat, light and power		720	
Depreciation		1,000	
Inspection cost		80	
Production overhead		2,000	
Reworking of faulty production		40	
Customer support		200	
Marketing and administrative expenses		424	
Total fixed overheads			4,464
Operating profit			576

Statement of financial position as at 30 November 20X3

	£000	£000
Non-current assets at cost		8,000
Cumulative depreciation		2,000
Carrying amount		6,000
Inventory	1,440	
Receivables	2,400	
Cash	960	
Payables	(1,200)	
Net current assets		3,600
		9,600
Financed by		
Debt		6,000
Equity		3,600
		9,600

- The number of production employees in the company is 180.
- Production labour is a variable expense.
- The demand for Zetas in the year to 30 November 20X3 was 390,000 but not all could be produced and sold due to poor quality materials. Any orders not completed this year can be completed next year.
- The only reason for the reworking of faulty production and customer support expenses was the poor quality of the materials.
- Material and heat, light and power are the only bought-in expenses.
- Payables relate entirely to material purchases.
- There are no inventories of finished goods or work in progress.
- Depreciation is based on the straight-line method.

Task

Prepare the following information for Marwa Eisha:

(a)	Selling price per Zeta:		
(b)	Material cost per Zeta:		
(c)	Labour cost per Zeta:		
(d)	Contribution per Zeta:		
(e)	Contribution percentage:		
(f)	Net profit (or revenue) margin:		
(g)	Return on capital employed:		
(h)	Asset turnover:		
(i)	Average age of receivables in months:		
(j)	Average age of inventory in months:		
(k)	Average age of payables in months:		
(l)	Added value per employee		
	Revenue:		
	Material:		
	Heat, light and power:		
		————	
	Added value:		
		————	
	Added value per employee:		

(m)	**Average delay in completing an order in months**		
	Order volume:		
	Sales volume:		
		———	
	Backlog:		
		———	
	Average delay:		
(n)	**Cost of quality**		
	Inspection:		
	Reworking:		
	Customer support:		

Test your understanding 20

The actual and budgeted operating results for the sale and production of executive desks for the year to May 20X4 are set out below.

	Actual	Budget
	£	£
Revenue	2,750,000	3,000,000
Cost of sales		
Opening finished goods inventory	200,000	200,000
Cost of production	2,329,600	2,400,000
Closing finished goods inventory	(240,000)	(200,000)
Cost of sales	2,289,600	2,400,000
Gross profit	460,400	600,000
Distribution and administration costs	345,000	360,000
Operating profit	115,400	240,000

Other data for the production and sale of executive desks for the year to May 20X4 is as follows:

	Actual	**Budget**
Number of desks sold	11,000	12,000
Number of desks produced	11,200	12,000
Direct labour hours	58,200	60,000
Net assets employed	£1,075,400	£1,200,000

Task

(a) Calculate the following actual and budgeted performance indicators:

	Actual	**Budget**
Gross profit margin		
Operating profit margin		
Return on capital employed		
Inventory turnover (in months)		

(b) Write a memo to Sam Thomas. Your memo should include ONE course of action the company could take to improve EACH performance indicator.

MEMO

To:

From:

Date:

Subject:

(i) **Gross profit margin**

(ii) **Operating profit margin**

(iii) **Return on capital employed**

(iv) **Inventory turnover**

Sam Thomas has been on a course on product management. Sam was particularly interested in the concept of value engineering or value analysis. This was explained to be a process which involves different specialists to evaluate a product's design. The objective of the process is to identify how a product may be redesigned to improve its value.

Task

Write a brief memo to Sam Thomas. Your memo should describe how value engineering or value analysis may be used to reduce the production cost of an item such as an executive desk.

MEMO

To:

From:

Date:

Subject:

12 Summary

As you have seen, there are numerous possible performance indicators and their relevance will depend upon the type of organisation and the aspect of performance being assessed.

The most important ratios for you to be able to compute (and interpret) are as follows:

Profitability:	Return on capital employed (ROCE)
	Gross and operating profit margins
Efficiency:	Inventory holding period
	Receivable period
	Payable period
	Working capital cycle period
	Any cost as a percentage of revenue
	Asset turnover

Remember that a ratio on its own is not particularly useful information; it needs to be compared, internally or externally.

Many of the ideas covered in earlier chapters will have relevance here (e.g. variance analysis and the use of indices).

Make sure you are quite clear about the necessary attributes of a cost unit (or unit of activity) in order for it to provide a useful basis for measurement. This is particularly important for service activities. Try to think of services you have had experience of yourself and how the various aspects may be measured.

There will rarely be a unique right or wrong answer, so do not be afraid to use your imagination!

Answers to chapter test your understandings

Test your understanding 1

WH Limited

REPORT

To: Senior Management Committee

From: Assistant Accountant

Date: Today

Subject: Profitability and asset turnover ratios

We have received the Trade Association results for year 4 and this report looks in detail at the profitability and asset turnover ratios.

(a) **What each ratio is designed to show**

(i) Return on capital employed (ROCE)

This ratio shows the percentage rate of profit which has been earned on the capital invested in the business (i.e. the return on the resources controlled by management). The expected return would vary depending on the type of business and it is usually calculated as follows:

Return on capital employed =

$$\frac{\text{Profit before finance costs and tax}}{\text{Capital employed}} \times 100$$

Other profit figures can be used, as well as various definitions of capital employed.

(ii) Net operating profit margin

This ratio shows the operating profit as a percentage of revenue. The operating profit is calculated before finance costs and tax and it is the profit over which operational managers can exercise day to day control. It is the amount of revenue remaining after all direct costs and overheads have been deducted.

$$\text{Net operating profit margin} \frac{\text{Operating profit}}{\text{Revenue}} \times 100$$

(iii) Asset turnover

This ratio shows how effectively the assets of a business are being used to generate sales:

$$\text{Asset turnover} \frac{\text{Revenue}}{\text{Capital employed}}$$

If the same figure for capital employed is used as in ROCE, then ratios (i) to (iii) can be related together as follows.

(i) ROCE = (ii) Net operating profit margin × (iii) Asset turnover

(iv) Gross margin

This ratio measures the gross profit compared to revenue:

$$\text{Gross margin} \frac{\text{Gross profit}}{\text{Revenue}} \times 100$$

The gross profit is calculated as the revenue less the cost of goods sold and this ratio therefore focuses on the company's manufacturing and trading activities.

(b) **WH Limited's profitability and asset turnover**

WH Limited's ROCE is lower than the trade association average, indicating either poor profitability (as measured by the net profit margin) or poor asset utilisation (as measured by the asset turnover) or both.

WH Limited's operating profit margin is higher than the trade association average, despite a lower than average gross profit margin. This suggests that overheads are lower relative to revenue in WH Limited.

WH Limited's asset turnover ratio is lower than the trade association average. This may mean that assets are not being used as effectively in our company as they could be.

WH Limited's gross profit margin is lower than the trade association average. This suggests either that WH's direct costs are higher than average, or that selling prices are lower.

(c) **Limitations of the ratios and of inter-company comparisons**

There are a number of limitations of which you should be aware before drawing any firm conclusions from a comparison of these ratios:

(i) The ratios are merely averages, based on year-end balance sheet data, which may not be representative.

(ii) One particular factor which could affect these ratios is if there has been any new investment during the financial year. This investment would increase the value of the assets or capital employed, but the profits from the investment would not yet have accumulated in the income statement. Generally, newer assets tend to depress the asset turnover and hence the ROCE in the short term, as the assets have been purchased at cost and have not been depreciated. It is possible that this is the cause of our company's lower asset turnover and ROCE.

(iii) Although the trade association probably makes some attempt to standardise the data, different member companies may be using different accounting policies, for example in calculating depreciation and valuing inventory.

(iv) Our company's analyst may have used a different formula for calculating any of the ratios. For example, as noted above, there are a variety of ways of calculating capital employed. However, it is likely that the trade association would provide information on the basis of calculation of the ratios.

(v) The member companies will have some activities in common, hence their membership of the trade association. However, some may have a diversified range of activities, which will distort the ratios and make direct comparison difficult.

Test your understanding 2

Two working capital ratios are inventory turnover and receivable days.

Test your understanding 3

(a) **Target ratios**

Return on capital employed	= 66/250 × 100	= 26.4%
Operating profit percentage	= 66/820 × 100	= 8%
Asset turnover	= 820/320	= 2.6 times
Working capital period	= 70/754 × 365	= 34 days
Percentage room occupancy	= 5,900/(18×365) × 100	= 90%
Revenue per employee	= 820,000/20	= £41,000

Key ratios for 20X4

	Stately Hotels plc target	Homely Limited actual
Return on capital employed	27%	26.4%
Operating profit percentage	13%	8%
Asset turnover	2.0 times	2.6 times
Working capital period	20 days	34 days
Percentage room occupancy	85%	90%
Revenue per employee	£30,000	£41,000

(b)

MEMORANDUM

To: Management Accountant, Stately Hotels plc

From: Assistant to the Management Accountant

Date: Today

Subject: Initial assessment of the performance of Homely Limited

I have carried out an initial assessment of Homely Limited, based on an extract from their accounts for 20X4. I have calculated their key accounting ratios and compared them with our company's target ratios and my conclusions and recommendations are as follows.

Return on capital employed (ROCE)

At 26.4% the ROCE is below the target which we set for the hotels in our chain. Management action will be necessary to improve the return on capital employed, through improved profitability of operations, increased asset turnover, or both.

The main limitation in the use of this ratio is that the valuation of the capital employed can have a considerable effect on the apparent ROCE. For example, if the capital employed is undervalued, this will artificially inflate the ROCE.

Operating profit percentage

This is considerably below the target ratio set by Stately Hotels plc and it is the cause of the depressed ROCE. Management action will be necessary to improve this, either by increasing prices or by controlling operating costs relative to revenue. Since the former action may depress demand in Homely Limited's market, it is likely that management will need to focus on the control of operating costs.

A limitation in the use of this ratio is that Homely's operations may not be comparable to the average hotel in the Stately group. For example, they may not have conference facilities, which would affect the profile of their costs.

Asset turnover

At 2.6 times this is higher than the target ratio, indicating that, although Homely's operations are not as profitable, they generate more revenue per £ of capital employed. It may be that Homely has a different basis of operating, i.e. charging lower prices, and thus reducing the profitability of revenue, but in the process generating a higher revenue for the level of capital employed.

The main limitation of this ratio stems from the limitation of the ROCE, i.e. its accuracy relies on the correct valuation of capital employed.

Working capital period

This is 34 days of operating costs, almost double the level which we require in our target performance ratios. Working capital levels are probably unacceptably high and need to be reduced. This will require more attention to receivables control, reduction in inventory of, for example, consumable materials and foodstuffs, and an investigation into whether full use is being made of available credit facilities.

A limitation of this ratio is that it relies on the accurate valuation of working capital. For example, although inventories should not account for a high proportion of working capital in a hotel, their valuation can be very subjective.

Another major limitation is that the ratio is based on statement of financial position data, which depicts the working capital level on a single day. This may not be representative of the year as a whole and therefore incorrect conclusions may be drawn from the analysis.

Percentage room occupancy

Homely Limited is achieving a room occupancy rate which is above the level expected in our organisation's target ratios. This is a healthy sign, which is encouraging.

Revenue per employee

Homely Limited's revenue per employee is also healthy. However, we must ensure that customer service and quality are not suffering as a result of operating with a lower level of staffing.

Overall, Homely Limited seems to have some strengths which would be worth exploiting. However, their control of operating costs and of working capital needs some attention.

Test your understanding 4

Task 1

Diamond Ltd
Performance report – Branch 24
Year ended 31 December 20X9

(a)	Return on capital employed	57.6/240.0	24%
(b)	Gross profit margin	360.0/720.0	50%
(c)	Asset turnover	720.0/240.0	3 times
(d)	Net profit margin	57.6/720.0	8%
(e)	Average age of receivables	(96.0/720.0) × 12	1.6 months
(f)	Average age of payables	(51.0/340.0) × 12	1.8 months
(g)	Average age of inventory	(60.0/360.0) × 12	2.0 months

Task 2

		£
Revised revenue	£240,000 × 4	960,000
Cost of sales = 50%		480,000
Gross profit		480,000
Fixed costs		302,400
Operating profit		177,600
Revised return on capital employed	£177,600/£240,000	74%

Test your understanding 5

(a) **Value added statements**

	20X2	*20X3*
Revenue	£m	£m
	6.1	6.5
Less bought in materials and services	2.0	2.1
Value added	4.1	4.4

(b) **Value added per £ of employee costs**

	20X2	*20X3*
Value added	£m	£m
	4.1	4.4
Employee costs	1.8	1.9
Value added per '£' of employee costs	£2.28	£2.32

Bought in materials and services are consumed by value adding activities which are driven by labour and other resources to produce finished goods or services rendered. These outputs have a value in the form of revenue and when offset by the bought in items create a pool of wealth we know as value added.

Labour is a major resource which contributes to this wealth and therefore we can measure labour's productivity as:

$$\frac{\text{Value added}}{\text{Labour cost}}$$

If the productivity of labour increases then this ratio will increase.

In the case of Sandsend Engineering Ltd above, the ratio has improved from £2.28 to £2.32 – showing an increase in labour productivity.

Test your understanding 6

Cost control performance ratios

Cost per mile
Cost per tonne carried
Cost per journey
Cost per tonne/mile

} each of these ratios could be calculated for fixed and variable costs separately

Fixed cost per available day
Fixed cost per working day

Usage performance ratios

Tonne/miles per period
Days available as a percentage of total working days
Days used as a percentage of available days
Tonnes carried per available day
Journeys made per available day
Tonnes/miles per journey

Test your understanding 7

B External failure costs include the costs of product recalls.

Test your understanding 8

The correct answer is A.

There is no evidence that AV has breached confidentiality in this scenario. However, AV has produced an inaccurate profit figure, compromising integrity. AV is also breaching objectivity, by allowing self-interest to bring bias into the work done. AV's actions, if discovered, would also bring the profession into disrepute, meaning that AV is not displaying professional behaviour.

Test your understanding 9

B The balanced scorecard includes the financial perspective.

Test your understanding 10

(a) The four perspectives within the 'balanced scorecard' view of performance are:

- **The financial perspective**

  This is concerned with satisfying shareholders and measures used include the return on capital employed and the profit margin.

- **The customer perspective**

  This attempts to measure how customers view the organisation and how they rate customer satisfaction. Examples include the speed of delivery and customer loyalty.

- **The internal business process perspective**

  This measures the quality of the organisation's output in terms of technical excellence and consumer needs. Examples include unit cost and total quality measurement.

- **The innovation and learning perspective**

  This emphasises the need for continual improvement of existing products and the ability to develop new products to meet customers' changing needs. In a 'for profit' organisation, this might be measured by the percentage of revenue attributable to new products.

(b) **Financial perspective:**

Shareholder satisfaction

Return on capital employed

$$\frac{\text{Operating profit}}{\text{Assets employed}} \times 100$$

$$\frac{1.14}{6.30} \times 100 \quad = \quad 18.1\%$$

Customer perspective:

Customer satisfaction

% of revenue to established and existing customers

$$\frac{4.90}{6.85} \times 100 \quad = \quad 71.5\%$$

Internal business process perspective:

Quality assurance costs as a % of total cost

$$\frac{0.35}{5.71} \times 100 \quad = \quad 6.1\%$$

Innovation and learning perspective:

Revenue generated by new products as a % of total revenue

$$\frac{2.00}{6.85} \times 100 \quad = \quad 29.2\%$$

Test your understanding 11

5 × £50,000 = £250,000

ROCE = Operating profit/Capital employed × 100%

20% = Operating profit/£400,000

Operating profit = £80,000

Gross profit margin = Gross profit/Sales revenue × 100%

20% = Gross profit × £1,000,000

Gross profit = £200,000

Receivable days = Receivables/Sales revenue × 365

80 = £400,000/Sales revenue × 365

Sales revenue = £1,825,000

Value added = Sales revenue – Cost of materials and bought in services

Value added = £950,000 – £400,000 – £200,000

Value added = £350,000

Payable days = Payables/Cost of sales × 365

30 = Payables/£700,000 × 365

Payables = £57,534

Test your understanding 12

(a) **Return on capital employed**

$$= \frac{\text{Net profit before finance costs and tax}}{\text{Net assets}} \times 100$$

20X2	**20X3**
0.95/3.12× 100	0.86/3.47 × 100
= 30.45%	= 24.78%

Asset turnover

= Revenue/net assets

20X2	**20X3**
5.38/3.12	6.68/3.47
= 1.72 times	= 1.93 times

Net profit before finance costs and tax as a % of revenue

$$\frac{\text{Net profit before finance costs and tax}}{\text{Revenue}} \times 100$$

20X2	**20X3**
$\frac{0.95}{5.38} \times 100$	$\frac{0.86}{6.68} \times 100$
= 17.66%	= 12.87%

Receivables collection period

$$\frac{\text{Receivables}}{\text{Revenue}} \times 365 \text{ days}$$

20X2

$$\frac{0.88}{5.38} \times 365 \text{ days}$$

= 60 times

20X3

$$\frac{1.19}{6.68} \times 365 \text{ days}$$

= 65 times

Payables payment period

$$\frac{\text{Trade payables}}{\text{Purchases}}$$

20X2

$$\frac{0.66}{3.21} \times 365 \text{ days}$$

= 75 days

20X3

$$\frac{0.82}{4.32} \times 365 \text{ days}$$

= 69 days

Finished goods inventory days

$$\frac{\text{Inventories (finished goods)}}{\text{Cost of sales}} \times 365 \text{ days}$$

To improve our estimation of Cost of Sales we can add back the distribution and admin expenses to the operating costs.

20X2

$$\frac{0.43}{(4.43 - 0.49 - 0.22)} \times 365 \text{ days}$$

= 42 days

20X3

$$\frac{0.45}{(5.82 - 0.61 - 0.27)} \times 365 \text{ days}$$

= 33 days

Labour cost % of revenue

20X2

$$\frac{0.98}{5.38} \times 100$$

= 18.22%

20X3

$$\frac{1.25}{6.68} \times 100$$

= 18.71%

Operating costs % of revenue

20X2	**20X3**
$\frac{4.43}{5.38} \times 100$	$\frac{5.82}{6.68} \times 100$
= 82.34%	= 87.13%

Distribution costs % of revenue

20X2	**20X3**
$\frac{0.49}{5.38} \times 100$	$\frac{0.61}{6.68} \times 100$
= 9.11%	= 9.13%

Admin costs % of revenue

20X2	**20X3**
$\frac{0.22}{5.38} \times 100$	$\frac{0.27}{6.68} \times 100$
= 4.09%	= 4.04%

Value added per '£' of employee costs

Value added:

	20X2	**20X3**
	£m	£m
Revenue	5.38	6.68
Bought in materials and services	3.21	4.32
Value added	2.17	2.36

Value added per '£' of employee costs

20X2	**20X3**
$\frac{2.17}{0.98}$	$\frac{2.36}{1.25}$
= £2.21	= £1.89

(b) **Return on capital employed**

The company has experienced a significant decline in profitability in 20X3 to a level below that for the sector as a whole. However, a return of 24% may be considered a good level of performance but a further decline may be the sign of longer term problems.

Asset turnover

The company has increased its volume of sales to net assets ratio, but is not generating the volume experienced by the sector.

Profit margin

One reason for the reduction in the primary ratio (the ROCE) is highlighted here. There has been a significant fall in the profit margin so, although sales volume has increased, there has been a reduction in the margin.

The return to sales is now approximately 13% compared with 15% for the sector.

Receivables collection period

The receivables day period has increased and is currently 65 days compared with 60 days average for the sector.

Tighter controls are required here and if the trend continues upward the company may be exposing itself to the incidence of bad debts.

Payables payment period

The company's period is typical of the sector as a whole. There has been a fall in payable days as the company has utilised some of its excess cash flow in this area.

Finished goods inventory in days

The company is now holding around one month's supply of finished inventory. It is not sacrificing liquidity by tying up excess working capital in the form of inventory.

The company's inventory management controls are now tighter than those for the sector.

Labour costs % of revenue

There has been a marginal increase here but the ratio is still at an acceptable level of control.

Operating costs % of revenue

There has been a significant increase here which indicates that operating overheads and some other direct costs need tighter controls. It may be that the company has an ageing plant and maintenance charges are on an upward trend.

If these assumptions are not the case, there may have been a significant shift in product mix which can influence product profitability.

An analysis of the above factors needs to be carried out to assess fully the change in this measure of efficiency.

Distribution and admin costs to revenue

These measures are well in line with the sector average and indicate good sound controls in these areas of cost.

Value added per '£' of employee costs

The effectiveness and efficiency of the human asset resource has been offset by the adverse factors highlighted above.

The productivity of labour is now some 3% less than the sector average.

Test your understanding 13

(a) **Net operating margin**

(£324,000/£6,480,000) × 100	5%

(b) **Return on capital employed**

(£324,000/£800,000) × 100	40.5%

(c) **Asset turnover**

(£6,480,000/£800,000)	8.1 times

(d) **Average age of inventory**

(£120,000/£1,080,000) × 12	1.33 months

(e) **Average age of payables** 2 months

(£180,000/£1,080,000) × 12

(f) **Added value per employee**

Revenue	£6,480,000	
Less: Material A10	£1,080,000	
Less: Other material and bought in services	£108,000	
Added value	£5,292,000	
Added value per employee (£5,292,000/140)		£37,800

(g) **Wages per production employee**

(£1,296,000/140) £9,257

(h) **Contribution per Alpha**

Selling price per unit (£6,480,000/10,800) =

Marginal cost per unit (£2,484,000/10,800) =

Contribution per Alpha = £370

Test your understanding 14

(a) Gross profit margin:

£221,760/£633,600 × 100 35%

(b) Net profit margin:

£76,032/£633,600 × 100 12%

(c) Return on capital employed:

£76,032/£95,040 × 100 80%

(d) Asset turnover:

£633,600/£95,040 6.67 times

(e) Number of passengers in the year:

£633,600/£1 633,600 passengers

(f) Total cost per mile:

(£633,600 – £76,032)/356,400 £1.56

(g) Number of journeys per day:

356,400/(18 miles × 360 days) 55 journeys

(h) Maintenance cost per mile:

£28,512/356,400 £0.08

(i) Passengers per day:

633,600/360 — 1,760 passengers

(j) Passengers per journey:

1,760/55 — 32 passengers

(k) Number of drivers:

£142,000/£14,200 — 10

MEMO

To: Chief Executive

From: Management Accountant

Date: Today

Subject: Performance of Travel Bus Ltd

I refer to your observations relating to the performance of Travel Bus Ltd and detail my comments below.

(a) **Relationship between productivity and profitability**

Productivity is the measure of outputs against inputs and is often a nonfinancial measure.

An example of productivity is output per employee. Increases in productivity do not always lead to an increase in profitability. Profits may fall if finished goods or services rendered are sold at a market price less than previously charged. Cost increases not passed on in increased prices may also adversely affect profitability, even though productivity may have risen.

(b) **Driver productivity**

One measure of driver productivity is miles driven per driver. There has been a reduction in this measure from 40,500 miles per driver in 20X1 to 35,640 in 20X2. These results do not support the drivers' claims.

(**NB:** An alternative measure could have been passengers per driver.)

(c) **Reasons for improved profitability**

Both volume and price have increased, passengers per day and per journey have increased together with fare per passenger journey.

These factors have resulted in fixed costs being recovered faster by an increase in contribution.

Volume has increased and may be the effect of the free parking supported by council policy.

(d) **Indicator of passenger satisfaction**

The number of journeys per day has increased from 50 to 55. This indicates that there was a decrease in waiting time between journeys.

The figures provided do not indicate any measure of the punctuality of the service.

(**NB:** Other comments could include the number of passengers having to stand throughout the journey and the catering for disabled passengers.)

(e) **Possible safety indicators**

Maintenance cost per mile is an indicator of safety issues. The maintenance cost per mile has fallen from £0.10 to £0.08 and as the fleet is a further year older the question of safety needs to be reviewed.

One additional safety indicator is the provision of security facilities at both the car park and the bus terminal.

(**NB:** Accidents per year would also be a useful measure.)

Test your understanding 15

(a)	Return on capital employed:	10.00%
	(£1,188,000/£11,880,000) × 100	
(b)	Asset turnover:	2.50 times
	£29,700,000/£11,880,000	
(c)	Revenue (or net profit) margin:	4.00%
	£1,188,000/£29,700,000 × 100	
(d)	Actual number of return flights per year:	2,160
	6 × 360	
(e)	Actual number of return passengers per year:	108,000
	£29,700,000/£275	
(f)	Average seat occupancy:	62.50%
	108,000/(2,160 × 80) × 100	
(g)	Actual number of passenger-miles:	
	108,000 × 300	32,400,000
(h)	Cost per passenger mile:	
	£28,512,000/32,400,000 miles	£0.88

MEMO

To: Carol Jones

From: Management Accountant

Date: Today

Subject: Competitive advantage

I outline below the forecast performance for SeaAir for the year to 31 May 20X1.

(a) Forecast number of passengers:

9 flights × 80 seats × 55.00% occupancy × 360 days =	142,560

(b) Forecast net profit for the year to 31 May 20X1:

	£000
Revenue: 142,560 flights × £275	39,204
Fuel and aircraft maintenance: £14,580,000 × 9/6	21,870
Take-off and landing fees at Waltonville: £2,160,000 × 9/6	3,240
Aircraft parking at Waltonville: £2,880,000 × 50%	1,440
Depreciation of aircraft	600
Salaries of flight crew: £380,000 + £58,000	438
Home airport costs	8,112
Net profit	3,504

(c) Revised return on capital employed:

(£3,504,000/£11,280,000) × 100 — 31%

(Net assets: £11,880,000 – £600,000 extra depreciation = £11,280,000)

(d) SeaAir has a competitive advantage as its route to Waltonville is over the sea and therefore cannot be threatened by other rail or road transport. This allows SeaAir to charge an economic fare. Also, with a lower seat occupancy, SeaAir customers may have a better choice of flights.

(e) One major expense which does not add value in the eyes of a customer is the cost of aircraft parking at Waltonville.

Test your understanding 16

(a) Return on capital employed:

(£48,000 ÷ £200,000) × 100 — 24%

Scorecard: financial perspective.

(b) Revenue (net profit) margin percentage

(£48,000 ÷ £240,000) × 100 — 20%

Scorecard: financial perspective (and possibly internal perspective as partly measuring unit cost).

(c) Asset turnover:

£240,000 ÷ £200,000 — 1.2 times

Scorecard: internal perspective, demonstrating intensive use of assets and, hence, unit cost

(d) Research and development as percentage of production:

(£15,900 ÷ £53,000) × 100 — 30%

Scorecard: innovation and learning perspective.

(e) Training as percentage of labour costs:

(£5,200 ÷ £26,000) × 100 — 20%

Scorecard: innovation and learning perspective.

(f) Average age of finished inventories:

(£13,000 ÷ £52,000) × 12 — 3 months

Scorecard: internal business process perspective as the greater the amount of finished inventory, the less efficient the business is (working capital is tied up).

Test your understanding 17

Performance indicators for ALV (West) Ltd

(a) Asset turnover:
£2,520/£2,100 — 1.2 times

(b) Net profit margin:
(£378/£2,520) × 100 — 15%

(c) Return on capital employed:
£378/£2,100 × 100 — 18%

(d) Wages per employee:
£260,000/20 — £13,000

(e) Production labour cost per unit:
£260,000/30,000 — £8.67

(f) Output per employee:
30,000/20 — 1,500 units

(g) Added value:
£2,520,000 – £1,020,000 = £1,500,000
Added value per employee:
£1,500,000/20 — £75,000

(h) Profit per employee:
£378,000/20 — £18,900

Test your understanding 18

(a)	Operating surplus/fee income	(£35,200/£1,760,000 × 100)	2%
(b)	Return on capital employed	(£35,200/£7,040,000 × 100)	0.50%
(c)	Average age of receivables	(£440,000/£1,760,000 × 12)	3 months
(d)	Average age of payables	(£96,000/(£128,000 + £160,000) × 12)	4 months
(e)	Number of children in school	(£1,760,000/£22,000)	80
(f)	Occupancy rate of school	(80/100 × 100%)	80%
(g)	Number of teachers	(80 children/4 children per teacher)*	20
(h)	Number of nursing and support staff	(80 children/2 children per member of staff)*	40
(i)	Total cash-based expenses= total expenses – depreciation	= £1,724,800 – £236,800	£1,488,000
***Alternative answers:**			
	Total teachers' salaries/average salary	(£600,000/£30,000)	20
	Total nursing and support staff salaries/average salary	(£480,000/£12,000)	40

Test your understanding 19

(a)	Selling price per Zeta: £14,400,000/360,000	£40
(b)	Material cost per Zeta: £5,760,000/360,000	£16
(c)	Labour cost per Zeta: £3,600,000/360,000	£10
(d)	Contribution per Zeta: £5,040,000/360,000	£14
(e)	Contribution percentage: £5,040,000/£14,400,000 × 100	35%
(f)	Net profit (or Revenue) margin: £576,000/£14,400,000 × 100	4%
(g)	Return on capital employed: £576,000/£3,600,000 × 100	16%
(h)	Asset turnover: £14,400,000/£3,600,000	4 times
(i)	Average age of receivables in months: £2,400,000/£14,400,000 × 12	2 months
(j)	Average age of inventory in months: £1,440,000/£5,760,000 × 12	3 months
(k)	Average age of payables in months: £1,200,000/£5,760,000 × 12	2.5 months

(l) Added value per employee

Revenue:	£14,400,000	
Material:	(£5,760,000)	
Heat, light and power:	(£720,000)	
Added value:	£7,920,000	
Added value per employee: £7,920,000/180		£44,000

(m) Average delay in completing an order in months

Order volume:	390,000	
Revenue volume:	360,000	
Backlog:	30,000	
Average delay: 30,000/360,000 × 12		1 month

(n) Cost of quality

Inspection:	£80,000	
Reworking:	£40,000	
Customer support:	£200,000	£320,000

Test your understanding 20

(a)

	Actual	Budget
Gross profit margin (W1)	16.7%	20.0%
Operating profit margin (W2)	4.2%	8.0%
Return on capital employed (W3)	10.7%	20.0%
Inventory turnover (in months) (W4)	1.3	1.0

Workings: Note that the workings only show the calculation of the actual figure. The budget is calculated in the same way.

1 $\frac{\text{Gross profit}}{\text{Revenue}} = \frac{460{,}400}{2{,}750{,}000} = 16.7\%$

2 $\frac{\text{Operating profit}}{\text{Sales}} = \frac{115{,}400}{2{,}750{,}000} = 0.0419 = 4.2\%$

3 $\frac{\text{Operating profit}}{\text{Net assets}} = \frac{115{,}400}{1{,}075{,}400} = 0.1073 = 10.7\%$

4 Inventory turnover (also called 'Inventory holding period')

$\frac{\text{Closing inventory}}{\text{Cost of sales}} \times 12 = \frac{240{,}000}{2{,}289{,}600} = 1.257 = 1.3$

(b)

MEMO

To: Sam Thomas

From: Accounting Technician

Date: Today

Subject: Performance indicators

(i) **Gross profit margin**

An increase in the selling price or a reduction in the cost of a desk will result in an increase in the gross margin. At present, however, the company is achieving the budgeted price of £250 per desk and it may not be possible to increase the price. If this is the case, efforts should be made to reduce the cost of production.

(ii) **Operating profit margin**

The operating profit margin will increase if the company can reduce its distribution and administration costs. The actual results are £15,000 below budget, so it may be difficult to make further savings in this area.

(iii) **Return on capital employed**

The return on capital employed will improve if operating profits improve with no increase in capital employed. The measures detailed above will, therefore, have the effect of improving the return.

One could also examine whether an asset disposal programme could be implemented and the proceeds distributed to shareholders. This would have the effect of reducing capital employed and improving the return on capital employed.

(iv) **Inventory turnover**

The current Inventory of desks represents 1.2 months' production. An increase in revenue volumes may lead to a reduction in the number of desks held in inventory and will consequently improve this indicator. Alternatively, the company should examine whether inventory levels can be reduced.

MEMO

To: Sam Thomas

From: Accounting Technician

Date: Today

Subject: Value Engineering Production cost of an executive desk

It is clear from the actual results for November that, although the budgeted revenue price has been achieved, the gross margin has not. Value engineering may be employed to examine ways in which production costs may be reduced.

Value engineering is the process of reducing costs by:

- simplifying the product design
- eliminating unnecessary activities in the production process.

Value engineering requires the use of functional analysis which involves the identification of the attributes of the executive desk. Once these are established, a price can be determined for each attribute.

Functional analysis may lead to a change in design and a reduction in the materials required for production. Also, if the product design is simplified, assembly time may be reduced and this will lead to lower labour costs.

Divisional performance

12

Introduction

In the previous chapter we looked at performance measures from an organisation wide perspective. We are continuing the performance measurement theme here with a look at how we do this where organisations have more than one division that they wish to report on.

We'll remind ourselves about different types of responsibility centres and the sorts of measures we can use for each type. Our main focus will be on investment centres and the two new measures that we can use for these; return on investment (ROI) ad residual income (RI). Neither is perfect, but they both have their uses.

We'll also consider how transfer prices work for sales between internal divisions.

ASSESSMENT CRITERIA

Divisional performance (LO 4.3)

CONTENTS

1 Responsibility centres

1.1 Introduction

Remember that in previous chapters we have discussed different responsibility centres, namely:

- cost centre
- revenue centre
- profit centre
- investment centre

Type of division	Description	Typical measures used to assess performance
Cost centre	Division incurs costs, but has no revenue stream, e.g. the IT support department of an organisation.	• Total cost and cost per unit • Cost variances • NFPIs related to quality, productivity & efficiency
Revenue centre	Division is only responsible for the generation of revenue.	• Total revenue and revenue per unit • Revenue (sales) variances
Profit centre	Division has both costs and revenue. Manager does not have the authority to alter the level of investment in the division.	All of the above PLUS: • Total sales and market share • Profit • Sales variances • Potentially working capital ratios depending on managers' responsibility for e.g. receivables collection.

		• NFPIs e.g. related to productivity, quality and customer satisfaction
Investment centre	Division has both costs and revenue. Manager does have the authority to invest in new assets or dispose of existing ones	All of the above PLUS: • ROI • RI These measures are used to assess the investment decisions made by managers and are discussed in more detail below.

Important point: For each of these, care must be taken to assess managers on controllable factors only. So, for example, the manager of a cost centre should only be assessed on controllable costs. Controllable costs are those which the manager has the ability to influence, such as the cost of the materials purchased by the department. A cost centre manager should not be held responsible for, say, the head office rental costs.

This chapter will first focus on the new measures that are mentioned in the previous table relating to investment centres.

2 Return on investment

2.1 Introduction to ROI

The first new measure we will consider is return on investment (ROI). This measure has some similarities with ROCE that we have already studied, which is an organisation wide measure. It is also similar to ARR that we will look at in a later chapter on investment appraisal decisions.

As such, ROI can be used to both measure performance, and also appraise investment decisions.

The calculation is as follows:

$$\text{Return on investment (ROI)} = \frac{\text{Controllable profit}}{\text{Capital employed}} \times 100$$

- Controllable profit is usually taken after depreciation but before tax. However, in the exam you may not be given this profit figure and so you should use the profit figure that is closest to this. Assume the profit is controllable, unless told otherwise.
- Capital employed is total assets less current liabilities, or total equity plus long term debt. Quite often capital employed is specifically given and there is no need to adjust it. It is also acceptable to use net assets if capital employed is not given in the question.

2.2 Decision making with ROI

In terms of investment decisions, the organisation may specify a specific target percentage for ROI that investment opportunities should meet, or it may leave it up to discretion of the manager.

If investment ROI > target ROI = accept

If investment ROI < target ROI = reject

Example 1

Division A of Babbage Group had investments at the year end of £56 million.

The profit of division A for the year was £6.2 million before deducting head office recharges of £800,000. Babbage Group have a target return of 12%.

Required:

What is the most appropriate measure of ROI for Division A for the year? Give your answer to two decimal places.

Solution

The figure for profit should be the controllable profit, to get this we need to add back the £800,000 of head office recharges, as these are not controllable by the division. Giving:

Controllable profit = £6,200,000 + £800,000 = £7 million.

ROI = £7 million/£56 million × 100 = 12.50%

As the controllable ROI is above the target of 12% division A would be perceived to be performing well.

ROI is a popular measure for divisional performance but has some serious failings which must be considered when interpreting results.

2.3 Advantages of ROI

- It is widely used and accepted since it is in line with ROCE, which is frequently used to assess overall business performance.
- As a relative measure it enables comparisons to be made with divisions or companies of different sizes.
- It can be broken down into secondary ratios for more detailed analysis, i.e. profit margin and asset turnover.

2.4 Disadvantages of ROI

- It may lead to dysfunctional decision making, e.g. a division with a current ROI of 30% would not wish to accept a project offering a ROI of 25%, as this would dilute its current figure. However, the 25% ROI may meet or exceed the company's target.
- ROI increases with the age of the asset if NBVs are used, thus giving managers an incentive to hang on to possibly inefficient, obsolescent machines.
- It may encourage the manipulation of profit and capital employed figures to improve results, e.g. in order to obtain a bonus payment.
- Different accounting policies can confuse comparisons (e.g. depreciation policy).

Test your understanding 1

Nielsen Ltd has two divisions with the following information:

	Division A	Division B
	£	£
Profit	90,000	10,000
Capital employed	300,000	100,000

Complete the following table by calculating the ROI for each division. Enter answers to two decimal places.

	Division A	Division B
ROI (%)		

Division A has been offered a project costing £100,000 and giving annual returns of £20,000. Division B has been offered a project costing £100,000 and giving annual returns of £12,000. The company's cost of capital is 15%. Managers have discretion to select or reject their own projects.

Divisional performance is judged on ROI and the ROI–related bonus is sufficiently high to influence the managers' behaviour.

Complete the following table by calculating the ROI for the project opportunity each division has. Enter answers to two decimal places

	Division A	**Division B**
Project ROI (%)		

Considering the current ROI, the project ROI, Nielsen Ltd's target ROI and the bonus, select whether the managers will make a dysfunctional or goal congruent decision.

	Dysfunctional	**Goal congruent**
Division A		
Division B		

3 Residual income

3.1 Introduction to RI

The second new measure we will consider is residual income (RI). This measure gives an absolute figure, the idea being that the 'residual income' is the amount that the division is contributing to the wealth of the shareholders, after the financing costs of the division have been considered.

RI can also be used to measure the performance of a division and to help make investment decisions.

The calculation is as follows:

Residual income = controllable profit – notional interest cost

- Notional interest cost is calculated by taking the capital employed in the division and multiplying it by the cost of capital or the interest rate.

- Capital employed is calculated in the same way as for ROI.
- Notional interest represents the theoretical cost of financing the division or project being considered.

3.2 Decision making with RI

In terms of investment decisions, a positive RI is considered to be good, and a negative RI is bad:

If the RI > 0 = accept

If the RI < 0 = reject

Example 2

An investment centre has net assets of £800,000 and made profits before interest and tax of £160,000. The notional cost of capital is 12%.

Required:

Calculate and comment on the RI for the period

Solution

		£
Controllable profit		160,000
– Notional interest cost	£800,000 × 12%	(96,000)
RI		64,000

The RI is positive and so is financially viable.

Compared to using ROI as a measure of performance, RI has several advantages and disadvantages.

3.3 Advantages of RI

- It encourages investment centre managers to make new investments if they add to RI. A new investment might add to RI but reduce ROI. In such a situation, measuring performance by RI would not result in dysfunctional behaviour, i.e. the best decision will be made for the business as a whole.
- Making a specific charge for interest helps to make investment centre managers more aware of the cost of the assets under their control.

- Risk can be incorporated by the choice of interest rate used: different interest rates for the notional cost of capital can be applied to investments with different risk characteristics.

3.4 Disadvantages of RI

- It does not facilitate comparisons between divisions since the RI is driven by the size of divisions and of their investments.
- It is based on accounting measures of profit and capital employed which may be subject to manipulation, e.g. in order to obtain a bonus payment.

Test your understanding 2

An investment centre has the following information:

	£
Net assets	1,000,000
Controllable profits	350,000
Profit	200,000

The notional cost of capital is 15% and this is also the company's target return.

Calculate the RI for the investment centre.

RI (£) to the nearest whole number	

Test your understanding 3

An investment centre has the following information:

	£
Net assets	800,000
Controllable profits	160,000
Head office costs	60,000
Profit	100,000

The notional cost of capital is 12% and this is also the company's target return.

Calculate the RI and the ROI for the investment centre.

RI (£) to the nearest whole number	
ROI (%) to two decimal places	

An opportunity has arisen to invest in a new project costing £100,000. The project would have a four-year life, and would make profits of £15,000 each year

Complete the following table by calculating the RI and ROI for the opportunity.

Project RI	
Project ROI (%) to two decimal places	

Considering the current ROI, the project ROI, and the company target, select whether the manager will accept or reject the opportunity under the two methods.

	Accept	Reject
Division A		
Division B		

Test your understanding 4

Two divisions of a company are considering new investments. The first table below shows their most recent results.

	Division X	Division Y
Net assets	£1,000,000	£1,000,000
Current divisional profit	£250,000	£120,000

The company has a required ROI of 18%.

Calculate the RI and the ROI for the two divisions.

	Division X	Division Y
ROI (%) to two decimal places		
RI (£) to the nearest whole number		

The following data relates to the new opportunities for each division.

	Division X	Division Y
Investment cost	£100,000	£100,000
Projected profits from the new investment	£20,000	£15,000

Calculate the RI and the ROI for the opportunities the divisions have.

	Division X	Division Y
ROI (%) to two decimal places		
RI (£) to the nearest whole number		

Considering the calculations, and the company target, select whether the manager will accept or reject the opportunity under the two methods.

	Accept	**Reject**
Division X – ROI		
Division X – RI		
Division Y – ROI		
Division Y – RI		

4 Transfer pricing

4.1 Introduction to transfer pricing

A transfer price is the price at which goods or services are transferred from one division to another within the same organisation.

It is not an issue when the divisions are cost centres as they are not judged on revenue, only on costs, and any appropriate non-financial performance measures.

It is, however, a consideration for investment and profit centres. If one such division carries out work for another internal division, they will require an income for the products or services they have provided, as they would if they had carried out the work for an external customer. The important point we need to recognise here, is that the fee charged internally, between the two divisions, can have a significant impact on the revenue of the division providing the product or service and on the costs of the division receiving the service or product.

 **Example**

Galburys makes chocolate cookies. They have two divisions, Division chunk (Chunk) and Division biscuit (Biscuit).

Chunk is the supplying division and makes chocolate to go in the cookies. Chunk can also sell the chocolate it produces in a bar form to the external market.

Biscuit is the receiving division and buys the chocolate for the cookies it sells from Chunk. Biscuit then adds the chocolate to the cookies.

Biscuit then sells the chocolate cookies in the external market.

Both divisions, Chunk and Biscuit, are profit centres and want to maximise their profits.

The price that Chunk charges to Biscuit for the chocolate will have an impact on the profitability of both divisions. It will be a revenue stream in Chunk and part of the costs in Biscuit.

The amount of chocolate that Chunk sells to Biscuit will also impact the amount of resources that are available to sell to their external market too.

4.2 Objectives of a transfer pricing system

Goal congruence

The decisions made by each profit centre manager should be consistent with the objectives of the organisation as a whole, i.e. the transfer price should assist in maximising overall company profits.

A common feature of exam questions is that a transfer price is set, which results in sub-optimal behaviour.

Performance measurement

The buying and selling divisions will be treated as profit centres. The transfer price should allow the performance of each division to be assessed fairly. Divisional managers will be demotivated if this is not achieved.

Autonomy

Autonomy is the ability of a person to make their own decision. The system used to set transfer prices should seek to allow profit centre managers to make their own decision about where they buy their products or services from. If autonomy is maintained, managers tend to be more highly motivated but sub-optimal decisions may be made.

Recording the movement of goods and services

In practice, an extremely important function of the transfer pricing system is simply to assist in recording the movement of goods and services.

4.3 Transfer pricing; the basic situation

One division (the supplier) provides a component to another division (the receiver) within the same organisation, the receiver then processes the component further and sells it on to the external market.

Both divisions are profit centres and so will be judged on both costs and revenues.

Example

Division A is the supplying division and makes a component that costs £4 in terms of direct material, £5 for direct labour and £1 of variable overheads.

Division B is the receiving division and buys this component from division A, modifies it and then sells it on to the external market. The costs B incurs to modify the component are £1.50 for materials, £3 for labour and £0.50 for overheads.

Division B can then sell this product in the external market for £40.

Both divisions, A and B, are profit centres and want to maximise their profits.

(a) What is the minimum transfer price charged by division A that could be set?

(b) What is the maximum transfer price at which division B would still cover all of its costs?

(c) What is the range of acceptable transfer prices for Division A and B?

Solution

(a)

	Division A
	£
Direct material	4.00
Direct labour	5.00
Variable overheads	1.00
Variable cost per unit	10.00

The minimum transfer price for division A would be the price that covers the variable costs that are incurred, £10 per unit.

(b)

	Division B
	£
Direct material	1.50
Direct labour	3.00
Variable overheads	0.50
Variable cost per unit	5.00

Division B incurs a cost of £5 to modify the component.

Division B can sell the product externally at £40, therefore, as long as the transfer price is no greater than £35 (£40 – £5 = £35) then division B will cover its costs. The maximum transfer price B will pay, and still cover all of its costs, is £35.

(c) The acceptable range for the transfer price is between the lowest price that A will accept (which is £10), and the highest price that division B will accept (which is £35).If the price is below £10 then A will not cover its costs, and it if is above £35 then B's costs will be greater than the price at which they can sell to the external market.

Minimum transfer price = £10

Maximum transfer price = £35

4.4 The impact on divisional profitability

In the previous example we identified an acceptable range for the transfer price. The price chosen within that range will impact the amount of profit each division will make from the work performed.

Example

Using the same figures as the previous example, Division A is the supplying division, and has a variable cost of £10 per unit.

Division B is the receiving division and buys this component from division A, modifies it, and then sells it on to the external market. The costs B incurs to modify the component are £5 per unit.

Division B can sell this product in the external market for £40.

Both divisions A and B are profit centres and want to maximise their profits.

(a) What is the contribution per unit in division A and B if the transfer price is set at £25 per unit?

(b) What is the contribution per unit in division A and B if the transfer price is set at £20 per unit?

(c) Would Division B prefer a transfer price of £15 or £30?

Solution

(a)

	Division A	Division B
	£	£
Selling price	25.00	40.00
Variable costs	10.00	(W1) 30.00
Contribution per unit	15.00	10.00

(W1) The variable cost in B is the transfer price of £25 plus their modification costs of £5.

(b)

	Division A	Division B
	£	£
Selling price	20.00	40.00
Variable costs	10.00	(W2) 25.00
Contribution per unit	10.00	15.00

(W2) The variable cost in B is the transfer price of £20 plus their modification costs of £5.

(c) Considering the answer to parts (a) and (b) we can see that Division B made a higher contribution per unit when the transfer price is lower, so Division B is likely to prefer a transfer price of £15 per unit. At this price it would make a contribution per unit of £20. At a transfer price of £30 the contribution per unit would be only £5.

The transfer price influences the contribution per unit for each division and therefore the profitability of each division but, in the example we have looked at so far, the overall contribution per unit for the organisation that division A and B are part of is unaffected. There is an example of this below.

Also, notice that we are considering the contribution per unit. As we saw earlier when we looked at relevant costing, fixed overhead costs per unit are not relevant as they are a period related cost and do not vary with production levels.

Example

Using the same figures as in the previous examples, Division A is the supplying division, and has a variable cost of £10 per unit. The fixed cost per unit is £2.

Division B is the receiving division and buys this component from division A, modifies it, and then sells it on to the external market. The costs B incurs to modify the component are £5 per unit.

Division B can sell this product in the external market for £40.

Both divisions A and B are profit centres and want to maximise their profits.

(a) What is the contribution per unit for the overall business if the transfer price is £25 per unit?

(b) What is the contribution per unit for the overall business if the transfer price is £20 per unit?

Solution

(a)

	Division A	Division B	Overall business
	£	£	£
Selling price	25.00	40.00	40.00
Variable costs	10.00	30.00	(W1) 15.00
Contribution per unit	15.00	10.00	25.00

(W1) The variable cost for the overall business is the £10 per unit cost in division A and the £5 per unit cost in division B.

(b)

	Division A	Division B	Overall business
	£	£	£
Selling price	20.00	40.00	40.00
Variable costs	10.00	25.00	15.00
Contribution per unit	10.00	15.00	25.00

Test your understanding 5

PD Ltd has several divisions, two of which work closely together.

Division X makes component A that it can either sell externally or transfer to division Y. Division Y would like to order 15,000 units of component A from division X.

The following information is available from division X relating to component A.

Material cost per unit	£5.00
Labour cost per unit	£10.00
Variable overhead cost per unit	£2.00
Fixed overhead cost per unit	£4.00

What should be the minimum per unit transfer price, charged by division X for the 15,000 units?

Enter your answer to two decimal places.

	£
Per unit transfer price for component A	

4.5 Considering capacity levels

So far we have looked at the basic concept of a transfer price and how the contribution per unit in each division changes at different transfer prices. Another key consideration in setting a transfer price is the capacity levels, particularly within the supplying division and the demand levels.

If the supplying division can sell their output internally and externally then we will need to apply relevant costing principles to the calculation of the transfer price.

If there is spare capacity in the supplying division then they would not be doing anything else with the product and they would therefore be happy/willing to transfer the spare units to the internal division'.

If there is no spare capacity – that is, all of their output could be sold externally – then they would have to forego external sales in order to fulfil the internal transfer and so we would need to consider the opportunity cost.

Example

Using the same figures as the previous examples, Division A is the supplying division, and has a variable cost of £10 per unit.

Division B is the receiving division, and buys this component from division A, modifies it, and then sells it on to the external market. The costs B incurs to modify the component are £5 per unit.

Division A can sell their output externally for £25 per unit. They have capacity to manufacture 100,000 units per annum.

Division B can sell their product in the external market for £40. The maximum demand for this product is 40,000 units and division B has the capacity to manufacture to this level.

Both divisions A and B are profit centres and want to maximise their profits.

(a) If the external demand for the component produced by division A is 60,000 units per annum, what would be the transfer price?

(b) If the external demand for the component produced by division A is 100,000 units per annum, what would be the transfer price?

(c) What would division B do if the transfer price was set at the level of (b)?

Solution

(a) As division A has spare capacity, then as long as they cover the additional costs they incur, they would be in the same position as they were if they didn't manufacture them. So, the basis for the transfer price should be the variable cost of £10.

The business may choose to give them a small benefit to help cover fixed costs and make further profit, but £10 is the most likely outcome so that division B can take advantage of the demand for their product.

(b) In this situation, division A has no spare capacity and could sell all of its output externally, for £25 per unit.

	Division A
	£
External selling price	25.00
Variable costs	10.00
Contribution per unit from an external sale	15.00

Therefore, from division A's perspective, if they sell internally then they forego an external sale, and so the internal transfer price needs to provide the same benefit as the external sale would have done.

Transfer price = standard variable cost + opportunity cost

Transfer price = £10 + £15 = £25

(c) Division B would prefer the transfer price in part (a) of £10, but they will still make a positive contribution of £10 (£40 – £5 – £25 = £10) if the transfer price is set at £25, and so would be willing to accept the transfer price.

4.6 Savings from avoiding the external market

Sometimes there are additional costs to supply to an external customer. These could be from distribution, packaging, advertising or the risk that an external party may default on the payment.

As such, there may be some savings from making an internal transfer rather than an external sale that we need to take into account when setting the transfer price.

Example

Using the same figures as the previous examples, Division A is the supplying division, and has a variable cost of £10 per unit.

Division B is the receiving division, and buys this component from division A, modifies it, and then sells it on to the external market. The costs B incurs to modify the component are £5 per unit.

Division A can sell their output externally for £25 per unit. They have capacity to manufacture 100,000 units per annum.

Division B can sell their product in the external market for £40. The maximum demand for this product is 40,000 units and division B has the capacity to manufacture to this level.

Both divisions A and B are profit centres and want to maximise their profits.

The external demand for the component produced by division A is 100,000 units per annum.

Some of the material costs would be saved if division A transferred internally to division B, as the packaging would not need to be so elaborate or durable. This saving amounts to £0.75 per unit.

What would the transfer price be?

Solution

In this situation, division A has no spare capacity and could sell all of its output externally for £25 per unit.

	Division A £
External selling price	25.00
Variable costs	10.00
Contribution per unit from an external sale	15.00

Therefore, from division A's perspective, if they sell internally then they forego an external sale, and so the internal transfer price needs to provide the same benefit as the external sale.

Transfer price = standard variable cost + opportunity cost

This time, however, the standard variable cost for the internal transfer is lower, it is only £9.25 (£10 less the saving on materials of £0.75).

Transfer price = £9.25 + £15 = £24.25

Test your understanding 6

TP has two divisions. Division S makes product WW that it can either sell externally or transfer to division R. Division R would like to order 25,000 units from Division S.

The following information is available from Division S relating to product WW.

Maximum capacity	150,000 units
Maximum external sales	100,000 units
External selling price per unit	£70.00
Standard direct material cost per unit	£15.00
Standard direct labour cost per unit	£8.00
Standard variable overhead cost per unit	£2.50
Standard fixed overhead cost per unit	£5.00

Complete the following table to show:

Spare capacity in division S (units to nearest whole number)	
Minimum transfer price per unit for WW (£ to two decimal places)	
Total internal sales revenue generated for division S by selling product WW to division R at the minimum transfer price (£ to the nearest whole pound)	

 Test your understanding 7

ZZ has two divisions. Division T makes product YY that it can either sell externally or transfer to division V. Division V would like to order 25,000 units from Division T.

The following information is available from Division T relating to product YY.

Maximum capacity	100,000 units
Maximum external sales	120,000 units
External selling price per unit	£85.00
Standard direct material cost per unit	£25.00
Standard direct labour cost per unit	£12.00
Standard variable overhead cost per unit	£5.50
Standard fixed overhead cost per unit	£25.00

The standard direct material cost includes some costs relating to packaging that would be saved completely for an internal transfer. These packaging costs are £0.50 per unit.

Complete the following table to show:

Spare capacity in division T (units to nearest whole number)	
Minimum transfer price per unit for YY (£ to 2 decimal places)	

The approach we have considered so far is often referred to as the market-based approach.

Advantages of this method:

- The transfer price should be deemed to be fair by the managers of the buying and selling divisions. The selling division will receive the same amount for any internal or external sales. The buying division will pay the same for goods if they buy them internally or externally.
- The company's performance will not be impacted negatively by the transfer price because the transfer price is the same as the external market price.

Disadvantages of this method:

- There may not be an external market price.
- The external market price may not be stable. For example, discounts may be offered to certain customers or for bulk orders.
- Savings may be made from transferring the goods internally. For example, delivery costs will be saved. These savings should ideally be deducted from the external market price before a transfer price is set, giving an "adjusted market price".

4.7 Cost based approach

Cost plus pricing is also an option.

The transferring division would supply the goods at **cost plus a % profit**. A standard cost should be used rather than the actual cost since:

- Actual costs do not encourage the selling division to control costs.
- If a standard cost is used, the buying division will know the cost in advance and can therefore put plans in place.

Another complication is that there are a number of different standard costs that could be used:

- Full cost.
- Marginal (variable) cost.
- Opportunity cost.

4.8 Other options for transfer prices

As with a lot of management accounting concepts, there is no perfect 'one size fits all' solution to the transfer pricing conundrum. The following are some other alternatives.

Negotiated prices

- Divisional managers negotiate a transfer price until a compromise is reached.
- While this is good training for managers who may then have to negotiate with external parties, it can lead to an experienced manager taking advantage of an inexperienced manager and negotiating a transfer price that favours their own division too much.

Two-part tariff

- Products or services are supplied at standard marginal cost, but a fixed annual fee is charged by the supplying division to recover fixed costs.
- The issue with this approach is how the fixed annual fee is decided upon to ensure that it is fair to both divisions.

Dual pricing

- The supplying division is credited with a different price to the one which has been debited to the receiving division.
- This is very appealing from a performance management point of view, but will create additional work to eliminate the differences for the financial accounts. It would also lead to discrepancies between internal payments and receipts.

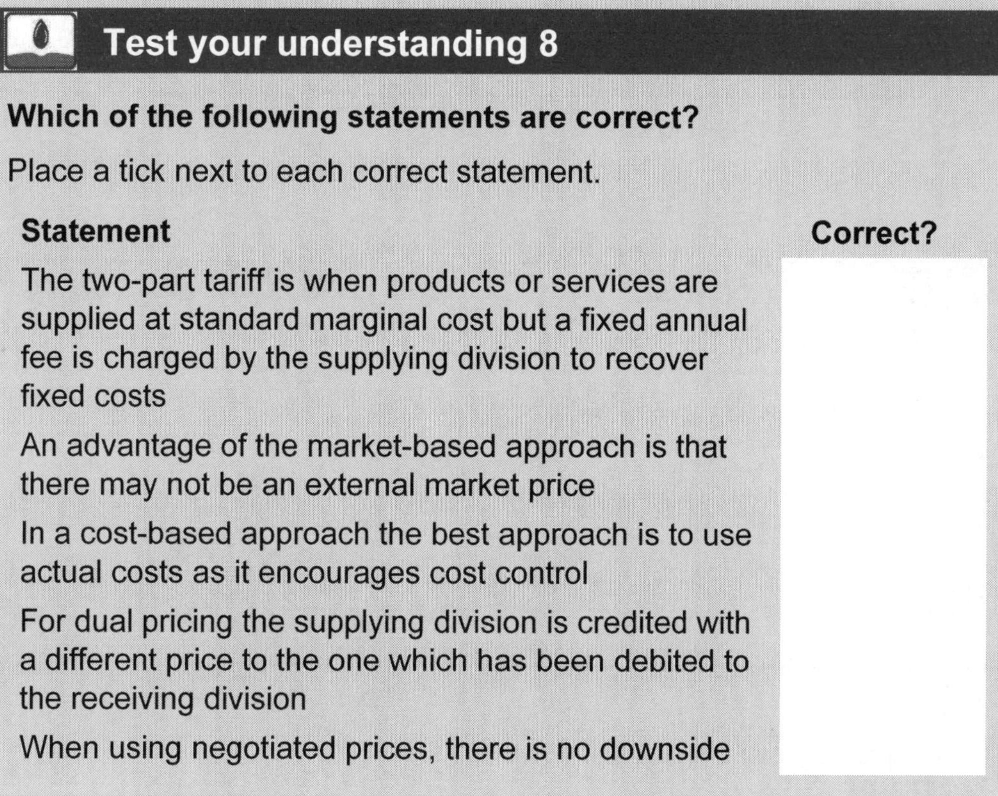

Test your understanding 8

Which of the following statements are correct?

Place a tick next to each correct statement.

Statement	Correct?
The two-part tariff is when products or services are supplied at standard marginal cost but a fixed annual fee is charged by the supplying division to recover fixed costs	
An advantage of the market-based approach is that there may not be an external market price	
In a cost-based approach the best approach is to use actual costs as it encourages cost control	
For dual pricing the supplying division is credited with a different price to the one which has been debited to the receiving division	
When using negotiated prices, there is no downside	

5 Summary

In this chapter we have considered the impact that having a divisionalised organisation has on the way performance is measured. In particular we have looked at the different types of division, with a particular focus on investment centres and the specific measures that might be used in these types of responsibility centres, which are ROI and RI.

Finally, we also considered transfer pricing and how that can impact divisional performance. The key areas here are the options available when setting the transfer price and the potential issues that may occur with each option.

Test your understanding answers

Test your understanding 1

	Division A	Division B
ROI (%)	**30.00**	**10.00**

Workings:

Division A = 90,000/300,000 × 100 = 30%

Division B = 10,000/100,000 × 100 = 10%

	Division A	Division B
Project ROI (%)	**20.00**	**12.00**

Workings:

Division A = 20,000/100,000 × 100 = 20%

Division B = 12,000/100,000 × 100 = 12%

	Dysfunctional	Goal congruent
Division A	☑	
Division B	☑	

Division A will reject the project as it is below their current ROI, so would reduce their performance against this target. As it is above the company target of 15%, from the company perspective, they should accept it. This makes their decision to reject the project a dysfunctional decision.

Division B will accept the project as it is above their current ROI, so would improve their performance against the target. 12% is below the company target ROI however, so from the company perspective they should reject it. This makes their decision to accept the project a dysfunctional decision.

Test your understanding 2

RI (£) to the nearest whole number	**200,000**

Workings:

	£
Controllable profit	350,000
– Notional interest (1,000,000 × 15%)	(150,000)
RI	200,000

Test your understanding 3

RI (£) to the nearest whole number	**64,000**
ROI (%) to two decimal places	**20.00**

Workings:

RI	£
Controllable profit	160,000
– Notional interest (800,000 × 12%)	(96,000)
RI	64,000

ROI = 160,000/800,000 × 100 = 20%

Project RI	**3,000**
Project ROI (%) to two decimal places	**15.00**

Workings:

RI	£
Controllable profit	15,000
– Notional interest (100,000 × 12%)	(12,000)
RI	3,000

ROI = 15,000/100,000 × 100 = 15%

	Accept	**Reject**
RI	✓	
ROI		✓

RI – as it is a positive RI, the manager will accept it.

ROI – as the ROI is below the current level the manager would reject it.

This is an example of RI being less likely to lead to a dysfunctional decision.

Test your understanding 4

	Division X	Division Y
ROI (%) to two decimal places	**25.00**	**12.00**
RI (£) to the nearest whole number	**70,000**	**(60,000)**

Workings:

Division X ROI = 250,000/1,000,000 × 100 = 25%

Division Y ROI = 120,000/1,000,000 × 100 = 12%

RI	Division X	Division Y
	£	£
Controllable profit	250,000	120,000
– Notional interest (1,000,000 × 18%)	(180,000)	(180,000)
RI	70,000	(60,000)

	Division X	Division Y
ROI (%) to two decimal places	**20.00**	**15.00**
RI (£) to the nearest whole number	**2,000**	**(3,000)**

Workings:

Division X ROI = 20,000/100,000 × 100 = 20%

Division Y ROI = 15,000/100,000 × 100 = 15%

RI	Division X	Division Y
	£	£
Controllable profit	20,000	15,000
– Notional interest (100,000 × 18%)	(18,000)	(18,000)
RI	2,000	(3,000)

	Accept	**Reject**
Division X – ROI		✓
Division X – RI	✓	
Division Y – ROI	✓	
Division Y – RI		✓

While the ROI of the project in division X is greater than the company target it is lower than their current ROI so it would reduce the overall ROI for the division.

For division Y, the ROI is below the target, but it is above their current ROI so it would improve their ROI, hence they would accept it.

Both of these are examples of dysfunctional decisions.

Test your understanding 5

The minimum transfer price is the standard variable cost per unit:

= £10 + £5 + £2

	£
Per unit transfer price for component A	**17.00**

Test your understanding 6

Spare capacity in division S (units to nearest whole number)	**50,000**
Minimum transfer price per unit for WW (£ to two decimal places)	15 + 8 + 2.50 = **25.50**
Total internal sales revenue generated for division S by selling product WW to division R (£ to the nearest whole pound)	25.50 × 25,000 = **637,500**

Test your understanding 7

Division T is already operating at full capacity and cannot meet external sales demand.

Spare capacity in division T (units to nearest whole number)	**0**
Minimum transfer price per unit for YY (£ to 2 decimal places)	**84.50**

The transfer price will be the standard variable cost plus the opportunity cost of a lost external sale.

The opportunity cost is the lost contribution:

85 – 25 – 12 – 5.50 = 42.50

The variable cost of an internal transfer = 25 – 0.50 (saving from avoiding external market) + 12 + 5.50 = £42

Therefore TP = 42 + 42.50 = 84.50

Test your understanding 8

Statement	Correct?
The two-part tariff is when products or services are supplied at standard marginal cost but a fixed annual fee is charged by the supplying division to recover fixed costs	✓
An advantage of the market-based approach is that there may not be an external market price	
In a cost-based approach the best approach is to use actual costs as it encourages cost control	
For dual pricing the supplying division is credited with a different price to the one which has been debited to the receiving division	✓
When using negotiated prices, there is no downside	

Long-term decision making

13

Introduction

In this chapter the focus is on long-term investment decisions – usually lasting **more than one year**. This could vary from the decision to build a new factory, to whether or not to discontinue a product range.

The investment appraisal techniques that are discussed in this chapter are payback period, accounting rate of return, net present cost, net present value, discounted payback and internal rate of return.

We also briefly revisit life cycle costing from earlier in our studies.

ASSESSMENT CRITERIA

Discount cash flows (LO 3.5)

Appraisal methods for long-term decisions (LO 3.6)

Life cycle costing (LO 2.5)

CONTENTS

1 Long-term investments

1.1 Introduction

The key characteristic of a capital investment project as opposed to a short term decisions is the tying up of capital for a number of years, or for the long term, in order to earn profits or returns over the period.

1.2 What will the capital be invested in?

The most common investment you will encounter will be in **tangible non-current assets**, such as a new machine, factory or premises from which to operate a new service business.

Other intangible forms of investment include **research and development**, **patent rights or goodwill** obtained on the purchase of an existing business.

1.3 What form will the returns take?

The purchase of a new non-current asset will often be with the intention of starting a new line of business – say the manufacturing of a new product, or the provision of a new or extended service. The returns will be the **net income** generated by the new business.

Alternatively, the investment may be to benefit the existing operations, such that **sales are increased** (where existing products/services are improved technologically or in quality) or **costs are reduced** (where production processes are updated or personnel reorganised). The returns will be measured as the **increase in net income or net reduction in costs** resulting from the investment.

1.4 Authorisation for a capital project

For projects involving a significant amount of capital investment, **authorisation** will be required. This authorisation will usually be given by the main board, or a sub-committee formed from the board for this purpose. Smaller projects (such as the replacement of an existing machine) may be within the authorisation limits of the manager of the area of business involved.

1.5 Importance of non-financial factors

Although these appraisal methods will usually give a basis for a **recommendation as to whether or not the project should be accepted,** they will only be able to take account of monetary costs and benefits. **Qualitative factors** will also need to be considered when reaching a final decision – such as possible effects on staff morale (for example, if the project involves increased automation or considerable overtime), the environment, customer satisfaction and the business's status/reputation.

2 Investment appraisal and cash flows

2.1 Introduction

Any potential investment will need to be evaluated with regards the costs and revenues that will occur i.e. the net cash flow received from the investment activity. This will involve estimating the cash flows for sales, costs, capital expenditure and disposal proceeds.

As with short term decision making it is important to ensure that the calculations are made knowing as much detail as possible or that any assumptions are stated. This will maintain the integrity of the information and should demonstrate professional competence.

2.2 The cash flows under consideration

When estimating future cash flows we want to identify what difference the project will make, therefore we only consider **future incremental cash** flows to be relevant. For example, if a new machine was to be purchased, the factory rent may be unaffected and so this cost would not need to be included when assessing the investment. However the purchase cost of the new machine itself is relevant and so would be included.

As well as knowing what the future cash flows will be, we also need to know when they will occur. The time the investment starts is called time or year 0 or t = 0. Subsequent future cash flows are assumed to happen at year-ends, e.g. all of the sales revenues and costs for the first year are assumed to be paid at the end of the first year this is called time or year 1 or t = 1.

If we do this for all the future cash flows of the project, then we will typically end up with a table like the following:

	t = 0 £000	Year 1 (t = 1) £000	Year 2 (t = 2) £000	Year 3 (t = 3) £000	Year 4 (t = 4) £000	Year 5 (t = 5) £000
Initial Investment	(100)					
Scrap value						30
Sales revenues		40	50	60	50	40
Variable costs		(10)	(12)	(15)	(13)	(11)
Net cash flow	(100)	30	38	45	37	59

2.3 Methods of capital investment appraisal

Capital investment appraisal is an analysis of the expected financial returns from a capital project over its expected life. There are several methods of carrying out a capital expenditure appraisal such as:

- Payback
- Accounting rate of return
- Net present value method of discounted cash flow
- Discounted payback
- Internal rate of return method of discounted cash flow.

3 Payback period

3.1 Calculation

Definition

The **payback period** is the length of time a project takes to recoup the initial money invested in it. This is the time which elapses until the invested capital is recovered.

Payback is commonly used as an initial screening method, and projects that meet the payback period are then evaluated using another investment appraisal method.

When the annual cash flows are constant, then the calculation is very straightforward e.g. if £100,000 is invested and £20,000 cash in received each year, then it will take £100,000/£20,000 = 5 years to recover the investment cost.

However, if the annual cash flows vary, then we need to calculate the cumulative net position at the end of each year.

Example 1

A machine costs £100,000 now. We expect the following cash flows:

	Year 1 (t = 1) £000	Year 2 (t = 2) £000	Year 3 (t = 3) £000	Year 4 (t = 4) £000	Year 5 (t = 5) £000
Scrap value					30
Sales revenues	40	50	60	50	40
Variable costs	(10)	(12)	(15)	(13)	(11)

Calculate the payback period for the investment.

Solution

Time	**Net cash flow** £000	**Cumulative position** £000	**Working to calculate the cumulative position**
t = 0	(100)	(100)	
t = 1	30	(70)	(100) + 30
t = 2	38	(32)	(70) + 38
t = 3	45	13	(32) + 45
t = 4	37	50	13 + 37
t = 5	59	109	50 + 59

From this table we can see that the initial investment would be recovered sometime in the third year as this is when the cumulative position initially becomes positive.

If cash flows are assumed to occur at the end of each year the payback period would 3 years.

If we assume that cash flows accrue evenly through the year i.e. there is an equal amount of sales revenue each month and an equal amount of costs each month, we are then able to estimate at what point during the year break even occurs.

From the figures above we can see that the outstanding amount at the start of year 3 is £32,000 (*) and that during the third year there is a total of £45,000 (**) cash flow. See extract of table below:

Time	Net cash flow £000	Cumulative position £000
t = 2	38	**(32)***
t = 3	**45****	13

The payback period is therefore calculated as follows:

Calculate the cash flow per month

£45,000/12 = £3,750

Calculate how many months are needed to cover remaining investment

£32,000/£3,750 = 8.533 months

Payback is 2 years and 8½ months

This could also be calculated as follows:

= 2 $^{32}/_{45}$ or 2.71 years

0.71 of a year is 8½ months

Note: In the exam the payback period is rounded **up** to the nearest whole month. The payback period is therefore 2 years and 9 months.

The payback period is then compared with the target payback that has been set, e.g. this company may have decided only to accept projects with paybacks lower than four years, in which case this project is acceptable.

Test your understanding 1

A machine costs £100,000 now. We expect net cash flows of £30,000 in one year's time, £40,000 in two years' time, £60,000 in three years' time and £10,000 in four years' time.

Calculate the payback period for the investment by filling in the table below:

Time	Net cash flow £000	Cumulative cash flow £000
t = 0	(100)	
t = 1	30	
t = 2	40	
t = 3	60	
t = 4	10	

Payback is __________ years and _________ months.

Test your understanding 2

Highscore Ltd manufactures cricket bats. They are considering investing £30,000 in a new delivery vehicle which will generate savings compared with sub-contracting out the delivery service. The vehicle will have a life of six years, with zero scrap value.

The accounting technician and the transport manager have prepared the following estimates relating to the savings.

The net cash flows from the project are:

Year	£
1	9,000
2	11,000
3	10,000
4	10,500
5	10,200
6	10,100

Calculate the payback period in year(s) and months.

3.2 Advantages of payback period

(a) It is simple to calculate.

(b) It is understandable for non-financial managers.

(c) It is **less affected by uncertainty** as the cash flows that are being considered are earlier forecasts.

(d) It is very useful in specific circumstances, such as when the company has **liquidity problems** i.e. if cash is only available for a limited length of time it provides an estimate of how long cash will be tied up in the investment for.

3.3 Disadvantages of payback period

(a) Cash **flows outside of the payback period are ignored**. If we consider the previous example, if the cash flow in the fifth year had been £20,000 the payback period would be unaltered at 2 years 8½ months.

(b) The **timing of flows within the payback period** are ignored. If, again for the same example, the first two years' receipts had been:

1st year £50,000

2nd year £20,000

Again, the payback period would be unaltered at 2 years 8½ months.

(c) It **ignores the time value of money** i.e. the interest that capital can earn. We shall see the relevance of this in the next sections on discounted cash flow.

(d) It does not provide a monetary value for the return available from the investment.

4 Accounting rate of return

4.1 Introduction

One of the criticisms of the previous method was that the flows outside of the payback period are ignored. An alternative, and very different, approach that resolves this issue is the **accounting rate of return** (ARR). This method is very similar to ROCE that we looked at earlier, as such it uses profits rather than cash flows.

The ARR is an expression of the profits that a project is forecast to make as a percentage of the capital invested in the project.

There are two possible ways of calculating the ARR. One uses the initial capital costs:

$$ARR = \frac{\text{average annual profits before interest and tax}}{\text{initial capital costs}} \times 100$$

The alternative approach is to use the average value of the capital invested:

$$ARR = \frac{\text{average annual profits before interest and tax}}{\text{average capital investment}} \times 100$$

The average investment can be calculated in a similar way to most averages by adding the investment cash flows together and dividing by the number of flows. This is usually an initial investment value plus a residual value at the end of the investment, often referred to as a scrap value.

$$\text{Average capital investment} = \frac{\text{initial investment + scrap value}}{2}$$

These formulas are not given in the exam and must be learnt.

Example 2

A machine costs £100,000 now. We expect the following cash flows:

	Year 1 (t = 1) £000	Year 2 (t = 2) £000	Year 3 (t = 3) £000	Year 4 (t = 4) £000	Year 5 (t = 5) £000
Scrap value					30
Sales revenues	40	50	60	50	40
Variable costs	(10)	(12)	(15)	(13)	(11)

Calculate the ARR for the investment, giving your answer to 1DP, using:

(a) the initial value of the investment

(b) the average value of the investment

Solution

(a) First of all calculate the cumulative total profits of the project:

Cumulative sales revenue (£000) = 40 + 50 + 60 + 50 + 40 = 240

Cumulative variable costs (£000) = 10 + 12 + 15 + 13 + 11 = 61

Total depreciation across the project (£000) = 100 – 30 = 70

Profit (£000) = 240 – 61 – 70 = 109

Therefore the average annual profit (£000) = 109/5 = 21.8

ARR = 21.8/100 × 100 = **21.8%**

(b) The average annual profit will be the same (£000): 21.8

The average value of the investment (£000) = (100 + 30)/2

= 130/2

= 65

ARR = 21.8/65 × 100 = **33.5%** (1DP)

From this we can see that the ARR based on the average value of the investment is greater than the initial value of the investment. As the average value will invariably be lower than the initial value of the investment this will usually be the case.

Note: In the exam the question may ask you to advise whether the investment should be undertaken.

The ARR is then compared with either a target level or the current ROCE (for the organisation) or the ROI (for the division) e.g. this company may have decided only to accept projects with ARR higher than 20%, in which case, regardless of the approach used, this project is acceptable.

Test your understanding 3

A machine costs £800,000 now. We expect net cash flows as follows:

Year	1	2	3	4	5	6	7
Cash inflows (£000)	100	200	400	400	300	200	150

In addition, at the end of the seven year period, project assets initially purchased will be sold for £100,000.

Required:

Complete the following table:

	£
Total cash inflow	
Total depreciation	
Total profit for the investment	
Average annual profit	
Average capital invested	

Use the figures calculated above to calculate the ARR (to 2DP) for the investment using:

	%
ARR using initial investment	
ARR using the average value of the investment	

Test your understanding 4

HSL manufactures CB. They are considering investing £30,000 in a new machine which will generate savings compared with leasing the machine. The machine will have a life of six years, with zero scrap value.

The accounting technician and the production manager have prepared the following estimates relating to the savings.

The net cash flows from the project are:

Year	**£**
1	9,000
2	11,100
3	10,000
4	10,500
5	10,200
6	10,100

Required:

Complete the following table to calculate the ARR return under each method to 2DP.

	%
ARR using the initial value of the investment	
ARR using the average value of the investment	

4.2 Advantages of ARR

(a) It is considered simple to calculate.

(b) It links to other accounting measures, as we have discussed it is very similar to ROCE, and therefore ROI.

(c) It is a % so enables comparisons to the overall business or division.

4.3 Disadvantages of ARR

(a) **Timings of the benefits are not considered**. Returns further into the future are more uncertain, but in this method all returns are added together and valued equally.

(b) In contrast to all the other methods in this chapter it uses **profits rather than cash flows** and these can be manipulated by different accounting policies.

(c) It **is a percentage measure** and so does not measure absolute returns of the project.

(d) There is no definitive rule about what is acceptable and so the target level for acceptance is arbitrary.

5 Discounting

5.1 The time value of money

A key concept in long-term decision-making is that money received today is worth more than the same sum received in the future, i.e. it has a **time value**.

Suppose you were offered £100 now or £100 in one year's time. Even though the sums are the same, most people would prefer the money now. The £100 in the future is effectively worth less to us than £100 now – the timing of the cash makes a difference.

The main reasons for this are as follows:

- **Investment opportunities**: the £100 received now could be deposited into a bank account and earn interest. It would therefore grow to become worth more than £100 in one year.
- **Inflation**: the £100 now will buy more goods than £100 in one year due to inflation increasing the cost of goods.
- **Cost of capital**: the £100 received now could be used to reduce a loan or overdraft and save interest.
- **Risk**: the £100 now is more certain than the offer of money in the future.

To do calculations using the time value of money it needs to be expressed as an interest rate (often known as a cost of capital, a required return or a **discount rate**).

Suppose we felt that £100 now was worth the same to us as £110 offered in one year's time due to the factors above. We could say that our time value of money was estimated at 10% per annum.

Therefore £100 now is worth the same as £110 offered in one year. Alternatively we say that the £110 in one year has a present value of £100 now. This process of taking future cash flows and converting them into their equivalent present value now is called **discounting**.

To calculate the present value of any future cash flow we multiply the cash flow by a suitable discount factor (or present value factor):

Present value = future cash flow × discount factor

Discount factors are provided in the assessment so you do not need to be able to calculate them, but you will need to know how to use them.

For example, with a 10% discount rate, the discount factor for a cash flow at t=1 is 0.909. Thus the offer of receiving £110 in one year's time is worth, in today's terms

Present value = £110 × 0.909 = £99.99

The use of the discount rate enables a more accurate prediction of the return an investment will give. Future incremental cash flows can be discounted to present values and the values can then be netted off against the initial investment to see what the overall return from the investment will be.

6 Net present value/cost

6.1 Net Present Value (NPV)

Definition

The net present value is the net benefit or loss of benefit in present value terms from an investment opportunity. The NPV represents the surplus funds earned on a project.

There is a step by step procedure for completing an NPV calculation:

Step 1 Calculate the future incremental net cash flows.

Step 2 Discount the net cash flows so they are in today's terms (present values).

Step 3 Add up the present values and add them to the initial investment out flow to give a net present value or NPV.

Step 4 If the NPV is positive, then it means that the cash inflows are worth more than the outflows and the project should be accepted.

Example 3

A machine costs £100,000 now. We expect the following cash flows:

	Year 1 (t = 1) £000	Year 2 (t = 2) £000	Year 3 (t = 3) £000	Year 4 (t = 4) £000	Year 5 (t = 5) £000
Scrap value					30
Sales revenues	40	50	60	50	40
Variable costs	(10)	(12)	(15)	(13)	(11)

Calculate the net present value of the investment if a discount factor of 10% is used.

Solution

	t = 0 £000	Year 1 (t = 1) £000	Year 2 (t = 2) £000	Year 3 (t = 3) £000	Year 4 (t = 4) £000	Year 5 (t = 5) £000
Net cash flow	(100)	30	38	45	37	59
Discount factor at 10%	1.000	0.909	0.826	0.751	0.683	0.621
Present value	(100)	27.3	31.4	33.8	25.3	36.6

The Net Present Value = (100) + 27.3 + 31.4 + 33.8 + 25.3 + 36.6 = 54.4

The NPV = £54,400 positive, so the project should be undertaken.

Test your understanding 5

Four projects have been assessed using NPV. Assuming that we can invest in only one project which one of the following projects should be chosen for investment?

A £12,500

B £33,450

C (£44,777)

D (£13,456)

Test your understanding 6

A machine costs £80,000 to buy now and will have no scrap value. The predicted sales revenue and operating costs for the following four years are as follows:

Year	Sales revenue	Operating cost
	£	£
1	40,000	20,000
2	70,000	20,000
3	80,000	40,000
4	90,000	80,000

The rate of interest applicable is 15%. Should we invest in the machine?

The relevant present value factors are:

	Year 1	**Year 2**	**Year 3**	**Year 4**
15%	0.870	0.756	0.658	0.572

	Year 0	**Year 1**	**Year 2**	**Year 3**	**Year 4**
Capital expenditure					
Sales revenues					
Operating costs					
Net cash flow					
PV Factor	1.000	0.870	0.756	0.658	0.572
Discounted cash flow					
Net present value					

The net present value is positive/negative*

*delete as appropriate

This means we should **accept/reject*** the investment.

*delete as appropriate

Test your understanding 7

Machine A costs £100,000, payable immediately. Machine B costs £120,000, half payable immediately and half payable in one year's time. Neither machine A or B will have any scrap value.

The net cash flows expected are as follows.

	A	B
	£	£
at the end of 1 year	20,000	–
at the end of 2 years	60,000	60,000
at the end of 3 years	40,000	60,000
at the end of 4 years	30,000	80,000
at the end of 5 years	20,000	–

With interest at 5%, which machine should be selected?

The relevant present value factors are:

	Year 1	Year 2	Year 3	Year 4	Year 5
5%	0.952	0.907	0.864	0.823	0.784

Machine A

	Year 0	Year 1	Year 2	Year 3	Year 4	Year 5
Capital expenditure						
Net cash flow						
PV Factor	1.000	0.952	0.907	0.864	0.823	0.784
Discounted cash flow						
Net present value						

The net present value of Machine A is positive/negative*

*delete as appropriate

Machine B

	Year 0	**Year 1**	**Year 2**	**Year 3**	**Year 4**	**Year 5**
Capital expenditure						
Net cash flow						
PV Factor	1.000	0.952	0.907	0.864	0.823	0.784
Discounted cash flow						
Net present value						

The net present value of machine B is positive/negative*
*delete as appropriate

Machine A/B* should be selected as it has the higher/lower* NPV
*delete as appropriate

6.2 Net present cost

In some cases you may be asked to look at only the **operating costs** of an investment rather than the costs and revenues associated with the investment. In this case the step by step procedure is exactly the same but you will need to decide which investment is cheapest to run.

Test your understanding 8

Machine A costs £100,000, payable immediately. Machine B costs £80,000, payable immediately. The running costs expected are as follows.

	A	B
	£	£
at the end of 1 year	20,000	20,000
at the end of 2 years	50,000	30,000
at the end of 3 years	30,000	40,000
at the end of 4 years	20,000	50,000
at the end of 5 years	10,000	60,000

With interest at 8%, which machine should be selected?

The relevant present value factors are:

	Year 1	Year 2	Year 3	Year 4	Year 5
8%	0.926	0.857	0.794	0.735	0.681

Machine A

	Year 0	Year 1	Year 2	Year 3	Year 4	Year 5
Capital expenditure						
Net cash flow						
PV Factor	1.000	0.926	0.857	0.794	0.735	0.681
Discounted cash flow						
Net present cost						

Machine B

	Year 0	Year 1	Year 2	Year 3	Year 4	Year 5
Capital expenditure						
Net cash flow						
PV Factor	1.000	0.926	0.857	0.794	0.735	0.681
Discounted cash flow						
Net present cost						

Machine **A/B*** should be selected as it has the **higher/lower*** net present cost

*delete as appropriate

6.3 Advantages of NPV/NPC

(a) It considers the **time value of money**.

(b) It uses cash flows which are less subjective than profits. Profit measures rely on such things as depreciation and other policies which are, to a certain extent, subjective.

(c) It considers the **whole life** of the project.

(d) It provides a monetary value for the return from an investment.

6.4 Disadvantages of NPV/NPC

(a) Cash flows are future predictions and we are **unable to predict** the future with accuracy.

(b) Discounted cash flow as a concept is **more difficult** for a non-financial manager to understand.

(c) It may be difficult to **decide on which discount rate** to use when appraising a project.

Test your understanding 9

Whitby Engineering Factors are considering an investment in a new machine tool with an estimated useful life of five years.

The investment will require capital expenditure of £50,000 and the accounting technician has prepared the following estimates of cash flow over the five-year period:

Year	£
1	18,000
2	20,000
3	21,000
4	22,000
5	18,000

The firm's cost of capital is considered to be 12% and it uses this rate to appraise any future projects.

Required:

Calculate the payback period and then prepare an appraisal of the project using the discounted cash flow (NPV method) technique.

The payback period is Year(s) and Months

	Year 0	Year 1	Year 2	Year 3	Year 4	Year 5
Capital expenditure						
Net cash flow						
PV Factor	1.000	0.893	0.797	0.712	0.636	0.567
Discounted cash flow						
Net present value						

The net present value is **positive/negative***
**delete as appropriate*

Accept/reject* investment
**delete as appropriate*

Test your understanding 10

An investment project has the following expected cash flows over its three-year life span.

Year	Cash flow
	£
0	(285,400)
1	102,000
2	124,000
3	146,000

Task

Calculate the net present value of the project at a discount rate of 20%.

The payback period is Year(s) and Months

	Year 0	Year 1	Year 2	Year 3
Capital expenditure				
Net cash flow				
PV Factor	1.000	0.833	0.694	0.579
Discounted cash flow				
Net present value				

The net present value is **positive/negative***
**delete as appropriate*

Accept/reject* investment
**delete as appropriate*

Test your understanding 11

Martinez Limited makes a single product, the Angel.

Martinez Limited has a long-term contract to supply a group of customers with 10,000 units of Angel a year for the next three years.

Martinez is considering investing in a new machine to manufacture the Angel. This machine will produce 10,000 units a year, which generate a profit of £8 per unit. The machine will cost £220,000 and will last for the duration of the contract. At the end of the contract the machine will be scrapped with no resale value.

Task

Calculate the present value of the machine project if a 10% discount rate is used.

The payback period is Year(s) and Months

	Year 0	Year 1	Year 2	Year 3
Capital expenditure				
Net cash flow				
PV Factor	1.000	0.909	0.826	0.751
Discounted cash flow				
Net present value				

The net present value is **positive/negative***
*delete as appropriate

Accept/reject* investment
*delete as appropriate

Test your understanding 12

Loamshire County Council operates a library service.

In order to reduce operating expenses over the next four or five years, there is a proposal to introduce a major upgrade to the computer system used by the library service. Two alternative projects are under examination with different initial outlays and different estimated savings over time. The computer manager has prepared the following schedule:

	Project A	Project B
	£	£
Initial outlay	75,000	100,000
Annual cash savings		
1st year	20,000	30,000
2nd year	30,000	45,000
3rd year	30,000	45,000
4th year	25,000	40,000
5th year	20,000	–

Assume that the cash savings occur at the end of the year, even though in practice they would be spread over the year. From a technical point of view, both systems meet the librarian's specification. It is assumed that there will be no further savings after year five. The county uses the net present value method for evaluating projects at a 10% discount rate.

Task

Project A

	Year 0	Year 1	Year 2	Year 3	Year 4	Year 5
Capital expenditure						
Net cash flow						
PV Factor	1.000	0.909	0.826	0.751	0.683	0.621
Discounted cash flow						
Net present value						

The net present value is **positive/negative***
*delete as appropriate

The payback period is Year(s) and Months

Project B

	Year 0	Year 1	Year 2	Year 3	Year 4
Capital expenditure					
Net cash flow					
PV Factor	1.000	0.909	0.826	0.751	0.683
Discounted cash flow					
Net present value					

The net present value is **positive/negative***
*delete as appropriate

The payback period is Year(s) and Months

Invest in **A/B***
*delete as appropriate

 Test your understanding 13

A transport company is considering purchasing an automatic vehicle-cleansing machine. At present, all vehicles are cleaned by hand.

The machine will cost £80,000 to purchase and install in year 0 and it will have a useful life of four years with no residual value.

The company uses a discount rate of 10% to appraise all capital projects.

The cash savings from the machine will be:

Year	£
0	–
1	29,600
2	29,200
3	28,780
4	28,339

Task

As assistant management accountant, you are asked to carry out an appraisal of the proposal to purchase the machine and prepare a report to the general manager of the company. Your report should contain the following information:

1 the net present value of the cash flows from the project

2 the payback period of the proposal

3 a recommendation as to whether or not the proposal should be accepted.

	Year 0	Year 1	Year 2	Year 3	Year 4
Capital expenditure					
Net cash flow					
PV Factor	1.000	0.909	0.826	0.751	0.683
Discounted cash flow					
Net present value					

The net present value is **positive/negative***
*delete as appropriate

The payback period is Year(s)

Accept/reject* project
*delete as appropriate

Test your understanding 14

A company is considering setting up a small in-house printing facility.

Machines costing £14,400 will be purchased in year 0. They will last for four years and will have no value at the end of this time.

The cash savings associated with the machines will be:

Year	£
0	–
1	6,920
2	6,920
3	6,920
4	6,920

Task

(a) Calculate the net present value of the cash flows from the proposal, using a 12% discount rate over four years.

Assume that all cash flows occur at the end of the year.

(b) Calculate the payback period for the proposal assuming that cash flows occur evenly through the year.

	Year 0	Year 1	Year 2	Year 3	Year 4
Capital expenditure					
Net cash flow					
PV Factor	1.000	0.893	0.797	0.712	0.636
Discounted cash flow					
Net present value					

The net present value is positive/negative*
*delete as appropriate

The payback period is Year(s) and Months

Accept/reject* project
*delete as appropriate

7 Discounted payback

7.1 Introduction

When we initially looked at payback in section 3 of this chapter, one of the disadvantages that we highlighted was that we had not considered the time value of money. Well, now we know how to discount cash flows, this disadvantage is easily remedied by calculating the discounted payback.

The discounted payback period (DPP) is the amount of time that the project's cumulative NPV takes to turn from being negative to positive.

Example 4

A project is expected to have the following cash flows.

Year	Cash flow (£000)	Discount factor @ 10%
0	(1,500)	1
1	500	0.909
2	500	0.826
3	400	0.751
4	600	0.683
5	300	0.621

What is the expected discounted payback if the cost of capital is 10%?

Solution

Year	Cash flow	Discount factor @ 10%	Present value	Cumulative present value
	£000		£000	£000
0	(1,500)	1	(1,500)	(1,500)
1	500	0.909	454.5	(1,045.5)
2	500	0.826	413	(632.5)
3	400	0.751	300.4	(332.1)
4	600	0.683	409.8	77.7
5	300	0.621	186.3	

The DPP is towards the end of year 4. As we are assuming that the cash flows occur at the end of each year when discounting, we do not work out the exact time as we did with the original payback calculation.

As it is a slight extension of the payback period, the advantages and disadvantages are fairly similar, with the ones relating to the timings and time value of money flipping to an advantage.

7.2 Advantages of payback period

(a) It is simple to calculate.

(b) It is understandable for non-financial managers.

(c) It is **less affected by uncertainty** as the cash flows that are being considered are earlier forecasts.

(d) It is very useful in specific circumstances, such as when the company has **liquidity problems** i.e. if cash is only available for a limited length of time it provides an estimate of how long cash will be tied up in the investment for.

(e) The **timing of flows within the payback period** are now considered. The decreasing discount rates will make earlier cash flows more worthwhile.

(c) It **considers the time value of money** i.e. the interest that capital can earn. We have seen the relevance of this in the previous sections on discounted cash flow.

7.3 Disadvantages of payback period

(a) Cash **flows outside of the payback period are still ignored**. If we consider the previous example, if the cash flow in the fifth year had been £1,000,000, the payback period would be unaltered at towards the end of year 4.

(b) It does not provide a monetary value for the return available from the investment.

Test your understanding 15

Highscore Ltd manufactures and delivers cricket bats. They are considering investing £30,000 in a new delivery vehicle which will generate savings compared with sub-contracting out the delivery service. The vehicle will have a life of six years, with zero scrap value.

The accounting technician and the transport manager have prepared the following estimates relating to the savings.

The net cash flows from the project are:

Year	£
1	9,000
2	11,000
3	10,000
4	5,850
5	6,200
6	5,100

The cost of capital is 8%

	Year 1	Year 2	Year 3	Year 4	Year 5	Year 6
8%	0.926	0.857	0.794	0.735	0.681	0.630

Required:

Complete the following table (round all numbers to the nearest £):

Year	£	Discount factor @ 8%	Present Value £	Cumulative present value £
0	(30,000)	1		
1	9,000	0.926		
2	11,000	0.857		
3	10,000	0.794		
4	5,850	0.735		
5	6,200	0.681		
6	5,100	0.630		

The discounted payback is closest to ___ years.

8 Internal rate of return

8.1 The internal rate of return (IRR)

Definition

The **IRR** calculates the **rate of return** (or discount rate) that one project is expected to achieve if it **breaks even** i.e. no profit or loss is made. The IRR is therefore the point where the **NPV of an investment is zero**.

For one investment, a graph of NPV against discount rate looks like the following:

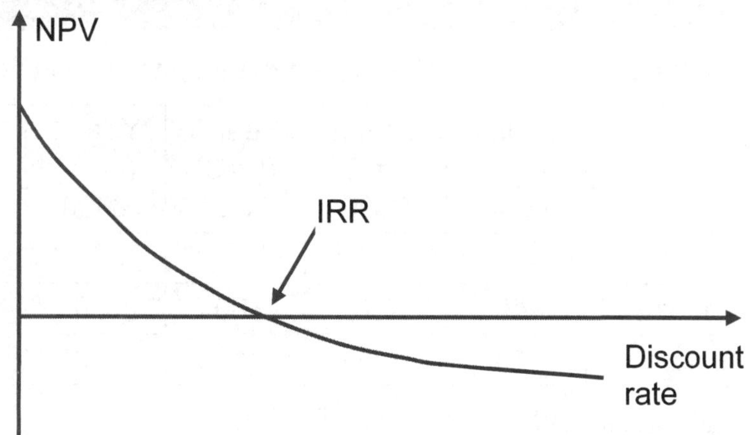

As the discount rate gets higher, the NPV gets smaller and then becomes negative. The cash flows are being discounted by a higher percentage therefore the present value of the cash flows becomes less.

The internal rate of return (IRR) is the discount rate that will cause the cash flow of a project to have a net present value equal to zero.

To decide on whether to invest using the IRR you need to compare the IRR with the discount rate that the company would like to use. If the chosen discount rate was somewhere between 10% and 15%, and the IRR of a project was 22% then we can still accept the project as our rate is less than the IRR, giving a positive NPV.

Test your understanding 16

If the company's cost of capital is 16% and the IRR is 14% the investment should go ahead.

True or false?

8.2 Estimating of the IRR

The method used to **estimate** the IRR is as follows:

- Calculate two NPVs for the investment at different discount rates.
- Estimate the IRR with reference to the NPV values.

Example 5

A machine costs £150,000 now. We expect the following cash flows:

	Year 1 (t = 1) £000	Year 2 (t = 2) £000	Year 3 (t = 3) £000	Year 4 (t = 4) £000	Year 5 (t = 5) £000
Scrap value					30
Sales revenues	40	50	60	50	40
Variable costs	(10)	(12)	(15)	(13)	(11)

1 NPV with a discount rate of 10% = £4,400

2 NPV at a discount rate of 20% = –£31,000

Estimate the IRR of the investment.

Solution

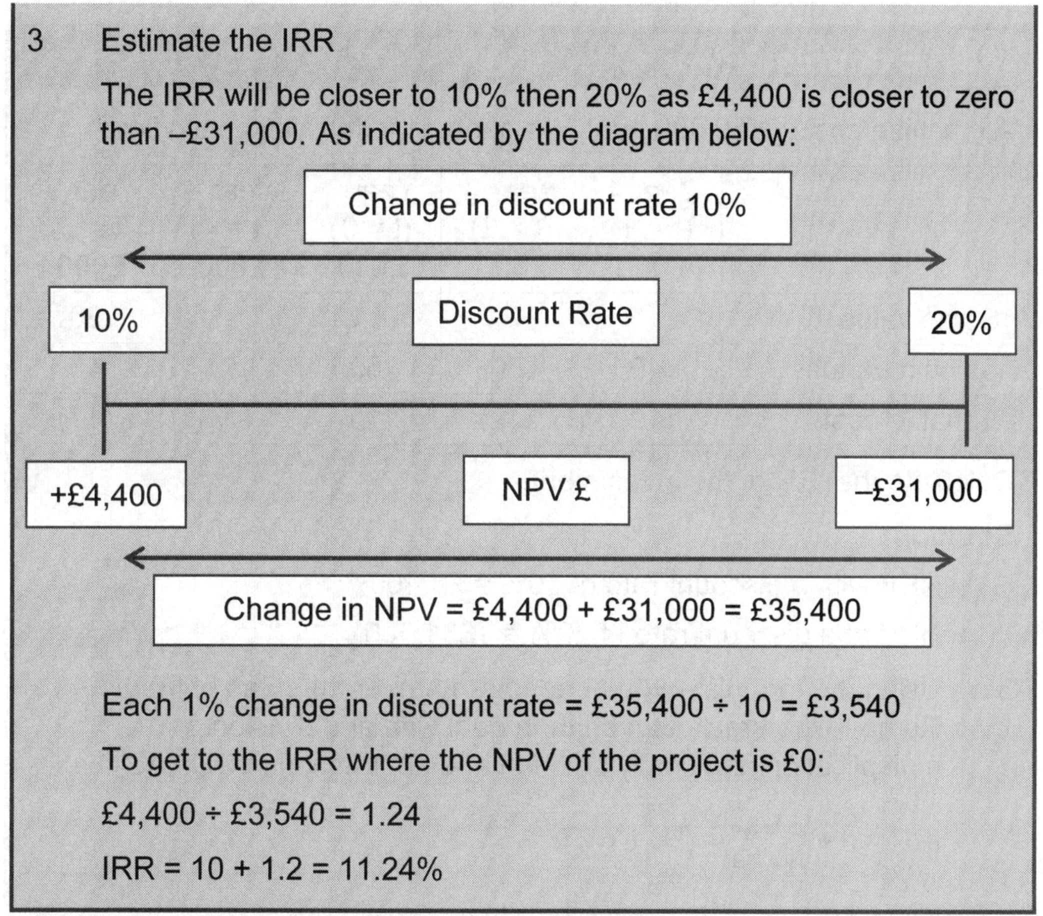

3 Estimate the IRR
The IRR will be closer to 10% then 20% as £4,400 is closer to zero than –£31,000. As indicated by the diagram below:
Change in discount rate 10%
10%
Discount Rate
20%
+£4,400
NPV £
–£31,000
Change in NPV = £4,400 + £31,000 = £35,400
Each 1% change in discount rate = £35,400 ÷ 10 = £3,540
To get to the IRR where the NPV of the project is £0:
£4,400 ÷ £3,540 = 1.24
IRR = 10 + 1.2 = 11.24%

The IRR of an investment can also be calculated using linear interpolation i.e. it uses two known points on a graph and joins them with a straight line. The point where the line crosses the x-axis will be calculated to provide the IRR.

8.3 Calculation of the IRR

The method used to **calculate** the IRR is as follows:

- Calculate two NPVs for the investment at different discount rates.
- Use the following formula to find the IRR:

$$IRR\ \% = L + \frac{N_L}{N_L - N_H} \times (H - L)$$

Where:

L = Lower rate of interest

H = Higher rate of interest

N_L = NPV at lower rate of interest

N_H = NPV at higher rate of interest

Example 6

A machine costs £150,000 now. We expect the following cash flows:

	Year 1 (t = 1) £000	Year 2 (t = 2) £000	Year 3 (t = 3) £000	Year 4 (t = 4) £000	Year 5 (t = 5) £000
Scrap value					30
Sales revenues	40	50	60	50	40
Variable costs	(10)	(12)	(15)	(13)	(11)

Calculate the IRR of the investment.

Solution

1 NPV with a discount rate of 10% = £4,400

2 NPV at a discount rate of 20% = –£31,000

3 Using the formula – you need to remember the rules of maths. Remove the brackets first, then deal with and division or multiplication and finally addition and subtraction (BODMAS).

$$IRR = L + \frac{N_L}{N_L - N_H} \times (H - L)$$

$$IRR = 10 + \frac{4,400}{4,400 - -31,000} \times (20 - 10)$$

(remember minus minus becomes a plus, this is a very common issue when using the IRR formula)

$$IRR = 10 + \frac{4,400}{35,400} \times 10$$

IRR = 10 + 0.1243 × 10

IRR = 10 + 1.243 = 11.24%

Test your understanding 17

A business undertakes high-risk investments and requires a minimum expected rate of return of 17% per annum on its investments.

A proposed capital investment has the following expected cash flows:

	£
Year 0	(50,000)
Year 1	18,000
Year 2	25,000
Year 3	20,000
Year 4	10,000

1 Calculate the NPV using 15% cost of capital and 20% cost of capital.

The relevant present value factors are:

	Year 1	Year 2	Year 3	Year 4
15%	0.870	0.756	0.658	0.572
20%	0.833	0.694	0.579	0.482

NPV @ 15%

	Year 0	Year 1	Year 2	Year 3	Year 4
Capital expenditure					
Net cash flow					
PV Factor	1.000	0.870	0.756	0.658	0.572
Discounted cash flow					
Net present value					

NPV @ 20%

	Year 0	Year 1	Year 2	Year 3	Year 4
Capital expenditure					
Net cash flow					
PV Factor	1.000	0.833	0.694	0.579	0.482
Discounted cash flow					
Net present value					

2 Using the NPVs you have calculated, estimate the IRR of the project.

3 Should the company proceed with the investment?

8.4 Advantages of IRR

(a) It considers the **time value of money** as NPVs are used in the calculation process.

(b) It uses cash flows which are less subjective than profits. Profit measures rely on such things as depreciation and other policies which are, to a certain extent, subjective.

(c) It considers the **whole life** of the project.

(d) It provides a **percentage return** that is easier for non-financial managers to understand.

(e) It can be calculated without deciding on the desired cost of capital.

8.5 Disadvantages of IRR

(a) Cash flows are future predictions and we are **unable to predict** the future with accuracy.

(b) It does not provide a monetary value for the return available from the investment.

8.6 Conflict between payback, NPV and IRR

NPV is considered the most robust of the project appraisal techniques, therefore if there is a conflict between payback, NPV and IRR then the result of the NPV should be used to make the final decision with regards to the investment.

Test your understanding 18

Data

RBG plc is a large quoted company using a 25% rate of interest for appraising capital projects. One of its divisional directors has put forward plans to make a new product, the AI. This will involve buying a machine specifically for that task. The machine will cost £600,000 and have a life of 5 years. However, because of the nature of the product, the machine will have no residual value at any time.

The annual cash flows will be as follows:

	£
Sales revenues	380,000
Material costs	90,000
Labour costs	30,000
Overhead costs	20,000

Task

You are asked to appraise the divisional director's proposal by calculating:

(a) the net present value

(b) the payback period.

	Year 0	Year 1	Year 2	Year 3	Year 4	Year 5
Capital expenditure						
Net cash flow						
PV Factor	1.000	0.800	0.640	0.512	0.410	0.328
Discounted cash flow						
Net present value						

The net present value is positive/negative*
*delete as appropriate

The payback period is Year(s) and Months

Further information

The IRR is 28%.

The new product should be/should not be* purchased
*delete as appropriate

Test your understanding 19

Mickey

Mickey is considering two mutually-exclusive projects with the following details.

	A	B
	£	£
Initial investment	450,000	100,000
Year 1	200,000	50,000
Year 2	150,000	40,000
Year 3	100,000	30,000
Year 4	100,000	20,000
Year 5	100,000	20,000

At the end of the five years each project has a scrap value. Project A's scrap value is £20,000 and Project B's scrap value is £10,000.

1 Calculate the payback period of each project.

2 Calculate the NPV of each project to the nearest £000 using a cost of capital of 10%.

The relevant present value factors are:

	Year 1	Year 2	Year 3	Year 4	Year 5
10%	0.909	0.826	0.751	0.683	0.621

Project A

	Year 0	Year 1	Year 2	Year 3	Year 4	Year 5
Capital expenditure						
Net cash flow						
PV Factor	1.000	0.909	0.826	0.751	0.683	0.621
Discounted cash flow						
Net present value						

Project B

	Year 0	Year 1	Year 2	Year 3	Year 4	Year 5
Capital expenditure						
Net cash flow						
PV Factor	1.000	0.909	0.826	0.751	0.683	0.621
Discounted cash flow						
Net present value						

If Project A is appraised using a cost of capital of 20% the NPV is £25,000 negative. If Project B is appraised using a cost of capital of 20% the NPV is £8,500 positive.

3 Calculate the IRR of each project.

4 Which project should Mickey invest in and why?

9 Lifecycle costing

9.1 Discounted approach

Earlier on we looked at life cycle costing and considered the non-discounting approach to working out the total cost associated with a products over the products life. We could also use discounting.

Remember, lifecycle costing is the forecasting of costs for assets over their entire life, so that decisions concerning the acquisition, use or disposal of the assets can be made in a way that achieves the optimum asset usage at the lowest possible cost to the entity. (It is simply a net present cost (NPC).)

For example, when buying a machine, a business might be offered either a poor quality machine for £20,000 or a high quality machine for £50,000. If the poor quality machine is expected to continually break down and need to be repaired all the time, while the high quality machine is expected never to break down, then life cycle costing might argue that the high quality machine should be bought, despite it being more expensive initially, since its total cost of ownership over its entire life will be less than the poor quality alternative.

Test your understanding 20

A company is going to renew a machine and is undecided between two options.

Machine A costs £50,000 immediately while machine B costs £80,000. Both machines will last 4 years. They will generate net savings after maintenance costs of:

	Machine A	Machine B
Year 1	£20,000	£30,000
Year 2	£20,000	£20,000
Year 3	£20,000	£20,000
Year 4	£10,000	£20,000

At the end of their lives they will be disposed of, generating an inflow of £10,000 for machine A and £30,000 for machine B.

Task

Calculate the Life Cycle Cost (LCC) of the two proposals when the interest rate is 10%.

The relevant present value factors are:

	Year 1	**Year 2**	**Year 3**	**Year 4**
10%	0.909	0.826	0.751	0.683

	Cashflow	DF	PV	Cashflow	DF	PV
Y0						
Y1						
Y2						
Y3						
Y4						
		LCC	£		LCC	£

Therefore machine ______________ is the better option.

Test your understanding 21

A company is considering whether to buy a machine for £20,000 today with maintenance costs of £1,000 per year for 3 years. It will be sold at the end of the third year for £3,000. The company uses a discount rate of 10%.

Discount factors are:

Year	**1**	**2**	**3**
	0.909	0.826	0.751

What is the net present cost?

Test your understanding 22

The net present cost for two projects has been calculated. For Project A it is (£12,000) and for Project B it is (£15,000).
On financial grounds, which project should be accepted?

10 Summary

In this chapter we have considered the mechanics and the advantages and the disadvantages of various investment appraisal techniques. In the context of an examination, you must be able to **calculate** the **payback period, ARR, the net present value, net present cost the IRR and the discounted life cycle cost of a project**.

The payback period, ignoring discounting, calculates how long it will take to recover the initial investment in a project. If this is longer than expected then the project should be rejected. We also looked at the discounted payback period, as this overcomes one of the weaknesses of the basic payback period.

The ARR uses profits rather than cash flows and is comparable to the ROCE or ROI from earlier chapters.

The net present value is an appraisal technique that takes discounted cash flows and calculates the return from an investment in monetary terms. The project is viable if the NPV is positive.

The net present cost also uses discounted cash flows but without any inflows, just considering the operating costs. When faced with more than one option, then on financial grounds we should choose the option with the cheapest net present cost.

The IRR of a project is the discount rate at which a project has a NPV equal to zero. A cost of capital (or discount rate) which is less than the IRR will give rise to a positive NPV (and is therefore considered to be an 'acceptable investment').

If there are conflicts between payback, NPV and IRR investment appraisal methods then the NPV is the strongest measure so the **NPV result will overrule the payback and IRR**.

Finally, we considered how the technique of life cycle costing that we looked at in an earlier chapter could also use discounting.

Test your understanding answers

Test your understanding 1

Time	**Cash flow** £000	**Cumulative position** £000	**Working** £000
t = 0	(100)	(100)	
t = 1	30	(70)	(100) + 30
t = 2	40	(30)	(70) + 40
t = 3	60	30	(30) + 60
t = 4	10	40	30 + 10

Payback period is **2** years and **6** months.

$= 2\frac{30}{60}$ or 2.5 years

or

£60,000/12 = £5,000

£30,000/£5,000 = 6 months

Test your understanding 2

The payback period is **3** Year(s) and **0** Months

Year	Cash flow	Cumulative cash flow
0	(30,000)	(30,000)
1	9,000	(21,000)
2	11,000	(10,000)
3	10,000	0

Test your understanding 3

	Workings (£000)	£
Total cash inflow	100 + 200 + 400 400 + 300 + 200 + 150 =	**1,750,000**
Total depreciation	800 – 100 =	**700,000**
Total profit for the investment	1,750 – 700 =	**1,050,000**
Average annual profit	1,050/7 =	**150,000**
Average capital invested	(800 + 100)/2 =	**450,000**

		%
ARR using initial investment	150,000/800,000 × 100 =	**18.75**
ARR using the average value of the investment	150,000/450,000 × 100 =	**33.33**

Test your understanding 4

	%
ARR using the initial value of the investment	**17.17**
ARR using the average value of the investment	**34.33**

Workings

The savings will increase the profit.

Total savings (£): 9,000 + 11,100 + 10,000 + 10,500 + 10,200 + 10,100 = 60,900

Total depreciation (£) = 30,000 – 0 = 30,000

Total profits = 60,900 – 30,000 = 30,900

Average annual profit = 30,900/6 = 5,150

ARR using initial value = 5,150/30,000 × 100 = 17.166667%

Average value of the investment = (30,000 + 0)/2 = 15,000

ARR using the average value of the investment = 5,150/15,000 × 100 = 34.333333%

Test your understanding 5

Project B has the highest NPV and should be selected.

Test your understanding 6

	Year 0	Year 1	Year 2	Year 3	Year 4
Capital expenditure	(80,000)				
Sales revenues		40,000	70,000	80,000	90,000
Operating costs		(20,000)	(20,000)	(40,000)	(80,000)
Net cash flow	(80,000)	20,000	50,000	40,000	10,000
PV Factor	1.000	0.870	0.756	0.658	0.572
Discounted cash flow	(80,000)	17,400	37,800	26,320	5,720
Net present value	7,240				

The net present value is positive.

This means we should **accept** the investment.

Test your understanding 7

Machine A

	Year 0	Year 1	Year 2	Year 3	Year 4	Year 5
Capital expenditure	(100,000)					
Net cash flow	(100,000)	20,000	60,000	40,000	30,000	20,000
PV Factor	1.000	0.952	0.907	0.864	0.823	0.784
Discounted cash flow	(100,000)	19,040	54,420	34,560	24,690	15,680
Net present value	48,390					

The net present value of Machine A is positive.

Machine B

	Year 0	Year 1	Year 2	Year 3	Year 4	Year 5
Capital expenditure	(60,000)	(60,000)				
Net cash flow	(60,000)	(60,000)	60,000	60,000	80,000	0
PV Factor	1.000	0.952	0.907	0.864	0.823	0.784
Discounted cash flow	(60,000)	(57,120)	54,420	51,840	65,840	0
Net present value	54,980					

The net present value of Machine B is positive.

Machine B has the higher NPV therefore the return from using this machine is better than machine A. Machine B should be selected.

Test your understanding 8

Machine A

	Year 0	Year 1	Year 2	Year 3	Year 4	Year 5
Capital expenditure	100,000					
Net cash flow	100,000	20,000	50,000	30,000	20,000	10,000
PV Factor	1.000	0.926	0.857	0.794	0.735	0.681
Discounted cash flow	100,000	18,520	42,850	23,820	14,700	6,810
Net present cost	206,700					

Machine B

	Year 0	**Year 1**	**Year 2**	**Year 3**	**Year 4**	**Year 5**
Capital expenditure	80,000					
Net cash flow	80,000	20,000	30,000	40,000	50,000	60,000
PV Factor	1.000	0.926	0.857	0.794	0.735	0.681
Discounted cash flow	80,000	18,520	25,710	31,760	36,750	40,860
Net present cost	233,600					

Machine A should be selected as it has the lower net present cost.

Test your understanding 9

The payback period is **2** Year(s) and **7** Months

Year	Cash flow	Cumulative cash flow
0	(50,000)	(50,000)
1	18,000	(32,000)
2	20,000	(12,000)
3	21,000	9,000
4	22,000	

£12,000/£21,000 × 12 = 7 months

	Year 0	**Year 1**	**Year 2**	**Year 3**	**Year 4**	**Year 5**
Capital expenditure	(50,000)					
Net cash flow	(50,000)	18,000	20,000	21,000	22,000	18,000
PV Factor	1.000	0.893	0.797	0.712	0.636	0.567
Discounted cash flow	(50,000)	16,074	15,940	14,952	13,992	10,206
Net present value	21,164					

The net present value is positive.

Accept.

 Test your understanding 10

The payback period is **2** Year(s) and **5** Months

Year	Cash flow	Cumulative cash flow
0	(285,400)	(285,400)
1	102,000	(183,400)
2	124,000	(59,400)
3	146,000	86,600

£59,400/£146,000 × 12 = 5 months

	Year 0	Year 1	Year 2	Year 3
Capital expenditure	(285,400)			
Net cash flow	(285,400)	102,000	124,000	146,000
PV Factor	1.000	0.833	0.694	0.579
Discounted cash flow	(285,400)	84,966	86,056	84,534
Net present value	(29,844)			

The net present value is negative.

This project has a negative NPV but still pays back within the life of the project. This project should be **rejected** as when the time value of money is considered there is not a return from the investment.

Test your understanding 11

The payback period is **2** Year(s) and **9** Months

Year	Cash flow	Cumulative cash flow
0	(220,000)	(220,000)
1	80,000	(140,000)
2	80,000	(60,000)
3	80,000	20,000

£60,000/£80,000 × 12 = 9 months

	Year 0	Year 1	Year 2	Year 3
Capital expenditure	(220,000)			
Net cash flow	(220,000)	80,000	80,000	80,000
PV Factor	1.000	0.909	0.826	0.751
Discounted cash flow	(220,000)	72,720	66,080	60,080
Net present value	(21,120)			

The net present value is negative.

This project has a negative NPV but still pays back within the life of the project. This project should be rejected as when the time value of money is considered there is not a return from the investment.

Test your understanding 12

Project A

	Year 0	Year 1	Year 2	Year 3	Year 4	Year 5
Capital expenditure	(75,000)					
Net cash flow	(75,000)	20,000	30,000	30,000	25,000	20,000
PV Factor	1.000	0.909	0.826	0.751	0.683	0.621
Discounted cash flow	(75,000)	18,180	24,780	22,530	17,075	12,420
Net present value	19,985					

The net present value is positive.

The payback period is **2** Year(s) and **10** Months

Year	Cash flow	Cumulative cash flow
0	(75,000)	(75,000)
1	20,000	(55,000)
2	30,000	(25,000)
3	30,000	5,000

£25,000/£30,000 × 12 = 10 months

Project B

	Year 0	**Year 1**	**Year 2**	**Year 3**	**Year 4**
Capital expenditure	(100,000)				
Net cash flow	(100,000)	30,000	45,000	45,000	40,000
PV Factor	1.000	0.909	0.826	0.751	0.683
Discounted cash flow	(100,000)	27,270	37,170	33,795	27,320
Net present value	25,555				

The net present value is positive.

The payback period is **2** Year(s) and **7** Months

Year	Cash flow	Cumulative cash flow
0	(100,000)	(100,000)
1	30,000	(70,000)
2	45,000	(25,000)
3	45,000	20,000

£25,000/£45,000 × 12 = 7 months

Project **B** should be invested in.

Project B should be recommended as it has the higher discounted cash flow, therefore the higher return from the investment. Payback is a cruder method of assessing future cash flows. No account is taken of flows after the payback period and equal weight given to flows within the payback period.

Test your understanding 13

	Year 0	Year 1	Year 2	Year 3	Year 4
Capital expenditure	(80,000)				
Net cash flow	(80,000)	29,600	29,200	28,780	28,339
PV Factor	1.000	0.909	0.826	0.751	0.683
Discounted cash flow	(80,000)	26,906	24,119	21,614	19,356
Net present value	11,995				

The net present value is positive.

The payback period is **2** Year(s) and **9** Months

Year	Cash flow	Cumulative cash flow
0	(80,000)	(80,000)
1	29,600	(50,400)
2	29,200	(21,200)
3	28,780	7,580

£21,200/£28,780 × 12 = 9 months

This project has a positive NPV and pays back within the life of the project. This project should be **accepted** as when the time value of money is considered there is a return from the investment.

Test your understanding 14

	Year 0	Year 1	Year 2	Year 3	Year 4
Capital expenditure	(14,400)				
Net cash flow	(14,400)	6,920	6,920	6,920	6,920
PV Factor	1.000	0.893	0.797	0.712	0.636
Discounted cash flow	(14,400)	6,180	5,515	4,927	4,401
Net present value	6,623				

The net present value is positive.

The payback period is **2** Year(s) and **1** Month

Year	Cash flow	Cumulative cash flow
0	(14,400)	(14,400)
1	6,920	(7,480)
2	6,920	(560)
3	6,920	6,360

£560/£6,920 × 12 = 1 month

This project has a positive NPV and pays back within the life of the project. This project should be **accepted** as when the time value of money is considered there is a return from the investment.

Test your understanding 15

Year	£	Discount factor @ 8%	Present Value £	Cumulative present value £
0	(30,000)	1	(30,000)	(30,000)
1	9,000	0.926	8,334	(21,666)
2	11,000	0.857	9,427	(12,239)
3	10,000	0.794	7,940	(4,299)
4	5,850	0.735	4,300	1
5	6,200	0.681	4,222	4,223
6	5,100	0.630	3,213	7,436

The discounted payback is closest to **4** years.

Test your understanding 16

False. The IRR is lower than the cost of capital therefore the investment will have broken even at 14% and be a negative NPV at 16%.

Test your understanding 17

1 Calculate the NPV using 15% cost of capital and 20% cost of capital.

NPV @ 15%

	Year 0	**Year 1**	**Year 2**	**Year 3**	**Year 4**
Capital expenditure	(50,000)				
Net cash flow	(50,000)	18,000	25,000	20,000	10,000
PV Factor	1.000	0.870	0.756	0.658	0.572
Discounted cash flow	(50,000)	15,660	18,900	13,160	5,720
Net present value	3,440				

NPV @ 20%

	Year 0	**Year 1**	**Year 2**	**Year 3**	**Year 4**
Capital expenditure	(50,000)				
Net cash flow	(50,000)	18,000	25,000	20,000	10,000
PV Factor	1.000	0.833	0.694	0.579	0.482
Discounted cash flow	(50,000)	14,994	17,350	11,580	4,820
Net present value	–1,256				

2 Using the NPVs you have calculated, estimate the IRR of the project.

$$IRR = L + \frac{N_L}{N_L - N_H} \times (H - L)$$

$$IRR = 15 + \frac{3,440}{3,440 - -1,256} \times (20 - 15)$$

$$IRR = 15 + \frac{3,440}{4,696} \times 5$$

$$IRR = 15 + 3.663 \quad = 18.7\%$$

3 Should the company proceed with the investment?

The IRR of the project is 18.7%. The company requires a return of 17%. The IRR is higher than the required return therefore the company should invest.

Test your understanding 18

	Year 0	Year 1	Year 2	Year 3	Year 4	Year 5
Capital expenditure	(600,000)					
Net cash flow	(600,000)	240,000	240,000	240,000	240,000	240,000
PV Factor	1.000	0.800	0.640	0.512	0.410	0.328
Discounted cash flow	(600,000)	192,000	153,600	122,880	98,400	78,720
Net present value	45,600					

The net present value is positive.

The payback period is **2** Year(s) and **6** Months

Year	Cash flow	Cumulative cash flow
0	(600,000)	(600,000)
1	240,000	(360,000)
2	240,000	(120,000)
3	240,000	120,000

£120,000/£240,000 × 12 = 6 months

The NPV is positive, the payback period well within the life of the project and the cost of capital is less than the IRR of 28%, and therefore the new product **should** be purchased.

Test your understanding 19

1 Calculate the payback period for each project.

Project A

	Cash flow	**Cumulative cash flow**
Year 0	(450,000)	(450,000)
Year 1	200,000	(250,000)
Year 2	150,000	(100,000)
Year 3	100,000	0

Payback is 3 years.

Project B

	Cash flow	**Cumulative cash flow**
Year 0	(100,000)	(100,000)
Year 1	50,000	(50,000)
Year 2	40,000	(10,000)
Year 3	30,000	20,000

Payback is 2 years 4 months.

2 Calculate the NPV for each project.

Project A

	Year 0	**Year 1**	**Year 2**	**Year 3**	**Year 4**	**Year 5**
Capital expenditure	(450)					
Net cash flow	(450)	200	150	100	100	120
PV Factor	1.000	0.909	0.826	0.751	0.683	0.621
Discounted cash flow	(450)	182	124	75	68	75
Net present value	74					

Project B

	Year 0	Year 1	Year 2	Year 3	Year 4	Year 5
Capital expenditure	(100)					
Net cash flow	(100)	50	40	30	20	30
PV Factor	1.000	0.909	0.826	0.751	0.683	0.621
Discounted cash flow	(100)	45	33	23	14	19
Net present value	34					

3 Calculate the IRR of each project.

Project A

$$IRR = 10 + \frac{74}{74 - -25} \times (20 - 10)$$

IRR = 17.5%

Project B

$$IRR = 10 + \frac{34}{34 - 8.5} \times (20 - 10)$$

IRR = 23.3%

4 Which project should Mickey invest in and why?

Project **A** should be invested in.

Project B has a shorter payback period and higher IRR but the NPV of Project A is the greater therefore providing the better return for the investment. NPV is the more robust of the investment appraisal techniques used as it considers the whole life of the project, includes the effect of the time value of money and also provides an absolute value for the return from the investment.

Test your understanding 20

	Cashflow	DF	PV	Cashflow	DF	PV
0	(£50,000)	1.000	(50,000)	(£80,000)	1.000	(80,000)
1	£20,000	0.909	18,180	£30,000	0.909	27,270
2	£20,000	0.826	16,520	£20,000	0.826	16,520
3	£20,000	0.751	15,020	£20,000	0.751	15,020
4	£20,000	0.683	13,660	£50,000	0.683	34,150
		LCC	£13,380		LCC	£12,960

Therefore machine A is the better option.

Test your understanding 21

The net present cost is: £20,233.

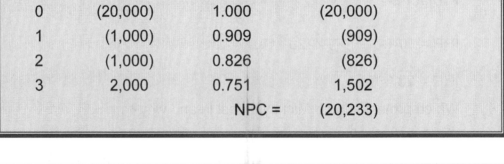

Year	Cost	DF @ 10%	PC
0	(20,000)	1.000	(20,000)
1	(1,000)	0.909	(909)
2	(1,000)	0.826	(826)
3	2,000	0.751	1,502
		NPC =	(20,233)

Test your understanding 22

Project A is the least cost and should be selected.

Impact of technology

Introduction

In this chapter will we introduce some of the key developments and technologies driving the new wave of innovation and increasingly changing the world around us.

Developments are happening all the time. One of the ultimate aims of these changes is that they make our lives easier, whether that is in our very own homes reminding us about important things we need to do, or even doing the tasks for us. This is also true in business; tasks are being simplified and streamlined and business awareness of what the consumer wants or needs is increasing too.

ASSESSMENT CRITERIA

Technology and its impact on operational control. (2.6)

CONTENTS

1 Technological advancements

1.1 Introduction

This chapter introduces a selection of technological advancements that have occurred in recent years, which have all had an impact on the way in which organisations operate. In lots of ways they have helped to change the world around us.

Specifically in AMAC we will consider the impact that the following have had on organisations:

- Cloud accounting
- Artificial intelligence
- Data analytics
- Visualisation

1.2 Benefits of technological advancements

Later in this chapter we will consider some benefits to specific to each development but more generally some of the benefits to organisations are:

- **Speed** – the use of technologies often enables an organisation to carry out processes more quickly. For example a computer can process data much more quickly than a person. Exam boards have utilised this by increasing the use of objective test questions that can be computer marked rather than marked by a human.
- **Automation** – often technology allows management to replace a process that was time consuming. For example many organisations have reduced the human involvement in a process allowing for a machine carry out an activity in the same speed and to the same standard every time, rather than the variability of a human carrying out the process.
- **Efficiency** – completely replacing human involvement is not always possible but technology can be used to improve efficiency, this can be both reduction in time taken and reduced wastage.
- **Focus** – reduction in time consuming processes can allow management additional time to focus on the core activities of the organisation. For example, some of the management accounting activities studied in the module are now carried out by software. This does not mean that a management accountant is no longer necessary, but that they are now able to free up more of their time to analyse data and provide more meaningful information to management to improve decision making.

1.3 Challenges faced by organisations in adopting technological advancements

As well as many potential benefits, there will also be challenges for organisations as they adopt technological advancements. These include:

- **Change management** – any adoption of new techniques will need employees to adopt the new processes. This can sometimes be difficult, as there may be a fear of the unknown or a fear that new technologies may replace them and that they may lose their job.
- **Skills and expertise** – linked into staffing issues, to use the technological advancement effectively may require hiring new staff with the appropriate skills and expertise to operate it.
- **Integration issues** – as technology develops it may not always be compatible with current systems and processes, meaning an organisation may not get the full benefit of the advancement.
- **Legislation** – increased data is not always a good thing. Holding too much, or unnecessary, data about customers could lead to issues with adherence to legislation like GDPR.
- **Cost benefit** – just because an organisation can measure something, or can automate something, doesn't mean that it should. Consideration of whether the technological advancement provides more benefit than it costs will be critical.
- **Cyber security** – the more an organisation relies on technology the greater the risk involved if either there is a fault on the system/network or software, or if someone tries to hack into the systems.
- **Staying up to date** – technology is constantly changing and updating, whether that is to protect it from known flaws or new forms of cyber-attack or it could also relate to further technology advancements that mean a previous advancement is no longer the best option. For example high definition very quickly became replaced by even better pictures and ultra-high definition.

2 Cloud accounting

2.1 Introduction

Cloud computing is computing based on the internet. It avoids the need for software, applications, servers and services being stored on physical computers. Instead, it stores these with cloud service providers who store these things on the internet and grant access to authorised users.

2.2 Cloud accounting software

Cloud accounting is using is accounting software that is hosted on remote servers. It is sometime referred to as cloud based accounting software and it works in essentially the same way as all other cloud based software. Due to the information being stored in such a way that it is always accessible, users can log in and perform accounting practices on any computer on the planet with an Internet connection.

Using cloud computing accounting software means that the business does not have to pay for, install, manage or protect software on individual machines.

2.3 Benefits of cloud computing to the organisation

- **Store and share data** – cloud services can often store more data than traditional, local physical drives, and the data can be shared more easily (regardless of physical location).
- **On-demand self-service** – users can gain access to technology on demand. For example, every time you download an app from iTunes or the Play store you are downloading it from a cloud service where it is stored.
- **Flexibility** – work can be done more flexibly as employees no longer need to be 'plugged into' work networks or facilities to access the data they need.
- **Collaboration** – the cloud facilitates better workforce collaboration – documents, plans etc. can be worked on by many different users simultaneously.
- **More competitive** – smaller firms can get access to technology and services that, without significant financial investment, may otherwise only be available to the largest organisations. This can allow small organisations to compete better with larger rivals.

- **Easier scaling** – cloud services provide high levels of flexibility in terms of size, number of authorised users etc. This means that the service can grow as the business grows, and allows businesses to scale up much more easily.
- **Reduced maintenance** – there is no longer need on the part of the organisation for regular maintenance and (security or software) updates of IT services; the cloud provider will take care of this.
- **Back-ups** – it can be used to back up data. This adds an extra layer of security and removes the need for physical devices to store backed-up data.
- **Disaster recovery** – this means that it can also aid disaster recovery. Using cloud technology makes this faster and cheaper.
- **Better security** – the cloud can increase security of data. For example, if in the past an employee were to lose a laptop with sensitive data on it, this would be a high risk security event for the organisation. Keeping data stored in the cloud should reduce such risks associated with hardware.

3 Artificial intelligence

3.1 Introduction

Artificial Intelligence (AI) is an area of computer science that emphasises the creation of intelligent machines that work and react like human beings.

A common definition from Kaplan and Haenlein describes AI as a "**system's ability to correctly interpret external data, to learn from such data, and to use those learnings to achieve specific goals and tasks through flexible adaptation**". This is often considered in the context of human-type robotics but reaches much further than this, and is set to transform the way in which we live and work.

Some of the more advanced activities and skills that AI can now master, and therefore present huge opportunity for developers and companies alike, include:

- Voice recognition
- Planning
- Learning
- Problem solving

Example

There are increasing examples of AI in our lives, but one of the most popular ones is that companies such as Apple and Amazon have developed and marketed voice recognition systems, either to be built into an existing product (such as Apple with its Siri system) or developed new products whose main function is voice recognition (such as Amazon and 'Alexa').

A further simple example is that of Facebook and its process of recommending new friends for users to connect with.

There are many, more complex examples of AI, but a common factor to both the simple and the more involved is that they are designed to make our lives easier and they involve machine learning.

3.2 Machine learning

Machine learning is a subset of AI where AI computer code is built to mimic how the human brain works. It essentially uses probability based on past experiences through data, events and connections between events. The computer then applies this learning to a given situation to give a fact driven, plausible outcome. If the conclusion that the computer reaches turns out to be incorrect this will act to add more experience and enhance its understanding further, so in future the same mistake will not be repeated.

Essentially machine learning algorithms detect patterns and learn how to make predictions and recommendations rather than following explicit programming instruction. The algorithms themselves then adapt to new data and experiences to improve their function over time.

An **algorithm** is a process or set of rules to be followed in calculations or other problem-solving operations, especially by a computer

Example

It is possible to use an algorithm to teach a computer to play a variety of games that involve a repetitive process and a finite number of options.

In fact, as early as 1961, artificial intelligence researcher Donald Michie effectively taught a pile of matchboxes to play noughts and crosses (tic-tac-toe). Each matchbox represented the state of the board and contained a coloured bead representing the possible moves that could be made from that position.

If the matchboxes went on to win the game, they would be rewarded for the moves they made, the reward was extra beads of the colour move they made. If they went on to lose the game, they would be penalised by removing the colour of bead representing the move they made.

This is an example of a reinforcement loop, and through this reinforcement gradually the matchboxes "learnt" the correct moves to make at each stage of the game.

Another game where a lot of time and money has been invested in teaching a computer algorithm to play the game is chess.

3.3 Benefits of AI

There are many benefits of AI, including:

- **Cost saving** – organisations can save the cost of employing staff to undertake low level, routine, repetitive tasks. This doesn't necessarily mean redundancies, as current staff can be retrained to do tasks that add more value or require more creativity.
- **Competitive advantage** – the detection of patterns that enables predictions and recommendations can lead to improved targeting of customers and therefore additional sales opportunities.

4 Data analytics

4.1 Introduction

Data analytics is the process of collecting, organising and analysing large sets of data to discover patterns and other information which an organisation can use to inform future decisions.

Data analytics generally includes three stages:

- Collection of data – organisations have access to greater quantities of data available from a number of internal and external sources.
- Organisation of data – once the data has been captured it needs to be organised and stored for future use, often using data warehousing facilities.
- Analysis of data – data mining software uses statistical algorithms to discover correlations and patterns to create useful information.

4.2 Big data

Big data describes data sets so large and varied they are beyond the capability of traditional data-processing

The key features of big data are described as the 4Vs:

- **Volume** – considers the amount of data that feeds into the organisation.

  Does the organisation have the resources available to store and manage this data?
  Or does it have the financial resources required to invest in or upgrade IT/IS?

- **Velocity** – considers the speed that data feeds into the organisation, and in some cases how quickly that data changes.

  Are systems able to capture and process 'real time' data?
  Does the organisation have the skills to provide timely analysis of this data?

- **Variety** – considers the various formats that the data can be received in.

  Are systems compatible and capable of accepting various forms of data?
  Legally, is the data owned by the organisation or by the third party?

- **Veracity** – considers the reliability of the data that is being received into the organisation.

  Can the organisation challenge data received from third parties?
  Is the data received fully representative of the whole data population?

 **Example**

Applying Gartner's 4Vs to Match.com, part of The Match Group, provide services to help people connect.

Volume – The Match Group is a community of over 20 million singles in 25 countries and across five continents. Match.com estimates that it has 70 terabytes of data about its customers.

Variety – Match.com (with user permission) also gathers data on users' browser and search histories, viewing habits and purchase histories to build an accurate view of the sort of person the customer might like to date.

Velocity – New customers will join the service, or existing customers will find their needs and wants from a partner may change. Match.com needs to continually gather data to ensure that they are able to deal with this.

Veracity (truthfulness) – Match.com has found that when gathering customer data, customers may lie to present themselves in the most positive light possible to prospective partners. This will lead to inaccurate matches. Using non-biased sources of information (such as purchasing or web browser histories) rather than relying solely on customer feedback is therefore important.

4.3 Sources of big data

Big data comes in two main forms: structured and unstructured. Structured data is deliberately produced and collected for a specific purpose and therefore exhibits a clear, deliberate structure. For instance feedback data when people have been asked to rate a service or product. Unstructured data, on the other hand, is captured passively without a clear purpose. Social media posts and 'likes' are an example of this. Its format is highly variable and non-standard.

The principal sources of these two forms of data are classified as follows:

- **Human-sourced data** – billions of data points are produced every day from social media, text messages, web browsing, emails etc.
- **Machine-generated data** – smart technologies and the internet of things is a growing source of data. Sensors built in to all aspects of modern technology, log and upload data constantly. Home assistants, smart meters, TV boxes and cars are a small selection of items producing machine-generated data.
- **Processed data** – traditional data, held on databases of businesses and organisations recording customers, transactions and company assets.
- **Open data** – publically available data stemming from sources such as governments, the public sector and national statistics agencies.

4.4 Benefits of big data

Big data has several stated benefits to the organisation, including:

- **Driving innovation** by reducing the time taken to answer key business questions and therefore make decisions.
- **Gaining competitive advantage** by identifying trends or information that has not been identified by rivals.
- **Improving productivity** by identifying waste and inefficiency, or identifying improvements to working procedures.

4.5 How data analytics improve the effectiveness of management accounting

Data analytics is contributing to the development of effective management control systems and budgeting processes. For example:

- The use and analysis of data can aid cost management and control across all areas of the production process through improved information.
- Analysis of data can enhance inventory management leading to lower costs.
- Analysing data from purchases can improve purchasing processes to lower expenditure.
- Building up customer profiles can lead to improved personalisation of product offering and increase sales.
- Proposed changes can be assessed in terms of their predicted benefits by using data from previous changes.

5 Visualisation

5.1 Introduction

Data visualisation allows large volumes of complex data to be displayed in a visually appealing and accessible way that facilitates the understanding and use of the underlying data.

The growing significance of data has seen a rise in the importance of being able to access and understand the data in clear, concise way. This is where data visualisation fits in. The tools of today's market leaders Tableau and Qlik, go far beyond the simple charts and graphs of Microsoft Excel. Data is displayed in customisable, interactive 3D formats that allow users to manipulate and drill down as required. Central to data visualisation is understanding and ease of use; the leading companies in the field look to make data easier and more accessible for everyone.

Essentially it aims to remove the need for complex extraction, analysis and presentation of data by finance, IT and data scientists. It puts the ability to find data in to the hands of the end user, through intuitive, user friendly interfaces.

The most common use of data visualisation is in creating a dashboard to display the key performance indicators of a business in a live format. This helps immediate understanding of current performance and potentially prompting action to correct or amend performance accordingly.

An effective data visualisation tool should display these five features:

- **Decision making ability** – results focused, it should aid decision making
- **Effective infrastructure** – the output is reliant upon sufficient quantity and quality of data
- **Integration capability** – with existing systems and the business overall
- **Prompt discovery of rules and insights** – live data is vital and delay can render any insight useless
- **Real time collaboration** – users must interact with each other and the data

5.2 Benefits of visualisation

Visualisation has several benefits to organisations, including:

- **Understanding and ease of use** are core to the benefits of visualisation. Making sure that complex data is displayed in an appealing and accessible way.
- **Reduces the need for complex and time consuming extraction analysis and display work.** The systems allow intuitive and user friendly extraction of key data.
- **Improving performance** as key performance indicators are more accessible and updated constantly so it is easier to identify when corrective action needs to be taken.

Test your understanding 1

Which ONE of the following is an advantage of data analytics?

A Increased risk of non-compliance with legislation

B Easier access to back ups

C Improved productivity

D Inability to integrate systems

Test your understanding 2

Which ONE of the following is the most common name for the delivery of on-demand computing resources?

A Artificial intelligence

B Data visualisation

C Data analytics

D Cloud computing

Test your understanding 3

Sara has recently started looking at ways of gathering big data for her business. She is concerned that some of the sources of data she has chosen are unreliable and may therefore lead her to inaccurate conclusions.

Which of ONE of Gartner's features may be missing from Sara's big data?

A Variety

B Velocity

C Veracity

D Volume

Test your understanding 4

Dollar Co is a chain of banks. It collects data from customers who visit the banks in person, and also from online transactions. For the online banking system, customers need to log in via the website using their login and password. Recently Dollar Co invested in a system that promoted certain products to customers when they were online, based on past transactions and banking history.

Which ONE of the following is this an example of?

A Data visualisation

B Cloud accounting

C Artificial intelligence

D Voice recognition

Test your understanding 5

Which THREE of the following statement relating to data analytics are true?

A Big data refers to any financial data over £1 billion

B The defining characteristics of big data are velocity, volume, veracity and variety

C Managing data analytics effectively can lead to increased competitive advantage

D Data analytics is computing based on the internet

E Data analytics can contain both financial and non-financial data

Test your understanding 6

Which ONE of the following is a potential challenge that an organisation may face when adopting technological advancements?

A Allowing large volumes of complex data to be displayed in a visually appealing and accessible way that facilitates the understanding and use of the underlying data.

B Gaining competitive advantage by identifying trends or information that has not been identified by rivals

C As technology develops it may not always be compatible with current systems and processes

D The use and analysis of data can aid cost management and control across all areas of the production process through improved information

Test your understanding 7

PL is a global firm that manufactures and sells to both retailers and individual customers. The company currently uses cost plus pricing, but is considering switching to target costing, especially for a new product it is developing.

PL have carried out some research into this new product, to identify the appropriate features and acceptable selling price of the product. They believe to make sure it has the relevant features that the market research suggests the customers value that they will need 3 different types of material.

Identify FOUR advantages to PL of adopting the use of data analytics for this and other product innovations.

Test your understanding 8

Which of the following statements are correct?

Place a tick next to each correct statement.

Statement	Correct?
Technological advances are always better.	
Cloud accounting is using accounting software that is hosted on remote servers.	
There are 4Ds of big data.	
Data analytics generally includes three stages: Collection of data Organisation of data Analysis of data.	
Artificial Intelligence (AI) is an area of computer science that emphasises the creation of intelligent humans that work and react like machines.	

6 Summary

In this chapter we have looked at how technology has created opportunities for organisations to improve understanding, efficiency, cost control and other areas too.

Technological advancements will no doubt continue and offer even more opportunities for organisations in the future.

Although, it is important to remember, that just because something is new and in theory better, it won't necessarily be appropriate or beneficial for all organisations and proper cost benefit analysis should be considered.

Test your understanding answers

Test your understanding 1

The correct answer is C.

Increased data means there is an increased risk of data privacy legislation breaches, this is a potential disadvantage of data analytics.

Easier access to back-ups is an advantage of cloud computing.

A risk of technological advancements is that the new technology may not be compatible with the current systems or processes is a disadvantage of technological advancements.

Test your understanding 2

The correct answer is D.

Cloud computing is where software that is hosted on remote servers is accessed on-demand.

Test your understanding 3

The correct answer is C.

Veracity refers to the accuracy and truthfulness of the data. If this is missing, it can lead to inaccurate conclusions being drawn.

Test your understanding 4

The correct answer is C.

Artificial intelligence has algorithms that process data and can use it to make recommendations.

Data visualisation allows complex data to be viewed in a visually appealing way.

Cloud accounting is using accounting software that is hosted on remote servers.

Voice recognition is another aspect of artificial intelligence, but there is no mention of its use in this situation.

Test your understanding 5

The correct answers are B, C and E.

Option A is incorrect as big data does not refer to any specific financial amount.

Option D is also incorrect, cloud computing is computing based on the internet.

Test your understanding 6

The correct answer is C.

Option A is a benefit of data visualisation.

Option B and D are advantages of using data analytics.

Test your understanding 7

Data analytics can aid understanding of the production process which could lead to improvements in cost management and control, thus reducing the cost per unit of the new product.

Data analytics can help improve inventory control enabling a reduction in costs associated with inventory management, helping PL achieve its target cost.

The use of data analytics could also improve their understanding of their purchasing needs for each of the three key materials, this could also lead to potential cost savings.

Data analytics linked into customer behaviour will help improve customer profiling and enable them to target likely purchasers more effectively.

For future products, data analytics can help predict and anticipate likely needs and wants of customers and also measure the potential impact of any changes they make to products.

Test your understanding 8

Statement	Correct?
Technological advances are always better.	
Cloud accounting is using accounting software that is hosted on remote servers.	✓
There are 4Ds of big data.	
Data analytics generally include three stages:	✓
Collection of data	
Organisation of data	
Analysis of data.	
Artificial Intelligence (AI) is an area of computer science that emphasises the creation of intelligent humans that work and react like machines.	

Technological advances are not always better, they may cost more than the benefit they provide, or system integration issues may lead to benefits not being achieved.

There are 4Vs of big data.

Artificial Intelligence (AI) is an area of computer science that emphasises the creation of intelligent machines that work and react like human beings

MOCK ASSESSMENT

1 Mock Assessment Questions

Task 1 (12 marks)

This task is about budgetary processes, responsibilities and uncertainties.

(a) **Match each item of budget data below with its appropriate source.** **(4 marks)**

Budget data	Appropriate source
Global Economic Trends	Customer Relationship Management (CRM) system
Likely future government policy	World Bank, International Monetary Fund
UK Inflation Trends	Market research
Details of orders placed by your company's customers	Office for National Statistics SWOT Analysis
	Political consultancies/ commentators

(b) **Match each task with the individual or group that you will need to contact for information.** **(3 marks)**

Task	Contact
You want to know plans to disrupt the firms' operations	Firms' customers
You want to identify the firm's production capacity	Suppliers
You want to check the availability of a raw material	Competitors' price lists
	Pressure groups
	Production planning manager

(c) **Select the appropriate term to match each of these descriptions. (5 marks)**

A cost that fluctuates in direct proportion to changes in activity

- Variable cost
- Fixed cost
- Semi-variable cost
- Stepped cost

Detailed budgets prepared by functional managers are collated to form a master budget

- Top-down budgeting
- Bottom up budgeting
- Invariable budgeting
- Zero based budgeting

How functional managers may feel when an organisation uses an imposed budgeting approach

- Excited
- De-motivated
- Motivated
- Energised

A financial measure of the difference between budget and actual performance

- Flexed budget
- Financial difference
- Inequality
- Variance

Where a periodic budget is set by considering the previous budget or actual performance and adjusting it for changes in volume and inflation

- Zero based budget
- Rolling budget
- Incremental budget
- Activity based budget

Task 2 (24 marks)

This task is about budget preparation, evaluation and revision.

(a) **Complete the following production forecast for product 'Mauve'. Round any decimal figures up to the next whole number of units, if necessary.** **(10 marks)**

Units of product Mauve

	Week 1	Week 2	Week 3	Week 4	Week 5
Opening inventory	16,000				
Good production					
Sales volume	68,000	69,000	67,000	70,000	72,000
Closing inventory					

Rejected production				
Total manufactured units				

Closing inventory should be 25% of the following week's forecast sales. 5% of all production fails quality control checks and is rejected.

(b) The quarterly production requirements for product B are shown below.

3% of production fails the quality checks and must be scrapped.

How many items of product B must be manufactured to allow for waste? **(2 marks)**

	Month 1	Month 2	Month 3
Required units	50,600	49,500	49,800
Manufactured units			

(Round **up** to nearest whole unit)

(c) **Raw material purchases**

50,000 items of product G are to be manufactured in April.

Each requires 1.5 metres of raw material.

20% of raw material is wasted during manufacture.

The opening inventory will be 10,000 metres.

The closing inventory will be 11,000 metres.

How much material must be purchased? **(1 mark)**

Select from

94,750m 94,550m 94,900m 95,000m 96,750m

(d) **Labour hours**

114,000 units of product X are to be manufactured in May.

Each one takes 2 minutes to produce.

20 staff will each work 160 hours basic time.

How many overtime hours must be worked to complete the production? **(2 marks)**

Select from

600 200 360 300 3,800

(e) Department C manufactures three products, D, E and F.

Calculate the machine hours required to manufacture these in November.

Product	Units	Hours per unit	Hours required
D	50	1.5	
E	130	2.0	
F	250	2.5	
Total hours for department X			

There are seven machines in the department.

Each machine can be used for 120 hours in November. Additional machines can be hired if required.

How many additional machines should be hired?

(5 marks)

(f) **The budget committee has set the sales volume growth and pricing assumptions for years 2, 3, 4 and 5 in the form of indices. Complete the sales revenue forecast below.**

Do not show decimals. Round each figure to the nearest whole number. **(4 marks)**

	Year 1	Year 2	Year 3	Year 4	Year 5
Sales volume index	110	111	115	116	119
Sales price index	112	115	120	122	125

Sales revenue	Actual Year 1 £	Forecast Year 2 £	Forecast Year 3 £	Forecast Year 4 £	Forecast Year 5 £
At Year 1 prices	350,000				
At expected prices					

Task 3 (18 marks)

This task is about flexed budgets or standard costing.

A company provides you with the following budget and actual information:

Budgeted output	2,500 units
Standard cost information	
Direct material	10 kg @ £7.50 per kg
Direct labour	2 hours @ £6.00 per hour
Fixed overheads	£16 per unit

Actual information

Output and sales		2,400 units
Revenue		£286,800
Direct material	24,550 kg	£184,616
Direct labour	5,040 hours	£30,492
Fixed overheads		£38,500

Additional information

- Budgeted fixed overhead for the year is £40,000.
- Production is anticipated to be evenly spread throughout the year.
- Budgeted selling price for the year is £120 per unit

(a) Calculate the following:

Standard GP per unit	£	
	£	F / A
Sales price variance		
Sales volume variance		
Direct labour rate variance		
Direct labour efficiency variance		
Direct material price variance		
Direct material usage variance.		
Fixed overhead expenditure variance		
Fixed overhead volume variance		

(15 marks)

(b) **Answer the following question about variances.** **(3 marks)**

Which of the following situations would probably cause an adverse materials usage variance?

better quality materials / higher grade labour / an increase in the minimum quality standards / purchase of new machinery

Which of the following situations would probably cause a favourable labour rate variance?

better quality material / better quality workers / poorer quality materials / decrease in the need for overtime

Which of the following situations would probably cause an adverse fixed overhead capacity variance?

decrease in annual rent / purchase of additional machinery / higher grade labour / strike action by workers

Task 4 (20 marks)

This task is about costing systems to aid control.

Yarrow Limited manufactures two products, the Marrow and the Barrow.

The overhead activities for these, machine set ups and special parts handling, have budgets of £400,000 and £200,000 respectively.

It takes 2 hours 30 minutes of labour to make a Marrow and 3 hours 30 minutes of labour to make a Barrow.

Other information about the Marrow and Barrow is below.

	Marrow	Barrow
Direct materials – £ per unit	4	6
Direct labour – £ per unit	12.50	17.50
Number of special parts	300	100
Number of machine set ups	150	50
Budgeted production units	10,000	50,000

(a) **Calculate the fixed overheads assuming they are absorbed on a budgeted labour hours basis.** **(2 marks)**

	Marrow (£)	Barrow (£)
Fixed overheads		

(b) **Complete the table below using Activity Based Costing (ABC) principles.** **(6 marks)**

	£	Marrow (£)	Barrow (£)
Cost driver rate – special parts handling			
Cost driver rate – machine set ups			
Total special parts			
Total machine set ups			

(c) **Using the information from (a) and (b) calculate the total cost per unit using traditional absorption costing and using ABC. Give you answers to two decimal places.** **(4 marks)**

	Marrow	Barrow
Total unit cost – Absorption costing		
Total unit cost – ABC		

(d) **Discuss the potential issues that Yarrow could have switching from absorption costing to activity based costing.** **(8 marks)**

Task 5 (20 marks)

This task is about short term decision making.

A company manufactures two products, the Shola and the Sammy. The information below relates to the upcoming reporting period.

	Shola (£)	Sammy (£)
Direct materials at £8 per kg	12	16
Direct labour at £5 per hour	5	7.5
Variable overheads	2	3
Fixed production overhead	1.50	2.50
Selling price	30	40
	Units	**Units**
Sales demand	3,000	6,000

As a result of the recent storms and subsequent transportation issues materials are limited to 20,000 kg and labour hours are limited to 9,750 hrs.

(a) **Complete the table below for the upcoming period to calculate the optimal production plan. (10 marks)**

	Shola	Sammy
Total materials required (kg)		
Total labour hours required		
Contribution per unit (£)		
Contribution per limiting factor (£) (to TWO decimal places)		
Optimal production (units)		

(b) **What is the maximum extra premium that would be paid for each of the following? (2 marks)**

1,500 kg of extra material £ [ ] .

1,500 hrs of extra labour £ [ ] .

(c) **Discuss why you have decided on the production plan in (a) and the implications of not using it for this company. (5 marks)**

Bonanza Ltd is considering purchasing a new machine to improve efficiency.

	Current performance	**New machinery**
Direct materials per unit	2 kg at £6	Usage would reduce by 10%
Direct labour per unit	4 hours at £8	Time taken would reduce by 25%
Sales	4,000 units at £100	No change in sales units, but the price would be 1% higher
Fixed costs	£100,000	Increase by 20%

(d) **Calculate the profit figures for the current and proposed situations and indicate whether or not the equipment should be purchased. (3 marks)**

	Current situation (£)	**Expected situation with new machinery** (£)
Profit		

It would/would not be beneficial to purchase the new machinery.

Task 6 (14 marks)

This task is about long term decision making.

One of the painting machines in the Finishing department is nearing the end of its working life and Icon Ltd is considering purchasing a replacement machine.

Estimates have been made for the initial capital cost, sales revenue and operating costs of the replacement machine, which is expected to have a working life of three years:

	Year 0 £000	**Year 1** £000	**Year 2** £000	**Year 3** £000
Capital expenditure	1,900			
Other cash flows:				
Sales revenue		1,620	1,860	2,300
Operating costs		1,120	1,150	1,190

The company appraises capital investment projects using a 15% cost of capital.

(a) Complete the table below and calculate the net present value of the proposed replacement machine (to the nearest £000). **(11 marks)**

	Year 0 £000	**Year 1** £000	**Year 2** £000	**Year 3** £000
Capital expenditure				
Sales revenue				
Operating costs				
Net cash flows				
PV factors	1.0000	0.8696	0.7561	0.6575
Discounted cash flows				
Net present value				

The net present value is **positive/negative**.

(b) Calculate the payback of the proposed replacement machine to the nearest whole month. **(2 marks)**

The payback period is ______Year(s) and ______ Months

(c) What is the approximate internal rate of return (IRR) of the project? **(1 marks)**

A 0%

B 10%

C 15%

D 20%

Task 7 (20 marks)

This task is about analysing business performance.

(a) Menmuir Ltd has a receivables balance of £200,000, and their receivables collection period is 32 days. They have a gross profit margin of 28% and the split of their cost of sales is 65% variable production costs & 35% fixed production costs. The net profit margin is 8%.

Payables payment period is 40 days and the cash balance is £50,000.

Complete the table below using the performance indicators given for Menmuir Ltd.

Enter all figures as positive numbers – do not enter negative figures. **(9 marks)**

	£
Sales	
Variable production costs	
Fixed production costs	
Cost of sales	
Gross profit	
Net profit	
Payables	
Receivables	

(b) **Complete the statements below by selecting one of the following phrases for each statement:**

financial / customer / internal business / innovation and learning

(4 marks)

Revenue growth would be most likely classified under the [ ] perspective of the balanced scorecard.

Numbers of new products developed would be most likely classified under the [ ] perspective of the balanced scorecard.

The measurement of the time taken to complete the production cycle would be most likely classified under the [ ] perspective of the balanced scorecard.

Profit would be most likely classified under the [ ] perspective of the balanced scorecard.

(c) **Tarana Ltd has the following performance indicators for the last two years.**

	20X1	20X2
Gross profit margin %	21.01	23.46
Operating profit margin %	10.81	12.73
Expenses as a % of revenue	10.20	10.73
ROCE %	15.94	18.52
Asset turnover (times)	1.99	2.68
Average spend per transaction (£)	£15.25	£18.10
Number of new products launched	2	0
% of customers who complain	1.05	5.62

Using the performance indicators, analyse the performance of Tarana Ltd over the period. (7 marks)

Task 8 (12 marks)

This task is about divisional performance and forecasting.

(a) The table below contains the last three months cost per litre for a product.

Jan	Feb	Mar
Actual price was £6.00	Actual price was £6.00	Actual price was £6.30
Seasonal variation was –10p	Seasonal variation was –15p	Seasonal variation was +10p

The trend in prices is an increase of £ [ ] per month.

(2 marks)

(b) **Complete the following sentences: (2 marks)**

Seasonal variation is the [ ] data at a point less the trend data at the same point.

actual / budgeted / indexed / forecast

A change in the economy that affects sales of a product is an example of a [ ].

random variation / underlying trend / seasonal variation / cyclical variation

(c) A company has provided the following information:

	Jan	Feb	Mar
Total cost	£15,000	£20,000	£22,320
Total quantity purchased	2,000 m	2,500 m	2,480 m

The cost index for March, based upon January being the base period with an index of 100, is:

A 120

B 124

C 133

D 149 **(2 marks)**

(d) **Complete the following sentences:** **(2 marks)**

To calculate an index number, divide the current period figure by the [ ] figure.

base / future / trend / independent

The RPI can be used to remove distortion in a set of figures to help aid [ ] .

absorption / life cycle costing / comparison / extrapolation

(e) The Production Director has asked for your help. She has been given an equation and information to estimate the cost of asphalt for the coming three months.

The equation is Y = a + bX, where

X is the time period in months

The value for X in May 20X1 is 18

Y is the cost of asphalt

Constant 'a' is 100 and constant 'b' is 2.7.

The cost of asphalt is set on the first day of each month and is not changed during the month.

The expected price of asphalt per tonne for June 20X1 is £ [ ] and for July 20X1 is £ [ ] **(2 marks)**

(f) **Complete the following sentences:** **(2 marks)**

One of the assumptions of linear regression is that the data used is representative of future [ ]

indexes / targets / standards / trends

In the equation Y = a + bX, Y is the [ ] variable

independent / index / cyclical / dependent

2 Mock Assessment Answers

Task 1

(a)

Data	Answer
Global Economic Trends	World Bank, International Monetary Fund
Likely future government policy	Political consultancies/ commentators
UK Inflation Trends	Office for National Statistics
Details of orders placed by your company's customers	Customer Relationship Management (CRM) system

(b)

Task	Answer
You want to know plans to disrupt the firms' operations	Pressure groups
You want to identify the firm's production capacity of the firm	Production planning manager
You want to check the availability of a raw material	Suppliers

(c) A cost that fluctuates in direct proportion to changes in activity: Variable cost

Detailed budgets prepared by functional managers are collated to form a master budget: Bottom up budgeting

How functional managers may feel when an organisation uses an imposed budgeting approach: De-motivated

A financial measure of the difference between budget and actual performance: Variance

Where a periodic budget is set by considering the previous budget or actual performance and adjusting it for changes in volume and inflation: Incremental budget

Task 2

(a)

Units of product Mauve

	Week 1	Week 2	Week 3	Week 4	Week 5
Opening inventory	16,000	17,250	16,750	17,500	
Good production	69,250	68,500	67,750	70,500	
Sales	68,000	69,000	67,000	70,000	72,000
Closing inventory	17,250	16,750	17,500	18,000	

Rejected production	3,645	3,605	3,566	3,711
Total manufactured units	72,895	72,105	71,316	74,211

Workings

We start by calculating the values for the 'closing inventory' row.

- 'Closing inventory' in week 1 = 25% of week 2 sales
  = 25% × 69,000
  = 17,250
- 'Closing inventory' in week 2 = 25% of week 3 sales
  = 25% × 67,000
  = 16,750
- 'Closing inventory' in week 3 = 25% of week 4 sales
  = 25% × 70,000
  = 17,500
- 'Closing inventory' in week 4 = 25% of week 4 sales
  = 25% × 72,000
  = 18,000

We can then fill in the **'opening inventory'** row: the opening inventory in week 2 is the same as closing inventory in week 1, and so on and so forth.

Once this has been done, we may calculate, for each week, the **'Good production'** numbers as follows:

Good production units = sales units + closing inventory – opening inventory.

For example, in week 1:

Good production units = sales units 68000 + closing inventory 17250 – opening inventory 16000 = 69,250

Then, to calculate the **'total manufactured units'**, we take the 'good production' units that are only 95% of the total production, and we calculate what 100% of the total production would be. For example, in Week 1, we have 69,250 good units and they represent only 95% of the total production, so the total production is

$$\frac{\text{69,250 good units}}{0.95} = \text{72,895 units}$$

Finally, to calculate the 'rejected production' units, we deduct the 'good production units' from the 'total manufactured units'. For example in Week 1:

Rejected production units = Total manufactured units – good production

Rejected production units = 72,895 – 69,250 = 3,645 units.

(b)

	Month 1	**Month 2**	**Month 3**
Required units	50,600	49,500	49,800
Manufactured units	52,165	51,031	51,341

(Round **up** to nearest whole unit)

(c) 94,750m

Working

50,000 items @ 1.5 metres = 75,000 metres.

75,000m × 100/80 (wastage) = 93,750m

Plus 11,000m closing inventory less 10,000m = 94,750m

(d) 600

Working

114,000 × 2/60 = 3,800 hrs required.

3,800 – (20 × 160) = 600 hrs overtime needed.

(e)

Product	Units	Hours per unit	Hours required
D	50	1.5	75
E	130	2.0	260
F	250	2.5	625
Total			960

How many additional machines should be hired? 1

(f) The budget committee has set the sales volume growth and pricing assumptions for years 2, 3, 4 and 5 in the form of indices. Complete the sales revenue forecast below.

Do not show decimals. Round each figure to the nearest whole number.

	Year 1	Year 2	Year 3	Year 4	Year 5
Sales volume index	110	111	115	116	119
Sales price index	112	115	120	122	125

Sales revenue	Actual Year 1 £	Forecast Year 2 £	Forecast Year 3 £	Forecast Year 4 £	Forecast Year 5 £
At Year 1 prices	350,000	353,182	365,909	369,091	378,636
At expected prices		362,642	392,045	402,045	422,585

Workings for the 'Forecast Year 2' column

In Year 2 we have a sales volume index of 111, compared to a sales volume index of 110 in Year 1. To calculate the numbers to enter in the 'Forecast Year 2' column, we can:

- First, multiply our actual sales of £350,000 in Year 1 by 111 (= £38,850,000), then divide this number by 110.

  $\frac{£350,000}{110} \times 111 = £353,182$. These are the forecast sales for Year 2 before we adjust for the sales price index.

- Then, to adjust for the sales price index forecast in Year 2, we take our forecast sales of £353, 182 at Year 1 prices, then divide them by 112% to get a '1%' of that total:

  $\frac{£353,182}{112} = £3,153.411$ (you should leave this number in your calculator)

  We can then multiply this by the index of 115 for Year 2:

  £3,153.411 × 115 = £362,642.

Task 3

(a)

Standard GP per unit = £120 – £75 – £12 – £16 = £17	£	17.00
	£	F / A
Sales price variance AS × AP = £286,800 AS × SP = 2,400 × £120 = £288,000	1,200	A
Sales volume variance AS × Std Cont = 2,400 × £17 = £40,800 BS × Std Cont = 2,500 × £17 = £42,500	1,700	A
Direct labour rate variance AQ × AP = 5,040 × AP = £30,492 AQ × SP = 5,040 × £6 = £30,240	252	A
Direct labour efficiency variance AQ × SP = 5,040 × £6 = £30,240 SQ × SP = 2,400 × 2 × £6 = £28,200	1,440	A
Direct material price variance AQ × AP = 24,550 × AP = £184,616 AQ × SP = 24,550 × £7.50 = £184,125	491	A
Direct material usage variance. AQ × SP = 24,550 × £7.50 = £184,125 SQ × SP = 2,400 × 10 × £7.50 = £180,000	4,125	A
Fixed overhead expenditure variance Actual = £38,500 Budget = £40,000 (2,500 × £16)	1,500	F
Fixed overhead volume variance Budget = £40,000 (2,500 × £16) AQ × SR = 2,400 × £16 = £38,400	1,600	A

(b) Which of the following situations would probably cause an adverse materials usage variance?

an increase in the minimum quality standards

Which of the following situations would probably cause a favourable labour rate variance?

decrease in the need for overtime

Which of the following situations would probably cause an adverse fixed overhead capacity variance?

strike action by workers

Task 4

(a) Labour hours: (10,000 × 2.5) + (50,000 × 3.5) = 200,000

OAR = 600,000/200,000 = £3 per labour hour

Marrow: 25,000 hrs × £3 = £75,000

Barrow: 175,000 hrs × £3 = £525,000

	Marrow (£)	**Barrow** (£)
Fixed overheads	75,000	525,000

(b) Cost driver rates:

Special parts = 200,000/(300 + 100) = £500 per special part

Machine set ups = 400,000/(150 + 50) = £2,000 per set up

Special parts:

Marrow = £500 × 300 = £150,000

Barrow = £500 × 100 = £50,000

Machine set ups:

Marrow = £2,000 × 150 = £300,000

Barrow = £2,000 × 50 = £100,000

Year	£	**Marrow** (£)	**Barrow** (£)
Cost driver rate – special parts handling	500		
Cost driver rate – machine set ups	2,000		
Total special parts		150,000	50,000
Total machine set/ups		300,000	100,000

(c) Absorption cost per unit:

Marrow = 4 + 12.5 + (75,000/10,000) = 24

Barrow = 6 +17.5 + (525,000/50,000) = 34

ABC cost per unit:

Marrow = 4 + 12.50 + (150,000/10,000) + (300,000/10,000) = 61.50

Barrow = 6 + 17.50 + (50,000/50,000) + (100,000/50,000) = 26.50

	Marrow (£)	**Barrow** (£)
Total unit cost – Absorption costing	24.00	34.00
Total unit cost – ABC	61.50	26.50

(d) The problems Yarrow could have all relate to the complexity of activity based costing.

ABC can be time consuming and costly, the benefits obtained from ABC might not justify the costs.

ABC will be of limited benefit if the overhead costs are primarily volume related or if the overhead is a small proportion of the overall cost.

It is impossible to allocate all overhead costs to specific activities.

The choice of both activities and cost drivers might be inappropriate.

The staff at Yarrow Limited may not understand ABC and the benefits it provides, this could mean that it is not implemented properly. Training would help with this, but would add to the costs.

Task 5

(a) Material required:

Shola: 12/8 = 1.5 kg per unit, 3,000 × 1.5 = 4,500

Sammy: 16/8 = 2 kg per unit, 6,000 × 2 = 12,000

Labour hrs required:

Shola: 5/5 = 1 hr per unit, 3,000 × 1 = 3000

Sammy: 7.5/5 = 1.5 per unit, 6,000 × 1.5 = 9000

Contribution per unit:

Shola = 30 – 12 – 5 – 2 = 11

Sammy = 40 – 16 – 7.5 – 3 = 13.50

Contribution per limiting factor:

The limiting factor is labour hours as 12,000 are needed to meet the demand for both products and only 9,750 are available.

Shola = 11/1 hr per unit = £11 per hr

Sammy = 13.50/1.5 hrs per unit = £9 per hr

Optimum production plan:

As the Shola makes the highest contribution per hour this should be made first.

3000 units, using 1 hour each, which leaves 6750 hours to make Sammy.

6750/1.5 hrs per unit = 4,500 units.

	Shola	Sammy
Total materials required (kg)	4,500	12,000
Total labour hours required	3,000	9,000
Contribution per unit (£)	11	13.50
Contribution per limiting factor (£) (to TWO decimal places)	11	9
Optimal production (units)	3,000	4,500

(b) 1500 kg of extra material £0.

They already have more than enough material to meet the demand, so there would be no benefit in getting any extra.

1500 hrs of extra labour £13,500.

Labour is the limiting factor, so with 1,500 extra hours they could make another 1000 units of the Sammy giving £13.50 each unit. so that is the extra premium they would pay on top of the current costs for it to be financially viable.

(c) The companies aim is to maximise profits and as fixed costs do not change the aim will be to maximise contribution.

To make the total sales demand they would need 16,500 kgs of material (which they have) and 12,000 labour hours (which they don't have).

As labour hours are the limiting factor they must make best use of these.

Shola is the best use of the labour hours and so they make this first.

The plan recommended will yield the highest contribution, any other option would reduce the overall contribution.

They may consider this if a major customer requested a significant order of Sammy to make sure that longer term they kept the customer happy.

(d) Current situation:

Sales: 4,000 × 100 = 400,000

Materials: 4,000 × 2 × 6 = 48,000

Labour: 4,000 × 4 × 8 = 128,000

Profit = 400,000 – 48,000 – 128,000 – 100,000 = 124,000

Expected situation:

(400,000 × 1.01) – (48,000 × 0.9) – (128,000 × 0.75) – (100,000 × 1.2) = 144,800

	Current situation (£)	**Expected situation with new machinery** (£)
Profit	124,000	144,800

It **would** be beneficial to purchase the new machinery.

Task 6

	Year 0 £000	**Year 1** £000	**Year 2** £000	**Year 3** £000
Capital expenditure	(1,900)			
Sales revenue		1,620	1,860	2,300
Operating costs		(1,120)	(1,150)	(1,190)
Net cash flows	(1,900)	500	710	1,110
PV factors	1.0000	0.8696	0.7561	0.6575
Discounted cash flows	(1,900)	435	537	730
Net present value	(198)			

The net present value is **negative**.

(b) The payback period is **2** years and **8** months.

Year	Cash flow	Cumulative cash flow
0	(1,900)	(1,900)
1	500	(1,400)
2	710	(690)
3	1,110	420

(690/1,110) × 12 = 7.5 months

(c) **10%**

The NPV is negative at 15% so the IRR will be lower.

Task 7

(a) Receivables days = receivables/sales × 365

32 = 200,000/sales × 365

(32/365) × sales = 200,000

Sales = 200,000/(32/365)

Sales = 2,281,250

Gross profit = 2,281,250 × 28% = 638,750

Cost of sales = 2,281,250 – 638,750 = 1,642,500

Var prod cost = 1,642,500 × 65% = 1,067,625

Fix prod cost = 1,642,500 – 1,067,625 = 574,875

Net profit = 2,281,250 × 8% = 182,500

Payables:

Payables day = payables/cost of sales × 365

40 = payables/1,642,500 × 365

40/365 × 1,642,500 = payables

180,000 = payables

	£
Sales	2,281,250
Variable production costs	1,067,625
Fixed production costs	574,875
Cost of sales	1,642,500
Gross profit	638,750
Net profit	182,500
Payables	180,000
Receivables	200,000

(b) Revenue growth would be most likely classified under the **financial** perspective of the balanced scorecard.

Numbers of new products developed would be most likely classified under the **innovation and learning** perspective of the balanced scorecard.

The measurement of the time taken to complete the production cycle would be most likely classified under the **internal business** perspective of the balanced scorecard.

Profit would be most likely classified under the **financial** perspective of the balanced scorecard.

(c) Most of the financial performance indicators have improved over the two years.

The only one that hasn't is 'expenses as a % of revenue' which has increased slightly.

Both the ROCE and the asset turnover have increased, this could be partly due to the age of the assets increasing and the NBV depreciating.

Part of the increased gross margin will have come from the increased average spend per transaction.

The most concerning aspect of the information relates to the significant rise in complaints in the second year.

The increased complaints could be linked to the higher average spend per transaction. Customers have a higher expectation of the purchases, and this leads to increased dissatisfaction.

The complaints could also be linked to the lack of innovation from Tarana Ltd. There have been no new products launched during the second year, customers may be bored with the offerings of Tarana Ltd.

If the non-financial issues are not resolved, then it indicates that the financial performance of Tarana may decline in the coming year, dissatisfied customers may not return, reducing the sales revenue.

Task 8

(a)

Jan	Feb	Mar
Actual price was £6.00	Actual price was £6.00	Actual price was £6.30
Seasonal variation was – 10p	Seasonal variation was – 15p	Seasonal variation was 10p
Trend £6.10	Trend £6.15	Trend £6.20

The trend in prices is an increase of **£0.05** per month.

(b) Seasonal variation is the **actual** data at a point less the trend data at the same point.

A change in the economy that affects sales of a product is an example of a **cyclical variation**.

(c) **A**

	Jan	Feb	March
Total cost	£15,000	£20,000	£22,320
Total quantity purchased	2,000 m	2,500 m	2,480 m
Cost per m	£7.50	£8.00	£9.00
Index	100		£9.00/£7.50 × 100 = 120

(d) To calculate an index number, divide the current period figure by the **base** figure.

The RPI can be used to remove distortion in a set of figures to help aid **comparison**.

(e) Y = 100 + (2.7 × 19) = **151.3** (June)

Y = 100 + (2.7 × 20) = **154.0** (July)

(f) One of the assumptions of linear regression is that the data used is representative of future **trends**.

In the equation Y = a + bX, Y is the **dependent** variable.

INDEX

N

O

P

Q

R

S